More Praise for Jalil Roshandel an
International Security:

"The authors of this welcome volume ask the hard questions about the ideology motivating global jihadists; they also provide some balanced and sensible policy recommendations. Both for its overview and its practicality, this book will stand apart from others. It deserves a wide readership, not just in government circles, but with all those concerned to understand how the war on terror is to be fought and won."
—*Bruce Lawrence*, Professor of Islamic Studies, Director, Duke Islamic Studies Center, Duke University

"Roshandel and Chadha have written a tough, hard nosed primer on al Qaeda and the global jihad movement. They provide a basic introduction to the network's history, actions, tactics, organization, and financing, as well as the methods that have been used to fight it. They also review al Qaeda's statements, ideology, philosophy, and interpretation of Islam."
—*Steven Spiegel*, Professor of Political Science, Director, Middle East Regional Security Program, Burkle Center for International Relations, University of California, Los Angeles

Jihad and International Security

Jalil Roshandel and Sharon Chadha

JIHAD AND INTERNATIONAL SECURITY
© Jalil Roshandel and Sharon Chadha, 2006

First published in 2006 by
PALGRAVE MACMILLAN™
175 Fifth Avenue, New York, N.Y. 10010 and
Houndmills, Basingstoke, Hampshire, England RG21 6XS
Companies and representatives throughout the world.

PALGRAVE MACMILLAN is the global academic imprint of the Palgrave Macmillan division of St. Martin's Press, LLC and of Palgrave Macmillan Ltd. Macmillan® is a registered trademark in the United States, United Kingdom and other countries. Palgrave is a registered trademark in the European Union and other countries.

ISBN-13: 978–1–4039–7191–3   hard back
ISBN-10: 1–4039–7191–9   hard back
ISBN-13: 978–1–4039–7192–0   paper back
ISBN-10: 1–4039–7192–7   paper back

Library of Congress Cataloging-in-Publication Data is available from the Library of Congress.

A catalogue record for this book is available from the British Library.

Design by Newgen Imaging Systems (P) Ltd., Chennai, India.

First edition: October 2006

10 9 8 7 6 5 4 3 2 1

Printed in the United States of America.

To our spouses

Contents

Preface

The purpose of this book is to give the reader a general understanding of the emergence of al Qaeda and the global jihad movement. To this end, we have traced the movement's roots; dissected its most important published statements; explored its interpretation and use of Islam; examined its important ideological sources; reviewed the way in which jihadists conduct themselves on the battlefield; attempted to understand their self-justification; reviewed what government analysts and the media have been able to uncover about its sources of funding and sponsorship; and tried to understand the way in which the United States and other countries have tried to counter the threat the movement poses to national and international security.

While we made a concerted effort not to insert our personal views into this account, we acknowledge that something of our own biases must surely have seeped into our analysis. We have also refrained from offering any of our own policy prescriptions and have left that for later discussions or other analysts. We took this approach because, first, we wanted to provide what we feel is a concise accounting of the evolution of the global jihad movement that is as free as possible from political bias. Second, we also discovered, while writing this book that we, the coauthors, do not necessarily share the same view as to how this new threat to international security should be countered.

Thus we hope that though we may have not been able to deliver an accounting of our personal views we do believe we have provided a correct accounting of the views and actions of the principal players (and some of the minor ones as well) that have effected this global phenomenon.

Some call this evil Islamic radicalism; others, militant Jihadism; still others, Islamo-fascism. Whatever it's called, this ideology is very different from the religion of Islam. This form of radicalism exploits Islam to serve a violent, political vision: the establishment, by terrorism and subversion and insurgency, of a totalitarian empire that denies all political and religious freedom.

President George W. Bush, October 6, 2005

CHAPTER 1

Where Is Jihad Being Fought?

This battle is not between al Qaeda and the U.S. This is a battle of Muslims against the global crusaders.

Usama bin Laden, in an October 2001 interview with al-Jazeera correspondent, Tayseer Alouni, who was later sentenced to seven years in prison by a Spanish court for collaborating with al Qaeda.

When the second airplane hit the World Trade Center on September 11, 2001, a new and disturbing thought quickly spread across America: the nation was under attack.[1] September 11, 2001, it would turn out was not the first day of this new war, or to be precise this *jihad*—or Islamic holy war—against America. In fact, though most people had not noticed it, this jihad had been declared almost four years earlier, in February of 1998.[2] It had been announced in the form of a *fatwa*—or Islamic religious decree—that was published in a London-based Arabic newspaper.[3] Its author, Usama bin Laden, was a rich Saudi exile then living in Afghanistan. Though the fatwa urged Muslims to attack American civilians anywhere on the planet, it received almost no attention until the next summer, when bin Laden launched his first mass-casualty attack: the simultaneous suicide bombing of two American embassies in east Africa. But even this act of war would largely go unnoticed, as most of the casualties were African.

The U.S. government paid such little attention to the threat coming from bin Laden, that even on the morning of September 11, 2001, when the lead pilot of the North American Aerospace Defense Command was called into action, his first thought was that the United States had just been attacked by the Russians—as he recalled, "I'm thinking cruise missile threat from the sea. You know you look down and see the Pentagon burning and I thought the bastards snuck one by us."[4]

When it finally did emerge that bin Laden was behind the attacks, most Americans could only register a sense of confusion. Why was bin Laden urging Muslims to wage holy war against Americans? Or, as President Bush put it: "Why do they hate us?"[5]

The answer would not be obvious given the amount of blood and treasure Americans had committed over the past several decades defending Muslims. Americans had sent billions of dollars of aid and Stinger missiles to help Muslims drive the Soviets out of Afghanistan during the 1980s. In 1983, 241 Marines gave up their lives trying to establish peace between Muslims and Christians during Lebanon's civil war. Then in 1991, the United States spent tens of billions of dollars and 147 lives to liberate Kuwaiti Muslims from Iraqi Muslims. In 1993, another eighteen U.S. soldiers were killed trying to deliver famine relief to Muslims in Somalia. Then in 1995 Americans defied the international community to intervene on behalf of Muslims in Bosnia and again in Kosovo in 1999. Not to mention the billions of dollars American taxpayers sent every year to benefit Muslims in Egypt and Jordan. When most Americans read this history they were only more perplexed: Why was bin Laden telling his coreligionists they had a religious duty to attack Americans? Shouldn't he be ordering them instead to thank the Americans for their sacrifice? Even more astonishing was the fact that other Muslims were apparently taking him seriously. What was the real story here?

According to bin Laden, the case against America was threefold: the American military presence in Saudi Arabia; the fact the United States was a loyal ally to Israel; and the crippling sanctions that the United Nations had imposed on Iraq. According to bin Laden, as he wrote in his fatwa, these three "crimes and sins" were the reasons that Muslims ought to, "kill the Americans and plunder their possessions wherever he finds them and whenever he can."[6]

In fact, bin Laden had been urging Muslims to attack American forces in Saudi Arabia as early as 1996 even though the only reason the United States forces were in the Arabian Peninsula in the first place was because they had been invited there at the behest of the Saudi king, who first asked them to protect the kingdom's oil fields from the designs of Saddam Hussein in the run-up to the Gulf War and who then continued to request their presence there ever since. But as far as bin Laden was concerned, the presence of the American forces was objectionable because given the fact they were non-Muslims, they were prohibited from being permanently stationed in the holy lands of Islam.

In his fatwa, an astute reader would have noticed, bin Laden referred to Americans as "Crusaders,"[7] in the manner Muslims sometimes pejoratively refer to Western Christian civilization. By calling Americans "Crusaders," bin Laden was reminding his coreligionists that the modern-day Americans were only the descendants of the Christian armies of the Middle Ages, the armies who had sought but failed to reclaim the birthplace of their religion from the Muslims, who had conquered these same lands during the eighth century. By using such a pejorative, bin Laden was essentially telegraphing his fellow Muslims that once again the Muslim armies would prevail, even if these modern "Crusaders" were no longer fighting under the banner of Christianity but under the star-spangled banner of the American flag.

In the fatwa, bin Laden would also remind Muslims that they had a religious duty to reclaim Jerusalem from the Jews. But what was curious about bin Laden's statement was that he did not specify that Muslims should target

Israelis, or even Zionists—the term for Jews who support the state of Israel—but that he was advising Muslims to kill Jews, and not just in Israel or the lands called Palestine but wherever Muslims could find them, anywhere on earth. Why he was urging his followers to wage unlimited war against the Jews would not become clear until much later, in an interview with Al-Jazeera, the Arabic satellite-television channel, when he would explain that Muslims had to kill Jews not just because of what they had done to Palestine, but because the Prophet Mohammed, the founder of the Muslim religion, Islam, had prophesied this. Or as bin Laden himself put it:

> The prophet has said, "The end won't come before the Muslims and the Jews fight each other till the Jew hides between a tree and a stone. Then the tree and stone say, 'Oh, you Muslim, this is a Jew hiding behind me. Come and kill him.'" He who claims there will be a lasting peace between us and the Jews is an infidel. He'll be denouncing the book and what's in it.[8]

Curiously, at the same time that bin Laden was issuing this declaration of jihad, signaling to Muslims that they must now play out their final battle, many Americans were also of the mindset that they were living in an end-stage of history.[9] But the end-stage Americans that Americans imagined themselves in was one in which they would never again have to be called to pick up arms to defend themselves or their friends and families. The Americans who believed themselves part of this post-conflict world were of course not so ill-informed to think that *everyone* in the world was able to live like this. They were surely aware that there were still wars going on in the world, but these were wars that happened in other places, places like Africa and the Middle East, for example, or maybe even as close to home as Eastern Europe, but never in the United States or even Western Europe, not since World War II and the Cold War. No, thanks to the unrivaled power of the American military, a substantial number of Americans and West Europeans (who also lived under American protection though they did not have to pay for it) believed that they would never again have to pick up a weapon in order to defend themselves or their homeland. In this new post-conflict era, at least for Americans and most West Europeans, military service would be a strictly voluntary affair and war would be an option—something Americans and Western European could elect or decline to participate in strictly at their own leisure.

One of the reasons for this happy state was that in the new post-conflict world of the liberal secular West, religion was no longer something that had to be reckoned with: if religion was not altogether a spent force—as it was for the most part in Europe—then religion, specifically Christianity, had certainly been defanged. Even if the intellectual class liked to amuse themselves with the notion that rightwing evangelicals were on the verge of taking over the United States, the last thing that anyone sophisticated enough to even contemplate this sort of thing believed they would have to take seriously in this new day and age was a call for a holy war, and one from as far away and as impoverished and dysfunctional a place as Afghanistan at that. And so, had anyone in America's thinking class even heard of bin Laden's fatwa—and, again, very few did—most would have simply dismissed it as something akin to the delusional rantings of a homeless crazy person. And so, for a few more years, America's best and brightest could still worry about the really important things that earnest and serious people worried about in the post-conflict era, things like starting dot.com companies, curing breast cancer and AIDS, slowing down global warming, where to go on the next vacation, winning that Academy Award, writing that bestseller, or when to climb the world's seven highest summits or visit the world's last remaining aboriginal peoples.

Even the U.S. government did not take bin Laden's threat all that seriously. Although the fatwa would help to motivate President Clinton to agree to promote one Richard Clarke to a newly created position of national coordinator for security and counterterrorism, because of concerns raised by his Attorney General Janet Reno, Clarke's new authority would have to be limited to providing advice on budgets and coordinating interagency efforts to come up with some stronger counterterrorism programs.[10] In other words, Clarke should confine his counterterrorism efforts to monitoring bureaucrats in Washington, such was the Clinton administration's perception of the real threat the nation faced.

But bin Laden was not just addressing the secular progressive and well, smug West in his fatwa. He was also sending a message to his followers, the Muslim armies, as he liked to call them, telling them that now was the time for them to deploy, to once and for all destroy the myth that was American superpower and that in the end they should expect to triumph and at last realize Islam's divine mandate to rule the world.

And so it was for his Muslim audience that bin Laden included in his message a citation from the *Koran*, the sacred text of Islam, and not just any verse either, but the famous Sword Verse, the verse which commands Muslims to "fight and slay the pagans wherever ye find them, seize them, beleaguer them, and lie in wait for them in every stratagem (of war)."[11] This verse, according to a long line of Islamic scholars going back at least a millennium, is the final pronouncement on how Muslims should deal with non-Muslims. And so in this way, using no less an authority than God's word, bin Laden officially declared jihad on Americans and Jews.

It should have also been noticed that other people as well added their signatures to bin Laden's declaration: specifically a couple of Egyptians, a Pakistani, and a Bangladeshi. While the names themselves would have probably not registered, the fact that they were announcing the formation of an international alliance unified around the idea of killing Americans and Jews should have caused at least some pause. Then again, further research would have only revealed that these men and their organizations were at best only small-scale terrorists, hardly in possession of capabilities that could seriously threaten the world's greatest superpower. Serious declarations of war, after all, were the province of industrialized nations in command of powerful armies, motivated by serious ideologies like fascism, Nazism, nationalist militarism, and communism. A ragtag alliance of religious extremists from some underdeveloped, dysfunctional countries would have hardly been taken as a serious threat.

And yet, some six months later, this new alliance—later called *al Qaeda*—would launch its first mass-casualty attack on American interests, the nearly simultaneous bombing of two U.S. embassies in east Africa, in which two hundred people would be killed—mostly Africans—and thousands injured. When bin Laden was asked if he was responsible for the attacks, he told the Time Magazine reporter that he had indeed issued a "crystal-clear fatwa calling on the Islamic nation to carry on jihad" to liberate the "holy sites" and that he was fully confident that Muslims would "be able to end the legend of the so-called superpower that is America."[12]

These attacks were enough to provoke CIA director George Tenet to issue a directive in December 1998, addressed to CIA officials stating: "We are at war. I want to resources or people spared in this effort, either inside CIA or the Community" but as the 9/11 Commission, the independent bipartisan commission tasked by Congress in 2002 to "create a full and complete account of the circumstances surrounding the September 11, 2001, terrorist attacks"[13] learned, Tenet's "memorandum had little overall effect on mobilizing the CIA or intelligence community."[14] During the 2000 presidential election campaign, presidential candidate Al Gore who was then the vice president, never introduced a serious discussion of bin Laden or al Qaeda into the presidential campaign.[15] Surely he would have done so had the Clinton White House really considered the threat to be something that had to be seriously dealt with during this period.

Richard Clarke, Counterterrorism Coordinator for the National Security Council in the Clinton administration and then under the Bush administration, summed up the situation in a memo addressed to his new boss, National Security Advisor, Condoleeza Rice, dated September 4, 2001, just days before the attacks, the "real question" for the White House, he wrote, was "are we serious about dealing with the al Qida threat? . . . Is al Qida a big deal?" and then as the 9/11 Commission paraphrased the memo:

> One school of thought, Clarke wrote in this September 4 note, implicitly argued that the terrorist network was a nuisance that killed a score of Americans every 18–24 months. If that view was credited, then current policies might be proportionate. Another school saw al Qaeda as the "point of the spear of radical Islam." But no one forced the argument into the open by calling for a national estimate or a broader discussion of the threat. The issue was never joined as a collective debate by the U.S. government, including the Congress, before 9/11.[16]

The African embassies bombings were not, as Clarke implied in his memo, the first time Americans had been targeted by "radical Islam." In November of 1990, El Sayyid Nosair, described at the time as a Muslim supremacist, shot and killed the leader of the Jewish Defense League in New York, Rabbi Meir Kahane. Though investigators would find boxes of jihadist literature in his possession and learn that he was a follower of a well-known jihadist, a sightless Egyptian cleric, Sheik Omar Abdel Rahman, also called the Blind Sheik, they would insist that the killing of Kahane was the act of a lone gunman.

The Blind Sheik, it would turn out, was the spiritual advisor of one of the groups who signed off on bin Laden's 1998 fatwa. By the time the fatwa was issued, however, the Blind Sheik was serving a 240-year prison sentence in the United States for having conspired to blow up landmarks in New York City, including the United Nations. Earlier, in February of 1993, other followers of his had attempted to blow up the World Trade Center, though they only succeeded in creating a multistory hole in the basement of the building, and in the process, killed six and injured thousands, including a pregnant woman. Nosair, the "lone gunman" who killed Rabbi Kahane, would turn out to be one of the conspirators in the landmarks plot. As Michael Cherkasky, the prosecutor's lead investigator in the Kahane case, noted when evidence first emerged linking the rabbi's killer to the World Trade Center bombers: "We should have understood that we had more than just a one-man fanatical shooter."[17] The CIA, for its part, dismissed the 1993 World Trade Center bombing as an "anomaly," according to Robert Baer, a former CIA operative who later told *Vanity Fair* that in his view, there was "a good degree of bigotry" involved in the agency's thinking—"these people are ragheads" was how he characterized the general sentiment at the time.[18]

There were also other attacks against the United States: In 1993, Somalian militias trained by bin Laden attacked U.S. famine-relief forces in Somalia and killed eighteen U.S. service personnel.[19] In 1995, bin Laden associates would claim credit for the truck bombing of a U.S.-operated training center of the Saudi National Guard in Riyadh in which seven people were killed. And in 1996, U.S. investigators would conclude al Qaeda was somehow involved in the truck bombing of the Khobar Towers, a military housing complex in Saudi Arabia, in which 19 U.S. military personnel were killed (the major player in this bombing is believed to be Iranian-backed Saudi Hezbollah).[20]

In fact, since 1979, the year the modern global jihad movement was born, al Qaeda has been but one—albeit the strongest—of the many players who have declared and waged jihad. In the years that followed, as we shall see, jihads raged all over the globe in the form of interstate wars, liberation struggles, secessionist movements, civil wars, insurrections, insurgencies, and terrorist acts. Nor have Americans and Jews been the only targets of this new movement. Nations and peoples from the Middle East to Southeast Asia to India to Europe have all been targeted as can be seen from the following list of modern jihads:

Interstate wars:
- Arab-Israeli wars
- Iran-Iraq War (1980–1988)
- Gulf War (1991)

Liberation struggles:
- Palestine (The First Intifada 1987–1993; The al-Aqsa Intifada, which started in 2000)
- Afghanistan-Soviet War (1979–1989)

Secessionist movements:
- Southern Sudan (1980s–2005)
- Kashmir (since 1989)—this can also be classified as an interstate conflict
- Bosnia (1992–1995)
- Chechnya (since 1994)

- Philippines (since 1995)
- Kosovo (1996–1999)
- Dagestan (since 1999)
- Indonesia (since 2000)
- Thailand (since 2004)

Civil wars:
- Algeria (1991–1998)

Insurrections:
- Afghanistan:The Northern Alliance versus The Taliban (1994–2001)

Insurgencies:
- Egypt (1992–1997 and from 2004)
- Uzbekistan (since 1998–1999)
- Afghanistan after the Taliban (since 2002)
- Iraq after Saddam (since 2003)
- Saudi Arabia (since May 12, 2003)

Sectarian and communal conflicts:
- India (decades)
- Pakistan (decades)
- Nigeria (since 2000)
- Darfur, Sudan (since 2003) and Nuba, Sudan (since 1992)
- Somalia (since 2006)

Major terrorist attacks outside "conflict zones":
- August 7, 1998, two U.S. embassies in east Africa are bombed
- October 12, 2000, al Qaeda bombs a US Naval destroyer, the USS Cole, harbored in Yemen
- September 11, 2001, attacks on New York and Washington
- April 11, 2002, a suicide bomber attacks the Ghriba synagogue in Tunisia.
- May 16, 2003, suicide bombers attack Jewish and Western targets in Casablanca, Morocco
- November 15, 2003, suicide bombers attack two synagogues and five days later hit the British consulate and a bank in Istanbul, Turkey
- March 11, 2004, ten explosions occur on four commuter trains in Madrid, Spain
- July 7, 2005, suicide bombers attack the London public transportation system
- November 9, 2005, bombs explode at three hotels in Jordan, killing 57 people including 17 guests attending a wedding

From the above list, we can see that the global jihad movement began decades before bin Laden declared his jihad in 1998 and that jihads have been fought against the Soviets in Afghanistan, Christians and animists in Sudan, the Indian government in Kashmir, Orthodox Serbs in Bosnia and Kosovo, Russian rule in Chechnya and Dagestan, Christians in Indonesia, and Buddhists in Thailand.

Contemporary jihads have also been waged against Muslims themselves. In the case of the Iran-Iraq war, jihad was fought between two Muslim states. During the Gulf War, Iraq declared a jihad against the U.S.-led coalition that included many Muslim nations. In Algeria, Egypt, Saudi Arabia, Iraq (after Saddam Hussein) and Afghanistan (after the Soviets left), there have been jihads waged that pitted Muslims against Muslims.

This observation brings up a critical point. The word *jihadist* is a neologism meant to denote someone who supports jihad, specifically the militant form of jihad. Though all jihadists define themselves to be Muslims, and believe that theirs is a correct interpretation of Islam, not all Muslims define themselves to be jihadists. Though accurate statistics are not available, jihadists are generally not believed to represent more than a small (albeit energetic) minority of the world's population of Muslims. We should state at the outset that in this book, the authors will not take a position as to whether the jihadists are correct in their interpretation of Islam. That is a question only other Muslims can answer. Rather, the aim of this particular book will be to explore what experts have come to call the global jihad movement.

We should also note that in this book, a given conflict will be determined to be a jihad if someone somewhere claiming to have sufficient Islamic authority has declared it so. Again, the authors will not presume any authority to vet such claims and will not opine as to the validity of the issuer's authority or his call (and so far it is always a his; while females have enlisted in the global jihad movement, the authors are not aware of any instance in which a female has taken it upon herself to declare a jihad). Again, whether or not a particular jihad should have been declared is an issue that will be left up to Muslims themselves to decide.

Year Zero: 1979

While there have been many calls to jihad in modern times—most notably in both the world wars of the twentieth century—perhaps the most resoundent call to jihad in modern times occurred on January 21, 1979. This was just after America's staunchest ally in the Middle East, the shah of Iran, fled into exile following a populist revolt led by an Islamic cleric. The Ayatollah Khomeini, who had led the revolution from Paris, announced that the next target, would be America: "US imperialism must get out of our nation. The people have absolute confidence in their victory in this holy war (jihad-e moqaddas)."[21]

Under Khomeini, Iran was now the "Islamic Republic of Iran" and its constitutional mandate would be to export Islamic revolution. As the Ayatollah wrote, "All secular power, no matter what form it takes, is the work of Satan," and Muslims must "stop it in its tracks."[22]

Though the Islamic Republic of Iran was a Shiite state, and only about 10 to 15 percent of the world's Muslims could be categorized as Shiites, those Sunni Muslims who longed to live under an Islamic state as opposed to secular nation states found inspiration in the Ayatollah's revolution. What they took from the Iranian revolution was the notion that Islam had now proven itself to be the world's most potent revolutionary force. Only Islam—and not communism or any other political ideology—had succeeded in bringing down the shah of Iran, who was not only rich and well-armed in his own right, but had also become the symbol of American power in the Middle East.

Incidentally, in this book, we shall use the term *Islamist* to describe the subset of Muslims who see Islam as not just a religion (whatever that means) but also as a comprehensive political solution. The "ist" ending is meant to suggest that the person adheres to the political ideology summarized by the slogan "Islam is the answer" in the same way a communist adheres to the teachings of, say, Karl Marx.

The next watershed event in the emerging jihad movement was when the Egyptian president Anwar Sadat signed a peace accord with Israel in March 1979. While the international community would grant Sadat and the other parties to the agreement the Nobel Peace Prize for their efforts, as far as Egypt's radical Islamists were concerned, Sadat had just signed his own death warrant.

At the time of the signing, Egypt had been under the domain of a military-dominated regime since 1952. The only opposition force that had ever been even remotely successful in challenging Egypt's one-party rule had been the Islamist movement, which traced its origins back to 1928, to the founding of the Muslim Brotherhood, a movement whose goal was to mobilize society in order to establish an Islamic order.

Gamel Abdul Nasser, who led the military coup in 1952, had used the Islamists to gain power, but a power struggle soon ensued and in 1954, he banned the Muslim Brotherhood and put at least a temporary stop to the ascending Islamist movement in Egypt.

Arab nationalism, the ideology Nasser adopted instead, sidelined Islam and to unify Arabs, drew instead on the region's shared language and culture so as not to exclude the region's Christians, who were the primary theoreticians of the ideology. Arab nationalism, which combined notions of racial supremacy, along with militarism and socialism, dominated Egyptian and Arab politics up until the Arab nationalist armies were defeated by the state of Israel during the 1967 Six Day War. That the tiny Jewish state took less than a week to defeat the Arab nationalist armies that had by then been training for nearly two decades effectively ended any hope that Arab nationalism could ever deliver Palestine back to the Arabs.

This provided an opportunity for the Islamists to make another play. They argued that the Arab cultural identity was never the force the Arab nationalists made it out to be. They argued that the true source of unifying power in the region came from Islam and that only by reverting back to the principles advocated by the Prophet and his followers, would the Arab nations be able to resume their rightful place in human history, which was to dominate mankind. They contrasted the early history of the religion when in less than a hundred years, the Muslims had conquered an empire that extended all the way from Europe to the Indus River in what is today's Pakistan, with the modern period when in the last two hundred years, Muslims had been suffering all sorts of humiliating defeats at the hands of the Western powers.

Hence when the radical Islamists saw the Egyptian president Sadat shaking hands with the Israeli prime minister Menachem Begin and the American president Jimmy Carter to cement the peace accord between Egypt and Israel they failed to see did not see this as a sign of hope for peaceful coexistence. Instead they interpreted the gesture as a violation of the tenets of Islam that said that any lands that had ever been conquered by Muslims must forever remain under the dominion of Islam and that no ruler other than God could ever give them up. Thus, to the Islamists, Egypt's peace agreement with Israel represented no more than a repudiation of Islam.

Sadat well understood that his having made peace with Israel would only enrage the Islamists. To try and the now rapidly growing movement, which was especially popular on Egypt's university campuses, Sadat banned Islamist student organizations and prohibited women from wearing the *niqab*, or face veil on Egypt's campuses. Sadat correctly perceived that one of the most conspicuous signs of Islam's growing power was that droves of university and middle class women were now expressing their new found religious enthusiasm by going back to the *hijab*, or modest Islamic dress. Woman whose grandmothers had enthusiastically adopted Western dress were now choosing to cover their hair with a headscarf or even going to the extreme of donning an all-encompassing black robe and covering their faces with a niqab. Sadat correctly saw the increasing use of niqab as a showing of solidarity with the radical Islamists who were threatening his hold on power. But once again Sadat's gesture only signaled to the radicals that Sadat had repudiated Islam. Under a traditional reading of Islamic law (or *Sharia* in Arabic) this was an offense punishable by death. Now Sadat had two fatal strikes against him.

Not unpredictably, within two years, Sadat would meet his fate at the hands of a radical Islamist. Sadat was assassinated during a parade commemorating Egypt's surprise attack on Israel, an attack that launched the 1973 Middle East war. When he was asked why he killed him, Sadat's killer responded "because he did not rule in accordance with the shari'ah, because he concluded sulh [conciliation] with peace, and because he insulted the scholars of Islam."[23]

Among those who the Egyptian government suspected of having plotted Sadat's assassination was a young Egyptian doctor by the name of Ayman al-Zawahiri. He had founded a clandestine splinter group of the Muslim Brotherhood, whose goal was to launch a surgical strike that would destroy the Egyptian regime and make way for a new Islamic order. At his trial, Zawahiri famously addressed the TV cameras and proclaimed, "We are . . . the real Islamic opposition against Zionism, Communism, and imperialism!" "And then his codefendants chimed in saying. The army of Muhammad will return, and we will defeat the Jews!"[24] Prosecutors failed to link Zawahiri to the assassination and he was only convicted on weapons-related charges. After he was released from prison in 1984, he found his way to jihad in Afghanistan.

The third seminal event in the global jihad movement occurred in November 1979, when 200 Islamic fundamentalists seized the Grand Mosque in Mecca during the annual hajj and held hundreds of pilgrims hostage. With the help of French security forces, the Saudis were able to bring the situation under control though 250 people died and many more were wounded.

The notion that a group of radicals had penetrated the holiest site of Islam during the sacred hajj, shook the Saudi regime to its very core. For the first time since the founding of the nation-state in 1932, the ruling family had to acknowledge that their hold on power was slipping.

The Saud family had ruled the Arabian Peninsula for most of the last several centuries. They first came to prominence in the mid-1700s, when an ancestor, Muhammad bin Saud, created an alliance with a Muslim cleric, Muhammad ibn Abd Wahhab (1703–1792), who was known for wandering around the Arabian Peninsula, imploring his fellow Muslims to rebel against the Ottoman rulers because of their failure to implement Sharia. Wahhab was also adamantly opposed to the then popular practice of grave worshipping, which he saw as a form of idol worship and a breach of the Islamic injunction that Muslims only acknowledge one God. He was also contemptuous of Shiite and Sufis, whom he regarded as heretics. Wahhab urged his fellow Muslims to get their house in order—that is, rid the community (or *Umma*) of any Muslims who did not sub-scribe to his view of Islam—namely the grave worshippers, Shiites, and the Sufis. As Islamic law expert Khaled Abou El Fadl put it, Wahhab "argued that Muslims who engaged in acts of shirk (heresy) must be fought and killed."[25]

This was exactly the take on religion that Muhammad bin Saud, a tribal warlord was looking for. By adopting an austere and unforgiving version of Islam, Muhammad bin Saud would be able to rally the Muslim masses to take on his rival warlords as well as the Ottomans who were then in control of Islam's holy lands. This interpretation of Islam would later be dubbed Wahhabism, and always been seen as the core strength of the descendents of ibn Saud and ibn Wahhab who would go on to found the Kingdom of Saudi Arabia in 1932. So in 1979, when the Saudi royal family felt that they were losing their grip on power, it was to this source that they looked to to shore up their legitimacy.

Since oil had become an important commodity, and particularly since 1973, when the world's petroleum exporters punished the United States, Western Europe, and Japan for supporting Israel during the 1973 Ramadan-Yom Kippur War with an oil embargo that pushed oil prices sky high, the Saudi royal family had become famously impious in the enjoyment of their unprecedented oil wealth. The excesses of Saudi princes had become legendary in the gambling casinos and resorts of Europe and America. Many Muslims bristled at the idea that these self-designated custodians of their holy sites were squandering what they believed was the oil wealth that Allah had provided for the benefit of all Muslims, not just the Saudi nation, and certainly not just for the benefit of these extravagant Saudi royals. The newly revolutionized Iranians were particularly harsh in their criticism of the corruption and lack of piety of the royal family.

To appease such critics, the Saudis turned to the clerics. They were given con-trol of the educational system. By this point, many of them were Egyptian exiles—members of the Muslim Brotherhood that fled Nasser's Egypt after he dis-covered that the group was plotting to assassinate him. If Nasser saw the Muslim

Brotherhood as a threat to his power, the Saudis saw them as a way to counter the rise of Arab nationalism. By the time 1979 rolled around and the Saudis needed a cadre of Sunni Islamists to counter the threat coming from the Shiite revolutionary movement in Iran, they had plenty of Muslim Brothers they could call upon.

The religious police were given a freer hand to enforce the strict Islamic code of conduct which had relaxed somewhat along with the influx of petrodollars. Now all signs of Western influence were being discouraged. Islamic dress codes were being enforced even in stores serving the international community. Contact with foreigners was curtailed.

To make sure that it would be the Saudi version of Islam that would prevail—as opposed to the Shiite interpretation coming from Iran—the Saudis also began earnestly promoting Wahhabism. Over the next few decades, the Saudis would spend billions building mosques and Islamic centers and schools worldwide and publishing pamphlets and books to spread the Wahhabi message. One of the most ambitious projects the Saudis would undertake would be to fund the Muslim holy warriors or *mujahidin* who would soon be called to fight the godless Soviets in Afghanistan.

And so we arrive at what would be the last but by no means least of the events that would mark 1979 as year zero in the global jihad movement: the Christmas Eve Soviet invasion of Afghanistan.

The Soviets are said to have chosen this particular time to mount their invasion because they were certain that they could get away with it. They calculated that Washington would be too distracted by the hostage crisis in Iran to launch any kind of serious retaliation. That November, a band of Iranian students had seized control of the U.S. embassy in Tehran only to announce that they were going to hold everyone hostage until the United States agreed to send their former ally, the ousted shah, back to the Islamic Republic of Iran so that he could stand trial for his crimes against the Iranian people. At the time, the shah was seeking treatment for his terminal case of cancer at a New York hospital.

The Soviets had designs on Afghanistan because they wanted to add the Central Asian state to their empire to create a corridor all the way to the warm water ports and shipping lines of the Arabian Sea, through which most of the world's oil supply passed. The Soviets, however, made a grave miscalculation. Instead of quietly adding to their sphere of influence, the invasion would ultimately cost them their empire.

The American president Jimmy Carter immediately cancelled all negotiations related to crucial wheat sales to the Soviet Union, called for a boycott of the upcoming 1980 Olympics which were to be held in Moscow and then quietly summoned the CIA to offer its covert support to the Afghan resistance in order to counter the Soviet invasion. That an American president would offer covert support to anticommunist forces was certainly nothing new. This was generally the way in which the United States fought the Cold War against the Soviets. What was different about this situation was that this time the anticommunist forces in Afghanistan coalesced under a different ideology—Islamism.

Countries in the Middle East, particularly Saudi Arabia, jumped at the chance to send their newly radicalized youth to fight jihad in Afghanistan, based on the notion that it would be better to have the Islamist radicals fight the Soviets in far away Afghanistan than remain at home and create havoc in the kingdom. Other Arab nations applied the same rationale and for the next decade, jihad in Afghanistan became a sort of regional safety valve, a place where Arab nations could send their young militants to avoid having them mount Islamist revolutions back home. As a senior Pakistani intelligence officer at the time would later recall for the Los Angeles Times, "What Saudi Arabia did during the Afghan jihad was it encouraged these youngsters, these militants, to come over" to Pakistan, adding that the Saudis gave the mujahidin "money, tickets, air fare and the necklace that would bring them martyrdom if they died in jihad. . . . They sent them here to kill them. It was very simple. This was a ploy."[26]

Other Muslims offered their support to the jihad in Afghanistan in the form of money, arms, military training, or compensation for the families of fallen warriors. As the Egyptian doctor, who would later become bin Laden's second-in-command, recalled the situation in his own memoirs, "The United States wanted the war to be a war by proxy against the Russians, but, with God's assistance, the Arab mujahidin turned it into a call to revive the neglected religious duty, namely jihad for the cause of God."[27]

The young men who answered this worldwide call to jihad—and there were anywhere from ten to fifty thousand of these young men from as many as forty different countries (estimates vary)—were called "Arab Afghans" in spite of the fact that they were by no means all Arab. Non-Arab Muslims from the Philippines, Indonesia, Central Asia, Europe, and even North America all came to fight jihad in Afghanistan. The Muslim fighting forces called themselves the *mujahidin*, using the Arabic word for Islamic holy warriors. (The singular word for a person who engages in jihad is *mujahid*.)

The leader of the mujahidin was a Palestinian-Jordanian cleric by the name of Abdullah Azzam. He had attended the prestigious al-Azhar University in Cairo where he became radicalized under the influence of the Muslim Brotherhood. Eventually he ended up teaching at the King Abdul Aziz University in Jeddah, Saudi Arabia, where one of his students was an engineering student by the name of Usama bin Laden.

While Abdullah Azzam never achieved the worldwide fame that bin Laden did, it was Azzam who first popularized the idea of jihad in Afghanistan. Azzam spent the 1980s traveling the world, promoting the idea that Muslims had a duty to wage jihad. It was Azzam who created the operative motto of the mujahidin in Afghanistan: "Jihad and the rifle alone: no negotiations, no conferences and no dialogues."[28]

Azzam was also responsible for recruiting bin Laden to fight jihad in Afghanistan, where bin Laden distinguished himself by performing heroically in battle and because he used his own wealth and personal resources to build a system of bunkers and tunnels and training camps in the Hindu Kush mountains. Together with Azzam, he created the basis of a global Islamic army that later came to be known as *al Qaeda* (Arabic for the base).[29]

At this point in time, Americans were not concerned about the Islamic radicalism that was fomenting in Afghanistan. They had no idea that the Arab Afghans would ultimately parlay their experience in Afghanistan into an international jihad movement that would eventually target Americans. At this time the mujahidin were "freedom fighters" because they were seen to be reliable allies in the fight against communism, the central concern of American foreign policy at the time.

A persistent myth is that the CIA created the mujahidin and specifically bin Laden. Milton Bearden, who was for a time head of the CIA's covert action plan in Afghanistan denies the existence of any direct link and claims that, "despite what has often been written, the CIA never recruited, trained, or otherwise used the Arab volunteers who arrived in Pakistan."[30] Instead, Bearden contends that any money or training was only supplied to Pakistan's intelligence service, who then funded and trained the Afghans and the mujahidin. Bearden's account has been corroborated by other CIA officials as well as by Zawahiri in his memoirs.[31]

In any case, by the mid-1980s, including the mujahidin, the Afghans had a fighting force of more than 250,000, double the number of Soviet forces in the country. Yet because of the Soviet's superior air power, they were retaining the military advantage and it seemed at the time that the United States, in the words of Bearden, "was fighting the Soviets to the last Afghan in a confrontation that could run on indefinitely."[32]

Eventually, Congress would decide that it could longer stand by and passively watch the massive casualties that the Afghans were taking and decided to arm them with American-made Stinger antiaircraft missiles, their only hope to effectively counter the superior Soviet airpower. Over the next two years, armed with the thirty-five pound, five-foot long shoulder-fired missiles and their heat-sensing capability, the Afghans would down hundreds of Soviet aircraft and change the course of the war.

By April of 1988, the Soviets had suffered so many losses that they were finally willing to completely agree to withdraw their forces by February of the following year. By the time they actually pulled out of Afghanistan, more than a million Afghans—or some 10 percent of the prewar population—had been been killed in the war, hundreds of thousands had been wounded, and almost half the prewar population had fled or become refugees. The Soviet casualties were not minimal—they numbered hundreds of thousands.

The human toll, however, was not the extent of the Soviet's losses. The war had taken a heavy financial toll on the Soviet Union, severely weakening the world's second superpower. Within months, the Soviet empire would fall apart. First Hungary would open its borders with Austria to the West; the anti-Soviet Solidarity movement would achieve a majority in Poland; on November 9, 1989 East Germans tore town the Berlin Wall which had separated them from West Germany for almost thirty years; and, by December of 1989, Vaclav Havel was heading up a nonviolent "Velvet Revolution" in Czechoslovakia. The invasion of Afghanistan, originally launched to expand the Soviet empire, had so drained the second greatest superpower, that it became the catalyst that led to its demise.

American triumphalism would last throughout much of the 1990s. It would not be until the attacks of September 11, 2001, that Americans would even sense that the mujahidin in Afghanistan who had played such a starring role in bringing about the demise of the Soviet Union and the end of the Cold War would reconstitute themselves into a global jihad movement and emerge as the next great threat to international security.

The importance of what happened in Afghanistan during the 1980s cannot be understated. As bin Laden himself told CNN in March of 1997, the experience the mujahidin gained in Afghanistan, "cannot be measured by tens of years but rather more than that." According to him the greatest lesson that the mujahidin learned there was "that the myth of the superpower was destroyed not only in my mind but also in the minds of all Muslims."[33] When the Soviets pulled out of Afghanistan, the al Qaeda leadership debated where to go next to fight jihad. Bin Laden, now under the influence of Zawahiri, wanted to the mujahidin to fan out and bring about regime change back home, in places like Saudi Arabia and Egypt. Azzam, on the other hand, wanted the Muslim army to first establish an Islamic state in Afghanistan and once that was accomplished, he wanted the mujahidin to go and liberate his homeland, Palestine.[34]

Before the al Qaeda leaders were forced to face the possibility that they would have to split into separate factions, Azzam was taken out of the debate. On November 24, 1989, he and his two sons were blown up on their way to a mosque in Peshawar, Pakistan, when the car they were in drove over a land mine. Though the crime was never solved, bin Laden and Zawahiri were named as primary suspects, along with other rivals, Afghan warlords, the Pakistani intelligence service, the CIA, and, as is always the case in this part of the world, the Israeli intelligence service, Mossad.[35]

With Azzam gone, bin Laden returned home to Saudi Arabia where he worked for a while in the family business and attempted to wage a clandestine jihad against the Saudi monarchy. Whatever plans he had, would have to undergo significant changes when in the next year, the Iraqi dictator, Saddam Hussein, invaded his oil-rich neighbor, Kuwait.

Expanding Fronts

At the time of the Kuwait invasion, the Iraqi economy was in dire shape, struggling to recover from the country's eight-year war with Iran (1980–1988). Saddam was furious that his oil-rich neighbors were pressuring him to repay the billions they had lent him to fund the war with Iran.

Saddam invaded Iran on September 22, 1980 because he wanted to contain the Shiite revolution in Iran and he thought that the sooner he acted the easier it would be. Iran had been actively trying to incite the Shiite majority inside Iraq to rise up against Saddam and he had uncovered various Iranian plots targeting Iraqi officials both at home and abroad. He thought that it would be an easy victory as the military had been purged of its many loyalists to the shah and he assumed it would not be in any state of preparedness for war.

Initially, the war plan went just as Saddam had predicted and the Iraqi forces made easy headway into Iran. But Saddam had underestimated just how inspirational a leader Khomeini could be. To get the support of the Iranian people, Khomeini cast the battle as a jihad whose goal was to extend the Islamic republic into Baghdad and then ultimately liberate Jerusalem. "We shall get to Lebanon, and to Jerusalem through Iraq," Khomeini reportedly told his aides, "but first we have to defeat [Hussein]."[36]

Saddam also defined the battle as a "heroic jihad and martyrdom for the cause of right," adding that "the heroic Iraqi armed forces and the great Iraqi people are fighting today against a clique linked by inheritance, thoughts and activity to the Persian empire that was destroyed by Islam." [37] By referring to the "clique linked to inheritance," Saddam was calling attention to the unIslamic pride the Iranians took in their pre-Islamic history. He was also reminding the Sunnis—the bulk of his supporters—that the Iranians were Shiites. The Shiites believe that only the descendants of the Prophet are capable of leading the Muslims, while Sunnis contend that the only criteria for leadership is merit. Thus Saddam was suggesting that the Iranians were not "true" Muslims and that Muslims were now obliged to fight not just for Iraq but also to defend "the ideals for which the prophet Mohammed and his great supporters waged holy war."[38]

Khomeini's call to jihad incited thousands of Iranian teenagers to volunteer for martyrdom missions, where they were given red headbands inscribed with the words "Sar Allah" ("Blood for God") and small metal keys to symbolize the belief that should they be killed, they would be granted immediate entrance into Paradise. On the battlefield, the teen brigades were tied together in groups of twenty or so (to prevent defections) and sent to the front to clear minefields or facedown machine-gun fire to pave the way for the Iranian tanks lined up behind them.[39]

To counter Iran's ground offensives, Saddam deployed chemical weapons.[40] Not surprisingly, the death toll was devastating. The eight-year war resulted in a over a million casualties and ruined the economies of both countries.[41] The Iraqi invasion may have contained the Shiite revolution, but it also turned Iraq into a pariah state, when in a desperate move to recover his war debts, Saddam decided he had no choice but to annex Kuwait.

Saddam was perturbed that Kuwait and the other Gulf monarchies were pressuring him to repay his loans because he firmly believed that the only reason they had lent him money in the first place was because they too saw the threat coming from Iran, and saw Iraq as having one of the few militaries capability of containing it. Moreover, Saddam was upset that the Gulf monarchies were keeping oil production levels so high that oil prices were depressed, further impeding Iraq's ability to recover from the war, and he also suspected that Kuwait was stealing Iraqi oil through its underground pumps.

Again Saddam would label his aggression as a jihad in defense of Islam. This caused the official clergy of the Muslim states that had lined up with the U.S.-led coalition to issue counter-claims saying that it was those who were acting on behalf of Kuwait who had the legitimate claim to jihad as they were the ones who were acting in defense of Muslims.[42]

When the Saudi royal family rejected bin Laden's proposal to have the mujahidin veterans of the Soviet War in Afghanistan defend the kingdom's oil fields, opting instead to use American troops, bin Laden took the decision as an act of heresy. Saddam for his part did not miss the opportunity to convene a conference of religious scholars who would condemn this "infidel" presence in the Muslim holy lands.[43]

It was at this point that bin Laden began to take his case against the royal family to the public. The royal family countered by taking away his passport, but he still managed to slip away to Sudan.

Sudan

To bin Laden, Sudan was not a bad place to launch his Islamic revolution. Since 1989, the African country had been in the process of its own "Islamic experiment," as the country's leader, Sorbonne-educated legal scholar, Hassan al-Tourabi, liked to describe the effort.[44] Just prior to seizing control of the government, he had declared, "It is either sharia or it is jihad."[45] For years he had been encouraging bin Laden to relocate his organization in Sudan.

This is how Amnesty International would later describe the "Islamic experiment" in Sudan:

> [The regime] has resorted to repression to maintain control. Hundreds of prisoners of conscience from all walks of life have been arrested and detained without charge or trial. Torture and degrading treatment in secret detention centres, known locally as "ghost houses," have been widespread and sometimes fatal . . . Suspected political opponents have been sacked from their jobs and lost their homes, had their property confiscated and their civil rights restricted. In 1991 the government introduced a penal code which provides for cruel, inhuman and degrading penalties: flogging, amputation and stoning to death.[46]

For years the Muslims in the Sudanese north had been waging jihad against the largely Christian-Animist south. But in 1992, just after bin Laden moved there, the Sudanese regime extended the call to jihad to include the country's Nuba Muslims as well because they opposed the fundamentalist vision of the ruling party.[47] The government declared that anyone who resisted the regime was an apostate and would be sentenced to death.[48]

This was the regime in which bin Laden was eager to invest—in exchange for refuge, he would help the regime build needed infrastructure such as roads. In time bin Laden would be joined by Dr. Zawahiri, his old comrade from Afghanistan, who was not exactly welcome in his homeland of Egypt because of his earlier involvement in the Sadat assassination plot. As far as Zawahiri was concerned, neighboring Sudan was an even better place to wage jihad against the Egyptian regime as he would be out of reach of the Egyptian authorities yet still close enough to manage all the logistics.[49]

Egyptian Jihad

During his time in prison back in Egypt, Zawahiri had gotten to know the "Blind Sheik," Omar Abdel Rahman, the spiritual head of the Egyptian Islamic Group (EIG), Egypt's largest Islamist group. The Blind Sheik was charged with having provided the religious justification that gave Sadat's assassins the green light to kill him. Though the Sheik would be acquitted of these charges, he enjoyed the fact that he had been linked to Sadat's assassination and approved of the deed.[50]

The Blind Sheik also gave his followers permission to kill Christians and attack their businesses since, according to him, Muslims and Christians were in a perpetual state of war.[51] With this rationale, the Blind Sheik's followers burned and bombed movie theaters, banks, bookstores, and tourist spots throughout the early 1990s. One of his followers later justified the death and destruction to *The New Yorker*, "We believe in the principle of establishing Sharia [Islamic law], even if this means the death of all mankind."[52]

Ultimately, the Islamist insurgency in Egypt claimed some 1,200 lives.[53] It would end with a cease-fire in 1997, after members of the Blind Sheik's group gunned down and then hacked to death fifty-eight foreign tourists and four Egyptians at an ancient site in Luxor, Egypt.

The Egyptian jihad even spilled over into the United States. By 1993 the Blind Sheik was operating out of mosques in New York and New Jersey where a group of his followers truck bombed the World Trade Center, killing six and injuring a thousand. The mastermind of the operation, Ramzi Yousef, later told law-enforcement authorities that he had wanted to kill at least a quarter million[54] and promised that he would return with more money to "bring those towers down."[55] He never did return. In 1998, he was sentenced to 240 years in prison. Perhaps he was able to draw some comfort from the fact that it was his uncle, Khalid Sheik Mohammad, who was able to finish the job as the mastermind of the 9/11 attacks.

Yousef told investigators he had learned to use explosives in the training camps of Afghanistan and his ultimate goal was the liberation of Palestine. A boyhood friend told investigators that Yousef selected the World Trade Center as his target because he was told that a lot of Jews worked there.[56]

The Blind Sheik also wanted to punish the United States for its support of Israel, according to prosecutors at his trial in New York, where he was convicted of conspiring to blow up various New York City landmarks. The government linked the Blind Sheik to jihad organizations in Egypt, Sudan, Pakistan, and Afghanistan[57] and played the jury tape recordings of his sermons where he could be heard calling Muslims to "strike terror into the hearts of the enemies."[58]

Later, during a 2004 trial in which the Blind Sheik's former lawyer, translator, and paralegal were convicted of having helped him wage jihad from his prison cell, it emerged that just after his 1995 conviction, he had issued a fatwa calling on Muslims everywhere to kill Americans, even children, "to treat them with brutality," and to "drown their ships, shoot down their airplanes, kill them on earth, in the sea or in the sky, kill them everywhere you find them" until he was released from a U.S. prison.[59] Bin Laden was alleged to have told a reporter that he had used this fatwa as the basis of his own 1998 declaration of jihad against Americans and Jews.

In 1995, followers of the Blind Sheik tried to assassinate the Egyptian president, Hosni Mubarak, on a state visit to Ethiopia. Egyptian authorities discovered that bin Laden's group was helping them. This evidence increased pressure on the Sudanese regime to expel bin Laden. The Sudanese offered to turn him over to the Saudis, they declined the offer as they had already revoked his citizenship and frozen his assets.[60]

The Sudanese government informed bin Laden that they were no longer interested in harboring him and suggested that he find another sanctuary. By this time, bin Laden was broke and a man without a country. There was no place left to go but Afghanistan, which, though he still had some contacts there, had descended into a state of chaos, with various warlords fighting for control of the territory.[61]

Algeria

Around the time bin Laden was forced out of Saudi Arabia in 1991, other Arab Afghans were having some success waging jihads in their own homelands—in Algeria, for example.

After Algeria gained independence from France in 1962, one political party effectively dominated the system—the National Liberation Front. However, in 1991, an Islamist party, the Islamic Salvation Front (FIS), became so popular that the Algerian regime decided that it had to cancel what would have been the nation's first multiparty elections or it would risk losing power. The regime justified this antidemocratic move by arguing that if the FIS gained power, that would be the last election anyway. A group of Islamists immediately declared jihad against the regime.[62]

Soon a more radical faction emerged—the Armed Islamic Group (GIA). The GIA quickly became notorious for throat-slitting masses of ordinary villagers, including women and children. The GIA justified their slaughter by arguing that the villagers had lost their immunity as a defensive jihad had been declared and that any Muslim who did not actively oppose the regime could be considered an apostate, including children and the elderly. "There is no neutrality in the war that we are waging," Antar Zouabri, the GIA leader pronounced, "Apart from those who are with me, all others are apostates and deserve death."[63] The GIA also burned hundreds of schools and killed scores of teachers since, according to an official statement, "Keeping educational institutions open in such circumstances means inhibiting the Jihad."[64]

In 1996, the GIA also condemned to death any Algerian caught failing to pray five times daily or give charity to Muslim causes. Women who refused to wear hijab or who were caught working or attending school were also condemned to death, according to this GIA pronouncement:

> The GIA bans the Muslims' daughters and wives from going out without a veil and from indulging in obscenity and sin by showing their hair and faces . . . They must not work, and neither must they study . . . For those among them who will conform,

all will be well and good, but for those who refuse to comply and whose hearts, ears and eyes are impervious to God, death will be the punishment for their depravity.[65]

The GIA also claimed credit for beheading seven Trappist monks who lived in Algeria for decades serving the Algerian poor. According to the GIA, the Trappist monks deserved their fate because they had been "mixing with [the Algerian people], living with them, and blocking the way of Allah by calling people to Christianity."[66] Over the course of the jihad in Algeria, which lasted from 1991 until 1998, some 70,000 civilians were killed.[67]

The conflict even spilled over into France where Algerian jihadists allegedly carried out a series of bombings in Paris that killed twelve and wounded some 200 during 1995–1996.[68] French civilians were deemed to be legitimate targets because the French government supported the Algerian regime.

Tunisia

In neighboring Tunisia, in 1991–1992, Islamists tried to assassinate the Tunisian president, Zine Abidine ben Ali, but the Tunisian government responded with a severe crackdown, arresting over 20,000 suspected radicals and sentencing dozens to death.[69]

At the time, most Western governments and human rights monitors were appalled. The Tunisians, however, remained firm. "You cannot live in peace with these people," was the response of Abdallah Kallel, Tunisia's interior minister, adding that "The West doesn't want to understand that their action is directed essentially against the free world, against the West, and if Islam succeeds in taking over North Africa, they will next declare *jihad* (holy war) against the West."[70]

Tunisia would be largely spared Islamist violence until 2002, when a German convert to Islam, Christian Ganczarski with close ties to al Qaeda would launch an attack on a Tunisian synagogue, killing twenty-one, mostly German tourists.

Bosnia

During the early 1990s, the mujahidin also heard the call to jihad in Bosnia, where Muslims were reportedly being raped and slaughtered by the Serbs. The Serbs had taken up arms in 1992 just after Bosnia and Herzegovina had declared independence from the former Yugoslavia. They wanted to establish an independent "Greater Serbia." Muslims from all over the world were appalled that the international community was refusing to lift an arms embargo, making it virtually impossible for the Bosnian Muslims to defend themselves.

Clerics from all over the world were issuing statements that the war in Bosnia was a defensive jihad, and telling Muslims that it was obligatory for them to come to the defense of their fellow Muslims. Hundreds of mujahidin from at least a dozen different countries heeded the call to assist the Bosnian Muslims.[71] Though the mujahidin reportedly fought with distinction along side the

Bosnian Muslims, they eventually came to be resented because of their fanaticism and disdain for the more secular-minded locals.

In the end it was when President Bill Clinton finally gave the go-ahead to the NATO air forces that the conflict was brought to an end. By then, however at least a hundred thousand people had lost their lives and the American effort was essentially considered too little too late. Bin Laden summed up the general sentiment in much of the Muslim world when he wrote in his 1996 fatwa:

> Massacres in . . . Bosnia-Herzegovina took place, massacres that send shivers in the body and shake the conscience. All of this and the world watch and hear, and not only didn't respond to these atrocities, but also with a clear conspiracy between the USA and its' [sic] allies and under the cover of the iniquitous United Nations, the dispossessed people were even prevented from obtaining arms to defend themselves.[72]

Thus bin Laden and his associates added the Bosnian intervention to the list of grievances against America.

Chechnya

In 1992, just after the dissolution of the Soviet Union, Chechnya, a Russian republic, following the lead of other former Soviet republics, decided that it too would declare its own independence. The successor state to the Soviet Union, Russia, was in no position to respond. It would not be until 1994 that the Russian president, Boris Yeltsin, would do something about the renegade republic and then perhaps only because he thought it would bolster his popular appeal in time for the 1996 presidential elections.[73] In any case, he dispatched 40,000 Russian troops into the Muslim republic ignoring the warning from the Chechen president that the only purpose a Russian invasion would serve would be to provoke jihad.[74]

Indeed, as soon as the Russians invaded, calls to jihad went out and Arab Afghans and would-be mujahidin from all over the world descended on Chechnya to defend their fellow Muslims. At first the Chechnyans were not exactly thrilled by all the outside support, especially from those they considered to be religious fanatics. After the many years spent under communism, most Chechens were now only nominally Muslim and rejected the idea that they were suddenly supposed to martyr themselves for Islam.[75]

A radical element did eventually emerge among the Chechnyans. In 1995, for example, one faction seized a hospital in the north and held some 1,500 patients and hospital staff hostage in order to secure an escape route for their rebel commander, one Shamil Basayev, which resulted in scores of innocent deaths. Nevertheless the rebels took the hospital seizure to be a victory because it so effectively demonstrated to the Russian public the powerlessness of the regime in Moscow. In 1996, when the rebels finally drove the Russians out of Chechnya, Basayev was even deemed a war hero and named as Chechnya's new prime minister. Soon after, however, reminiscent of what happened when the

Russians left Afghanistan, Chechnya descended into a state of feudalism and lawlessness.

In 1999, Basayev now allied with an Arab jihadist, Amir Khattab, decided to launch jihad in next door Dagestan. They had the support of at least one cleric there, Mullah Bagauddin, who proclaimed that Dagestan would be happy to remain part of Russia but only if Russia became an Islamic state.[76]

Zawahiri details the jihadist plan for the region in his 2001 memoirs:

> The liberation of the Caucasus would constitute a hotbed of jihad (or fundamentalism as the United States describes it) and that region would become the shelter of thousands of Muslim mujahidin from various parts of the Islamic world . . . If the Chechens and other Caucasus mujahidin reach the shores of the oil-rich Caspian Sea, the only thing that would separate them from Afghanistan will be the neutral state of Turkmenistan. This will form a mujahid Islamic belt to the south of Russia that will be connected in the east to Pakistan, which is brimming with mujahidin movements in Kashmir. The belt will be linked to the south with Iran and Turkey . . . Furthermore the liberation of the Muslim Caucasus will lead to the fragmentation of the Russian Federation and will help escalate the jihad movements that already exist in the republics of Uzbekistan and Tajikistan.[77]

Unfortunately for them, the jihadist plan for Dagestan backfired and only provoked Russia to send its armies back into Chechnya and regain control of the renegade republic.

In October 2002, Chechnyan separatists, again led by Basayev, struck Russia another time. This time they seized a Moscow Theatre and held 800 people hostage. Three days into the seizure, Russian troops used noxious gas to try to pacify the situation and ended up poisoning about 170 people. Half of the forty-one hostage-takers were the Chechen "black widows"—women who concealed themselves in black hijab, out to avenge the death of loved ones killed in the separatist violence. Russian authorities would later claim the black widows were trained by Arab instructors.[78]

In September 2004, Chechen separatists again led by Basayev seized control of a school, in Beslan and held more than a thousand children and teachers, hostage for several days. In the end some 330 people ended up dead, including 156 children.[79] One of the hostage-takers told Russian state television that Basayev and another rebel leader had told him that the school takeover was a necessary "to start a war across the Caucasus"[80] so that they could establish an Islamic state there.[81]

S. Frederick Starr, chairman of the Central Asia-Caucasus Institute at Johns Hopkins University and one of America's foremost experts on Chechnya estimates that Chechnya has lost a quarter of its population in the conflict.[82]

Philippines

After carrying out the World Trade Center bombing in 1993, Ramzi Yousef, the mastermind, eventually ended up in the Philippines, where in the mid-1990s, he could be found in the midst of several plots. He had plans to assassinate both Pope John Paul II and President Bill Clinton during their upcoming visits to the

Philippines and he was eager to simultaneously blow up a dozen passenger airplanes as they flew over the Pacific. Helping him in this plot, which he nicknamed "Bojinka," was his uncle, Khalid Sheik Mohammad–or KSM as he came to be called by investigators, when it was discovered that it was he who had masterminded the 9/11 attacks.

The Philippines police uncovered the Bojinka plot after a Manila detective was called in to investigate a fire that had broken out in Yousef's apartment, when he was experimenting with bomb-making chemicals.[83] Though both Yousef and KSM managed to avoid arrest at the time, the police apprehended one of their coconspirators, after he came back to the apartment to retrieve the laptop computer Yousef left behind in which details of the plot were stored.

The Bojinka plot would not have been the island nation's first experience with Islamist terrorism—nor its first experience with Yousef. He had already succeeded in exploding a bomb aboard a Philippines airliner that blew apart the Japanese passenger under whose seat the bomb had been placed.

Moreover, in just the previous year alone there had been at least fifty incidents of Islamist terror—Roman Catholic priests were a favorite target, bombings had occurred on trains, a Wendy's hamburger stand, and at a movie theater. The radicals wanted to establish an Islamic state on the southern island of Mindanao.[84]

One of the groups at the center of the conflict, the Abu Sayyaf group, was funded by one of bin Laden's brother-in-laws, Mohammad Jamal Khalifa. The founder of the group, a cleric by the name of Abdurajak Janjalani, had fought with bin Laden in Afghanistan.[85] In March 2000, the group drew international attention when it kidnapped fifty-one tourists in the Philippines and threatened to kill them unless the United States released the Blind Sheik and Yousef from prison, who were both by then serving out life sentences for their terrorism plots. In spite of the fact that the U.S. government refused to accede to the kidnappers' demands, most of the hostages were eventually released, although two were beheaded and four remain missing and are presumed dead.

The Philippines government has yet to get the situation under control. By April 2005, there were so many Islamist radicals in Mindanao that a U.S. embassy official in Manila warned that the island was so lawless that it verged on "becoming an Afghanistan situation."[86] The Philippines government has acknowledged that the Mindanao is home to various radical groups, including the Jemaah Islamiyah (JI), an al-Qaeda affiliate that operates throughout Southeast Asia and that was responsible for the terror attacks in Bali.[87]

Saudi Arabia

On November 13, 1995, five Americans and two Indians were killed when a truck bomb exploded at the American-operated Saudi National Guard training center in Riyadh. The following year, on June 25, 1996 another truck bomb hit the Khobar Towers, a U.S. military residence, in Dharan, Saudi Arabia, killing nineteen U.S. servicemen.

Just after the bombings, bin Laden gave this explanation to British reporter Robert Fisk: "The Saudis now know their real enemy is America," he said, "The explosion at Khobar did not come as a direct result of American occupation but as a result of American behaviour against Muslims." He claimed Americans were complicit in the plight of the Palestinians and that "the deaths of 600,000 Iraqi children after UN sanctions were placed on Iraq" represented America's "crusade against Islam."[88]

In another interview with the same journalist, bin Laden warned that Muslims were emboldened by their victory against the Soviets and now prayed that they would also defeat America, "to make it a shadow of itself," adding:

> We . . . believe that our battle against America is much simpler than the war against the Soviet Union, because some of our mujahedin who fought here in Afghanistan also participated in operations against the Americans in Somalia—and they were surprised at the collapse of American morale. This convinced us that the Americans are a paper tiger.[89]

In his 1996 fatwa, bin Laden said that Muslims should use "swift and light forces" and work in "complete secrecy" to counter the superior American military power and emphasized that ridding the Arabian Peninsula of American forces was now "the most important duty" for Muslims, second only to their "belief in God."[90]

Regroupment in Afghanistan

At the time bin Laden issued his 1996 fatwa, he was back in Afghanistan, having been expelled from the Sudan. By this time, a large swath of the country was under the control of the Taliban, a group of religious students led by a one-eyed cleric, Mullah Mohammad Omar. The Taliban were rumored to have gained the support of the Afghans when they put an end to the squabbling of two rival warlords who were fighting over who had the sexual right of a certain boy, according to journalist Peter Bergen author of the book *Holy War, Inc.: Inside the Secret World of Osama Bin Laden*.[91] The West also initially hoped that the Taliban would also bring order to Afghanistan, which had been in a chaotic state since the Soviet pullout in 1989.

While the Taliban would indeed bring order to Afghanistan, it would be an extreme form of order. The Taliban's first move was to reinstitute traditional Islamic punishments including stoning to death, amputation, and beheading. Women were now compelled to wear an all-encompassing garment that covered them from head to toe. Even their eyes were to be covered with a piece of mesh to enable them to see, but just barely. All women, even widows who were the sole source of support of their families, were forbidden from working. Girls schools were closed. The Taliban banned movies, television and radio, video cassettes; even songbirds and children's toys. Soccer matches were occasionally permitted, but cheering or any other public display of happiness was forbidden and the soccer stadium was often used to conduct public stonings and beheadings. Because of their dismal human rights record, only three countries would recognize the Taliban as the legitimate government of Afghanistan: Saudi Arabia, the United Arab Emirates, and Pakistan.

Bin Laden, however, was enjoying life under the Taliban. When he first moved back to Afghanistan, he was apprehensive about how he would fit in. Fortunately, he got along well with his new guardians. They even afforded him a degree of freedom he had not had in Sudan, where the government was still eager to be accepted by the international community. Among the Taliban's virtues, in his mind, was the fact that they did not care what the rest of the world thought of their strict Islamic state.[92]

On August 6, 1998, after some Islamist radicals were arrested in Eastern Europe, a London-based Arabic daily published a statement from Zawahiri, warning that Americans would soon receive a message which would be written "in a language they will understand."[93]

One day later, on the anniversary of the U.N. sanctions against Iraq, as well as the day the first President Bush first sent U.S. forces into the Arabian Peninsula, al Qaeda bombed the two U.S. embassies in east Africa. Less than three weeks later, on August 20, President Clinton retaliated, launching seventy-nine Tomahawk cruise missiles at al Qaeda training camps in Afghanistan and at a manufacturing plant in Sudan, where the administration believed VX nerve gas was being made using Iraqi precursor materials. Neither strike had any real impact: the al Qaeda leaders had already left the camps in Afghanistan and the manufacturing plant turned out to be a pharmaceutical factory. In fact, when bin Laden took to the radio to announce that he was still alive, his legend grew even larger: he was now seen as someone whom God had blessed in his jihad against America.[94]

The next day, Zawahiri would cap off the failure of the air strikes when he delivered another ominous message, this time to a reporter in Pakistan:

> Tell the Americans that we aren't afraid of bombardment, threats, and acts of aggression. We suffered and survived the Soviet bombings for ten years in Afghanistan and we are ready for more sacrifices. The war has only just begun; the Americans should now await the answer.[95]

Kashmir

By the mid-1990s, the mujahidin were also answering the call to yet another jihad: this time in Kashmir, a Muslim-majority state high in the Indian Himlayas.

At the time of partition of the Indian subcontinent into two states: the Muslim state of Pakistan and the secular state of India in 1947, the Hindu monarch of the predominantly Muslim state of Kashmir opted to become part of India instead of Pakistan. Pakistan, however, was not happy about the situation and the two new nations went to war to resolve the issue. India eventually asked the United Nations to intervene, though it never fully accepted all of the terms of the U.N.-devised solution. Thus in 1965, the two countries once again found themselves in a full-scale war over the Himalayan state. Though this war was also relatively short, in 1999, tensions again flared up and this time, the two nations, nearly came to a nuclear stand-off. As far as Kashmiris themselves were concerned, most wanted nothing to do with either Pakistan or India. What they wanted was to be independent.

After the Soviets pulled out of Afghanistan in 1989, some of the mujahidin fanned out to Kashmir and suddenly the Kashmiri independence movement was co-opted by the global jihad movement. Since that time some 35,000 people have lost their lives in the jihad in Kashmir.[96]

Kashmiri jihadist groups have also been linked to terrorist attacks outside Kashmir. In 1994, Kashmiri jihadists kidnapped U.S. and British nationals in New Delhi. In 1999, they hijacked an airplane en route from Nepal to Afghanistan and held 155 passengers hostage until one of their leaders was released from an Indian jail. In 2000, they attacked an army installation in New Delhi. Indian officials claim that Kashmiri terrorists were behind the suicide bombing of the Indian parliament in December of 2001, which killed fourteen people died, including the six attackers. They have also been linked to the February 2002 kidnapping and beheading of Wall Street Journal reporter Daniel Pearl in Pakistan, as well as a series of attacks on Pakistani Christians in the same year. In March 2002, a senior al Qaeda lieutenant, Abu Zubaydah, was captured at a safe house operated by Lashkar-i-Taiba ("Army of the Pure" or "LET"), a Kashmiri jihadist group whose stated mission is to "plant Islamic flags in Delhi, Tel Aviv, and Washington."[97] Even in the United States, in 2004, a group of Virginia residents, dubbed the "Virginia jihad network," were convicted of associating with the LET in order to prepare for what they were told would be a global war against Islam in the wake of the 9/11 attacks.[98] In 2005, another member of the "Virginia Jihad Network," Ahmed Omar Abu Ali, an American citizen, was convicted of providing material support to al Qaeda and conspiracy to assassinate President Bush, kidnap members of Congress, pirate aircraft, and plot terrorist acts in the United States. Abu Ali claimed that the charges against him arose as a result of a confession he made while being tortured in Saudi Arabia where he was being detained in connection with the May 12, 2003 bombings in Riyadh that resulted in twenty-three deaths. He was sentenced to thirty years in prison.

Yemen

On October 12, 2000 two suicide bombers attacked an American warship, the U.S.S. Cole while it was refueling at a port in Yemen by detonating a small boat filled with 500 pounds of explosives. Seventeen U.S. sailors were killed and more than forty injured. The Aden-Abyan Islamic Army, an organization linked to al Qaeda, claimed credit for the attack.[99]

A month before the Cole bombing, bin Laden, Zawahiri and a member of the EIG, Rifai Ahmad Taha, released a videotape in which they vowed to spill American blood unless the Blind Sheik was released from U.S. prison.[100]

In 1998 just after this appeal was made the Aden-Abyan Islamic Army kidnapped sixteen Western tourists , including two Americans in Yemen. The group demanded the establishment of an Islamic state in Yemen and "an end to the aggression against Iraq and the withdrawal of the U.S. and British forces from the Gulf region."[101] At his trial, the mastermind of the kidnapping, Abu Hassan, confessed that he had planned other operations against Western targets and added "I hope God strikes you all."[102]

During the kidnapping investigation, it was learned that in December 1998, Yemeni authorities had arrested five British Muslims and a French-Algerian who had been plotting a series of bombings intended to strike the capital Aden, during the Christmas holidays. According to a U.S. indictment, the plotters were all recruited by Abu Hamza al-Masri, an Egyptian veteran of the Soviet-Afghan War, who had been granted British citizenship and was now the imam (or prayer leader) of the Finsbury Park mosque in London. Later this mosque would make headlines when it was discovered that Zacarias Moussaoui attended the mosque. Moussaoui is to date the only person to have been convicted in the U.S. in connection with the 9/11 attacks. Another famous attendee would be Richard C. Reid, the "shoe-bomber" who was arrested after he tried to blow up an American Airlines flight from Paris to Miami in December 2001 using explosives hidden in his shoes.

In 2006, British authorities charged the hook-fisted, one-eyed Abu Hamza who was convicted of inciting others to kill or hate Jews and non-Muslims and for possession of the "Encyclopedia of the Afghan Jihad" and other al Qaeda literature. In the United States, in addition to the kidnapping-related charges, he was indicted for trying to set up a terrorist training camp in Oregon and otherwise providing material assistance to al Qaeda and the Taliban. So far Britain has refused to honor the U.S. extradition request. He is also wanted in Yemen on terrorism charges.

9/11

On September 11, 2001, nineteen members of al Qaeda hijacked four commercial aircraft. Two of the planes crashed into the twin towers of the World Trade Center in New York, one hit the Pentagon, and the fourth, which was intended to strike either the U.S. Capitol Building or the White House, crashed into a field in Shanksville, Pennsylvania after the passengers, who had by then been alerted to the day's events, tried to commandeer the aircraft away from the hijackers. The 9/11 attacks were the most lethal strike in U.S. history. The final death toll was 2,986, and included citizens from some ninety countries.[103]

In response, the next month, the United States, along with Britain, Australia, Canada and the Northern Alliance, a group opposing the Taliban, attacked Afghanistan in order to destroy al Qaeda's safe haven. Calls for jihad against the U.S.-led coalition came from as far away as Kenya, where a group called itself the Friends of Al-Aqsa, organized a demonstration to declare its support.[104] In Malaysia, the 800,000-strong Islamic opposition party, the Parti Islam SeMalaysia (PAS), issued a statement saying that its members should assume that they were obligated to do their part.[105] Even some Canadians are believed to have tried to travel to Afghanistan in order to join the jihad against the U.S.-led coalition.[106]

In 2002, after the U.S.-led forces successfully routed the Taliban from Afghanistan, Golboddin Hekmatyar, the leader of an Islamist party, the Hezb-e

Eslami, whom the Taliban had driven out returned to Afghanistan to declare his own jihad, even going so far as to offer six-figure rewards for the capture of any Western military personnel.[107] Hekmatyar also reminded Muslims that, "Islam does not permit a Muslim to live in submission under infidels and aggressors," and cautioned that "the fate of the Islamic world" hung in Afghanistan. As he put it, what was going on now was a "war between civilizations" that would "continue forever" only because the West wants its "civilization to be the dominant one in the world." He further warned that "the slogans of reconciliation and cooperation are Western slogans" and that Muslims should resist falling for them.[108]

Indonesia

On October 12, 2002, Indonesian Islamists linked to al Qaeda exploded car bombs in the nightclub district on the resort island of Bali killing 202 people, mostly foreign tourists. This was the first time that foreigners had been targeted in the island nation, though for years Indonesian Islamists had been attacking Christians and other non-Muslims in the eastern islands of Maluku and Sulawesi and in the Aceh province.

Jemaah Islamiyah (JI), the group responsible for the Bali blasts, aims to establish a pan-Islamic state extending from Malaysia to southern Thailand, Indonesia, Singapore, and into the Philippines.[109] Singapore authorities foiled a JI plot to attack U.S., Israeli, British and Australian embassies and diplomatic missions in Singapore in December 2001. The JI has also attacked Christians and Buddhists in Thailand in an effort to establish an Islamic state in the nation's southern region.

The alleged mastermind of the Bali bombings, an Indonesian who goes by the name Hambali, turned out to be a close friend of KSM, the 9/11 planner. As al Qaeda expert Rohan Gunaratna put it, "In the post-9/11 world, there is no such thing anymore as a local Muslim struggle," adding, "Be it al-Qaeda or one of its affiliates, some part of the international Islamic militant movement will move in with logistical help, training and, above all, money."[110]

In July 2001, the Indonesian Islamists celebrated their first real political success when the government granted the Aceh provincial government enough autonomy to implement Islamic law. Among the changes, women must now don hijab, contact with the opposite sex outside of family or marriage is an offense punishable by caning, and elsewhere in Indonesia, Islamists continue to attack tourist spots, churches and "deviant" mosques.

Jihad Against "Renegade" Muslim Rulers

In February 2003, bin Laden urged Muslims to "liberate themselves from those nd renegade ruling regimes, which are enslaved by the United States" in "establish the rule of God on earth." He included a list of countries that ied were "the most qualified regions for liberation," naming Morocco, Nigeria, Pakistan, Saudi Arabia, and Yemen.[111]

A few months later, on May 12, 2003, suicide bombers attacked three residential compounds in Riyadh, the Saudi capital, killing thirty-five, including the nine attackers, nine Americans, seven Saudis, and at least one person each from Australia, Britain, Ireland, Jordan, Lebanon, the Philippines, and Switzerland.

On May 16, only four days later, Morocco was hit. Twelve suicide bombers attacked Jewish and tourist sites in Casablanca, killing forty-five, along with themselves. At first counterterrorism officials in both countries could not see any connection between the Riyadh and the Casablanca bombings. Later, however, officials in both countries would conclude that Moroccan al Qaeda operatives, Karim El-Mejjati and Hussein Mohammed Haski, were behind the attacks. A third member of their group, Amer Azizi, would later be linked to the Madrid train bombings.[112]

Later that year, on November 8th, Saudi Arabia was hit again when a suicide truck bomber drove into another foreign housing complex in Riyadh, killing eighteen, mostly Muslim and Arab guest workers from Egypt and Lebanon.

A week later, on November 15, 2003 suicide bombers attacked two synagogues in Istanbul, Turkey, killing twenty-seven people, mostly Turkish Muslim bystanders. Five days later, al Qaeda struck Turkey again. Two truck bombs exploded—one outside a London-headquartered bank and the other at the British Consulate, killing thirty and wounding hundreds. Again most of the dead were Turkish Muslims.

Jihad Against Israel

Perhaps the longest-running jihad in today's world is the struggle to reclaim Israel for the Muslims. During World War II, the highest ranking Islamic cleric of Jerusalem, the Grand Mufti Hajj Amin el-Husseini, was forced to flee to Nazi Germany after he tried to organize a pro-Axis coup in Iraq. He supported the Axis Powers because he was promised that they would respect Arab sovereignty and independence and were willing to abolish the Jewish National Homeland in Palestine.[113] In Berlin, the mufti was only too eager to collaborate with and assist the Nazis in the Final Solution.[114] In radio broadcasts directed at the Arab world from Berlin, the Grand Mufti famously urged Muslims to "Kill the Jews wherever you find them."[115] He also helped recruit Bosnian Muslims for the German SS[116] and worked to prevent further immigration to Palestine thus ensuring that many Jews would end up in death camps instead.[117]

In 1948, a month before the Arab states declared war on the new state of Israel, the ranking cleric of Egypt, Hasanayn Muhammad Makhluf, issued a fatwa declaring that all Muslims should participate in the jihad to "rescue" Palestine because the true intention of the "Jewish zionists" was to "dominate all Islamic states and to eliminate their Arabic character and their Islamic culture."[118]

Even the avowed secularist, Yasser Arafat, issued a call to jihad to rally his fellow Muslims when he urged a crowd of pilgrims at the annual Hajj to Mecca in 1978 to wage "holy war" to liberate Jerusalem. As Pakistani leader

General Zia-ul-Haq observed, "If the two million Moslem pilgrims who came" to Mecca that year decided to "march unarmed, barefoot and naked to liberate Jerusalem, then no power on earth" would be able to "stand in their way."[119]

In 1979, the Palestinians would have their first sole-purpose jihad organization when a local physician and a preacher got together to found the Palestinian Islamic Jihad (PIJ). The doctor and the cleric claimed to have been inspired by the Iranian revolution. They decided that it was time that the Palestinians tapped the power of Islam instead of relying on Arab nationalism, which had thus far clearly failed them. The PIJ set its mission to be the destruction of the state of Israel, which would be accomplished—as the group's name would suggest—through jihad. The PIJ's ultimate goal would include the overthrow of all nation-states in the region in favor of a pan-Islamic state.[120] To accomplish its aims, the PIJ would engage in scores of attacks and kill some 208 people, mostly Israeli civilians.[121]

The most prominent Islamic terror organization in Palestine, however, would end up being Hamas, a group comprised of a social welfare organization as well as a military wing, allowing it to create a much more substantial profile than the PIJ. Hamas was founded in 1987 by a group that included Sheikh Ahmed Ismail Yassin, the most prominent member of the Muslim Brotherhood in Gaza, as well as Abdullah Azzam, the leader of the jihad in Afghanistan.[122] The mission of Hamas was summed up in its motto: "Allah is its goal, the Prophet its model, the Quran its Constitution, Jihad its path and death for the sake of Allah is the loftiest of its wishes."[123]

Hamas believes that Muslims have a sacred obligation to restore back to Muslims all territory that was ever under the domain of Islam because, in their words, "an Islamic Waqf [property is] consecrated for future Muslim generations until Judgement Day."[124] According to Hamas, Palestine is not the only "Islamic Waqf"; other "lands conquered by Muslims by force, during the times of (Islamic) conquests" are also "Waqf lands" and must be restored through jihad.

In pursuit of its stated goals, since launching its first suicide attack in Israel in 1993, Hamas has been linked to hundreds of terrorist attacks.[125] Hamas won 74 out of 132 seats in the January 1996 parliamentary elections in the Palestinian Authority and as of this writing is the majority party of the legislative body.

Jihad in Iraq

Given this context, it is not surprising that in the run up to the U.S.-led war in Iraq, many calls to jihad could be heard.

Sheikh Yousef Al-Qaradhawi, the host of a television show on Al-Jazeera, issued several statements supporting jihad in Iraq against the U.S.-led forces and urged Muslim governments not to make their airports, harbors or bases available to U.S. forces launching attacks on Iraq.[126]

In Bahrain, a member of the national parliament, Abdul Latif Al Sheikh, called for jihad to defend Iraq and cast the war as part of a long-running campaign by U.S. and Zionist forces to take over the resources of the Islamic world.[127] Other clerics echoed his call. "The Americans are fighting this war on behalf of Islam's enemies, especially Israel which continues to murder our brethren in Palestine while the world sits idle," opined one Bahraini cleric.[128]

In the hours before the invasion, the clerics from al-Azhar in Cairo, the Sunni world's most prestigious center of learning, declared that "Jihad is an individual duty for all Muslims if the U.S. launches a war against Iraq"[129] and Al-Azhar's leading cleric later pronounced that suicide operations against the invading forces would be justified under Islamic law.[130]

Syria's top cleric, Sheik Ahmad Kaftaro, also weighed in saying that Muslims should "use all means possible to thwart the aggression, including martyr operations against the belligerent American, British and Zionist invaders."[131]

In Russia, the Supreme Mufti of an Islamic council, Talgat Tadzhuddin, claiming to represent Russian Muslims, declared that the council had voted unanimously in favor of jihad against the United States, saying this was the first time Russian Muslims had declared war on another country since 1941, when they declared jihad against Nazi Germany.[132] Fear of inciting the country's estimated fifteen million Muslims is one of the reasons some observers believe that the Russian leader, Vladimir Putin, was unwilling to lend his support to the American-led invasion.[133]

In November 2004, during the lead-up to Iraq's first democratic elections in history, twenty-six state-supported Saudi clerics got together to issue a call for jihad against the occupying forces in Iraq. Indeed, a substantial portion of the foreign jihadists who have come to Iraq are believed to be Saudis.

The coalition forces are not the only target of jihad in Iraq. Shiites have also been targeted. In September 2005, Abu Musab al-Zarqawi, the head of al Qaeda in Iraq, and the main suspect in many terrorist attacks against Iraqi civilians declared an all-out war against the Iraqi Shiites.[134]

In a letter he purportedly wrote that was intercepted by American forces in January 2004 Zarqawi explained why the Shiites are a legitimate target:

> They, i.e., Shi'a, have declared a secret war against the people of Islam. They are the proximate, dangerous enemy of the Sunnis, even if the Americans are also an archenemy. The danger from the Shi'a, however, is greater and their damage is worse and more destructive to the [Islamic] nations than the Americans, on whom you find a quasi-consensus about killing them as an assailing enemy.[135]

In the same letter, Zarqawi threatens to launch "martyrdom operations and car bombs" against the Shiites and claims to have already launched twenty-five martyrdom operations.

Shiites in Pakistan have also been frequent targets of Sunni jihadists. In 2004, Sunni extremists attacked a Shiite mosque, killing some one hundred people and injuring thousands. One Sunni jihadist described his group's use of violence as "never random" adding that "the Koran says, 'Kill those who kill you'" and that his group's philosophy was "an Islamic one: either victory or martyrdom. Combat is an essential part of jihad and jihad is our duty."[136]

Saudi Arabia is believed to be the primary sponsor of the Sunni extremists in Pakistan, while Iran is alleged to be backing the Shiites, leading terrorism expert Jessica Stern to characterize the situation in Pakistan as a proxy war between the Saudis and the Iranians.[137]

Europe

On March 11, 2004, Europe experienced its first mass-casualty attack by jihadists when ten bombs detonated on four commuter trains in Madrid Spain, killing 191 people and wounding nearly 1,800.

At first, Spanish authorities suspected that Basque separatists were behind the attacks but later concluded that a group of jihadists linked to al Qaeda carried out the bombings.

When news of what had occurred in Madrid reached a Norwegian security analyst, Brynjar Lia, he recalled a 42-page Arabic document on an Islamist website that he had located months earlier. The document proposed ways to defeat the coalition in Iraq and was purportedly written by a group claiming to be the Media Committee for the Victory of the Iraqi People. In the proposal, the authors suggested that "painful blows" should be dealt to the weakest link in the coalition, the Spanish forces, in light of the fact that the vast majority of the Spanish public was opposed the Iraqi invasion. The authors suggested that the "blows" should be timed to influence the outcome of the upcoming general election.[138]

While the proposal's authors never suggested targeting Spain itself, the train bombings did have the desired effect. The Spanish public became incensed when the government kept insisting that Basque terrorists were responsible for the attacks even as information emerged indicating that Islamist militants were the more likely suspects. Just as the authors would have predicted, the Spanish public vented their frustration with Prime Minister Jose Maria Aznar and his party was voted out of office. One of the first things the new ruling Socialist party leader did after his election victory was to announce that Spanish troops would be pulled out of Iraq.

Spain's appeasement strategy of dealing with terrorism was challenged only two weeks later when an explosives-laden backpack was discovered at a Madrid train station. The only reason the bomb failed to explode was because of a faulty detonator. How to explain this aborted attack given that the Spanish had already essentially capitulated to al Qaeda's demands?

A clue was found the very next day when in the middle of a stand-off with police, suspected terrorists holed up in a Madrid apartment blew themselves up to avoid arrest. In the debris of the explosion, police found fragments of a video-tape in which a spokesman announced that the terror cell was part of "the brigade situated in Al Andalus" that was determined to wage jihad "until martyrdom in the land of Tariq ibn Ziyad."[139] As New Yorker writer Lawrence Wright points out, the speaker was using the Arabic name for the part of Spain that had been conquered by the Muslim armies in 711 under the command of a Berber general, one Tariq ibn Ziyad In the terms made popular by the the Palestinian organization Hamas, what the speaker was essentially saying was this part of Spain was "Islamic Waqf" and the cell was trying to restore it to the domain of Islam.

Later more evidence would emerge that the Madrid attacks had nothing to do with Spain's participation in the Iraq war as planning for them had to started as early as October 2000, long before the United States ever contemplated invading Iraq.[140]

Nor were the Madrid train bombings the first indication that jihadists were targeting Europe. Authorities all over the continent claim to have thwarted some thirty "spectacular" or "massive attacks" since 9/11,[141] attacks that were to have occurred in Germany, France, the United Kingdom, and Italy and would have targeted American military bases, embassies, and government buildings; NATO bases; parliament buildings; churches; synagogues; landmarks such as the Eiffel Tower; marketplaces, including traditional Christmas markets; local transportation systems; and tourist spots. Most of the known conspirators were found to be first or second generation North African Muslims, though there were also Arabs, Pakistanis, though there were also European converts to Islam involved. Many had been trained in al Qaeda camps in Afghanistan.[142]

On November 2, 2004, jihadists again struck Europe when a Dutch film-maker, Theo van Gogh, was gunned down as he rode his bike through the streets of Amsterdam because he had made a film that criticized the treatment of women in Muslim societies. Dutch investigators concluded that the Dutch-Moroccan killer was part of a jihadist group, called the Hofstad network, that was comprised primarily of Dutch Muslims of North African descent, linked to other groups in Spain and Belgium, all subscribing to the vision of al Qaeda.

At the time of his arrest, the filmmaker's killer, Mohammed Bouyeri, had on his person a last will and testament in which he expressed a desire to die in jihad. After trying to saw off his victim's head, he used his knife to pin a note to the corpse in which he predicted the demise of the West and the death of the film's screenwriter, a Dutch politician, Ayan Hirshi Ali, originally from Somalia, who has described herself as an "ex-Muslim" in spite of recognizing that repudiating Islam is a crime under Islamic law that is punishable by death.

In Bouyeri's apartment, investigators found another note he had written, this one addressed to the Dutch people, in which he warned them that God has instructed Muslims to kill "the non-believing people of the Netherlands" in "the fight for world dominion between belief and unbelief."[143]

On July 7, 2005, jihadists would hit Europe for the third time when four sui-cide bombers blew themselves up on London's mass transit system killing fifty-six and wounding hundreds. Al Qaeda claimed responsibility for the attacks. The British public was stunned to learn that three of the four bombers were British-born citizens of Pakistani descent; the fourth was a Jamaican-born convert to Islam.

London would learn about the bombers motives when on September 1, 2005, Al Jazeera aired a taped statement in which one of the suicide bombers tried to explain himself:

> I and thousands like me are forsaking everything for what we believe. Our drive and motivation doesn't come from tangible commodities that this world has to offer. Our religion is Islam, obedience to the one true God Allah and following the footsteps of the final prophet messenger

This is how our ethical stances are dictated.

Your democratically elected governments continuously perpetuate atrocities against my people all over the world. And your support of them makes you directly responsible, just as I am directly responsible for protecting and avenging my Muslim brothers and sisters.

Until we feel security you will be our targets and until you stop the bombing, gassing, imprisonment and torture of my people we will not stop this fight. We are at war and I am a soldier. Now you too will taste the reality of this situation.[144]

Egypt and Jordan

On July 23, 2005, suicide bombers struck the Sharm el-Sheikh resort area in Egypt, killing sixty-four. This was the second mass-casualty Islamist terrorist attack to occur in Egypt since a cease-fire had gone into effect in 1997 after followers of the Blind Sheik had shot and hacked to death sixty-two people, mostly foreign tourists, at an ancient site in Luxor. Authorities were able to link the attacks to the Blind Sheik via leaflets calling for his release from prison left behind at the scene—one was stuffed into slit torso of one of the victims. In 2000, the Blind Sheik's lawyer, a self-described radical leftist, Lynne Stewart shuttled a message from the sheik, then in prison, to Reuters news service in which he withdrew his support for the ceasefire agreement. In February of 2005, Stewart was herself convicted of having provided material support to terrorism because of the role she played in getting the Blind Sheik's message out to his followers in violation of a federal gag order.

On November 9, 2005, suicide terrorists blew themselves up at three hotels in Amman, Jordan killing fifty-seven. Zarqawi, the head of al Qaeda in Iraq, claimed responsibility. The attack was carried out by Iraqis, including a husband and wife team who planned to attack the wedding party. The wife, however, failed to detonate her explosives belt and was later arrested; her husband succeeded in blowing himself up and killing the fathers of the groom and the bride along with fifteen other guests. (The bride's mother died later.)

Among the victims were many Palestinians. This was the first time that Palestinians found themselves on the receiving end of mass-casualty suicide terrorism. For years the Palestinians had glorified suicide terrorists, celebrating them as martyrs fighting for the noble cause of Palestinian nationalism.

Jordanians, a majority of whom are Palestinians, responded to the attacks by taking to the streets and calling for Zarqawi to "burn in hell." Zarqawi tried to justify the attacks in a published statement on the Internet saying that the hotels were attacked because "they are centers for launching war on Islam" and were being used by NATO as a rear base and "from which the convoys of the crusaders and the renegades head back and forth to the land of Iraq where Muslims are killed and their blood is shed."[145] Ironically, the statement failed to mention Zarqawi's complicity in the deaths of Muslims in Iraq where he is believed to be responsible for most of the killings of Iraqi civilians.

Zarqawi, who was a Jordanian citizen, had long plotted against the Jordanian monarchy, even serving time in jail because of his radicalism in the 1990s. After being released from prison, he has primarily lived outside of Jordan, though he continued to be involved in various plots targeting Jordan. He was sentenced to death four times in absentia for his involvement in the millennium attacks against tourist spots, the assassination of an American diplomat in Amman in 2002, an attack on the Jordanian intelligence headquarters in 2004, and finally for his role in the 2005 bombings.

Zarqawi's goal was the establishment of a pan-Islamic state in the Middle East; his method was jihad. He was killed along with five others while he was staying in a safe house just north of Baghdad in a precision bombing strike by U.S. forces on June 7, 2006.

Conclusion

While the above survey is by no means intended to be an exhaustive account of jihad in the past several decades, it does demonstrate a few key points about this new global movement.

Jihads generally start out as local battles—regional conflicts, liberation struggles, secessionist movements, civil wars, or insurgencies. But since the creation of al Qaeda in 1988, these local struggles are eventually co-opted by what can be described as a global jihad movement.

Al Qaeda—or the global jihad movement—traces its origins to the Soviet War in Afghanistan (1979–1989). This was the first time in the modern era that Muslims from all over the world gathered together to defend fellow Muslims, the Afghans, in a defensive jihad against an infidel enemy—the Soviets. When the Soviets were driven out of Afghanistan and the Soviet Union then collapsed, the mujahidin became convinced that they had defeated the world's second superpower and caused its collapse because of their belief in Islam.

After they left Afghanistan, the now emboldened mujahidin—also called *jihadists*—fanned out across the world. Some went back home where they worked to overthrow the local regime in order to install an Islamic government; others went to free other Muslim lands, what choice was made often depended on where the best action was. Eventually the leader of this new global jihad movement, Usama bin Laden, set his sights on, as he put it, ending "the legend of the so-called superpower that is America."[146] Over time, the theater of jihad would expand to also include Europe. In short, jihad had gone global.

Why now? What was the ideology behind this phenomenon?

CHAPTER 2

What Is The Ideology of Jihad?

The ideology known as Islamic radicalism, militant Jihadism, or Islamo-fascism—
different from the religion of Islam—exploits Islam to serve a violent political
vision that calls for the murder of all those who do not share it. The followers of
Islamic radicalism are bound together by their shared ideology, not by any cen-
tralized command structure. Although they fight on scattered battlefields, these
terrorists share a similar ideology and vision for the world openly stated in videos,
audiotapes, letters, declarations, and websites.

A White House statement on the War on Terror[1]

From the beginning, the Bush administration hesitated to cast the new
threat as having anything to do with the religion of Islam as the last thing
the administration wanted to do was provoke a religious war. As President
George W. Bush said in a televised address to the American people on
September 20, 2001, "The enemy of America is not our many Muslim
friends . . . Our enemy is a radical network of terrorists, and every government
that supports them."[2] This enemy, he went on to elaborate, practiced "a fringe
form of Islamic extremism."[3] What was the "fringe form" of Islam that President
Bush was talking about? Where did it come from and how did it become so
powerful that it had managed to incite jihad on almost every continent?

Islamic Origins

The roots of jihad can be traced to the beginning of Islam. According to the
Islamic tradition, this would be the year 622 CE, the year of the hegira, when
the Prophet Muhammad and his small band of friends, relatives, and social outcasts emigrated from Mecca to what is today the Saudi city of Medina to escape
persecution. There in Medina, this first group of Muslims would found, according to the Islamic understanding, the world's first community united around the
bonds of faith as opposed to the ties of kinship or clan. In the next ten-year
period, the early Muslims would fight in eighty-six military campaigns, twenty-
seven of which were commanded by the Prophet himself.[4] By the time of the

Prophet's death in 632, through battle, the Muslims would gain control of the entire Arabian Peninsula, a landmass roughly one third the size of the continental United States.

Even after the Prophet died, the Muslims would continue to expand their empire through militant jihad and within a hundred-year period, would manage to destroy the ancient Persian Empire and severely weaken the Byzantine Empire. They would hold territory from Europe (part of today's Spain) to North Africa, all the way to Asia, up to the Indus River in what is today's Pakistan. While scholars do not know what the early Muslims called these early battles, as David Cook, author of the book *Understanding Jihad*, points out, at some point in time, the Islamic tradition started regarding these early campaigns as the quintessential jihads.[5]

Even after the first one hundred years, jihad would remain a primary means of expansion in Islam. Under the banner of jihad, the Muslims conquered much of the Indian subcontinent by the eleventh century; extended their empire to what is today Turkey, seized control of Constantinople, the capital of Byzantium by1453, gaining control of much of eastern Europe; and captured most of west Africa by the early part of the nineteenth century.

The Arabic word for jihad is derived from the Arabic root *j-h-d*, which, in its verb form actually means to struggle or strive for something. This is why the term *jihad* can also be used to describe a moral or spiritual struggle, or even an effort to eliminate illiteracy or poverty. We however will confine our focus to the way in which bin Laden and his fellow jihadists mean the word jihad—that is, in the sense of armed struggle—or, as it is often translated into English, holy war.

It is important to note that Arabic uses another word—*harb*—to connote war. Understanding how the Islamic tradition differentiates war from jihad is in fact the key to understanding Islam. According to the Islamic tradition, *jihad* is a military effort waged on behalf of Islam, while *harb* is simply war—that is, war that has no Islamic or religious legitimacy. Islam, in fact, uses the notion of war to bifurcate the world into two distinct parts: that part of the world under the domain of Islam (*dar al-Islam*) versus the rest of the world which is referred to as the domain of perpetual war (*dar al-harb*). Roughly speaking, the mandate of Islam is to expand the domain of Islam until there is no longer perpetual war in the world and the way in which Muslims are to perform this fundamental obligation is to wage jihad.

Implied in this fundamental paradigm of the world is the notion that only under the domain of Islam can there ever be lasting peace in the world. The Arabic word *Islam*, in fact, comes from the same Arabic root (*-s-l-m*)-as the word *peace*. This is why Islam is often referred to as the "religion of peace." *Islam*, however, does not mean *peace*; rather it is more accurately translated as *submission*. Inherent in the name *Islam* then is the belief that only by submitting to God's plan for humanity—that is, Islam—can humanity achieve a state of lasting peace.

While Muslims believe that Islam is a continuation of the monotheistic creed that God first revealed to the Hebrew prophets beginning with Abraham, and continued revealing to such well-known figures as Moses and Jesus, the son of

God as far as Christians are concerned, Muslims believe that it was only the Prophet Muhammad who got the monotheistic message right. Thus, while Muslims accord their fellow monotheists at least a certain degree of respect, they are also advised that the Jews and the Christians ultimately garbled God's message. Hence, Muslims believe that while there is something to be learned from the Hebrew Bible and the New Testament, they are rife with human error and only their sacred text, the *Koran*, can be regarded as the actual word of God.

This is why Muslims believe that the Koran must be treated with a consideration not due to the other holy books. This is also why after *Newsweek* reported that U.S. interrogators had flushed a Koran down the toilet at Guantanamo Bay in April of 2005[6] that protests erupted throughout the Islamic world and in Afghanistan they even turned violent and resulted in some seventeen deaths. Though the *Newsweek* story would turn out to have been untrue and the magazine would indeed retract the article, the United States took the opportunity to issue public assurances to the Muslim world that the U.S. military is under strict orders to never not only desecrate the Koran, but to neither even casually touch the Korans the military routinely distributes to jihadist captives, as they would their own Bibles or Torahs, and that when handling the Koran they should always wear gloves and then use two hands in order to show respect and sensitivity to the Muslim belief that the Koran is unlike any other holy book.[7]

Because Muslims believe that the Koran *is* the word of God, and was codified in its present form just as the Prophet Muhammad received it, there is also a corresponding belief that it should never be translated from the original Arabic lest any human errors seep in. Now there are, of course, English translations. The way translators get around the prohibition is to never name their translations simply *The Koran*. Rather, they entitle their works with such names as *The Meaning of the Glorious Koran; The Koran Interpreted; The Holy Qur'an: Translation and Commentary; The Noble Qur'an in the English Language* so that they can never be criticized for having done the unthinkable, that is allowing themselves to do something so impossible as to translate God's word.[8] Hence, while there are many translations of the Koran, none are to be confused with *the* Koran, the Arabic book that is the actual, immutable word of God, that is according to the Islamic tradition.

In this book, incidentally, we will use the translation, *The Noble Qur'an in the English Language* by Muhammad Taqi al-Din al-Hilali and Muhammad Muhsin Khan. We selected this particular translation because it is said to be the one favored by today's global jihadists.[9] We fully recognize that this particular translation is objectionable to many university and reformist scholars of Islam because of its Muslim-supremacist overtones—the very reason, we suspect, that this translation is said to be the jihadists' favorite. Again, because we are largely concerned with how the jihadists view and use Islam, we decided that this was the translation that would best suit our purposes though it may not be either our or our colleagues preferred choice.

Now, after the Koran, it is important to understand that the next most authoritative source for Muslims—and jihadists—is the *Sunnah*, the collection of anecdotes about what the Prophet was alleged to have done and said during his lifetime. These anecdotes, called *hadith*, are believed to have been originally recounted by those early Muslims who actually knew the Prophet and his companions. (In English the word *hadith* is used as both a singular and a plural; although in Arabic, it is a singular for which the plural is *ahadith*.) Thus they are considered to provide important context and an indication of how exactly the Prophet himself interpreted the message he received from God.

For some two hundred years following the Prophet's death, hadith were circulated exclusively by word of mouth, as was the custom in those days. Anyone who was a good storyteller was undoubtedly tempted to entertain and possibly even manipulate their medieval audience by telling stories about the Prophet's life. Obviously, there was little to prevent an imaginative storyteller from interjecting all sorts of fabrications and distortions into their accounts.

Eventually, after a couple hundred years or so, now that the Islamic empire spanned several continents, some astute Islamic scholars recognized that unless they made a concerted effort to weed out all the false hadith, storytellers were in a position to completely undermine the Prophet's message. And so some scholars embarked on the long and arduous process of authenticating each of the hundreds of thousands of hadith that were by then in circulation.

To determine whether or not a particular hadith was authentic, these scholars had to examine both the plausibility of the hadith as well as the reliability of each link in the chain of transmission (namely the credibility of each person in the "he-said-she-said-he-said" chain through which the hadith was said to have become known). Eventually, there emerged six collections of authenticated hadith that were highly and widely regarded in the Sunni tradition (from which today's global jihadists spring—the Shiites have their own authoritative collections). These six collections of hadith came to be regarded as the second most authoritative source of Islamic guidance after the Koran and were now collectively known as the *Sunnah*. The Sunnah are studied in order to help Muslims make sense of the Koran, whose meaning can often be inscrutable as it often makes obscure references, changes tone and person, and often seems to contradict itself. The Sunnah tell how the Prophet himself and his early followers interpreted God's sometimes confusing instructions. They deal with all sorts of topics, including jihad, the subject of our particular interest.

However, just like the verses of the Koran, the hadith can also be contradictory, obscure or confusing, and thus throughout their history, Muslims—and including jihadists—have often had to turn to full-time Islamic scholars, what we would call learned experts, to help them sort out the meaning and implications of the Koran and the Sunnah in order to fully grasp the message of their religion. The guidance provided by such Islamic scholars is generally offered in the form of a *fatwa* or religious rulings, an opinion similar in tone, content, and arguing techniques to the fatwa bin Laden wrote to declare his jihad in 1998. (Again, fatwa is an anglicized plural of the Arabic singular *fatwa*.)

We will see that fatwas are written in the form of legal arguments and that most fatwas take as a starting point the opinions and writings of such religious scholars. In bin Laden's 1996 fatwa, for example, he cites the work of one Ibn Taymiyya (1263–1328), a renowned scholar of the Hanbali school, one of the four "classical" or established schools of Sunni Islamic jurisprudence (the others are the Maliki, the Hanafi and the Shafii schools; Shiites have their own schools). It will not be necessary for our purposes to understand the interesting and often subtle differences between these various schools of Islamic jurisprudence except to note that in accordance with the Islamic tradition, today's jihadists also use arguments enshrined in the traditional corpus of Islamic jurisprudence to bolster their calls to jihad. For example, in a call to jihad issued by the Shariah Council of the self-proclaimed Chechen Republic of Ichkeria, the council opens its fatwa with a review of the prevailing opinions among the classical schools regarding Muslims' fundamental obligation to perform jihad:

> Hanbali School defined it [jihad] as spending power and energy in the war in the way of Allah by personal participation, property, word, etc.
> Maliki School considers it a war (a battle) of a Muslim with a Kafir (an infidel) who has no treaty, to exalt the Word of Allah, or who trespassed on the territories of Muslims.
> Hanbalis say that this is a war against Kafirs (the infidels), unlike an armed fight with the Muslims bordering on being rebels, or brigands or robbers for example.[10]

By reviewing these classical definitions of jihad, the Chechens were probably trying to head off the criticism that they anticipated would be coming from Sufi scholars prevalent in Chechnyan Islam who would, unlike their Salafi brethren, generally oppose a fundamental association between jihad and holy war. What the Chechnyan council wanted to point out to the reader was that their interpretation, while it may not have been in accordance with the prevailing Sufi tradition, was however very much in line with the classical tradition and therefore should not be dismissed. The fact that such fundamental differences in interpretations of Islam occur among Muslims introduces an important concept, especially as it pertains to militant jihad.

This is because it is not only the Sufis who reject this primary association of jihad with holy war. This is also the view shared by many modern reformists and other Muslims who prefer to think of jihad as one's personal moral or spiritual struggle largely conducted against oneself in order to avoid sinning. This interpretation can be sourced to a hadith in which the Prophet is said to have declared upon returning from a raid (or militant jihad): "We have now returned from the Smaller Jihad to the Greater Jihad." In other words, the Prophet himself is said to have placed a greater value on the spiritual form of jihad as opposed to the militant form.

It is interesting to note that today's jihadists reject this notion—as does much of the Islamic tradition. Jihadists believe the notion that jihad is supposed to be primarily a spiritual struggle is a modern invention. They support their interpretation based on the fact that, as David Cook, author of *Understanding Islam*, points out, the hadith at the crux of the reformist argument is only found in one of Sunni Islam's six most authoritative collections of hadith[11] and all 199 references to jihad in the Bukhari collection, considered to be the most authoritative of the Sunni tradition, refer to jihad in the militant sense.[12] In any case, whatever the merits of the reformist case, the jihadist view is that militant jihad is a fundamental religious duty for Muslims.

The Jihadist Interpretation of the Koran

Now let us try to understand a bit how today's jihadists interpret what the Koran says about jihad. To aid us in our investigation, we can look to what is often called their "manifesto," the book *Milestones*, written by Sayyid Qutb (1906–1966), an Egyptian literary critic and educator who went on to become the chief ideologue of the Muslim Brotherhood, an organization that has been a potent force in revivifying Islam as a political solution. Qutb wrote his manifesto of jihad while he was serving out a prison sentence for his role in a foiled plot to assassinate the Egyptian president, Gamal Abdel Nasser.

In *Milestones*, Qutb writes that the Koran outlines four distinct phases of jihad:

> [Phase One] God held back Muslims from fighting in Mecca and in the early period of their migration to Medina, and told them, "Restrain your hands, and establish regular prayers, and pay Zakat." [Phase Two] Next, they were permitted when war was made, because they were oppressed, and God was able to help them. These were the people who were expelled from their homes without cause, except the next stage [Phase Three] came when the Muslims were commanded to fight against those who fight against them: "Fight in the cause of God against those who fight you." An [*sic*] finally, [Phase Four] war was declared against all the polytheists: "And fight against all the polytheists, as they all fight against you;" "Fight against those among the People of the Book who do not forbid what God and His Messenger have forbidden, and who do not consider the true religion as their religion, until they are subdued and pay Jizyah."[13]

During the first stage, when the Prophet and his small band of followers were still living in Mecca (up until 622), Muslims were not only barred from fighting with those who did not share their beliefs, they were advised not to even argue with Christians and Jews, "the people of the Scripture":

> And argue not with the people of the Scripture (Jews and Christians), unless it be in (a way) that is better (with good words and in good manner, inviting them to Islâmic Monotheism with His Verses), except with such of them as do wrong, and say (to them): "We believe in that which has been revealed to us and revealed to you; our Ilâh (God) and your Ilâh (God) is One (i.e. Allâh), and to Him we have submitted (as Muslims)." (Sura 29:46)

And to ignore the unbelievers—the polytheists, idolators, and disbelievers:

> Therefore proclaim openly (Allâh's Message Islâmic Monotheism) that which you are commanded, and turn away from *Al-Mushrikûn* (polytheists, idolaters, and disbelievers, etc.-see V.2:105). (Sura 15:94)

While God did severely restrict what the Muslims could do at this point, he did try to comfort them with the promise that the unbelievers would eventually get their due—that is they would be punished on Judgment Day:

> So leave them alone till they meet their Day, in which they will sink into a fainting (with horror). The Day when their plotting shall not avail them at all nor will they be helped (i.e. they will receive their torment in Hell). (Sura 52:45–46)

There are many, many verses in this category, verses in which God commands Muslims to live in peace with non-Muslims. In fact, of the 114 Suras (the anglicized plural of *Sura* or *chapter*) of the Koran, the vast majority—ninety are thought to have come from this Meccan period (610–622) and are principally concerned with matters of spirituality and faith in general. (There is some dispute among Muslim scholars as to whether certain verses should be classified as Meccan or Medinean verses so the exact number of Meccan verses cannot be precisely defined.) Had the Muslims been aggressive during this period, given their relative numbers, they most likely would have been easily wiped out.

Around 619, however, things began to change. First, Mohammad lost his beloved wife, a wealthy trader when he married her, who was some fifteen years his senior, and who would remain his only wife until her death. Not long after he also lost his powerful uncle, who had served as his protector since he had been orphaned as a small child. Now life became even more perilous for Mohammad whose revelation was challenging the status quo and by 622 things were so bad in Mecca that he and his small band of relatives, friends, and social outcasts decided they should seek refuge in the nearby city of what is today Medina and form what Muslims believe was the world's first community united simply around faith.

Muslims see the birth of this first Muslim community, the *ummah*, as *the* seminal event in world history. Thus they mark this to be the beginning of the period of enlightenment, when for the first time in human history a community was founded based on something other than kinship or tribe. Human history would now be forever divided into two distinct periods: *jahiliyya* or the period of ignorance before the dawn of Islam and the period after 622, when Muslims would begin to carry out God's plan for humanity.

During the early period in Medina, now that the Muslims were strong enough to have formed their own community, God would now permit them to defend themselves in the face of an attack:

> Permission to fight is given to those (i.e. believers against disbelievers), who are fighting them, (and) because they (believers) have been wronged, and surely, Allâh is Able to give them (believers) victory. (Sura 22:39)

Later, as the community grew even stronger and wealthier and thus became a more appealing target, God would tell Muslims that they *had* to fight to defend themselves and their community, even in case they were reluctant:

> *Jihâd* (holy fighting in Allâh's Cause) is ordained for you (Muslims) though you dislike it, and it may be that you dislike a thing which is good for you and that you like a thing which is bad for you. Allâh knows but you do not know. (Sura 2:216)

It was during this stage that, as our translators point out, the Arabic word for fighting (*qital*) is first mentioned in the Koran.

> And fight in the Way of Allâh those who fight you, but transgress not the limits. Truly, Allâh likes not the transgressors. (Sura 2:190)

Although Muslims are ordered that they must fight to protect themselves, they are also warned not to "transgress the limits"—not to fight in Mecca or during the "sacred month" and to show mercy if their opponents lay down their arms. It is notable that they were also given a waiver: If the enemy "transgresses the prohibition against you, you transgress likewise against him."[14] In other words, Muslims were told not to observe any limits if their enemies did not.

The last stage of jihad in the Koran—and to today's global jihadists, clearly the most important—begins after the Prophet and his followers have gathered enough strength to return to conquer Mecca (630), the birthplace of Islam. At this point the Muslim armies were now of sufficient force of faith to prevail even when seriously outnumbered and so armed with their superior faith, they were deemed ready, according to their prophet, to fight until there is no more "disbelief and polytheism":

> And fight them until there is no more *Fitnah* (disbelief and polytheism: i.e. worshipping others besides Allâh) and the religion (worship) will all be for Allâh Alone [in the whole of the world]. But if they cease (worshipping others besides Allâh), then certainly, Allâh is All-Seer of what they do. And if they turn away, then know that Allâh is your *Maulâ*(Patron, Lord, Protector and Supporter, etc.), (what) an Excellent *Maulâ*, and (what) an Excellent Helper! (Sura 8:39–40)

Let's review for a minute. We have just seen that the Koran offers a range of advice regarding how Muslims are to deal with unbelievers: first they are told to remain passive, then they are given the option to fight in self-defense, then they are commanded to protect themselves and finally they are told that it is their duty to wage all-out war to rid the world of *fitna* (disbelief and polytheism) and expand the domain of Islam. Naturally the question arises: What is a jihadist supposed to do, given all this essentially contradictory advice?

First, as we shall see, jihadists will be advised to recognize that the Islamic tradition is in almost universal agreement that the Koran's ultimate message regarding relations with unbelievers is contained in the famous Sword Verse, the verse with which bin Laden opened his 1998 fatwa, which like the aforementioned verse commands Muslims to wage all-out war with unbelievers. This is because the Islamic tradition holds that it was this verse, Sura 9:5, that was the last of the so-called jihad verses, or verses outlining relations with unbelievers, to be revealed to the Prophet. Now why would when a particular verse was revealed be of such significance?

The answer to this question, naturally resides in the Koran. As the following verse explains, should the Koran ever appear to contradict itself, whatever message was revealed last, should always be taken to trump whatever was the earlier guidance:

> And when We change a Verse [of the Qur'ân, i.e. cancel (abrogate) its order] in place of another, and Allâh knows the best of what He sends down, they (the disbelievers) say: "You (O Muhammad SAW) are but a *Muftari*! (forger, liar)." Nay, but most of them know not. (Sura 16:101)

This is what Koranic exegetes, not surprisingly, call the principle of abrogation. To confirm that this is also the view taken by today's jihadists, note that the Sword Verse is quoted in almost every declaration of jihad. Also consider what Sadat's assassins said about the Sword Verse in their pamphlet on jihad which they entitled *The Neglected Duty*:

> Al-Husayn ibn Fadl says: "This is the verse of the sword. It abrogates every verse in the Qur'an in which suffering the insults of the enemy is mentioned." It is strange indeed that there are those who want to conclude from Qur'an verses that have been abrogated that fighting and jihad are to be forsworn.
> The Imam Abu Abdallah Muhammad Ibn Hazm who died in 456 AH says . . . : "In 114 verses in 48 surahs everything is abrogated by the Word of God—Exalted and Majestic He is-: 'Slay the polytheists wherever ye find them.'[15]

Now because this verse is so important, let us review it again, this time more carefully:

> Then when the Sacred Months have passed, then kill the *Mushrikûn* wherever you find them, and capture them and besiege them, and prepare for them each and every ambush. But if they repent and perform *As-Salât*, and give *Zakât*, then leave their way free. Verily, Allâh is Oft-Forgiving, Most Merciful.(Sura 9:5)

What is meant by the phrase after the "Sacred Months have passed"? While most Islamic scholars have taken the "Sacred Months" to mean the time required for any pre-existing treaties to run out before Muslims can go out and fight the polytheists until they are converted or killed, others have argued that the phrase refers to a pre-Islamic tradition of not engaging in raids during certain "peace months." It would appear that today's jihadists, with their year-round killing sprees would appear to take the former and not the latter meaning.

It should be noted that later in the same chapter, Sura 9, God tells Muslims that they should fight their fellow monotheists, the Christians and the Jews, only until such time as they agree to pay a poll-tax (Jizyah) and live according to the laws of Islam.[16] In other words, unlike the polytheists or disbelievers, other monotheists are allowed to live in peace with Muslims—and even practice their religion—as long as they agree to a second class or *dhimmi* status in the Islamic order.

In the Koran, Muslims are further instructed that they have a duty to wage jihad "with their wealth and their lives"[17] and that those who fulfill this obligation can expect to go to Paradise in the afterlife:

> Verily, Allâh has purchased of the believers their lives and their properties; for the price that theirs shall be the Paradise. They fight in Allâh's Cause, so they kill (others) and are killed. It is a promise in truth which is binding on Him in the Taurât (Torah) and the Injeel (Gospel) and the Qur'ân. And who is truer to his covenant than Allâh? Then rejoice in the bargain which you have concluded. That is the supreme success. (Sura 9:111)

As this verse clearly states, this is the "bargain" Muslims "have concluded" with Allah: they are obliged to kill and be killed "in Allah's Cause." In Paradise, incidentally, Muslims are told that can at last enjoy all that is forbidden in life—including wine, virgins, fine clothing, and jewelry (i.e., silk and gold).[18]

Conversely, Muslims are advised that those who decline to fulfill their jihad duty should expect a "painful torment" in the hereafter:

> O you who believe! What is the matter with you, that when you are asked to march forth in the Cause of Allâh (i.e. Jihâd) you cling heavily to the earth? Are you pleased with the life of this world rather than the Hereafter? But little is the enjoyment of the life of this world as compared with the Hereafter. If you march not forth, He will punish you with a painful torment and will replace you by another people, and you cannot harm Him at all, and Allâh is Able to do all things. (Sura 9:38–39)

The Koran also advises that should a Muslim be faced with the stark reality of having to fight during the Sacred Months or abandon jihad, he should always choose jihad because to do otherwise would mean that he was essentially repudiating his faith and would then die as an unbeliever and be condemned to hell:

> They ask you concerning fighting in the Sacred Months (i.e. 1st, 7th, 11th and 12th months of the Islâmic calendar). Say, "Fighting therein is a great (transgression) but a greater (transgression) with Allâh is to prevent mankind from following the Way of Allâh, to disbelieve in Him, to prevent access to Al-Masjid-al-Harâm (at Makkah), and to drive out its inhabitants, and Al-Fitnah is worse than killing. And they will never cease fighting you until they turn you back from your religion (Islâmic Monotheism) if they can. And whosoever of you turns back from his religion and dies as a disbeliever, then his deeds will be lost in this life and in the Hereafter, and they will be the dwellers of the Fire. They will abide therein forever." (Sura 2:217).

It is interesting to note that once engaged in warfare, the Koran commands Muslims to be brutal, to "strike terror into (the hearts of) the enemies of God" though at the same time it instructs Muslims to make peace with those who "incline toward peace" with them.

> So if you gain the mastery over them in war, punish them severely in order to disperse those who are behind them, so that they may learn a lesson. If you (O Muhammad SAW) fear treachery from any people throw back (their covenant) to them (so as to be) on equal terms (that there will be no more covenant between you and them). Certainly Allâh likes not the treacherous. And let not those who

disbelieve think that they can outstrip (escape from the punishment). Verily, they will never be able to save themselves (from Allâh's Punishment). And make ready against them all you can of power, including steeds of war (tanks, planes, missiles, artillery, etc.) to threaten the enemy of Allâh and your enemy, and others besides whom, you may not know but whom Allâh does know. And whatever you shall spend in the Cause of Allâh shall be repaid unto you, and you shall not be treated unjustly. But if they incline to peace, you also incline to it, and (put your) trust in Allâh. Verily, He is the All-Hearer, the All-Knower. (Sura 8:57–61)

Other Koranic verses set limits on who is exempt from military service—namely, the sick, the weak, the poor, and the handicapped. (Suras 9:91 and 48:17)

In all, there are scores of verses spread over a dozen Suras that deal with jihad in the fighting and killing sense. There are also many hadith in the Sunnah which also encourage Muslims to fight and kill in the path of God. As we have previously noted, in the Bukhari collection alone, from which the above hadith are taken, there are 199 hadith that deal with the fighting form of jihad.

Jihadist Scholars: Taymiyya and Wahhab

While jihadists look to the Koran and Sunnah to guide them in their thinking, as we have already briefly noted they also rely on certain scholars—for example, a favorite scholar is the medieval cleric Ibn Taymiyya.

Ibn Taymiyya was born in Damascus in the mid-thirteenth century just after the Mongols sacked Baghdad in 1258. Interestingly, many scholars trace the sacking of Baghdad as the beginning of what would become the Muslim civilization's steep decline. Before the Mongol invasion, the Islamic empire was arguably the world's greatest civilization (certainly compared to the West) and Baghdad was its cultural and commercial center. After the Mongol invasion, however, the literate and sophisticated citizens of Baghdad would find themselves in the humiliating position of having been overrun by a people the Muslims regarded as an unwashed, uncivilized horde of nomadic horsemen from the Central Asian steppe. This is the degrading climate in which Ibn Taymiyya would come of age.

In his writings he would express profound dismay that the once glorious Muslims were now forced to live under the rule of a people they and especially he regarded as inferior heathens, even though by then the Mongol rulers were at least nominal Muslims. The fact that they had ostensibly converted to Islam only made things worse as far as Taymiyya was concerned because now they were not just unbelievers but heretics, people who because they refused to completely abandon their ancient shamanistic practices had effectively repudiated Islam and having done so, were even worse than unbelievers, who at least could claim to be ignorant. Moreover, Taymiyya believed that because they had failed to properly implant the Sharia, they had forfeited any claim to legitimacy and all pious Muslims should consider themselves obliged to rebel against them.

Taymiyya's case against the Mongols represented a distinct departure from the prevailing tradition as this was the first time that someone with religious authority was suggesting that Muslims could and should challenge the religious credentials of their fellow Muslims. The concept of judging the beliefs of other Muslims would later be expanded into the concept of *takfir*, or the practice of branding another Muslim as an apostate or heretic, a practice that would be adopted by the global jihad movement with zeal. This is how the GIA, Zarqawi, bin Laden, and others would rationalize killing their fellow Muslims in Algeria, Iraq, Saudi Arabia, the United States, and other places. Building on the foundation of ideas first introduced by Taymiyya, these radical jihadists or takfiris would decide that anyone who varied from their interpretation of Islam could and should be considered a candidate for execution.[19]

Secondly, until Taymiyya came on the scene, the Sunni tradition had always held that as long as Muslim rulers were at least nominally Muslim, the status quo should be accepted because stability was always preferable to the chaos and disorder that would surely accompany any kind of rebellion. With Taymiyya's innovation, however, Muslims would now be able to claim that it was a religious obligation to eliminate any Muslim leader who failed to implement Islamic law.[20] This would become particularly popular once jihad became associated with revolution in the twentieth century.

Ibn Taymiyya also popularized the notion that the most efficient way for Muslims to fulfill their destiny—that is to establish an Islamic order—would be for them to follow the example of their pious ancestors—the *Salafi*.[21] Taymiyya argued that Muslims needed to go back to their roots, to the time when the Islamic community was pure, having just embraced the Prophet's message of monotheism, before the community had split irreparably into two divisions: Sunnis versus Shiites.

The unbridgeable gap between Sunnis and Shiites arose over what was essentially a power dispute. Though the Prophet left detailed instructions on almost every aspect of life, the one instruction he failed to convey was who should succeed him as the leader of the Muslim community or *ummah* after his death. Those who took the position that the head of the Islamic state ought to be the person who was most qualified to lead became known as Sunnis. While those who believed that the descendents of the Prophet through his favorite daughter Fatima and his son-in-law and cousin Ali were most qualified to lead became known as Shiites.

The time of the pious ancestors, or *Salafi*, was also the time before the establishment of the clerical tradition. During this time, the only guidance the Muslim community could rely upon was what the Prophet himself had taught them—that is, the teachings that would become today's Koran, which was codified in its present book form sometime during the reign of the third Caliph, Uthman (644–656) and the anecdotes supplied by those who had firsthand experience of the sayings and doings of the Prophet—in other words, the early version of the Sunnah. Unlike their descendants, they could not yet rely on clerics or Islamic scholars to help them sort out the Prophet's message. They had only themselves and their own understanding of the Prophet's revelation and how he had lived his life.

Taymiyya believed that this is why the Salafi were divinely guided and advised Muslims to go back to this early approach and read the Koran and the

Sunnah for themselves and not rely on the clergy, who he believed—as the jihadists who would later follow him would as well—were no longer reliable, because most had been corrupted for one reason or another. This is why jihadists feel confident following someone like bin Laden who even though he may not have recognized credentials, he can claim a certain authority simply by virtue of his piety and devotion to the ancestors. This is also why today's jihadis prefer to be called *Salafi*, if they have to be differentiated from other Muslims. This is because they, following Taymiyya, look less to the tradition and instead prefer to rely on only the Koran and the Sunnah, for primary guidance.

Incidentally, it is important to bear in mind that not all Muslims who call themselves Salafi endorse what we think of as the global jihad movement. While these "reformist Salafis" do not fundamentally reject militant jihad, they contend that today's situation is analogous to the Meccan or early Medinean period, when Muslims were advised to focus on strengthening their own faith as opposed to worrying about the faith of those around them. While they may be willing to pick up arms in defense of Islam, they tend to believe that the community is not at the point where it can be fighting to expand the domain of Islam. In fact, this is why modern declarations of jihad are generally cast the call in terms of a *defensive* jihad in order to attract the most support.

Reformist Salafis argue that Muslims have not yet gathered sufficient strength to be waging jihad against the West or even their own local regimes. Muslims, they contend, have to get their own house in order, both as individuals and as a community before they try to establish an Islamic state. In their view, it would be only after this stage that the Muslims would be required to expand their domain through jihad. As one Egyptian reformist-Salafi, Muhammad Nasir al-Din al-Bani (d. 1999), observed: "We notice the mujahids call for whatever of the Muslims [*sic*] to join the fight, and [yet] when they go to fight, they find disagreements among themselves in matters of their faith and the basics of Islam. How do these people get ready for jihad when they are yet ·to understand what is obligatory on them of aqida [articles of faith]?"[22]

The Salafis, as we have noted, are often called Wahhabis, particularly in the West. The name *Wahhabi* is derived from the name of one of Taymiyya's followers, Muhammad ibn Abd al Wahhab (1703–1792) an itinerant Muslim cleric who wandered through Arab lands during the Ottoman period and with whom the founder of the Saud dynasty, in what is today's Saudi Arabia would form a critical alliance.

Following in the tradition of Taymiyya, he urged his fellow Muslims to follow the example of their pious ancestors. He railed in particular against the then popular practice of grave worship, denouncing it as idol worship and opposed any sort of innovation in the faith including Sufism, a mystical form of worship, or Shiism, which he regarded as a form of heresy. He made a name for himself when he ordered a woman who had confessed her adultery be stoned to death in line with Koranic teachings. Even back then the practice had largely been abandoned.[23]

In time, Wahhab forged an alliance with one Muhammad bin Saud, a local warlord who saw in the cleric's teachings the perfect ideology to rationalize having his fellow Muslims rise up against his rival warlords and claim their territory. Using the principle of *takfir* that Taymiyya had first introduced and Wahhab was now popularizing, Saud saw a creed that could be used to eliminate his opponents, and make certain that they would never rise again as thanks to Wahhab, they could now be denounced as infidels. Together they would conquer a large swath of the Arabian Peninsula.

The alliance the two men struck would even survive their deaths and that of their descendants. In 1932, the families of these two men, still aligned under this austere interpretation of Islam, would ultimately gain control of the Arabian Peninsula and establish the nation of Saudi Arabia. Hence the Saudis would become known as Wahhabis. Because the Salafi movement would also grow out of the same source as the Wahhabist interpretation—that is, Ibn Taymiyya—and because much of today's global jihad movement would end up being funded and promoted by Saudis (though not necessarily the regime), today's global jihadists would also be identified as Wahhabis, even though they themselves would probably prefer to be identified as simply *Muslims*, as again in the Taymiyya-Wahhabi tradition, they believe their interpretation is the only "true Islam."

Perhaps Taymiyya's most important legacy as far as the global jihad movement is concerned would be his promotion of the concept that jihad is a Muslim's most important duty. According to Taymiyya, jihad was even more important than a Muslim's other primary duties which included prayer five times a day, fasting during Ramadan, making the once-in-a-lifetime pilgrimage to Mecca and giving alms to the needy. The only duty which superseded jihad, according to Taymiyya, was the duty to believe in God and Islam. As he wrote in *Governance according to God's Law in Reforming both the Ruler and his Flock*:

> The command to participate in jihad and the mention of its merits occur innumerable times in the Koran and the Sunna. Therefore it is the best voluntary [religious] act that man can perform . . . Jihad implies all kinds of worship, both in its inner and outer forms. More than any other act it implies love and devotion for God, Who is exalted, trust in Him, the surrender of one's life and property to Him, patience, asceticism, remembrance of God and all kinds of other acts [of worship] . . . Since lawful warfare is essentially jihad and since its aim is that the religion is God's entirely and God's word is uppermost, therefore according to all Muslims, those who stand in the way of this aim must be fought.[24]

This was the legacy bin Laden cited when he quoted Ibn Taymiyya in his 1996 call for jihad against the American forces in Saudi Arabia:

> Clearly after Belief (Imaan) there is no more important duty than pushing the American enemy out of the holy land. No other priority, except Belief, could be considered before it; the people of knowledge, Ibn Taymiyyah stated: "to fight in defence of religion and Belief is a collective duty; there is no other duty after Belief than fighting the enemy who is corrupting the life and the religion."[25]

In April 2001, when bin Laden was trying to rally Muslims in Peshawar, Pakistan to support the Islamic state the Taliban had created in Afghanistan, he again made reference to Taymiyya when he declared that "The infidel world is not letting Muslims form a government of their own choice," adding, "They want to resist Jihad [holy war] and destroy the Islamic system," he said on the taped message played at the rally. "Therefore, under the present critical situation, Muslim unity is needed."[26]

Sadat's assassinations also made abundant use of Ibn Taymiyya's teachings in their pamphlet on jihad entitled, *The Neglected Duty*, which they circulated to explain why Muslims were now obligated to take up violence in order to bring about an Islamic state.[27] While Sadat's name is never specifically mentioned in the document, which is written as a discussion of general policy, as opposed to a justification for a specific act, it was widely understood to have been the rationale for the assassination. In the pamphlet, the author spells out the view that current Muslim leaders "are in apostasy" in that they "carry nothing from Islam but a name, even if they perform prayer ceremonies, or fast, or pretend to be Muslim" and for this reason they should be considered to be even more heretical than the Mongol rulers of Taymiyya's time because they have not just infused a few ancient beliefs into their practice of Islam but have actively sought to impose Western laws on Muslims and have thus repudiated Islam's teachings.[28]

While most traditional scholars would have advised against killing a Muslim leader, Sadat's assassins found just the religious justification they needed in the teachings of Ibn Taymiyya. When an Egyptian newspaper published the pamphlet, heralding it as "the complete text of the constitution of terrorism" it advised readers to take an interest in what was contained in the document as it showed that Sadat's assassins were not going to be satisfied by simply purging Muslims of their impious leaders, but they would also eventually target ordinary Muslims that they deemed had failed to live up to their Islamic obligations.[29]

As usual, the *Neglected Duty* opens with a verse from the Koran:

> It is not high time for those who have believed to humble their hearts to the Reminder of God and to the truth which He hath sent down; and that they should not be like those to whom the Book was formerly given and for whom the time was long, so that their hearts became hard, and many of them are reprobates? (Sura 57:16)

As Johannes Jansen, author of a scholarly analysis of the pamphlet, *The Creed of Sadat's Assassins*, points out, this verse is intended to address the question: Why should Muslims now suddenly resort to organized violence to rid the world of unbelief when earlier generations have not done so? As Jansen writes, the author calls on this particular verse because the "central element" is the injunction "not to be like earlier generations."[30]

In the pamphlet, Muslims are advised that it is no longer sufficient to be personally pious or try to establish an Islamic state by establishing Islamist political parties or social organizations. Rather, the author contends, Muslim history is full of evidence showing that violence is the only weapon that really works against unbelief.[31] Incidentally, this pamphlet had such an impact that its author, Abd al-Salam Faraj, was ultimately executed, along with those who actually carried out the assassination.

Abu Musab al-Zarqawi, the head of al Qaeda in Iraq, also called upon Taymiyya's logic to justify his attacks against the Shiite community. In a letter intercepted by U.S. forces in January 2004, purportedly written by Zarqawi and addressed to the leadership of al Qaeda, Zarqawi severely disparaged Shiite Muslims, describing them as "the most evil of mankind" who he blamed for the decline of Islamic civilization:

> One of the Orientalists spoke truth when he said that had the [Shiite] Safavid state not existed we in Europe would today be reading the Qur'an just as the Algerian Berber does. Yes, the hosts of the Ottoman state stopped at the gates of Vienna, and those fortifications almost collapsed before them [to permit] Islam to spread under the auspices of the sword of glory and jihad all across Europe. But these armies were forced to return and withdraw to the rear because the army of the Safavid state had occupied Baghdad, demolished its mosques, killed its people, and captured its women and wealth. The armies returned to defend the sanctuaries and people of Islam. Fierce fighting raged for about two centuries and did not end until the strength and reach of the Islamic state had waned and the [Islamic] nation had been put to sleep, then to wake up to the drums of the invading Westerner.

After detailing their various crimes against Islam, Zarqawi tried to lend gravitas to his conclusion that the Shiites must be neutralized by citing Taymiyya:

> Shaykh al-Islam Ibn Taymiyya spoke with truth and honesty when he said—after he mentioned their (Shi`a) thinking toward the people of Islam—"For this reason, with their malice and cunning, they help the infidels against the Muslim mass[es], and they are one of the greatest reasons for the eruption of Genghis Khan, the king of the infidels, into the lands of Islam, for the arrival of Hulagu in the country of Iraq, for the taking of Aleppo and the pillage of al-Salihiyya, and for other things."[32]

One can see Taymiyya's teachings at work when, in his letter, Zarqawi also railed against the Kurds for having "opened their land to the Jews"; "the masses" for daring "to look forward to a sunny tomorrow, a prosperous future, a carefree life, comfort, and favor"; the Muslims clerics for not endorsing "the spirit of jihad and the jurisprudence of martyrdom and disavowal of the infidel"; and even the Muslim Brotherhood for having "debased the horse, put aside arms, said 'no jihad.' "According to Zarqawi, only those who are willing to sacrifice themselves in jihad, can be said to be, in his words, "the quintessence of the Sunnis and the good sap of this country."

When Muslims Can Fight

In 1998, when bin Laden extended his 1996 declaration against the American forces guarding the oil fields of Saudi Arabia to all Americans "civilians and military" wherever they can be found, he quoted from the Koran to enjoin his fellow Muslims to "fight the pagans all together"[33] and not to stop "until there is no more tumult or oppression, and there prevail justice and faith in God."[34]

In the fatwa, bin Laden also lays out the reasons why Muslims are obliged to fight the Americans and the Jews:

First, for over seven years the United States has been occupying the lands of Islam in the holiest of places, the Arabian Peninsula, plundering its riches, dictating to its rulers, humiliating its people, terrorizing its neighbors, and turning its bases in the Peninsula into a spearhead through which to fight the neighboring Muslim peoples.

If some people have in the past argued about the fact of the occupation, all the people of the Peninsula have now acknowledged it. The best proof of this is the Americans' continuing aggression against the Iraqi people using the Peninsula as a staging post, even though all its rulers are against their territories being used to that end, but they are helpless.

Second, despite the great devastation inflicted on the Iraqi people by the crusader-Zionist alliance, and despite the huge number of those killed, which has exceeded 1 million . . . despite all this, the Americans are once against trying to repeat the horrific massacres, as though they are not content with the protracted blockade imposed after the ferocious war or the fragmentation and devastation.

So here they come to annihilate what is left of this people and to humiliate their Muslim neighbors.

Third, if the Americans' aims behind these wars are religious and economic, the aim is also to serve the Jews' petty state and divert attention from its occupation of Jerusalem and murder of Muslims there. The best proof of this is their eagerness to destroy Iraq, the strongest neighboring Arab state, and their endeavor to fragment all the states of the region such as Iraq, Saudi Arabia, Egypt, and Sudan into paper statelets and through their disunion and weakness to guarantee Israel's survival and the continuation of the brutal crusade occupation of the Peninsula.[35]

According to bin Laden, the above evidence leads to only one conclusion: "All these crimes and sins committed by the Americans are a clear declaration of war on Allah, his messenger, and Muslims." In other words, bin Laden is declaring a defensive jihad against Americans, because according to him, they have themselves already declared war on Muslims. Bin Laden wants to cast the jihad as a war in defense of Islam because, as he will point out, there is almost universal agreement in the tradition that in the event Muslims are attacked, it becomes an individual duty for every Muslim to come to the defense of their fellow Muslims. Or, as bin Laden writes in his fatwa:

All these crimes and sins committed by the Americans are a clear declaration of war on Allah, his messenger, and Muslims. And ulema have throughout Islamic history unanimously agreed that the jihad is an individual duty if the enemy destroys the Muslim countries. This was revealed by Imam Bin-Qadamah in "Al-Mughni," Imam al-Kisa'i in "Al-Bada'i," al-Qurtubi in his interpretation, and the shaykh of al-Islam in his books, where he said: "As for the fighting to repulse [an enemy], it is aimed at defending sanctity and religion, and it is a duty as agreed [by the ulema]. Nothing is more sacred than belief except repulsing an enemy who is attacking religion and life."

Thus bin Laden can call upon "every Muslim who believes in Allah" and expect that they will do whatever they can to help in the jihad against Americans (and Jews):

> We—with Allah's help—call on every Muslim who believes in Allah and wishes to be rewarded to comply with Allah's order to kill the Americans and plunder their money wherever and whenever they find it. We also call on Muslim ulema, leaders, youths, and soldiers to launch the raid on Satan's U.S. troops and the devil's supporters allying with them, and to displace those who are behind them so that they may learn a lesson.

To make sure that Muslims understand that this is in fact the pact they have made with God, he reminds them of what the Koran says by citing the following verses:

> Almighty Allah said: "O ye who believe, give your response to Allah and His Apostle, when He calleth you to that which will give you life. And know that Allah cometh between a man and his heart, and that it is He to whom ye shall all be gathered."[36] (Sura 8:24)
>
> Almighty Allah also says: "O ye who believe, what is the matter with you, that when ye are asked to go forth in the cause of Allah, ye cling so heavily to the earth! Do ye prefer the life of this world to the hereafter? But little is the comfort of this life, as compared with the hereafter. Unless ye go forth, He will punish you with a grievous penalty, and put others in your place; but Him ye would not harm in the least. For Allah hath power over all things."[37] (Sura 9:38)
>
> Almighty Allah also says: "So lose no heart, nor fall into despair. For ye must gain mastery if ye are true in faith."[38] (Sura 3:139)

Incidentally, this was the reason why so many Muslim nations were unable to lend support to the U.S.-led invasion of Iraq. Though the Muslim leaders may have despised Saddam Hussein and believed that the Iraqi people should be liberated, they simply could not get around the fact that infidel forces would be launching an offensive, or in the vocabulary of the Bush doctrine, a "preemptive war" against a Muslim country. Many Islamic scholars, in fact, ended up issuing declarations in support of waging jihad against the U.S.-led coalition in Iraq because, as Sadat's assassins put it back in 1981: "When the infidels descend upon a country, it becomes an individual duty for its people to fight them and drive them away."[39] By contrast, many Muslim nations supported the U.S. efforts in the Gulf War because in that instance, the case could be made that the coalition was acting in defense of a Muslim nation Kuwait, which had been invaded by Iraq.

Incidentally, Sadat's assassins, dismissed the notion that jihad should only be holy war in defense of Islam in their pamphlet, *The Neglected Duty*:

> Concerning this question it is proper that we should refute those who say that jihad in Islam is a defensive, and that Islam was not spread by the sword. This is a false view, which is (nevertheless) repeated by a great number of those who are

prominent in the field of Islamic missionary activities . . . Islam spread by the sword . . . It is obligatory for the Muslims to raise their swords under the very eyes of the Leaders who hide the Trush and spread falsehoods. If (the Muslims) do not do this, the Truth will not reach the hearts of Men.[40]

Proper Authority

Notice that bin Laden's 1998 fatwa was signed by four individuals: bin Laden himself; Zawahiri, his second in command, then head of Islamic Jihad in Egypt, a group involved in the assassination of Sadat; Abu-Yasir Rifa'a Ahmad Taha, a leader of a rival Islamist group in Egypt, the Egyptian Islamic Group, also involved in the assassination—the group's leader spiritual leader, Sheik Omar Abdel Rahman, was linked to several of the conspirators in the 1993 World Trade Center bombing and is currently serving a life sentence in an American prison for his role in a plot to blow up New York City landmarks; Taha would be later designated as a member of al Qaeda by the U.S. government; Shaykh Mir Hamzah, secretary of the Jamiat-ul-Ulema-e-Pakistan, or the Pakistani Society of Ulemas, a group that supported the Taliban and Fazlur Rahman, the head of the Jihad Movement in Bangladesh, a group whose members attacked a Bangladeshi poet with pickaxes in 1999.

As religious studies scholar, John Kelsay, points out, none of the signers have recognizable scholarly credentials. Bin Laden was trained as a civil engineer; Zawahiri is a physician; and little is known about Taha, Hamza and Rahman aside from their al Qaeda association. This is noteworthy because, as Kelsay writes,

> Historically, the textual nature of Shari'a reasoning gave rise to a class of scholars known as al-ulama, or "the learned." One becomes a member of this class by completing a long course of study in grammar, philology, history and logic, as well as in interpretation of the Qur'an and the hadith. Mastery of these fields qualifies one to issue opinions (fatwa) regarding the duty of Muslims in particular circumstances.[41]

How would someone like bin Laden, who has had only minimal religious training, have the confidence to issue such a decree when by doing so, he is clearly breaking from the Islamic tradition. Where was this confidence coming from?

Bin Laden was in fact taking advantage of the situation in Sunni Islam. Sunni Islam, unlike Shiite Islam, has no official religious hierarchy. That is, there is no priest class and no authority figure analogous to the ayatollah in Shiism (or the pope in Catholicism). Thus, anyone claiming to have religious authority is essentially free to issue an Islamic opinion, even one as serious as a declaration of jihad. The only question he had to ask himself was whether anyone would care what he thought was the Islamic solution to this particular problem. This is because the level of clerical authority in Sunni Islam is simply determined by the number of subscribers an "authority" is able to attract.

Note that, by now most Muslims states have designated an official clergy—called the *ulema*, whose job it is to help set (read justify) state policy in Islamic terms. Not surprisingly, the independence of these state-sanctioned clerics is regarded with a certain degree of skepticism. Most jihadists, in fact, regard them as having been entirely corrupted by the relationship with the state. This perception created the space for someone like bin Laden to enter, to stand simply on his personal piety and independence from the state. While bin Laden may not have been able to convince every Muslim that he was in a position to authorize a jihad, he was obviously able to persuade at least some.

Now while calls for jihad were traditionally issued by the head of the Islamic state, bin Laden was by no means the first non-state actor to have designated himself to be a person of sufficient Islamic authority to declare a jihad. Since the abolishment of the Caliphate, or the world's last pan-Islamic state (otherwise known as the Ottoman Empire), calls for jihad have been issued by a variety of non-state actors: There have been many calls for jihad to reclaim the state of Israel; there was the call to jihad to liberate Algeria from the French during Algeria's War of Independence (1954–1962); and the calls by Egyptian radicals, most notably the Blind Sheik. It was the Soviet invasion of Afghanistan, however, that was probably the most inspiring to bin Laden. This was the call to jihad issued by Abdullah Azzam that was written up in the pamphlet, *Join the Caravan* and *Defense of Muslim Lands*, and summarized by the slogan: "Jihad and the rifle alone. No negotiations, no conferences, and no dialogue."

While reformists have challenged the idea that jihad can be declared without a proper leader—that is a Caliph—this was a question that the jihad movement amply addressed in the *The Neglected Duty*, the self-justification produced by Sadat's assassins. In the pamphlet, they conclude that because the Prophet is said to have stated: "When three go out, make one of them *amir*, leader," this means Muslims are never truly absent a leader because "Muslims can (always) produce leaders from amongst themselves."[42]

Azzam himself addressed this concern. He wrote that even absent a Caliphate, Muslims not only can but must fight jihad as "abstract theories, amassed knowledge and studying" will never bring about the return of the Islamic state—only jihad has the capability.

> Yes we fight, and we haven't an Amir. None has said that the absence of an community of Muslims under an Amir cancels the Fard of jihad . . . We do not wait for the Caliphate to be restored. Because, the Caliphate does not return through abstract theories, amassed knowledge and studying. Rather, jihad is the right way to reform the divided authorities to the ultimate authority of the Caliphate.[43]

Where Jihad Should Be Waged

Azzam also gave a lot of thought to *where* they should begin their modern fight. He argued that while Arabs had a primary obligation to fight jihad in Palestine, the rest of the Muslim world, should begin by fighting in Afghanistan as there the battle was already underway:

> Whoever can, from among the Arabs, fight jihad in Palestine, then he must start there. And, if he is not capable, then he must set out for Afghanistan. For the rest of the Muslims, I believe they should start their jihad in Afghanistan.[44]

Azzam believed that Afghanistan was the best place to start because it was there (as opposed to Palestine), that the battle was clearly being waged under the banner of Islam, whereas in Palestine, people were fighting for a secular state: "Muslims, communists, nationalists and modernists Muslims . . . have [all] hoisted the banner of a secular state."[45]

Azzam, like Qutb, was opposed to the idea of a secular state. According to the jihadist view, communism presents a problem because it promotes atheism; nationalists try to create an identity other than Islam; and the secular state poses a problem because it vests authority to make law not with God but with the people.

Azzam, as we mentioned in chapter 1, was never able to succeed in his goal to liberate Palestine. After the Soviets agreed to leave Afghanistan, right in the middle of the debate over where the mujahidin should be deployed next, Azzam was killed in a car bombing on his way to the mosque. Among those suspected of having orchestrated his assassination, were bin Laden and Zawahiri both of whom argued that the mujahidin should first establish an Islamic state in the Arab heartland. In a letter dated July 9, 2005, Zawahiri, in the context of discussing the jihad in Iraq, explains why this is so important: "It has always been my belief that the victory of Islam will never take place until a Muslim state is established in the manner of the Prophet in the heart of the Islamic world, specifically in the Levant, Egypt, and the neighboring states of the Peninsula and Iraq."[46] In the letter he goes to state that once an "Islamic authority" has been established in Iraq, the jihad can be extended to the "secular countries neighboring Iraq," and while this process is going on, the Muslims can also confront Israel.[47]

While the U.S.-led invasion of Iraq did resuscitate the idea of trying to create an Islamic state in the Middle East, it is important to recognize that with his 1996 fatwa, bin Laden shifted the sights of the global jihad movement to the West, with the United States at the center of the focus. As Thomas Hegghammer, a Norwegian expert on jihadism points out, "Global jihadist ideologues [now] said that before an Islamic state could be established in Egypt, and before Palestine could be liberated, Muslims needed to defend the entire Islamic world against the imminent military threat posed by the US and the West."[48] In October 2004, Zawahiri issued a statement urging Muslims to attack any country which participated in the invasion of Iraq or Afghanistan, or which has, in his words, "facilitated Israel's existence."[49] Hegghammer has studied Islamist websites (most of them in Arabic) since 2002 and has concluded that Iraq is by now the most important jihad front by far in jihadist circles. To make his point, Hegghammer quotes from a statement issued by bin Laden in 2004: "To the mujahidin: There is now a rare and golden opportunity to make America bleed in Iraq, both economically and in terms of human losses and morale. Don't miss out on this opportunity, lest you regret it."[50]

Why Jihad Against The Jews?

As early as February 2003, bin Laden was warning his followers that if, in his words, "the new Crusader attack" in Iraq succeeds, it will "pave the way and prepare the region, after its fragmentation, for the establishment of what is known as 'the Greater State of Israel,' whose borders will include extensive areas of Iraq and Egypt, through Syria, Lebanon, Jordan, all of Palestine, and large parts of the Land of the Two Holy Places."[51]

In 1998 he included the liberation of the al-Aqsa Mosque in Jerusalem as part of his jihad, but after the 9/11 attacks, he will reveal the real reason Muslims have to fight the Jews to an an Al-Jazeera reporter (later convicted by a Spanish court of having collaborated with al Qaeda) on why Muslims have to confront the Jews:

> The prophet has said, "The end won't come before the Muslim and the Jews fight each other till the Jew hides between a tree and a stone. Then the tree and stone say, 'Oh, you Muslim, this is a Jew hiding behind me. Come and kill him.' He who claims there will be a lasting peace between us and the Jews is an infidel."[52]

In other words, bin Laden is casting the conflict between Muslims and Jews as an end-of-days struggle. This is also how the Palestinians are often told to see their struggle with the Jews, as can be seen in a May 2005 videotape of a sermon given by a prominent Palestinian cleric that was broadcast over the official Palestinian Authority television station:

> The day will come when we will rule Britain and the entire world—except for the Jews. The Jews will not enjoy a life of tranquility under our rule, because they are treacherous by nature, as they have been throughout history . . . Listen to the Prophet Muhammad, who tells you about the evil end that awaits Jews. The stones and trees will want the Muslims to finish off every Jew.[53]

Sayyid Qutb, in his "manifesto" of jihad, portrays the Jews as a perpetual threat, accusing them of conspiring to "perpetuate their evil designs" on the world, and singles them out for practicing usury or the charging of interest, a practice that is forbidden according to Islam. In *Milestones* he writes:

> [The goal of the Jews] is to eliminate all limitations, especially the limitations imposed by faith and religion, so that the Jews may penetrate into the body politic of the whole world and then may be free to perpetuate their evil designs. At the top of the list of these activities is usury, the aim of which is that all the wealth of mankind end up in the hands of Jewish financial institutions, which run on interest.[54]

As David Zeidan points out, Qutb "identifies modern secular philosophy as a trap laid by world-wide Judaism in order to destroy barriers of creed, weaken society, and enable Jews to penetrate every country with their 'satanic usurious activity' which will finally 'deliver the proceeds of all human toil into the hands of the great usurious Jewish financial institutions.' "[55]

We can see Qutb's influence in the mission statement of the Palestinian jihadist group, Hamas, which was founded by members of the Muslim Brotherhood. Recall that Qutb was their chief publicist and ideologue during the fifties and sixties. The Hamas mission statement describes a Jewish plot to dominate the world:

> For a long time, the enemies [the Jews] have been planning, skillfully and with precision, for the achievement of what they have attained. They took into consideration the causes affecting the current of events. They strived to amass great and substantive material wealth which they devoted to the realisation of their dream. With their money, they took control of the world media, news agencies, the press, publishing houses, broadcasting stations, and others. With their money they stirred revolutions in various parts of the world with the purpose of achieving their interests and reaping the fruit therein. They were behind the French Revolution, the Communist revolution and most of the revolutions we heard and hear about, here and there. With their money they formed secret societies, such as Freemasons, Rotary Clubs, the Lions and others in different parts of the world for the purpose of sabotaging societies and achieving Zionist interests. With their money they were able to control imperialistic countries and instigate them to colonize many countries in order to enable them to exploit their resources and spread corruption there.
>
> . . . They [the Jews] were behind World War I, when they were able to destroy the Islamic Caliphate, making financial gains and controlling resources. They obtained the Balfour Declaration, formed the League of Nations through which they could rule the world. They were behind World War II, through which they made huge financial gains by trading in armaments, and paved the way for the establishment of their state. It was they who instigated the replacement of the League of Nations with the United Nations and the Security Council to enable them to rule the world through them. There is no war going on anywhere, without having their finger in it. (Article 22)

It is not uncommon to hear jihadists refer to Christians and Jews as monkeys and pigs, especially in internal discussions or writings and sermons addressed to each other. This rather odd characterization (at least to Western ears) comes straight from the Koran as can be seen in the following verses:

> And indeed [addressing the Jews] you knew those amongst you who transgressed in the matter of the Sabbath (i.e. Saturday). We said to them: "Be you monkeys, despised and rejected." So We made this punishment an example to their own and to succeeding generations and a lesson to those who are *Al-Muttaqûn* (the pious-see V.2:2). (Sura 2:65–66)
>
> Say (O Muhammad SAW to the people of the Scripture): "Shall I inform you of something worse than that, regarding the recompense from Allâh: those (Jews) who incurred the Curse of Allâh and His Wrath, those of whom (some) He transformed into monkeys and swines, those who worshipped *Tâghût* (false deities); such are worse in rank (on the Day of Resurrection in the Hellfire), and far more astray from the Right Path (in the life of this world)." (Sura 5:60)
>
> So when they exceeded the limits of what they were prohibited, We said to them: "Be you monkeys, despised and rejected." (Sura 7:166)

While the Koran ridicules Jews, it also instructs them to protect them given that they are fellow monotheists. However, such protection is strictly dependent on their willingness to accept an inferior—or in Arabic, *dhimmi*—status in the Muslim order. This is another reason why jihadists take such a strong stance against the state of Israel, believing for example as Hamas does, that there cannot be a Jewish state at all in Muslim lands and that Israel must be destroyed. In their view, the Jews—a dhimmi people—simply cannot have dominion over what they regard as Muslim lands.

Inherent in the jihadists' interpretation is the notion that Islam cannot simply coexist with other faiths because it is superior. This is because only the Muslims—as opposed to the Jews or Christians—managed to get God's message right. This is why Muslims often call the Prophet Mohammed the "Seal of the Prophets." He was the last prophet God needed in order to deliver His monotheistic creed for humanity. This notion too comes directly from the Koran:

> Muhammad (**SAW**) is not the father of any man among you, but he is the Messenger of Allâh and the last (end) of the Prophets. (Sura 33:40)

Thus, the jihadists believe that it is Islam's mission to guide humanity back to God's plan, as it was revealed to the Prophet Mohammed. Because of this, in their view, Islam has to have dominion over all other faiths and belief systems. While other faiths can certainly coexist with Islam, especially given the instruction provided in this verse:

> There is no compulsion in religion. Verily, the Right Path has become distinct from the wrong path. Whoever disbelieves in *Tâghût* and believes in Allâh, then he has grasped the most trustworthy handhold that will never break. And Allâh is All-Hearer, All-Knower. (Sura 2:256)

As we have already discussed, in the famous Sword Verse, the Koran instructs that polytheists and disbelievers have to be converted or killed, while other verses indicate that monotheists, and monotheists alone, may survive and even practice their religions (Judaism and Christianity) but only if they agree to submit to the domain of Islam. In other words, Islam must be regarded as supreme and the other faiths must acquiesce to their subordination.

As it expanded, the Muslim empire eventually conferred dhimmi status on others including Zoroastrians, Hindus, and Sikhs. Perhaps, as some scholars have suggested, the empire recognized that it was more profitable to tax these groups than have to kill or convert them. The rights and obligations of dhimmi people would vary according to the Islamic tradition then in place. Typically, in addition to having to pay a poll tax, dhimmi men have been forbidden from marrying Muslim women (though Muslim men could freely marry dhimmi women) and dhimmis could expect to have their testimony accorded less weight, be punished more severely, and rewarded less compensation in Islamic courts than Muslims in similar circumstances.

The Goal of Jihad

Ultimately, the goal of the global jihad movement is to establish a worldwide Islamic order. For example, consider the Koranic quotation bin Laden cites in his 1996 fatwa:

> You are the best of the nations raised up for-the benefit of-men; you enjoin what is right and forbid the wrong and believe in Allah. (Sura 3:110)

During India's independence movement, an Indian journalist by the name of Abu al-A'la Mawdudi (1903–1979), rose to prominence because he was able to make the case that jihad was a revolutionary or liberation force. He argued that Muslims had to fight for political power and established what would be Pakistan's first Islamist party, the Jamaat-e-Islami in 1941 (which still survives). His writings would have a profound effect on the global jihad movement as he believed that Muslims should not "shrink from the use of force"[56] and that the goal of jihad was to establish a just society:

> Islam wants the whole earth and does not content itself with only a part thereof. It wants and requires the entire inhabited world. It does not want this in order that one nation dominates the earth and monopolizes its sources of wealth, after having taken them away from one or more other nations. No, Islam wants and requires the earth in order that the human race altogether can enjoy the concept and practical program of human happiness, by means of which God has honoured Islam and put it above the other religions and laws. In order to realize this lofty desire, Islam wants to employ all forces and means that can be employed for bringing about a universal all-embracing revolution. It will spare no efforts for the achievement of this supreme objective. This far-reaching struggle that continuously exhausts all forces and this employment of all possible means are called jihad.[57]

Qutb would continue Mawdudi's line of thinking: "Islam," he wrote in *Milestones*, "came into this world to establish God's rule on earth,"[58] and its vision should be applied universally:

> Islam is not a heritage of any particular race or country; this is God's religion and it is for the whole world. It has the right to destroy all obstacles in the form of institutions and traditions which limit man's freedom of choice. It does not attack individuals nor does it force them to accept its beliefs; it attacks institutions and traditions to release human beings from their poisonous influences, which distort human nature and which curtail human freedom.[59]
>
> Islam did not come to support people's desires, which are expressed in their concepts, institutions, modes of living, and habits and traditions, whether they were prevalent at the advent of Islam or are prevalent now, both in the East and in the West. Islam does not sanction the rule of selfish desires. It has come to abolish all such concepts, laws, customs and traditions, and to replace them with a new concept of human life.[60]

Thus while the near-term goals of the various jihads may be local and specific (ending occupation, overthrowing local regimes, restoring the pan-Islamic state in what was previously the Ottoman Empire, winning back the Iberian Peninsula, recapturing parts of Europe), there is plenty of evidence to suggest that the end-goal of the global movement is far-reaching and aims at establishing a global Islamic order.

As to what this new Islamic order would look like, consider what Qutb had to say about the United States, which he believed epitomized the "Western Jahiliyya" or "state of ignorance":

> Look at these concepts of the Trinity, Original Sin, Sacrifice and Redemption, which are agreeable neither to reason nor to conscience. Look at this capitalism with its monopolies, its usury and whatever else is unjust in it; at this individual freedom, devoid of human sympathy and responsibility for relatives except under the force of law; at this materialistic attitude which deadens the spirit; at this behavior, like animals, which you call "free mixing of the sexes"; at this vulgarity which you call "emancipation of women"; at these unfair and cumbersome laws of marriage and divorce, which are contrary to the demands of practical life; and at this evil and fanatic racial discrimination. Then look at Islam, with its logic, beauty, humanity and happiness, which reaches the horizons to which man strives but does not reach.[61]

According to Qutb the cure for Western civilization lies in the message of the Prophet—namely, Islam:

> Even the Western world realises that Western civilization is unable to present any healthy values for the guidance of mankind . . . The period of the Western system has come to an end primarily because it is deprived of those life-giving values which enabled it to be the leader of mankind.
>
> It is necessary for the new leadership to preserve and develop the material fruits of the creative genius of Europe, and also to provide mankind with such high ideals and values as have so far remained undiscovered by mankind, and which will also acquaint humanity with a way of life which is harmonious with human nature, which is positive and constructive, and which is practicable.
>
> Islam is the only system which possesses these values and this way of life.[62]

According to Qutb, once Muslims have eliminated the "tyrannical force" that is Western civilization, Islam will be able to install "a new social, economic and political system, in which the concept of freedom of man is applied in practice."[63] This is why Qutb says jihad is only defensive in the sense that it is "the defense of man" against other "beliefs and concepts, as well as political systems, based on economic, racial or class distinctions."[64]

The Importance of a Vanguard

How would this new Islamic order come about? Again Qutb provides guidance. In *Milestones*, he writes that this new world order will come about through the efforts of a small group of Muslims—a "vanguard"—who would set themselves apart from the corrupt and ignorant societies in which they lived and prepare to bring about this new order:

> Ii is necessary that there should be a vanguard which sets out with this determination and then keeps walking on the path, marching through the vast ocean of Jahiliyyah which has encompassed the entire world. During its course, it should keep itself somewhat aloof from this all-encompassing Jahiliyyah and should also keep some ties with it.
>
> It is necessary that this vanguard should know the landmarks and the milestones of the road toward this goal so that they may recognize the starting place, the nature, the responsibilities and the ultimate purpose of this long journey.[65]

This is why *Milestones* is referred to as the "manifesto" or handbook of the modern jihad movement. In *Milestones*, Qutb offers precise guidance as to what he believes this vanguard will need to do in order to carry out its missions—the *signposts* along the road that will guide them on their mission (signposts, incidentally is an alternative translation of the book's Arabic title). Note, however, that Qutb counsels his followers that it will not be enough for them to follow just his advice, rather, the most essential thing that they will have to do is become Salafis—that is, they will have to model themselves on the example set by the pious ancestors.

> The milestones will necessarily be determined by the light of the first source of this faith—the Holy Qur'an—and from its basic teachings, and from the concept which it created in the minds of the first group of Muslims, those whom God raised to fulfil His will, those who once changed the course of human history in the direction ordained by God.[66]

Azzam and bin Laden later took this concept of the vanguard and used it as the basis of establishing *al Qaeda*. As Azzam wrote:

> Every principle needs a vanguard (Tali'ah) to carry it forward and, while forcing its way into society, puts up with heavy tasks and enormous sacrifices. There is no ideology, neither earthly nor heavenly, that does not require such a vanguard that gives everything it possesses in order to achieve victory for this ideology. It carries the flag all along the sheer endless and difficult path until it reaches its destination in the reality of life, since Allah has destined that it should make it and manifest itself. This vanguard constitutes the solid base (al-Qa'ida al-Sulbah) for the expected society.
>
> As long as the ideology—even if it originates from the Lord of the Worlds—does not find this self-sacrificing vanguard that spends everything in its possession for the sake of making its ideology prevail, this ideology will be still-born, perishing before it sees light and life. The motto of those who carry this ideology forward must be:
>
> "Call your partners (of Allah), and then plot against me, and give me no respite. My protector is Allah, who has revealed the Book. He will choose and support the righteous." (Surat al-A'raf, 195–196)[67]

This is why we hear bin Laden using the nomenclature of the vanguard in his 1998 interview with ABC News:

> Tell the Muslims everywhere that the vanguards of the warriors who are fighting the enemies of Islam belong to them and the young fighters are their sons. Tell them that the nation is bent on fighting the enemies of Islam.[68]

To establish an Islamic hegemony, this vanguard, now called al Qaeda, will have to bring about the end of American superpower. In the words of bin Laden:

> Hostility toward America is a religious duty, and we hope to be rewarded for it by God . . . Osama bin Laden is confident that the Islamic nation will carry out its duty. I am confident that Muslims will be able to end the legend of the so-called superpower that is America.[69]

Local regimes such as Saudi Arabia, bin Laden warns, will also have to fall:

> We expect for the ruler of Riyadh the same fate as the Shah of Iran.[70]

But first, according to Zawahiri, "the jihad movement must adopt its plan on the basis of controlling a piece of land in the heart of the Islamic world on which it could establish and protect the state of Islam and launch its battle to restore the rational caliphate based on the traditions of the prophet."[71] This is key, Zawahiri writes in 2001, when he assumes he will not have long to live, and feels he must leave detailed instructions behind for those who will take up the vanguard: "Armies achieve victory only when the infantry takes hold of land. Likewise, the mujahid Islamic movement will not triumph against the world coalition unless it possesses a fundamentalist base in the heart of the Islamic world."[72]

Even in the short-term, Zawahiri goes on to argue, the United States must be dealt with, as in his view, it will never "allow any Muslim force to reach power in the Arab countries."[73] And so he warns his fellow jihadists to: "move the battle to the enemy's grounds to burn the hands of those who ignite fire in our countries."[74]

How Long Will Jihad Last?

As to the time-frame of the global jihad movement, Zawahiri cautions that the struggle may very well take centuries:

> [T]his is a goal that could take several generations to achieve. The Crusaders in Palestine and Syria left after two centuries of continued jihad. The Islamic nation at the time had jihad rulers and regular and discipline armies. It was led by prominent scholars . . . Despite this, the Crusaders did not leave in 30 or 50 years. The British occupied Egypt for 70 years. The French occupied Algeria for 120 years.[75]

In 1998, bin Laden sent a similar message in an ABC interview:

Allah has granted the Muslim people and the Afghani mujahedeen, and those with them, the opportunity to fight the Russians and the Soviet Union . . . They were defeated by Allah and were wiped out. There is a lesson here. The Soviet Union entered Afghanistan late in December of '79. The flag of the Soviet Union was folded once and for all on the 25th of December just 10 years later. It was thrown in the waste basket. Gone was the Soviet Union forever. We are certain that we shall—with the grace of Allah—prevail over the Americans and over the Jews, as the Messenger of Allah promised us in an authentic prophetic tradition when He said the Hour of Resurrection shall not come before Muslims fight Jews and before Jews hide behind trees and behind rocks.[76]

Sadat's assassins also warned that the battle would be long: As the author of *The Neglected Duty*, observed "The [Muslim] conquest of Constantinople came about more than 800 years after the Prophet's prediction. And also the conquest of Rome will be realized."[77]

CHAPTER 3

How Is Jihad Being Fought?

Yes, I am a terrorist. Write that down: I admit I am a terrorist. [The Koran] says it is the duty of Muslims to bring terror to the enemy, so being a terrorist makes me a good Muslim.

Marwan Abu Ubeida, an Iraqi training to
become a suicide bomber[1]

How exactly did the jihadists plan to prosecute their world domination plan? What tactics were they willing to employ? What is their overall strategy?

So far we have seen that, aside from some important exceptions (the Arab wars against Israel, the Iran-Iraq War, the Gulf War), today's jihads are waged by non-state actors—for example al Qaeda, Hamas, Jamaat al-Islamiyah—and depending on the situation, the battle involves a struggle against a local regime, an occupying power, a Western nation, or even the jihadists' fellow citizens (the Christians and Nuba in Sudan; the Shiites in Iraq, for example). The implication of this observation is that most jihads cannot be conducted using regular warfare—that is, open warfare conducted between states in command of uniformed armed forces and territory—if only because such non-state players have neither armies nor territories. This further means that today's non-state jihadists have essentially two means of fighting at their disposal: guerilla warfare or terrorism. Before we go further, we have to define by what we mean by these two often politicized terms.

Terrorism or Warfare

When we use the term *regular* (or alternatively *conventional*) warfare, we will be talking about warfare that is openly conducted between states abiding by the rules of war as expressed, for example, in the Geneva Conventions and the United Nations Charter. This series of international conventions protect civilians, prisoners of war, wounded or sick soldiers and sailors, prohibit the use of nerve gas or bacteriological agents, and regulate bombing. In addition, in regular warfare, armed services also are expected to follow *rules of engagement*, a code of conduct put in place at the command level that governs when and how much lethal force may be applied.

According to these internationally recognized rules of war, state-sanctioned armed forces must confine their targets to military installations or strategic civilian property. Legitimate military targets would be those which have been determined to be making a significant contribution to the opponent's war effort. Legitimate civilian targets, on the other hand, would include any property, the destruction of which would so advance a military objective that it would significantly outweigh the harm done to the civilian population.[2] For example, an electrical grid system supplying energy to a city could be targeted under this principle if it could be argued that by cutting off a city's electrical supply, it would significantly impact the enemy's morale or force strength. In this case, the military advantage—the possibility that this could bring about an earlier end to the conflict, could be reasonably argued to outweigh the damage to the civilian property—the temporary loss of electricity during wartime.

Some civilian targets—such as schools, hospitals, and religious sites—should never be targeted, unless these institutions have been converted by the enemy for military use, in which case they lose their immunity. But it is an internationally recognized rule of war that both sides in a conflict are expected to use their best efforts to segregate military installations and operations from the civilian population in order to minimize the possibility that civilians could be harmed in a cross fire. In other words, in no case are civilians ever to be used as human shields.

While civilian casualties often result as a consequence of military operations (in military parlance such casualties are called *collateral damage*), under the terms of the Fourth Geneva Convention, civilians are never to be the primary target of a military operation. Military operations in which civilians have been specifically targeted are classified as war crimes. (In cases where civilians are targeted away from the battlefield or outside of defined conflict zones, the perpetrators are not guilty of war crimes but rather of crimes against humanity.)

Irregular (or alternatively *guerilla*) warfare differs from regular or conventional warfare, in that guerilla warfare is that which is employed by non-state actors (Hezbollah, for example) against the regular forces of a state (in this case, Israel or the United States). Guerilla warfare is used in insurgencies, struggles against occupation, national liberation movements, and other types of conflicts where a non-state group is engaging in armed struggle against a state or an occupying power of a state. Guerillas operate very much like conventional forces in that they confine their targets to the armed and security forces of the enemy power, its military installations, or political leaders who have positions of command responsibility (for example the president or the intelligence organization). Guerillas can be distinguished from terrorists by one simple test: they have to refrain from targeting innocent civilians who have little or no ability to influence the outcome of a conflict. This is what distinguishes terrorism from guerilla warfare: terrorism uniquely targets civilians in order to achieve a political goal. If there is no political goal, the killing of innocents is defined as criminal activity. Because terrorism, by definition, involves the killing of innocents, the term *terrorism* has taken on a pejorative connotation, while *guerrilla warfare* has not.

Many people and countries have tried to make the case that defining who is a terrorist depends on one's politics. The commonly cited argument is: "one man's terrorist is another man's freedom fighter." The United Nations, for example, has never been able to issue a standard definition of terrorism because many member states resist the idea of endorsing any definition of terrorism that would criminalize or cast the Palestinian struggle for national liberation in a negative light.

We take the position that this view essentially conflates ends and means. We define a freedom fighter as one whose end-goal is the liberation of a people, while we contend that a terrorist is someone who is willing to use terrorism as a tactic to advance a political goal. That is, terrorism is a *tactic*, or a *means* to achieve an end-goal. If a freedom fighter confines his or her targets to ones that are ordinarily sanctioned in the rules of war (i.e., military targets and strategic civilian property) we will call him a *guerilla* or an *insurgent* or a *rebel*. If the freedom fighter, however, targets unarmed civilians to advance his cause, he becomes, by our definition, a *terrorist*. In other words, a freedom fighter fights for the goal of freedom and becomes a terrorist in the event that he willing to target civilians.[3] (But note: once a terrorist, always a terrorist, in our view.)

Our definition of terrorism, incidentally, is more or less in line with that of the United States State Department, or Title 22 of the United States Code, Section 2656f(d), which states:

- The term "terrorism" means premeditated, politically motivated violence perpetrated against noncombatant (1) targets by subnational groups or clandestine agents, usually intended to influence an audience.
- The term "international terrorism" means terrorism involving citizens or the territory of more than one country.
- The term "terrorist group" means any group practicing, or that has significant subgroups that practice, international terrorism.

(1) For purposes of this definition, the term "noncombatant" is interpreted to include, in addition to civilians, military personnel who at the time of the incident are unarmed and/or not on duty . . . We also consider as acts of terrorism attacks on military installations or on armed military personnel when a state of military hostilities does not exist at the site.[4]

While this definition may not pass muster everywhere (at the United Nations, for example), bin Laden himself would probably not object. In a 1998 interview with ABC, when he was asked to respond to allegations that he was a terrorist, he was unapologetic about the fact that his organization practiced terrorism:

Every state and every civilization and culture has to resort to terrorism under certain circumstances for the purpose of abolishing tyranny and corruption . . . The terrorism we practice is of the commendable kind for it is directed at the tyrants and the aggressors and the enemies of Allah, the tyrants, the traitors who commit acts of treason against their own countries and their own faith and their own prophet and their own nation.[5]

Other jihadists have also expressed a similar lack of hesitancy in using the word *terrorist* to describe themselves. The Blind Sheik, who was convicted of seditious conspiracy for waging a war of "urban jihad" against America was on record saying "We are terrorists and we wear the name proudly. We are commanded to strike terror into the hearts of the enemies of Islam, to shake the earth under their feet. Our main enemies, the United States of America and its allies. The United States of America, the master puppeteer pulling the strings of our oppressors—the Serbs, Hosni Mubarak, [the] State of Israel."[6] In 2005, Time magazine profiled an Iraqi suicide bomber who eagerly told his interviewer, "Yes, I am a terrorist," adding:

Write that down: "I admit I am a terrorist. [The Koran] says it is the duty of Muslims to bring terror to the enemy, so being a terrorist makes me a good Muslim." He quotes lines from the Surah known as Al-Anfal, or the Spoils of War: "Against them make ready your strength to the utmost of your power, including steeds of war, to strike terror into the enemy of Allah and your enemy."[7]

To get a sense of just how prevalent terrorism is in today's jihad campaigns, we can refer to TheReligionofPeace.com (TROP), a website that has kept track of all fatal terrorist attacks that have been reported in the Western media that have been committed in the name of Islam since September 11, 2001. Because the jihadists define *militant jihad* as violence carried out in the name of Islam, this list can serve as a log of jihadist attacks since 9/11. At the time of of this writing this book (up through May 30, 2006), 5,098 incidents of Islamic terrorism have been recorded, resulting in 16,958 deaths and 36,390 injured (again, statistics from the 9/11 attacks have not been included).[8] Bear in mind, however, that as the editors of TROP, duly note, the list:

[I]s incomplete because only a small percentage of attacks were picked up by international news sources, even those involving multiple loss of life. We included an attack if it was committed by Muslims in the name of Islam, and usually **only** if loss of life occurred (with a handful of exceptions where there were a very large number of injuries). In several cases, the victims are undercounted because deaths from trauma caused by the Islamists may occur in later days, despite the best efforts of medical personnel to keep the victims alive.[9]

Note that, TROP does not generally include attacks against armed forces in combat situations, such as in Iraq and Afghanistan, on its "List of Islamic Terror Attacks." The only time TROP does include such an attack is if it "involves particularly heinous terrorist tactics" or if it was entirely unprovoked and targeted military personnel carrying out police work as opposed to combat duties. This means that TROP's taxonomy is very much in line ours with respect to the classification of terrorism versus guerilla warfare.

After examining this list of jihadist attacks since 9/11, we noted some interesting trends in terms of targets. Among our findings

In Israel, jihadists evidence a strong preference for suicide attacks on soft targets such as buses, cafes, nightclubs, markets, and even a Passover celebration.

Tourist spots are favorite targets on other fronts as well. Nightclubs, cafes, restaurants, hotels and landmarks have been attacked everywhere from Africa to Indonesia to Egypt to Jordan to Morocco to Tunisia. Tourists have been kidnapped in places as far a field as Kashmir, Algeria, and the Philippines.

Synagogues, churches and Shiite mosques are favorite targets in Algeria, Egypt, India, Indonesia, Nigeria, Pakistan, Iraq, and the Philippines.

Trains and subways are the preference in Europe (London and Madrid), and they have also been hit in Dagestan (in Russia), Thailand, India, Pakistan and Algeria.

Schools, school buses, teachers and school administrators are considered fair game by jihadists using gunfire, bombs and arson in Afghanistan, Chechnya, India, Iraq, Israel, Pakistan, Philippines, and Thailand.

Beheading and throat-slitting have been used to terrorize the enemy in Iraq and also in Algeria and Thailand. Decapitated hostages have also been discovered in Algeria, Pakistan, Kashmir, the Phillippines, and Saudi Arabia, though this list is by no means exhaustive.

In *Iraq, jihadists favor suicide attacks of soft targets* such as the International Red Cross, Shiite mosques, markets, civilian neighborhoods, funeral processions and wakes, unarmed Iraqi police and army recruits, and even a hospital.

Justification of Tactics

How do these self-described pious Muslims justify killing their fellow Muslims while they attend mosque? How do they justify killing their fellow monotheists, the Jews, as they gather to celebrate the religious holiday of Passover? What is their religious justification for blowing up foreign tourists at a nightclub? Or killing local school teachers? How do jihadists rationalize the beheading of hostages or the throat-slitting of Muslim villagers? We do not have to speculate about their way of thinking. Just as in chapter 2, we can examine how the jihadists themselves explain their conduct, how they justify suicide attacks against unsuspecting and unarmed civilians going about their daily lives by reading their published statements.

But before we look at how jihadists have justified their use of terrorism, we need to understand that scores of Muslim clerics and intellectuals and Western Islamic scholars have gone on record to condemn the use of terrorism under the banner of Islam, and in particular the 9/11 attacks:

For example, Shaykh Yusuf al-Qaradawi, a cleric with his own show on Al-Jazeera, reminded Muslims that the Koran expressly forbids the killing of innocents:

> Islam, the religion of tolerance, holds the human soul in high esteem, and considers the attack against innocent human beings a grave sin, this is backed by the

Qur'anic verse which reads: "Who so ever kills a human being [as punishment] for [crimes] other than manslaughter or [sowing] corruption in the earth, it shall be as if he has killed all mankind, and who so ever saves the life of one, it shall be as if he had saved the life of all mankind." (Al-Ma'idah:32)[10]

Sheik Abdulaziz bin Abdullah al-Sheik, the grand mufti of Saudi Arabia, condemned the attacks with this statement: "Hijacking planes, terrorizing innocent people and shedding blood, constitute a form of injustice that cannot be tolerated by Islam which views them as gross crimes and sinful acts."[11]

Shaykh Muhammad bin 'Abdallah al-Sabil, a member of the Council of Senior Religious Scholars, Saudi Arabia, said Muslims should be protecting Christians and Jews, not attacking them. "Any attack on innocent people is unlawful and contrary to shari'a (Islamic law). . . . Muslims must safeguard the lives, honor and property of Christians and Jews. Attacking them contradicts shari'a."[12]

Even forty-six leaders of avowed jihadist groups and their sympathizers including Hamas, the Muslim Brotherhood in Egypt, and Jamaat-e-Islami in Bangladesh got together to issue a joint statement condemning the 9/11 attacks:

Mustafa Mashhur, General Guide, Muslim Brotherhood, Egypt; Qazi Hussain Ahmed, Ameer, Jamaat-e-Islami Pakistan, Pakistan; Muti Rahman Nizami, Ameer, Jamaat-e-Islami Bangladesh, Bangladesh; Shaykh Ahmad Yassin, Founder, Islamic Resistance Movement (Hamas), Palestine; Rashid Ghannoushi, President, Nahda Renaissance Movement, Tunisia; Fazil Nour, President, PAS—Parti Islam SeMalaysia, Malaysia; and 40 other Muslim scholars and politicians:

"The undersigned, leaders of Islamic movements, are horrified by the events of Tuesday 11 September 2001 in the United States which resulted in massive killing, destruction and attack on innocent lives. We express our deepest sympathies and sorrow. We condemn, in the strongest terms, the incidents, which are against all human and Islamic norms. This is grounded in the Noble Laws of Islam which forbid all forms of attacks on innocents. God Almighty says in the Holy Qur'an: 'No bearer of burdens can bear the burden of another.' (Surah al-Isra 17:15)"[13]

Omar Bakri, a self-described radical, who would later celebrate the 9/11 hijackers as the "magnificent 19,"[14] even condemned the attacks, saying they defied the teachings of Islam:

If Islamists did it—and most likely it is Islamists, because of the nature of what happened—then they have fully misunderstood the teachings of Islam. . . . Even the most radical of us have condemned this. I am always considered to be a radical in the Islamic world and even I condemn it.[15]

Bernard Haykel, a professor of Islamic studies at New York University, like many Western scholars of Islam, tried to show why the attacks were illegal in Islamic terms:

According to Islamic law there are at least six reasons why Bin Laden's barbaric violence cannot fall under the rubric of jihad: 1) Individuals and organizations cannot declare a jihad, only states can; 2) One cannot kill innocent women and children when conducting a jihad; 3) One cannot kill Muslims in a jihad; 4) One cannot fight a jihad against a country in which Muslims can freely practise their religion and proselytize Islam; 5) Prominent Muslim jurists around the world have condemned these attacks and their condemnation forms a juristic consensus (ijma') against Bin Laden's actions (This consensus renders his actions un-Islamic); 6) The welfare and interest of the Muslim community (maslaha) is being harmed by Bin Laden's actions and this equally makes them un-Islamic.[16]

Charles Kurzman, a sociologist at the University of North Carolina, for his part, collected dozens of such statements from Muslim clerics, Islamic scholars, and other intellectuals to show that the response to the attacks from leading Muslim clerics, Islamic scholars, and Muslim intellectuals was overwhelmingly negative.[17] So how did bin Laden and his followers justify the attacks? Moreover, since the 9/11 attacks—and all the criticism—there have been some 3,326 recorded incidents of Islamic terrorism directed at civilians in as many as thirty countries throughout the world.[18] Even an occasional reader of the world's newspapers over the past few years would have been able to see that not only have today's jihadists *not* abandoned the practice of targeting civilians—in spite of the rampant criticism—but have instead embraced the practice even *more* enthusiastically. This obviously begs the question, on just what Islamic basis are the jihadists acting?

Consider this excerpt from the authoritative Sahih Muslim collection of hadith, in which Abu Baker, the first "rightly-guided caliph" (or the first head of the Muslim state after the death of the Prophet) instructs the Muslim armies about the ten rules which they must be careful to observe on the battlefield:

> So great is the respect for humanly feelings in Islam that even the wanton destruction of enemy's crops or property is strictly forbidden. The righteous Caliphs followed closely the teachings of Allah and those of His Apostle in letter and spirit the celebrated address which the first Caliph Abu Bakr (Allah be pleased with him) gave to his army while sending her on the expedition to the Syrian borders is permeated with the noble spirit with which the war in Islam is permitted. He said: "Stop, O people, that I may give you ten rules for your guidance in the battlefield. Do not commit treachery or deviate from the right path. You must not mutilate dead bodies. Neither kill a child, nor a woman. nor an aged man. Bring no harm to the trees, nor burn them with fire, especially those which are fruitful. Slay not any of the enemy's flock save for your food. You are likely to pass by people who have devoted their lives to monastic services; leave them alone"[19]

Again, there is nothing in the above set of rules to suggest that Islam condones the mutilation of enemy corpses; the beheading of monks in Algeria or Thailand; or the bombing of fresh-air markets, Passover seders, discos, nightclubs, cafes, hotels, schools, or groups of children who are lining up to receive candy from American soldiers. That the above set of rules do not appear to have been adopted by the jihadists is more than a little curious as their source is no less an authority than the first "rightly-guided" caliph Abu Baker. Abu Baker was the first person selected to lead the Muslim community after the Prophet's death; he among all the other pious ancestors or *Salafi* was selected to become the first head of the Muslim community after the Prophet's death because of his outstanding personal piety. In other words, Abu Baker is the quintessential Salafi, someone who, by their own interpretation of Islam, the jihadists certainly ought to be following. So why would his rules no longer apply? Is there another set of guidelines in the Islamic tradition that the jihadists are following?

We begin our search for how the jihadists justify their use of terrorism by examining al Qaeda's response to all the criticism and condemnation it received for having carried out the 9/11 attacks. On April 24, 2002, al Qaeda issued a statement, entitled "A statement from *qaidat al-jihad* regarding the mandates of the heroes and the legality of the operations in New York and Washington."[20] The al Qaeda authors (who do not disclose their identity) begin their carefully crafted statement by citing a verse from the Koran:

> Fight against those who (1) believe not in Allâh, (2) nor in the Last Day, (3) nor forbid that which has been forbidden by Allâh and His Messenger (4) and those who acknowledge not the religion of truth (i.e. Islâm) among the people of the Scripture (Jews and Christians), until they pay the *Jizyah* with willing submission, and feel themselves subdued. (Sura 9:29)

By opening their fatwa with this verse, the authors are asserting that the 9/11 attacks were carried out as part of God's order to Muslims to fight both unbelievers (the polytheists or disbelievers) as well as Jews and Christians (or "the people of the Scripture") who have not yet submitted to the hegemony of Islam (that is, those who do not yet "feel themselves subdued")—in this particular case the occupants of the World Trade Center, the Pentagon, and those aboard the airliners.

The authors then go on to insist that the attacks were indeed a "success" because finally Muslims had humiliated "the Crusader enemy." They also warn the reader not to trivialize these attacks as they came at great sacrifice:

> Let all know as well that many souls died on account of these operations, the first among them the souls of the heroes. We should never think little of the passing of souls, especially the Muslims among them.

After acknowledging the cost in "souls," "after study and deliberation," the authors conclude, "we have found that operations like this are what will return its glory to the ummah and convince the oppressive enemy of the rights of the Islamic community." The authors are careful to point out that they did not reach this conclusion hastily but only, in their words, "after study and deliberation."

The authors express their indignation at all the criticism they received, singling out in particular those who on the one hand, readily support "martyrdom operations [suicide terrorism] against the Jews in Palestine" but then on the other hand oppose the same sort of attacks when they are directed at Americans. The authors are correct on this point: Many of those who readily condemned the 9/11 attacks were on record having justified against Israeli civilians.

Qaradawi, for example, the Al-Jazeera talk-show host and spiritual leader of the Muslim Brotherhood (see the September 14, 2001 statement that was signed by forty-six Muslim leaders) but has gone on record many times to endorse suicide terrorism against Israel which he calls heroic "martyrdom operations." Shortly after 9/11, in the wake of a series of bombings in Jerusalem that killed twenty-six people, Sheikh Mohammad Sayyed Tantawi, the head of Sunni Islam's most prestigious center of learning, al-Azhar, issued a statement condemning "any attack on innocent civilians" and expressing his disapproval of those "who justify attacks against children by reasoning that the children will join the army when they grow up."[21] To these remarks, Qaradawi dismissively replied, "Has fighting colonizers become a criminal and terrorist act for some sheikhs?" and went on to point out that "Israeli society was completely military in its make-up and did not include any civilians."[22] The jihadist organization Hamas, another critic of the 9/11 attacks, has not only condoned suicide attacks against Israeli civilians, it has executed them. As one Hamas militant explained, "We do not have tanks or rockets, but we have something superior—our exploding Islamic human bombs. In place of a nuclear arsenal, we are proud of our arsenal of believers."[23]

As the authors point out of al Qaeda's self-justification statement:

This inconsistency is very strange! How can one permit the killing of the branch and not permit the killing of the supporting trunk? All who permit martyrdom operations against the Jews in Palestine must allow them in America. If not, the inconsistency leads to nothing but a type of game playing with the legal ruling.

Addressing those who condemned the 9/11 attacks on the basis that Islam prohibits the killing of protected persons (women, children, and the elderly), the authors argue that such a prohibition should not be regarded as absolute and then go on to list the seven conditions under any one of which it is permissible to kill "protected ones":

First they claim that "[i]t is allowed for Muslims to kill protected ones among unbelievers as an act of reciprocity." Or, as they go on to say, "if the unbelievers have targeted Muslim women, children, and elderly," then, according to the authors logic "it is permissible for Muslims to respond in kind" because of the Koranic verse which says: "You may transgress against those who have transgressed against you just as they have transgressed against you." (Sura 2:194) The authors say that the proof that America is guilty of this offense—that is that America is targeting "children, women, and the elderly" can be seen in the "atrocious slaughter going on" in the West Bank cities of Jenin, Nablus, and Ramallah. (The claims of massacres and massive destruction going on in the West Bank during this period would later be determined by independent human rights organizations to have been wildly exaggerated.[24])

Next the al Qaeda authors argue that even if there *were* any innocent civilians among the dead on 9/11:

It is allowed for Muslims to kill protected ones among unbelievers in the event of an attack against them in which it is not possible to differentiate the protected ones from the combatants or from the strongholds. It is permissible to kill them incidentally and unintentionally according to the saying of the Prophet. When he was asked, as in al-Bukhari, about the offspring and women of unbelievers who stayed with the unbelievers and were killed, he said, "They are from among them." This indicates the permission to kill women and children because of their fathers if they can not be distinguished. In the account of Muslim he said, "They are from their fathers."

In other words, what the al Qaeda authors are saying here is that it is not incumbent upon Muslims to protect the innocents inside the enemy's stronghold, but rather it is the responsibility of "their fathers"—that is those who are supposed to protect them in their own homes. Earlier, in a 1998 interview with ABC News, bin Laden noted that Americans themselves had availed of methods in which it was impossible to differentiate between the civilian and the combatant populations, citing as an example the atomic bombing of Japan during World War II:

Through history, American [sic] has not been known to differentiate between the military and the civilians or between men and women or adults and children. Those who threw atomic bombs and used the weapons of mass destruction against Nagasaki and Hiroshima were the Americans. Can the bombs differentiate between military and women and infants and children?[25]

Next while the authors tacitly acknowledge that noncombatants (women, children, and the elderly) are generally protected under the Islamic rules of war law should any of these so-called protected persons fight Muslims or come to the aid of the enemy, they become legitimate targets. They cite the precedent of Abu Dawud, an Arab poet, who at the age of 120, was executed for having provided intelligence to the enemy in a war against the Muslims. According to the authors, this shows that in the Islamic tradition noncombatants lost their immunity if they assisted the enemy of the Muslims in any way. By citing this precedent, Quintan Wiktorowicz, a professor of international relations, and John Kaltner, a religious studies professor, point out, al Qaeda is asserting that anyone who has ever "assisted in combat, whether in deed, word, mind or any other form,"—including, journalists, academics, and businessmen—can therefore be considered fair targets in the jihad against Americans.[26]

Earlier in the letter, the authors go so far as to suggest that any American may be considered a legitimate target by virtue of the fact that as citizens of a democracy in which the people are supposed to be able to hold their government accountable, clearly they have not done enough to stop their government from waging this war against Islam and have thereby forfeited their immunity.

If the successive Crusader-Zionist governments had not received support from their people, their war against Islam and Muslims would not have taken such an obvious and conspicuous form. It is something that would not attain legitimacy except by the voices of the people.

Fourth, the authors argue that the World Trade Center and the Pentagon, symbols of American economic and military might, were legitimate targets because Islam permits the Muslim army to kill "protected ones" (noncombatants) if this means that the enemy's "stronghold" will be weakened to the extent that it will bring about the demise of the state. Just after the 9/11 attacks, bin Laden himself made this case in an interview with Al-Jazeera:

> I agree that the Prophet Mohammed forbade the killing of babies and women. That is true, but this is not absolute. There is a saying, "If the infidels killed women and children on purpose, we shouldn't shy way from treating them in the same way to stop them from doing it again." The men that God helped [attack, on September 11] did not intend to kill babies; they intended to destroy the strongest military power in the world, to attack the Pentagon that houses more than 64,000 employees, a military center that houses the strength and the military intelligence . . . The towers are an economic power and not a children's school. Those that were there are men that supported the biggest economic power in the world.[27]

Fifth, the al Qaeda authors assert the collateral damage argument: that the Muslim armies have always availed themselves of "heavy weapons" which are incapable of distinguishing between combatants and noncombatants, citing the Prophet's use of catapults or stone-hurling devices against his enemies in the battle of Taif. Just as the early Muslim armies were permitted to avail themselves of weapons that could not be so precisely targeted so as to eliminate the possibility of collateral damage, so today's Muslim army can also use imprecise weapons—hijacked commercial airlines for instance—that cannot distinguish between innocent civilians and those who are shoring up the enemy's stronghold.

Sixth, the authors argue, "When the enemy is shielded by their women or children" then the consensus of the Islamic tradition says Muslims may "kill the human shields." In other words, the secretaries and janitors killed in the 9/11 attacks should be regarded as a form of human shields.

Finally the al Qaeda authors wrap up their argument by saying that it is entirely within the bound of the Islamic tradition to kill civilians because this is what the Prophet himself did when he confronted the Bani Qariza, a Jewish tribe with whom the first Muslim community had a peace treaty while they were living in Medina. According to the tradition, when the minute the Prophet learned they had negotiated with the enemy, he turned his army against the tribe, killed the men and enslaved the women and children, and thus set the precedent demonstrating that Muslims may kill protected "ones in order to teach the unbelievers a lesson."[28]

Now the authors launch into their defense of what they clearly perceive to be an even hairier point. How to justify the fact that they may have killed fellow Muslims may have been killed in the attacks? Here the authors cite the six extenuating circumstances under which they contend that the Isalmic tradition says that Muslims can justify killing fellow Muslims:

First they assert—without offering any support—that in the event of a state of emergency, the killing of Muslims is permitted.

Second, they argue that there *were* no Muslims killed in the attacks:

> The majority opinion rests upon the idea that only unbelievers were present in the targets that were hit, and acting in accordance with the majority opinion in legal rulings is what a responsible party must do.

Notice that they offer no counter-evidence to refute the many press claims that Muslims were indeed killed in the attacks. Instead, they rely on "the majority opinion" which they argue, "is what a responsible party must do" in "legal rulings." Implicit in this statement is of course the logic that it is alright to kill "unbelievers."

But even Muslim lives may be sacrificed, the authors go on to assert, if that is the only way Muslims can continue fighting jihad:

> Third: Al-Shafii and the distinguished jurists in the Hanafi school believe it is permissible to burn, drown, and demolish a country of those who make war even if Muslims might be killed by such actions. This is so because holding back from the buildings that contain Muslims leads to an interruption in the jihad. The distinguished ones reply that the verse that begins, "For if believing men . . ." does not refer to prohibition. If that is so, the activities of this operation are allowed.
>
> Fourth: The indiscriminate and universal application of the aforementioned verse leads to the suspension of the practice of jihad against all warring nations because there does not exist a country today that does not contain a large number of Muslims. Today, wars kill large numbers of people. The application of the verse is absurd because it invalidates the practice of jihad without proof.

Thus the authors suggest that in the case where Muslim lives do have to be sacrificed in jihad, the families of Muslim victims should be paid "blood money" or some kind of compensatory damages, following the example of the Prophet:

> The solution is to pay half the blood money just as Muhammad ruled for those who killed the Muslims of Khatham who were living in the midst of a people of war. The Messenger paid half the blood money and did not cover up their killing, censure it, curse it, or rid them of it. Rather, he rid them of those who lived among them.

The authors end their self-rationalization by suggesting that any Muslims who would have died in the attacks were probably engaged in strengthening the unbelievers and thus would have had to face "eternal judgment" anyway.

Suicide Terrorism

What al Qaeda's April 2002 exculpation and most Islamic condemnations of the 9/11 attacks conspicuously have failed to address is whether Islam permits Muslims to carry out suicide attacks given that suicide is something that is clearly prohibited according to the verse in the Koran that says, "And do not kill yourselves." (Sura 4:29)

In spite of this injunction, however, suicide bombing is a tactic that has been widely adopted by the global jihad movement. After jihadists carried out the twin bombings of the U.S. Marine and French paratroopers' barracks in Lebanon in 1983 and caused the immediate withdrawal of the peacekeeping forces, suicide attacks became the weapon of choice against the Israeli Defense Forces then occupying Lebanon. While suicide attacks have not been exclusively the province of jihadists in the modern era—think of the Japanese kamikaze pilots during World War II and the Tamil Tigers in the 1980s, of the thirty-five groups that are actively employing suicide terrorism, thirty-one define themselves as Islamic.[29] Ihsanic Intelligence, an Islamic think tank which condemns suicide bombing, reports that more than twenty countries have experienced suicide attacks in the name of Islam since 1981, including Lebanon (1981), Kuwait (1983), Argentina (1992), Panama, Israel, and Occupied Palestinian Territories (1994), Pakistan, Croatia (1995), Saudi Arabia (1996), Tanzania, Kenya (1998), Yemen, Chechnya (2000), USA, Kashmir, Afghanistan (2001), Tunisia, Indonesia, Algeria (2002), Morocco, Russia, India, Iraq, Turkey (2003), and Uzbekistan and Spain (2004).[30] Added to their list would be the United Kingdom, Egypt, Jordan, and Bangladesh (2005).

Since 9/11, the incidence of suicide terrorism has risen sharply: Bruce Hoffman, the corporate chair in counterterrorism and counterinsurgency at the Rand Corporation, stated in August 2005 that according to data accumulated by Rand, 81 percent of all suicide attacks to have taken place in the past thirty years have occurred since 9/11.[31] In Iraq alone, since the U.S. invasion in March 2003 (through July 17, 2005) there have been some 400 suicide bombings. Ninety of these attacks occurred in May 2005 alone. Two out of three insurgent bombings during this period are believed to have been suicide missions.[32]

Given the prevalence of suicide attacks in jihad, it should come as no surprise that there have been many apologetics issued by sympathetic Islamic clerics and Muslim leaders endorsing such attacks:

- Sheikh Mohammad al-Tantawi, the head of al-Azhar University, the oldest and most prestigious center of Sunni learning, stated "suicide operations are of self-defense and a kind of martyrdom, as long as the intention behind them is to kill the enemy's soldiers, and not women or children."[33]
- The "Scholars of al-Azhar" and the "Al-Azhar Center for Islamic Research," issued their own fatwa which stated: "He who sacrifices himself [a *fidaai*] is he who gives his soul in order to come closer to Allah and to protect the rights, respect and land of the Muslims." Though they cautioned that anyone acting simply out of desperation or "to escape from life, and not for a higher goal, whether religious or national, or for the sake of the liberation of his robbed land" can expect to "lose his soul." But "when the Muslims are attacked in their homes and their land is robbed, the Jihad for Allah turns into an individual duty. In this case, operations of martyrdom become a primary obligation and Islam's highest form of Jihad."[34]
- Sheikh Yusuf al-Qaradawi, spiritual leader of the Muslim Brotherhood and television personality, also endorsed suicide terrorism: "These operations are the supreme form of Jihad for the sake of Allah, and a type of terrorism that is allowed by the *Shari'a*." Al-Qaradhawi backed up his opinion with a Koranic citation that said Muslims must "spread fear among one's enemies and the enemies of Allah," adding that "the term 'suicide operations' is an incorrect and misleading term, because these are heroic operations of martyrdom, and have nothing to do with suicide. The mentality of those who carry them out has nothing to do with the mentality of someone who commits suicide."[35]

- In December of 2002, in the lead-up to the war in Iraq, the then Hamas leader al-Rantisi urged Muslims to mount suicide attacks in Iraq, saying: "The enemies of Allah . . . crave life while the Muslims crave martyrdom. The martyrdom operations that shock can ensure that horror is sowed in the [enemies'] hearts, and horror is one of the causes of defeat."[36]

How do these clerics and the jihadists get around the Koranic injunction against suicide? To date, the most comprehensive statement justifying suicide attacks is arguably a fatwa believed to have been written by Saudi scholars, "The Islamic Ruling on the Permissibility of Martyrdom Operations," to rationalize sending Muslims on suicide missions after a Chechen woman (the first of the so-called black widows) blew herself up in an attack on Russian forces.[37]

In this so-called Chechen fatwa, which is noted for its scholarly precision, the anonymous authors (they refer to themselves as "we") start out with the admission: "Not every martyrdom operation is legitimate, nor is every martyrdom operation prohibited" and then go on to warn that any verdict they achieve will only apply to circumstances in which the exact same conditions are in force. With that caveat out of the way, the authors then dismiss the term "suicide-operations" as a misnomer "chosen by the Jews to discourage people from such endeavors." They contrast the difference between a suicide, which in their view, happens because of "unhappiness, lack of patience and weakness or absence of iman [faith]" versus martyrdom, which occurs when a "self-sacrificer" embarks on a mission for the positive reasons of "strength of faith and conviction, and to bring victory to Islam."

They then begin their Islamic exculpation by quoting the Koranic verse that they (and most scholars) contend defines the contractual relationship God made with Muslims:

> Verily, Allah has purchased from the believers their selves and their wealth, in return for Heaven being theirs. They fight in the path of Allah and they kill and are killed. (Sura 9:111)

The authors reason that this verse essentially gives Muslims permission to do whatever they need to in order to carry out their side of the bargain, even if it means killing or being killed while fighting in the path of Allah—or, as they put it, "any scenario in which the Mujahid offers the purchase price in order to attain the merchandise is permissible unless an evidence exists to specifically prohibit it."

The next source they cite is a verse which they contend shows that in asymmetric conflicts, anything goes:

> How many a small force has overcome a numerous force, by the permission of Allah. And Allah is with the steadfast ones. (Sura 2:249)

In other words, this verse suggests to the authors that God will allow what is otherwise prohibited in cases where the "steadfast ones" are greatly outnumbered, such as in the Chechen struggle against the more numerous Russian forces.

Next, the authors quote this verse from the Koran:

Among mankind is he who sells himself seeking the pleasure of Allah. And Allah is Pitying towards the servants. (Sura 2:207)

From which they conclude that "one who sells himself for the sake of Allah is not considered to have committed suicide, even if he immerses himself into 1,000 of the enemy forces without armour."

To further bolster their arguments, they go onto quote several hadith: In one, a Muslim woman who refuses to repudiate Islam at the behest of the Pharoah is forced to watch her children be tossed into a boiling cauldron and then is expected to jump into the pot herself. When she hesitates at the last minute, she is encouraged by her child who tells her: "O mother! Jump in, for the torture of this world is lighter than the punishment of the Hereafter." The lesson the authors draw is that sometimes jihad creates special circumstances in which a Muslim must proceed even when death is guaranteed.

The authors concede that in all of the classical precedents they were able to find, the martyr's death was caused by the enemy as opposed to the martyr's own hand as is the case in martyrdom operations today. Nevertheless, they claim these examples are still relevant to the current discussion because according to their logic "the former generations did not have knowledge of martyrdom operations in their current-day form, for these evolved with the changes in techniques of warfare, and hence they did not specifically address them."

After pointing out the difference between martyrdom (which is a shortcut to Paradise) and suicide (which condemns one to hell-fire), the authors summarize the conditions that must be met in order for a suicide operation to qualify for martyrdom: the mission has to be in the cause of Allah; one must be certain that the desired effect cannot be achieved without sacrificing one's life; one has to be sure that the operation will inflict pain on the enemy and conversely, embolden the Muslims; and finally, one must be sure that the operation will not interfere with any of the other strategic objectives of the Muslim army. Once these conditions have been met, the authors conclude, jihadists can be confident that suicide missions are permissible according to the Islamic tradition.

While the authors of this "Chechen" fatwa devote most of their exculpation to the religious justification of suicide terrorism, they could not resist listing its tactical advantages:

Suicide attacks, they note, uniquely terrorize the enemy: "As for the effects of these operations on the enemy, we have found, through the course of our experience that there is no other technique which strikes as much terror into their hearts, and which shatters their spirit as much."

They also point out their cost-effectiveness: "On the material level, these operations inflict the heaviest losses on the enemy, and are lowest in cost to us. The cost of equipment is negligible in comparison to the assault . . . The human casualty is a single life, who is in fact a martyr and hero gone ahead to the Gardens of Eternity, inshaa-Allah. As for the enemy, their losses are high."

Others have also noted the bottom-line logic of suicide terrorism, including Bruce Hoffman, a Rand Corporation expert, in a seminal *Atlantic Monthly* article:

> Suicide bombings are inexpensive and effective. They are less complicated and compromising than other kinds of terrorist operations. They guarantee media coverage. The suicide terrorist is the ultimate smart bomb. Perhaps most important, coldly efficient bombings tear at the fabric of trust that holds societies together.[38]

One Palestinian security official estimated that suicide attacks in Israel cost about $150: "Apart from a willing young man," he said, "all that is needed is such items as nails, gunpowder, a battery, a light switch and a short cable, mercury (readily obtainable from thermometers), acetone, and the cost of tailoring a belt wide enough to hold six or eight pockets of explosives. The most expensive item is transportation to a distant Israeli town."[39]

Suicide attacks are also uniquely effective because of the panic and fear they create in the target population. As Hoffman writes, "the perception is that it's impossible to guard against."[40] A special congressional report suggests that suicide attacks leave "the impression that the attacker is driven by a desperate determination."[41] This further increases the public's fear because they recognize that they are dealing with fanatics. As Daniel Benjamin, the coauthor of the book, *The Age of Sacred Terror*, points out, their willingness to kill themselves for their cause "is their way of saying they are much more determined than we are."[42] To illustrate his point he cites bin Laden's 1996 warning to Americans that "these youth love death as you love life." Bin Laden also like to remind his followers that in 1983, suicide bombers caused the withdrawal of American and French peacekeeping forces in Beirut after they carried out nearly simultaneous attacks that killed 241 U.S. marines and fifty-eight French paratroopers, while they were sleeping in their barracks.[43]

Jihadist organizations in general try to promote the image that they, unlike their less committed enemy have an abundance of members willing to make the ultimate sacrifice on behalf of their cause.

Hasan Nasrallah, the leader of Hizbollah, the organization behind the 1983 attacks in Beirut, coined the phrase "spider-web society" to describe what he asserted was the Israeli population's unwillingness to die for the national cause.

> The Israeli army is strong, Israel has technological superiority and is said to have strategic capabilities, but its citizens are unwilling any longer to sacrifice lives in order to defend their national interests and national goals. Therefore, Israel is a spider-web society: it looks strong from the outside, but touch it and it will fall apart.[44]

As Hoffman points out, "Al Qaeda, of course, has made a similar assessment of America's vulnerability."[45]

Moreover, relative to other types of attacks, suicide attacks are relatively simple to launch. Because the deployment agent is an intelligent being (relative to a missile), he or she can often get closer to the target and, if necessary, react to last-second changes. "If we look at what it takes to drive a bomb-laden vehicle into a crowd of people," commented Brig. Gen. Donald Aston, the U.S. military spokesman in Iraq, "it is not that challenging to perform that function—especially if you're willing to give your life."[46] Because the perpetrator is expected to die as part of a successful attack, as Hoffman points out, there is no need to plan an escape route or provide training on how to avoid compromising the organization if one is captured and tortured.

A Rand study revealed that suicide terrorism is roughly four times as efficient as other forms of terrorist attacks.[47] Robert Pape, author of *Dying to Win: The Strategic Logic of Suicide Terrorism*,[48] found that though suicide attacks represented only 3 percent of all terrorist attacks worldwide during the period 1980–2003, they accounted for 48 percent of the total fatalities, and his statistics did not even include the nearly 3,000 deaths that were recorded as a result of the 9/11 attacks.[49] The same phenomenon has been observed in Israel, according to Assaf Moghadam, a research fellow at Harvard's Belfer Center for Science and International Affairs. Moghadam found that though suicide attacks represented only 1 percent of the total number of attacks that were launched against Israelis during the period 2000–2002, they accounted for 44 percent of the total number of deaths.[50]

Suicide attacks also draw more attention to the attackers' cause. In the Palestinian areas, the deceased attacker is feted as a martyr and his death is celebrated as though it were a wedding (the brides being the virgins of Paradise)and not a funeral. After a suicide bomber carried out the August 2001 bombing of the Sbarro pizzeria in Jerusalem, a Hamas official recalled that his family had the typical reaction: "[They] distributed sweets and accepted their son as a bridegroom married to 'the black-eyed,' not as someone who had been killed and was being laid in the ground."[51] The following is a typical example of death notices published in a Palestinian newspaper: "With great pride, the Palestinian Islamic Jihad marries the member of its military wing . . . the martyr and hero Yasser Al-Adhami, to 'the black-eyed.' "[52]

This belief that "black-eyed" virgins await suicide bombers in Paradise comes directly from the Koran.[53] A member of Hamas cleric told Nasra Hassan, a relief worker who conducted an independent study on Palestinian suicide bombers, that in preparation for the bombing, Hamas handlers try to focus the recruit's attention "on Paradise, on being in the presence of Allah, on meeting the Prophet Muhammad, on interceding for his loved ones so that they, too, can be saved from the agonies of Hell, on the houris [the virgins of Paradise], and on fighting the Israeli occupation and removing it from the Islamic trust that is Palestine."[54]

In an Atlantic Monthly article, writer David Brooks elaborates on the preparation process suicide bombers go through:

> Recruits are sometimes made to lie in empty graves, so that they can see how peaceful death will be; they are reminded that life will bring sickness, old age, and betrayal. "We were in a constant state of worship," one suicide bomber (who somehow managed to survive his mission) told Hassan. "We told each other that if the Israelis only knew how joyful we were they would whip us to death! Those were the happiest days of my life!"[55]

In his study, Brooks concluded that by now martyrdom has been so zealously promoted that "Palestinian children grow up in a culture in which suicide bombers are rock stars, sports heroes, and religious idols rolled into one."[56]

Notice that while the al Qaeda apologetic defends the right to inflict collateral damage on Muslims (to inadvertently kill them in order to advance the cause of jihad), it does not take a stand on the permissibility of intentionally targeting Muslims, such has been done in jihads from Algeria, to Sudan, to Iraq. According to the website, TheRelgionofPeace.com, in the post 9/11 period though September 18, 2005, mosques have been targeted under the banner of Islam some 38 times, including 22 mosque attacks in Iraq which resulted in 257 deaths; 11 attacks in Pakistan, leaving 141 dead; 2 in Afghanistan, killing 7; and one each in India, the Philippines and Yemen, killing 3, 4, and 5, respectively. Summing up these figures, this means that Muslims have killed some 417 fellow Muslims while they were praying, entering or exiting mosques. The vast majority of the deaths in both Pakistan and Iraq involved Sunnis attacking Shiites.

While some of the mosque attacks may have been revenge or rivalry killings, most of the attacks are believed to have been carried out by Muslims fighting under the banner of jihad. This of course raises the question, just what is the Islamic rationale jihadists employ to justify their attacks on fellow Muslimas while they are at, say, a mosque?

To understand how the jihadists justify killing their fellow Muslims as they gather together to pray, we can refer to a letter purportedly written by Abu Musab al-Zarqawi, writing from Iraq to the leaders of al Qaeda. This letter was intercepted by the coalition forces in January 2004 and released to the public the following month.[57] In the letter, Zarqawi makes the case that the Shiites are not true Muslims because of their various heretical practices that range from, in his words, "patent polytheism, worshipping at graves, and circumambulating shrines, to calling the Companions [of the Prophet] infidels and insulting the mothers of the believers and the elite of this [Islamic] nation."

Zarqawi claimed that the Iraqi Shiites were angling "to take complete control over the economy like their tutors the Jews," and and cautions that this would be just the first stage of their plan. He went on to warn that their true intention was to "establish a Shi`i state stretching from Iran through Iraq, Syria, and Lebanon and ending in the Cardboard Kingdom of the Gulf." As far as Zarqawi is concerned: "These [Shiites have been] a sect of treachery and betrayal throughout history and throughout the ages. It is a creed that aims to combat the Sunnis."

Zarqawi then launched into what he saw was the Islamic case for targeting the Shiites. He wrote, "The Qur'an has told us that the machinations of the hypocrites, the deceit of the fifth column, and the cunning of those of our fellow countrymen whose tongues speak honeyed words but whose hearts are those of devils in the bodies of men—these are where the disease lies, these are the secret of our distress, these are the rat of the dike."

Not surprisingly, Zarqawi propped up his argument by citing the work of the medieval cleric Ibn Taymiyya, who was famously contemptuous of the Shiites of his day. According to Zarqawi, Ibn Taymiyya warned his followers in no uncertain terms that the Shiites "are the enemy" and Muslims should "beware of them" as "their hearts are full of vinegar and ire like no others with regard to Muslims old and young, godly and ungodly."

Anticipating that some Muslims would be reluctant to take up arms against their coreligionists, Zarqawi reminded his readers that they would not be the first Muslims to have been burdened with the task of cleaning up the religion:

Let the people of Islam know that we are not the first to have begun going down this road. We are not the first to have brandished the sword. These people (the Shi`a) are continuing to kill those who call for Islam and the mujahidin of the community, stabbing them in the back under cover of the silence and complicity of the whole world, and, regretfully, even of the symbolic figures beholden to the Sunnis.

It bears noting that Shiites are no means the only Muslims to have been targeted by the jihad movement. Fellow Sunnis are deemed to have committed heresy, blasphemy, or apostasy, have also been intentionally targeted. Under the jihadist interpretation of Sharia, such repudiations of the "true faith" are punishable by death. In Arabic, the word for pronouncing a fellow Muslim guilty of this capital sin is *takfir*. As the 9/11 Commission reports, "Among Arabs, Bin Ladin's followers are commonly nicknamed takfiri , or 'those who define other Muslims as unbelievers,' because of their readiness to demonize and murder those with whom they disagree."[58] Takfiris justify their uncompromising interpretation of the faith using the following Koranic verse:

What, do you believe in part of the Book, and disbelieve in part? (Sura 2:85)

This is how the GIA could rationalize killing ordinary Muslim villagers during the Islamist insurgency in Algeria in the 1990s; how the Egyptian Islamists have justified attacks on the tourist industry in Egypt; and how jihadists in Iraq can justify killing Muslims as they shop in markets, wait in line for jobs, or take their children to toy give-aways. Any Muslim who attends a mixed wedding, fraternizes with non-Muslims, or does not actively oppose an apostate or occupying power is not a true Muslim and can be taken out according to the jihadist view as expressed by Zarqawi.

Assassination, Throat-Slitting, and Beheading

Recall that this was also the logic promoted in the pamphlet, *The Neglected Duty*, distributed by Sadat's assassins in the months before the Egyptian president's death at the hand of an Islamist extremist. In this pamphlet, the author, Muhammad Abd al-Salam Faraj, argues that Islam is being menaced by a creeping Westernization that threatens to entice Muslims away from their religion. According to Faraj, the situation was becoming so urgent that all means were now necessary to protect the religion—in other words, every Muslim was now required to perform jihad. Like the authors of the Chechen fatwa, Faraj argued that the Islamic tradition permitted those waging jihad to perform actions that would otherwise be prohibited, such as killing protected persons or even other Muslims provided that such actions had a probability of advancing jihad. Though he never explicitly mentioned Sadat in his writings, Faraj made clear that any Muslim who failed to live up to the demands of his religion should be deemed guilty of apostasy and could expect to be marked for death.

Assassination is still apparently considered legal. Just since the attacks of 9/11, jihadists have assassinated or tried to kill politicians, rival clerics, secularists, and other leading activists in a variety of countries including Afghanistan, Chechnya, India, Iraq, Israel, Pakistan, Syria, Saudi Arabia, and Yemen.

Another tactic that is fairly commonly used in the global jihad movement that would appear to require some kind of religious justification is the practice of throat-slitting. Throat-slitting became popular during the jihad in Algeria in the 1990s, and even with the cessation of most hostilities, the practice has still continued. Since the attacks of 9/11 (through the period September 18, 2005), Algeria recorded more than a third of the total number of such incidents reported worldwide (31), attacks that resulted in 126 fatalities (group throat-slitting to maximize the victims' terror seems especially popular in Algeria). The tactic has also been popular in Iraq (though its use has declined since the fall of 2004, probably due to a certain amount of criticism of the practice, even by some jihadists).[59] There have been reported cases in Pakistan, India, and even in France. Included among the victims were a family of five, ages 8–50; a Jewish man in Paris, whose eyes were also gouged out; a man and his two teenage daughters in Algeria; and Daniel Pearl, the Wall Street Journal reporter, whose throat was slit before he was beheaded in January 2002. (Authorities suspect that KSM, the mastermind of the 9/11 attacks, may have dealt the fatal blow in Pearl's murder.)

Throat-slitting became a favored tactic in the Algerian jihad that began in 1991 after the government cancelled the country's first multiparty national elections because it was predicted that an Islamist party, the Islamic Salvation Front, would win and end democracy (the government invoked the slogan "one man, one vote, once" to garner support for having canceled the elections). A radical jihadist group emerged out of the conflict, the Armed Islamic Group, whose stated goal was to replace the regime with an Islamic state. Aside from the usual arsenal of car bombings, assassinations, and kidnappings, the GIA quickly took to raiding villages and slitting the throats of the locals, generally fellow Muslims. From the outset, it was the GIA's avowed policy to dispose of anyone—teachers, journalists, civil servants, or even villagers—who was deemed to have repudiated Islam for not actively participating in their jihad against the regime. Or, in the words of the GIA leader, Antar Zouabri: "There is no neutrality in the war we are waging. Apart from those who are with me, all others are apostates and deserve death."[60]

In March 1996, the GIA kidnapped and then beheaded seven Trappist monks who had been living in a monastery in the Atlas Mountains. Sensitive to the religious sensibilities of the local Muslim population, the monks had reportedly refrained from proselytizing, confining themselves to a life of prayer, work, and service to the local villagers. One of the monks served as the community physician. According to the GIA communiqué which explained the killings, the monks were beheaded because they were "mixing with [the Algerian people], living with them, and blocking the way of Allah by calling people to Christianity."[61]

The GIA became so keen on the practice of throat-slitting and beheading that they eventually recruited a butcher's apprentice, "Mohammad the Midget," who was reportedly so skillful that in one night in 1996, he is said to have cut off the heads of eighty-six people, including at least a dozen children.[62]

Jihadists in Chechnya also adopted the practice of beheading during their war for independence.[63] In the Philippines, the Abu Sayyaf group has also beheaded hostages. In one incident in 2000, they beheaded at least two hostages they were holding to demand the release from prison of Abdel Rahman, the spiritual leader of the 1993 World Trade Center bombers as well as the "Day of Terror" plotters who intended to blow New York City landmarks. However, it was arguably the videotaped beheading of Daniel Pearl that really popularized the practice and inspired a new wave of beheadings, also videotaped and posted on the Internet in order to compound the terror.

As Jerrold Post, a former CIA psychiatrist and now a professor of Political Psychiatry at George Washington University, put it, "The beheadings are designed to intimidate and convey a broader message of coercion, and it's unfortunately a strategy that is very clearly working."[64]

In spite of the fact that Islamic scholar Asma Afsaruddin of the University of Notre Dame says that "there is absolutely no religious imperative for" beheadings in Islam,[65] the record would suggest that this is not the interpretation of the Islamic sources shared by the jihadists.

Since 9/11 (through September 18, 2005) there have been some 55 recorded instances of beheading in ten countries with an estimated 182 victims (in some accounts, precise numbers were unclear—for example, the dead were counted but only "many" were found to have been beheaded). Iraq has recorded by far the most number of beheadings—some 25 incidents and an estimated 179 victims (mass beheadings seem to be particularly popular). India follows with 13 incidents (and 24 victims); Thailand recorded 7 incidents (with 7 victims); Afghanistan had 3 such incidents (but 14 victims); Algeria reported 2 such incidents (with 5 victims including a couple whose children's corpses were mutilated); and Bangladesh, Indonesia, Pakistan, the Philippines, and Saudi Arabia all recording one such incident with an average of 1 or 2 victims per incident.

Europe even recorded its first incidence of Islamic beheading in November 2004 when a radical Islamist tried to saw off the head of a Dutch filmmaker, Theo Van Gogh, after he shot and killed him in broad daylight on an Amsterdam street for having made a film critical of Islam. At his sentencing, the killer, Mohammed Bouyeri, a Dutch citizen of Moroccan descent, expressed no remorse, simply admitting, "I acted out of conviction and not out of hate," then going on to add, "if I'm ever released, I'd do the same again. Exactly the same." He said that he murdered the filmmaker because Islamic law "instructs me to chop off the head of everyone who insults Allah or the prophet."[66]

Was Van Gogh's killer right about this? Why are the practices of throat-slitting and beheading so common among today's jihadists? Is it just to invoke terror in the enemy? What is the religious justification, if any, for these practices?

The Koran mentions beheading in two verses, the first of which reads:

So, when you meet (in fight *Jihâd* in Allâh's Cause), those who disbelieve smite at their necks till when you have killed and wounded many of them, then bind a bond firmly (on them, i.e. take them as captives). Thereafter (is the time) either for generosity (i.e. free them without ransom), or ransom (according to what benefits Islâm), until the war lays down its burden. Thus [you are ordered by Allâh to continue in carrying out *Jihâd* against the disbelievers till they embrace Islâm (i.e. are saved from the punishment in the Hell-fire) or at least come under your protection], but if it had been Allâh's Will, He Himself could certainly have punished them (without you). But (He lets you fight), in order to test you, some with others. But those who are killed in the Way of Allâh, He will never let their deeds be lost. (Sura 47:4)

In the commentary on Sura 47:4 provided by the translator Abdullah Yusuf 'Ali (d. 1953), he suggests that this verse implies that "once the fight (Jihad) is entered upon," it should be carried out with "utmost vigour" or as he puts it, Muslims are told to "strike home your blows at the most vital points (smite at their necks), both literally and figuratively." Or, as he sums up the command, "You cannot wage war with kid gloves."[67] According to Timothy Furnish, a historian, Yusuf Ali's interpretation of the verse is consistent with most of the tradition.[68]

In the second verse in which beheading is mentioned:

(Remember) when your Lord inspired the angels, "Verily, I am with you, so keep firm those who have believed. I will cast terror into the hearts of those who have disbelieved, so strike them over the necks, and smite over all their fingers and toes." (Sura 8:12)

The goal of terrorizing the enemy is explicit. Again, we refer to the comments of the translator, Yusuf 'Ali, who says that here the practice of striking the neck is commanded because "the vulnerable parts of an armed man are above the neck" and "if he has armour it is difficult to get at his heart. But if his hands are put out of action, he is unable to wield his sword or lance or other weapon, and easily becomes a prisoner" and moreover, "a blow on the neck, face, or head, finishes him off."[69]

The classical Muslim jurist, Muhammad b. Jarir at-Tabari (d. 923 CE), suggested that God's command to strike "at the necks" of unbelievers was intentionally harsh because it was intended to demonstrate his opposition to unbelief.[70]

The jihadists have plenty of precedent for beheading and throat-slitting in Muslim history. Muhammad's earliest biographer, Ibn Ishaq, recounted that the Prophet himself ordered the beheading of some 700 male members of the Jewish Banu Qurayza tribe in Medina because they conspired against the Muslims.[71]

Then in 680 CE, when the Prophet's grandson, Hussein bin Ali, led a revolt against the Caliph Yazid, the Caliph's armies cut off his head in Karbala, Iraq and delivered it on a platter to the Caliph. This event (known as *Ashura*) is still celebrated by many Shiites in public demonstrations of self-flagellation, in which they cut their heads to cause bleeding and pound their bare chests to show their reverence for their beheaded leader.

Paul Fregosi, author of the book *Jihad in the West: Muslim Conquests from the 7th to the 21st Centuries*, writes that during the Muslim conquest of Spain, beheading was not uncommon. He recounts the story of the battle of Zalaca (1086) where the Muslim commander Yusuf ordered his men to behead the corpses of some 24,000 defeated Castilians. After having his soldiers arrange the heads in a mineret configuration, he had his muezzins stand on the "piles of headless" cadavers and called the faithful to prayer.[72] Afterward, Yusuf sent the detached heads on tour around Muslim Spain and North Africa to show his fellow Muslims they had nothing left to fear from the defeated Christians.

The Ottoman armies also famously beheaded European kings and war captives, including the Serbian nobleman who led the battle of Kosovo in 1389; the Hungarian king after the battle of Varna in 1444; and the Bosnian king and his sons in 1463 (the sultan bestowed the honor in this case on his highest-ranking cleric). Even as late as 1807, hundreds of Britons would lose their heads to the Ottomans on expedition to Egypt.[73]

Muslims armies have also been known to behead other Muslims—and not just in modern times. In sixteenth century India, Gujarati sultans beheaded the leaders of the Mahdavi movement, a cult who claimed to be divinely guided. Then in 1880, a self-proclaimed Mahdi or prophesied "rightful leader," Muhammad Ahmad of Sudan, took to beheading his enemy captives, in this case the armed forces of the Ottoman Empire and their British allies.[74] Even as late as the twentieth century, after Mustafa Kemal Ataturk declared an end to the last pan-Islamic state that was the Ottoman Empire, those wishing to reinstate the Caliphate stormed a Turkish army garrison, and decapitated the resident commander, whose head was then paraded about to demonstrate the impotence of the new secular government.[75] In 1979, after Islamic radicals stormed the Grand Mosque in Mecca during the annual hajj and called on all Saudis to rebel against the regime, the Saudis beheaded the rebel leader and put his followers in prison. Even to this day, beheading remains the execution method of record in Saudi Arabia, and is still carried out in public for offenses such as murder, drug trafficking, armed robbery, and other capital offenses.

Though the beheading of captives has been condemned by various religious leaders including the imam of the Great Mosque in Mecca,[76] as the record suggests, jihadists can simply look the Koran and the abundance of precedents in Muslim history to rationalize their actions.

Weapons of Mass Destruction

Because of the jihadists' willingness to use tactics that are illegal by Western standards of just war tradition, one of the greatest fears in the West is that the global jihad movement will come into the possession of and deploy weapons of mass destruction (WMDs)—otherwise known as biological, chemical, nuclear, and radiological devices (also called *dirty bombs*).

A *dirty bomb* is a conventional bomb wrapped in radiological material. It is detonated using a conventional explosive (as opposed to nuclear fission) and scatters the radioactive material in its blast. Though dirty bombs are relatively easy to construct (compared to nuclear bombs), there is still some risk to the bomb maker because of the danger involved in handling radioactive materials. The true difficulty in constructing such a device is the difficulty of obtaining the radioactive materials in the first place. While medical-use substances such as radium or cesium isotopes could conceivably be used, the bomb would be far more deadly if it were constructed with weapons-grade plutonium, uranium, or spent nuclear fuel—all of which are prohibited materials and therefore at least somewhat difficult to procure. There is concern, however, that sources of radioactive materials such as nuclear facilities, material storage sites, and medical labs are insufficiently secured throughout the world to the extent that committed terrorists could easily obtain these materials. Of particular concern to experts are stores in Pakistan, India, and Russia, according to the Council on Foreign Relations.[77] The good news is that radioactive substances are detectable and therefore not so easily transportable.

The amount of radioactive material used, wind and environmental conditions, along with the size of the blast, and the population density of the area in which the bomb is detonated all factor into a dirty bomb's ultimate power of destruction. Some experts estimate that aside from those that would be killed by the explosion, a dirty bomb containing one kilogram of plutonium detonated in the center of a city like Munich, Germany, could result in an additional 120 cancer cases.[78] Hence most experts believe that the detonation of a dirty bomb would cause more fear and panic than an actual increase in the number of mass casualties and that a large area surrounding the explosion would have to be evacuated until the extent of the radioactivity could be determined.

In May of 2002, the United States arrested one Jose Padilla, an alleged al Qaeda operative and American citizen when he landed at Chicago's O'Hare Airport en route from Pakistan on suspicion that he intended to build and use a radiological bomb against the United States. The source of the information was a captured al Qaeda leader, Abu Zubaydah, who told his interrogators that al Qaeda was close to building a "dirty bomb" and was hoping to smuggle such a device into the United States.[79] After years in detention as an "enemy combatant," in November 2005, the U.S. government finally indicted Jose Padilla, the so-called dirty-bomber on three counts alleging he conspired to murder, main and kidnap people overseas. Conspicuously absent in the government's action was any mention of a dirty-bomb plot.[80] According to *The New York Times*, the government declined to pursue these charges out of fears that the defense's right to discovery could possible compromise national security as well as their fear that because the evidence supporting such allegations had been obtained using harsh interrogation techniques, it would have likely been ruled inadmissible in court.[81]

In any case, the possibility that Padilla was involved in a dirty bomb plot recalled a serious of earlier remarks bin Laden made, in which he expressed the idea that Muslims had a religious duty to acquire and use WMDs.

In May of 1998, he purportedly issued a statement, *The Nuclear Bomb of Islam*, in which he urged Muslims to "prepare as much force as possible to terrorize the enemies of God."[82]

Later that year, in December, in response to an interviewer's question as to whether he was trying to acquire chemical and nuclear weapons, this was his response:[83]

> Acquiring weapons for the defense of Muslims is a religious duty. If I have indeed acquired these weapons, then I thank God for enabling me to do so. And if I seek to acquire these weapons, I am carrying out a duty. It would be a sin for Muslims not to try to possess the weapons that would prevent the infidels from inflicting harm on Muslims.

According to MEMRI, a Washington, DC-based service that tracks and translates Arabic-language media for items that may be of interest to non-Arabic speakers, the first Islamic authority to endorse Arab nuclear weapons was the Sheikh of Al-Azhar, Muhammad Sayyid Tantawi, in an opening address he gave to a conference on nuclear strategy that was held at an Egyptian university in October 1999. In his address, Tantawi remarked that "Islam calls for strength, but for logical and just strength that stands by the oppressed until he completely vanquishes the oppressor." Then citing the will of Abu Bakr, the first "rightly-guided Caliph," who is said to have advised the early Muslims to fight the enemy with the sword if that is what the enemy was using. Tantawi declared: "Had Abu Bakr lived today he would have said to Khaled ibn Al-Walid: 'If they fight you with a nuclear bomb, fight them with a nuclear bomb.' "Advising his fellow Muslims that "Strength is [one] of the traits of good and wise people who know their obligation towards their God and towards their homeland," he said that Muslims had an obligation to use their strength to "defend their faith and their homeland," adding, "this is the Sunna that was known to the forefathers of all times, and is known to us as well." Then citing the situation with Israel, he said: "If Israel has nuclear weapons, then it is the first to be doomed, because it lives in a world that does not fear death," adding, "[but] Israel's nuclear weapons do not frighten us; what does frighten us is [the possibility] that we will not wake up and [will] not advance." With this he urged his fellow Muslims to "Welcome the use of nuclear energy for purposes of peace!"[84]

In his first press interview after 9/11, Bin Laden echoed Tantawi's remarks when he told a Pakistani journalist, Hamid Mir: "I wish to declare that if America used chemical or nuclear weapons against us, then we may retort with chemical and nuclear weapons. We have the weapons as deterrents."[85]

There exists some evidence that Bin Laden had the capability to back up such a statement. During the 2001 trial in connection with the East African embassies bombings, one of the accused, a former bin Laden associate, Jamal Ahmed Al-Fadl, testified under oath that he had tried to purchase enriched uranium from a South African source for $1,500,000 on behalf of al Qaeda.[86]

Only a few days after Mir's interview with Bin Laden was published in November of 2001, *The Times* of London reported that documents written in a variety of languages had been found in an abandoned safe-house in Kabul, in which there were detailed plans on how to build nuclear weapons; in the same article, the newspaper said that it had been informed by intelligence sources that al Qaeda had already acquired nuclear materials from Pakistan.[87]

This was the context in which the Bush administration issued its call for pre-emptive war, *The National Security Strategy of the United States* in September 2002, in which the administration reserved the right to take preemptive action in order to stop rogue states from supplying terrorists with weapons of mass destruction. As the *Strategy* (also called the *Bush Doctrine*) stated:

> Rogue states and terrorists do not seek to attack us using conventional means. They know such attacks would fail. Instead, they rely on acts of terror and, potentially, the use of weapons of mass destruction—weapons that can be easily concealed, delivered covertly, and used without warning.[88]

This was also the climate in which shortly later, Congress approved the use of force against Iraq in the autumn of 2002. In the words of the resolution itself:

> Whereas Iraq's demonstrated capability and willingness to use weapons of mass destruction, the risk that the current Iraqi regime will either employ those weapons to launch a surprise attack against the United States or its Armed Forces or provide them to international terrorists who would do so, and the extreme magnitude of harm that would result to the United States and its citizens from such an attack, combine to justify action by the United States to defend itself.[89]

While the U.S. government was never able to definitively establish that Saddam was indeed collaborating with al Qaeda to obtain WMDs, in December of 2002, the Al-Azhar Religious Ruling Committee, perhaps the highest authority in Sunni Islam, made a resounding call to all Muslims that developing nuclear weapons was now to be considered a "religious obligation" for the entire Islamic nation. The head of the Al-Azhar committee explained the decision to a Kuwaiti newspaper:

> Current international circumstances confirm the need for this Fatwa, primarily at a time when Israel and all the enemies of the Islamic nation have this weapon. The Islamic nation's nuclear weapon must be used for self-defense, and for demonstrating power, so that none will [develop] covetous aspirations about the nation. What is happening to the Muslims in all countries of the world is the result of weakness, and if the Muslims obtain this weapon, no one will conspire against them . . . Obtaining nuclear weapons is a religious obligation, and anyone who gives up on [obtaining] this weapon is a sinner, according to religious law. Preparation in the face of the enemies, and employing all possible means to defend land and honor, should be considered a religious obligation.[90]

In May 2003, a Saudi cleric who is prominent in jihadist circles, Nasir bin Hamid al-Fahd, issued a similar fatwa. In his religious ruling he addressed the question of whether "Muslims engaged in jihad" are allowed to use weapons of mass destruction and under what circumstances.[91]

In his argument, one of the first things al-Fahd does is dismiss the moniker "weapons of mass destruction." He writes, "Surely the effect of several kilograms of TNT can be considered mass destruction if you compare it to the effect of a catapult stone of old. An RPG or mortar projectile can be considered mass destruction if you compare it to the shooting of arrows of old. Certainly, the infidels of our time have made these so-called weapons of mass destruction (deterrence weapons) only to frighten others."

Al-Fahd then goes on to ridicule the ban on WMDs imposed by international law: "Those who speak so pretentiously about combating the spread of weapons of mass destruction, America and Britain for example, were the first to have used these weapons: Britain used chemical weapons against the Iraqis in the World War I; America used nuclear weapons against Japan in World War II: and their arsenals—and those of the Jews—are full of such weapons!" He even disdains the basis of international law, that is, the Charter of Human Rights as well as the Geneva Conventions writing. "All these terms," he writes, "have no standing in Islamic law, because God Almighty has reserved judgment and legislation to Himself."

Al-Fahd then goes over what he describes as "the basic rules" of Islamic law regarding these matters. The first such law he cites is that "in killing" the Islamic sources, he says, command the Muslim to "put his victim at ease," and to "take the life as swiftly, easily, and desirably as possible."

The next basic Islamic law that must be observed, according to al-Fahd, is that one must "distinguish between the possible and the impossible." According to him, this means that—in his words:

1. One kills in a good manner only when one can. If those engaged in jihad cannot do so, for example when they are forced to bomb, destroy, burn, or flood it is permissible.
2. One avoids killing women and children only when one can distinguish them. If one cannot do so, as when the infidels make a night attack or invade, they may be killed as collateral to the fighters.
3. Similarly, killing a Muslim is forbidden and not permitted; but if those engaged in jihad are forced to kill him because they cannot repel the infidels or fight them otherwise, it is permitted, as when the Muslim is being used as a living shield.

He then makes the particularly vivid case that "anyone who considers America's aggressions against Muslims and their lands during the past decades will conclude that striking her is permissible merely on the basis of the rule of treating as one has been treated. No other arguments need be mentioned." He goes on to cite some statistics: "Some brothers," he asserts, "have totaled the number of Muslims killed directly or indirectly by their weapons and come up with a figure of nearly ten million." This would mean then, according to al-Fahd's logic that "We might need other arguments [only] if we wanted to annihilate more than this number of them!"

He then uses the analogy of the catapult to show that the Prophet himself sanctioned the use of WMDs. The catapult was a giant lever device that enabled medieval warriors to launch missiles from great distances. He argues that since the Sunnah is clear about the permissibility of catapults, and since catapults are analogous to WMDs because they too cannot "distinguish between women, children, and others" so al-Fahd concludes that "this proves that the principle of destroying the infidels' lands and killing them if the jihad requires it and those in authority over the jihad decide so is legitimate."

After reviewing the pronouncements of the classical legal schools of the Islamic tradition—the Hanafis, the Malikis, the Shafi'is, the Hanbalis, the Zahiris, and others—to make sure that he has addressed all the major issues, al-Fahd takes another pass at what he disdainfully terms "specious arguments" that ban killing women and children and concludes that it is indeed permissible to attack "the polytheists by night, even if their children are injured," and, even if Muslims are killed in such attacks.

In summing up his ruling al-Fahd concludes: "If the infidels can be repelled from the Muslims only by using such weapons, their use is permissible, even if you kill them without exception and destroy their tillage and stock."

In Jordan in 2004, authorities uncovered a plot involving some twenty tons of toxic chemicals and explosives intended to target the U.S. embassy, the Jordanian intelligence headquarters, and the prime minister's office. Government officials claimed that the attack was within days of being launched and that it would have released a deadly "toxic cloud."[92]

The suspected ringleader is said to have confessed almost immediately and in a videotaped confession broadcast on Jordanian state-run television admitted that he was responding to orders from Zarqawi: "I took explosives courses, poisons high level, then I pledged allegiance to Abu Musab al-Zarqawi, to obey him without any questioning."[93]

In an audio recording posted in May 2004, a man identifying himself as Zarqawi admitted that he was behind the plot but denied that it involved chemical weapons. Zarqawi and eight others were convicted and sentenced to death in February 2006 for their involvement in the plot. This was Zarqawi's third death penalty from a Jordanian court—in 2000 he was sentenced to death also in absentia for plotting to blow up a local hotel and other tourist locations and for the assassination of an American diplomat, Lawrence Foley, in 2002.

On November 9, 2005 Zarqawi dispatched four Iraqi suicide bombers to attack three hotels in the capital city of Amman. More than sixty people were killed because of the blasts, including many members of a wedding party—among them, both parents of the bride and the groom's father. The bombers included a recently married couple; the female half of which survived the attacks because her explosives failed to detonate due to a technical malfunction. Zarqawi later issued an audio taped statement claiming that the wedding was never directly targeted and that in fact the detonation occurred on the floor above it, though according to media accounts, the physical evidence was conclusive that the blast had occurred inside the wedding hall. The surviving bomber said in her videotaped confession that she and her husband were aware that they were about to bomb a wedding celebration and that they had dressed in formal clothes so as to less conspicuous. At least one cleric would rationalize the attacks, arguing outside of an Amman mosque after Friday prayers that any wedding in which the sexes were mixing should not be considered a Muslim wedding anyway.[94] In his audiotaped statement, Zarqawi went on to threaten to chop of the head of King Abdullah II, the Jordanian monarch and launch more attacks against tourist sites in the kingdom because Jordanians were guilty of "shooting the mujahedeen in the back as they go to perform Jihad."[95]

In the wake of the Amman attacks, Jordanians took to the streets en masse to wage a protest against terrorism, and around the same time, seventy-five members of Zarqawi's extended family, took out ads in leading Jordanian newspapers to be on record denouncing their relative. As their collective statement read: "We, the Al-Khalayilah tribesmen, disown him and renounce his actions, pronouncements, and whatever he approves of . . . until judgment day."[96]

In October 2005, the U.S. government released a letter that had been intercepted in Iraq and that was dated July 9, 2005. The letter was purportedly written by Zawahiri, bin Laden's second-in-command, and was addressed to Zaraqawi. In the letter, while Zawahiri concedes that the Shiites are indeed a genuine "danger to Islam" he cautions that "the majority of Muslims don't comprehend this" and that attacking the Shia will never become "acceptable to the Muslim populace however much you have tried to explain it."[97] Zawahiri suggests that Zarqawi learn from the mistakes of the Taliban who because they were unable to maintain their hold on power failed to, in his words, "have any representation for the Afghan people in their ruling regime, . . . when the invasion came, the amirate collapsed in days, because the people were either passive or hostile."

In this letter, Zawahiri lays out what he believes should be the strategy for Iraq, which he describes as "now the place for the greatest battle of Islam in this era." The mujahidin, he argues, first have to expel the Americans, then they have to establish an Islamic state in Iraq, then they have to "extend the jihad wave to the secular countries neighboring Iraq," and somewhere along the line they will also have to confront the "clash with Israel, because Israel was established only to challenge any new Islamic entity." This has to be the strategy, Zawahiri argues, because, as he puts it, "the Muslim masses—for many reasons, and this is not the place to discuss it—do not rally except against an outside occupying enemy, especially if the enemy is firstly Jewish, and secondly American . . . Therefore," Zawahiri concludes, "the mujahed movement must avoid any action that the masses do not understand or approve, if there is no contravention of Sharia in such avoidance, and as long as there are other options to resort to, meaning we must not throw the masses—scant in knowledge—into the sea before we teach them to swim."

CHAPTER 4

Who Is Fighting Jihad?

The religion was totally ingrained in her. She only lived for that.
Liliane Degauque, describing her daughter, the first
European female convert to Islam to carry out a
jihadist suicide mission.[1]

Who exactly is carrying out this global jihad? Who are the movement's leaders, who comprises the rank and file of this self-proclaimed Islamic army? How do jihadists make their way to the global jihad? Are they recruited? What inspires them? Are they motivated by a sense of desperation or a vision of a new world order?

Leadership

The leader of the global jihad movement is, of course, Usama bin Laden (b. 1957), the head of the movement's lead organization, al Qaeda. As we have already learned, al Qaeda grew out of the thousands of "Arab Afghans" who flocked to fight jihad in Afghanistan during the 1980s, to save their fellow Muslims from the Soviets. General Hamid Gul, the head of Pakistan's intelligence service, who played a role in unleashing these Arab Afghans, described them as "the first international brigade" of Muslims in "modern time," pointing out that "the Communists had their international brigades, the West has NATO," and then posed the rhetorical question, "Why should we Muslims not unite to one common front?"[2]

As we have already learned, this "international brigade" of Muslims originally came together under Abdullah Azzam (1941–1989), a Palestinian cleric who used the worldwide system of Sunni mosques, Islamic cultural organizations, professional unions, informal prayer circles, Koranic study groups, and Muslim student associations, and the new audio and videotape technology, to call his fellow Muslims to join a jihad against the godless communists who invaded Afghanistan in 1979. When the war with the Soviets finally wound down at the end of the 1980s, Azzam now joined by bin Laden, decided that instead of dismantling the force they had organized, they should build upon it as the foundation of a global Islamic army. Thus, over time, the "Bureau of Services" (or, in Arabic, the *Maktab al Khidmat*), the organization they had created to manage the flow of fighters into Afghanistan metamorphosed into a global jihad movement, or *al Qaeda*, which in Arabic means *the base*. By the time Azzam was murdered in a roadside bombing on his way to mosque in 1989, bin Laden was already the group's undisputed leader.

Who exactly is bin Laden and how did he come to head up the global jihad movement? Where did he learn his organizational skills? What do we know about his personality and the factors that motivate him?

Bin Laden first found his way to jihad soon after graduating from college in 1981. The wealthy young Saudi was the son of a Yemeni, Mohamed bin Laden (1895?–1968), who in 1930 trekked over a thousand miles through the harsh desert to the holy lands of Islam in order to escape what would have likely been his fate had he remained in his native Yemen: the back-breaking life of a dock-side laborer.[3]

In Saudi Arabia, the bin Laden patriarch first found work as a porter in Jeddah assisting pilgrims going to Mecca.[4] However, within only a couple of decades he was the head of his own construction company, winning contracts from the royal family to build palaces and reconstructing the highway between the holy cities of Mecca and Medina. "He couldn't read or write and signed his name with a cross all his life, but he had an extraordinary intelligence," recalled a French engineer who worked with him in the 1960s.[5]

The senior bin Laden also "changed wives like you or I change cars," according to the French engineer.[6] Under Islamic law, he was entitled to have up to four wives at a time as long as he treated them equally, both emotionally and financially. In all he is believed to have married some twenty-two women. He is alleged to have stayed married to the first three wives but kept the fourth-wife slot as a temporary post, using it to marry and divorce beautiful women, some as young as fifteen.

Bin Laden's mother was one of these revolving fourth wives, perhaps his tenth or eleventh. She was at the time of her marriage to Mohamed, a 22-year old Syrian beauty, who is said to have shown a preference for Chanel suits over the traditional Saudi veil. Though bin Laden was his father's seventeenth child out of a total of some fifty, he was his mother's only child with his father because soon after he was born, his parents divorced.

Bin Laden's mother later married one of her ex-husband's employees with whom she had another four children. There are conflicting accounts about his early childhood but the likelihood is that Bin Laden lived with his mother until the age of nine when, as is the law in Saudi Arabia, he went to live with his father. What is certain, however, is that any time he would have spent with his father was cut short because when he was just eleven, his father died in an airplane crash (some press reports contend it was a helicopter crash). Incidentally, Bin Laden would continue the practice of polygamy, marrying at least four times and fathering anywhere from a dozen to some twenty children. His first marriage to a cousin on his mother's side occurred when he was just seventeen.

Wisal al-Turabi, the wife of Hassan al-Turabi, bin Laden's host in Sudan, who claims that the two families socialized together when bin Laden was headquartered in Sudan, says that three of his wives were university lecturers whom he married to save them from what would otherwise probably have been a life of spinsterhood. "In Islam we do this. If you have a spinster, if you marry her, you will be rewarded for this in the afterworld, because you will bring up your offspring as Muslims," she is quoted as saying by Peter Bergen, author of book *The Osama bin Laden I know: An Oral History of al Qaeda's Leader*.[7]

Unlike many of his siblings, and contrary to many early press reports, most experts now believe that bin Laden never studied in the West. Instead they believe he stayed in Saudi Arabia for his education, attending at Al Thagher, an elite secondary school in Jeddah. One of his former English teachers at Al Thagher told New Yorker writer Steve Coll that bin Laden was "a nice fellow and a good student. There were no problems with him. . . . He was a quiet lad. I suppose silent waters run deep."[8]

At Al Thagher, Coll reports, bin Laden attended an Islamic study group run by a Syrian radical, perhaps a member of the Muslim Brotherhood, who used to mesmerize his young students with violent stories from the Sunnah, according to another student who attended the sessions for a while. The classmate also reportedly recalled that over time, bin Laden and the other boys in the study group began to adopt the style of Islamic activists, as Coll writes, "They let their young beards grow, shortened their trouser legs, and declined to iron their shirts (ostensibly to imitate the style of the Prophet's dress), and, increasingly, they lectured or debated other students at Al Thagher about the urgent need to restore pure Islamic law across the Arab world."[9]

For his graduate studies, he attended the prestigious King Abdul Aziz University in Jeddah from which he obtained either a degree in management or civil engineering, again accounts vary, but in either case, he is believed to have pursued courses of study that would be useful in the family business. At King Abdul Aziz University, bin Laden took courses from Mohammed Qutb, the brother of the famous Muslim Brotherhood ideologue, Sayyid Qutb, the author of *Milestones*, which as we have noted is referred to as the *manifesto* of the global jihad movement.[10] There he was also exposed to the teachings of Abdullah Azzam who was now actively urging Muslims to come fight jihad in Afghanistan. Thus, after graduating, that is precisely where bin Laden went.

Bin Laden would spend the rest of the eighties contributing to the jihad in Afghanistan, raising money for the mujahidin, organizing their flow to and from the front, and building a system of bunkers and tunnels in the Afghan mountains. He is even said to have participated in at least one battle, where the legend goes, he fought heroically. Though he made a name for himself, as one of his fellow Arab Afghans recalled, "You never knew he was so rich or the commander of everyone. We used to all sit down together and eat like friends."[11]

After the Soviets left Afghanistan, bin Laden, like most of his fellow mujahidin, returned home where he planned on continuing to wage jihad by working to replace the local regime with genuine Islamic governance. Very shortly, however, he made himself unwelcome by publicly criticizing the royal family for having invited infidel troops into the holy lands of Islam to defend the kingdom's oil wealth from the designs of Saddam Hussein, who had just annexed Kuwait. By 1991, the Saudis made it clear that they would no longer tolerate such a public display of dissidence and so he decided to take Hassan al-Turabi, the revolutionary leader in Sudan up on his longstanding offer to relocate his organization to, as Turabi liked to call it, the "Islamic experiment" that was now going on in Sudan. From Turabi's point of view, bin Laden was the ideal kind of refugee to have: deeply committed to the idea of the Islamic state and equipped with hundreds of millions of dollars that he was willing to invest in Sudan's embryonic infrastructure.

In Sudan, Bin Laden would soon be joined by his old friend Zawahiri and core members of his organization, Egyptian Islamic Jihad. Zawahiri's group thought Sudan would be an even better place than Egypt to carry on their seditious activities against the Egyptian government as the two countries shared a largely unguarded border and in Sudan they would be presumably out of reach of the state's security apparatus. The idea of tapping into bin Laden's reputed financial wealth was probably part of the appeal.[12]

Zawahiri was trained to be a surgeon and hailed from a prominent family. A 1995 obituary for one of his relatives published in a Cairo newspaper, reportedly mentioned thirty-one relatives in the medical profession along with an ambassador, a judge, and a member of parliament.[13] His great uncle was the ranking cleric at the prestigious Al-Azhar University. His maternal grandfather, Dr. Abd al-Wahab Azzam, variously served as the Egyptian ambassador to Pakistan, Yemen, and Saudi Arabia was also at one point the president of Cairo University and a founder and director of King Saud University in Riyadh, Saudi Arabia. A great uncle, Abdel-Rahman Azzam, was the founding secretary-general of the Arab League, the organization of Arab countries.

Incidentally, Zawahiri is by no means unique in having given up a promising career in medicine to perform jihad. Other famous examples of physicians turned jihadists include Hamas founder, Abdel-Aziz al-Rantissi, who was killed by an Israeli air strike in April 2004 and Dr. Mahmoud Zahar, who now leads the organization in Gaza; Islamic Jihad founder, Dr. Fathi Shekaki who was also killed by Israeli agents in Malta in 1995; Saad al-Fagih, a Saudi surgeon who was designated as a supporter of al Qaeda by both the U.S. Treasury Department and United Nations in December 2004; a Saudi medical student and son of a diplomat killed himself and 22 Americans in a suicide bombing in Mosul, Iraq in December 2004;[14] Karim El-Majjati, a former medical student is alleged to have orchestrated the May 2003 terror attacks in Saudi Arabia and Morocco; Rafiq Sabir a Florida doctor was indicted on charges of providing material support to al Qaeda during the period 2003–2005;[15] a London psychiatrist, Imran Waheed, is the head of Hizb ut-Tahrir, an avowedly nonviolent organization that nevertheless urges Muslims to kill Jews and praises suicide bombers;[16] and finally, the deputy commander of al Qaeda in Iraq killed by American forces in 2005 was a Syrian dentist, Khalid Suleiman Darwish.[17]

Many other highly educated and privileged individuals have also foregone promising career prospects to devote themselves to militant jihad. Marc

Sagemen, a psychiatrist and former CIA case officer posted in Afghanistan from 1986 to 1989 and author of the book *Understanding Terror Networks*,[18] analyzed open source data on 172 members of the global jihad movement. He found that most members of al Qaeda's core leadership (he called them the "Central Staff") were highly educated technocrats; 88 percent had earned at least an undergraduate degree and 20 percent had doctorates, the vast majority in science, engineering or medicine—but notably almost none from the humanities or social sciences faculties.[19] A University of Michigan anthropologist, Scott Atran, corroborated Sageman's findings, adding that U.S. government officials have told him that al Qaeda leaders detained in Guantanamo Bay, Cuba are generally from high-status, loving families, many having obtained graduate degrees and well-paying jobs, all of which they were willing to give up because they were committed to the idea that jihad was "the only way they're going to change the world."[20]

Zawahiri became radicalized as a young teenager, after he discovered the writings of Sayyid Qutb. In 1966, after the Egyptian authorities executed Qutb for his involvement in various sedition plots, Zawahiri who was then fifteen, organized a clandestine group to replace the Egyptian government with an Islamist regime. According to a former classmate, Zawahiri was a "mysterious character, closed and introverted . . . He could understand in five minutes what it would take other students an hour to understand. I would call him a genius."[21]

Zawahiri's first wife was the daughter of another prominent Cairo family, who, contrary to her family's practice, had taken to wearing the *niqab* or face veil while attending university. She would remain his only wife until her death—she and their children were killed in late 2001 during the U.S.-led invasion of Afghanistan. Months later, Zawahiri reportedly wed the two widows of a fallen comrade.[22] To the jihadists, marrying war widows is regarded as a form of social welfare.

Zawahiri became entranced by jihad in 1980, when he traveled to Afghanistan on a medical relief mission. When he returned to Cairo a few months later, he was a changed man, according to a family friend, Abdallah Schleifer, an American-Jewish convert to Islam, who at the time was running NBC's news bureau in Cairo. For some reason, his experience in Afghanistan pitted Zawahiri against the United States. Schleifer recalled having a conversation with him around this time in which he told the young doctor, "I don't understand. You just came back from Afghanistan, where you're cooperating with the Americans. Now you're saying America is the enemy?"[23]

In 1981, Zawahiri was imprisoned along with hundreds of other radicals for his suspected involvement in the assassination of the Egyptian president Anwar Sadat.

In prison, he claims to have been tortured and the experience is thought to have fundamentally changed him. Saad Eddin Ibrahim, an Egyptian democrat who also spent years in Egyptian prisons, says that many of those he saw who, in his words, "turn fanatic" did so after having been tortured. They were forced to seek solace in the religion and they also become extremely suspicious he reportedly told Wright.

Sageman, however, suggests that Zawahiri exhibited signs of an underlying personality disorder even before he was imprisoned, pointing to the fact that he formed his own splinter group as a possible sign that he had trouble even then getting along with others. Curiously, Sageman found that Zawahiri was the only jihad he studied who showed any sign of being paranoid before joining the movement, contrary to the popular belief that jihadists suffer from feelings or persecution or marginalization.[24]

During his time in Egyptian prison, Zawahiri got to know the Blind Sheik, whose followers would later bomb the World Trade Center (1993) and plot to blow up New York City landmarks, including the United Nations. Though Zawahiri and the Blind Sheik shared the goal of wanting to establish an Islamic order, the two did not get along especially well as Zawahiri would reportedly belittle the sheik for being, in his view, naïve enough to believe that humanity would eventually embrace Islam on its own. Zawahiri held the view that the Islamic state had to be imposed and that it would have to be done through violence. When he was released in 1984, Zawahiri and now thoroughly hardened from the experience and he was even less interested in settling down to practice medicine and raise a family. Instead he headed to where the real action was: the jihad in Afghanistan.

Sageman found that, like Zawahiri, most of the Egyptians who joined the global jihad had traversed much the same path: that is, they went from radicalism to prison to jihad in Afghanistan. Sagemen also observed that the Egyptians comprised the majority of al Qaeda's Central Staff (representing 63 percent). This led him to disavow himself of the popular misconception that the global jihad was Saudi or even Afghan in origin—instead he was forced to place the movement's roots in Egypt.[25]

Once back in Afghanistan, Zawahiri quickly forged a close relationship with bin Laden, who by that time had become a prominent player. Soon Zawahiri was having more influence over the impressionable Saudi than even Azzam, his old mentor. At least one Egyptian radical reportedly suspected that Zawahiri may have even resorted to dirty tricks to dislodge Azzam. Osama Rushdi, a former member of Egyptian Islamic Group who met Zawihiri when they were in prison, told Wright that the very night Azzam and his sons were killed in a roadside bombing on their way to mosque, Zawahiri had told him that there were rumors that Azzam was in fact an American spy.[26]

By 1993, al Qaeda would score its first victory against American military power when Somalian militias they claim to have trained shot down two U.S. helicopters in an incident made famous by the movie *Black Hawk Down*. When President Clinton responded by pulling the famine-relief forces out of Somalia, bin Laden later described it as a defining moment. Now the mujahidin saw for themselves, in his words, "the weakness, frailty, and cowardice of U.S. troops. Only eighteen U.S. troops were killed. Nonetheless, they fled in the heart of darkness."[27]

From their base in Sudan, the Egyptians were able to launch various assassination attempts on a number of Egyptian politicians. In November of 1993 when they tried to assassinate the Egyptian prime minister, they mistakenly killed an innocent bystander, a twelve-year-old schoolgirl. The public reacted with horror, though Zawahiri was nonplussed. As he later wrote in his memoirs, when he saw the Egyptian masses streaming behind the girl's funeral procession screaming "terrorism is the enemy of God," the only thought that crossed his mind was to wonder where their outrage was when hundreds of his followers had been arrested and or condemned to death.[28]

Zawahiri is widely regarded to be the brains behind bin Laden. Among the innovations he introduced to the global jihad movement was the use of martyrdom videotapes, the souvenir videos that suicide bombers leave behind to memorialize their act. He also is credited with having imposed a blind-cell structure on al Qaeda to ensure that in the event of a security breach, the members of one tactical unit do not have any information to give up about any other cell.[29]

What Zawahiri is said to lack, however, is the empathy that would be required for him to be a leader in his own right. His inability to comprehend the Egyptian public's reaction to the death of an innocent school girl is one example of this personality deficit. Another telling incident occurred when he was living in Sudan, when he learned that Egyptian security forces had videotaped two teenage Sudanese boys being sodomized in an effort to blackmail them into participating in an assassination plot against him. Given that he was their intended target, he convinced the Sudanese officials to release the boys into his custody so that he could question them. But instead he convened a Sharia trial, had the youngsters condemned to death, and then executed them, but not before videotaping their confession, which he then reportedly distributed as a warning to other potential traitors. The Sudanese officials saw this as the last straw and withdrew their offer of a safe harbor. Again, Zawahiri registered only confusion: "All we did was to apply God's Sharia," he wrote.[30]

Thus having worn out al Qaeda's welcome, bin Laden was now forced to relocate the group. By 1996, about their only option was to move to Afghanistan, which since the Soviets had pulled out had descended into a state of warlordism and there was no central authority coherent enough to block their move.

Just as bin Laden was moving back to Afghanistan, the Taliban was in the process of seizing control of the country and imposing their idea of an Islamic order. Under their interpretation, women were strictly forbidden from working outside the home, even widows with dependent children who were the sole source of support for their families. Girls were barred from attending school. Windows had to be blackened so that women could not be seen from outside the home. All forms of entertainment were banned, including videos, movies, and music; people were even forbidden from keeping songbirds as pets. Children were not allowed to fly kites or play with toys. Although soccer matches were still occasionally permitted—when the stadium was not being used for public beheadings or executions by stoning—cheering and public displays of emotion were strictly forbidden. The religious police would even walk through crowds to cane those who couldn't control themselves. Ironically, it would be under this regime that bin Laden, would find his greatest degree of latitude.

Though bin Laden had no prior connection to the Taliban before arriving back in Afghanistan in 1996, he quickly forged a relationship with the group's leader, Mullar Omar, a one-eyed recluse, who according to a U.S. intelligence report, gave the exiled Saudi the freedom to do whatever he wanted so long as he did not alienate Pakistan or Saudi Arabia, the Taliban's primary supporters.[31] Bin Laden would use his new freedom to issue his 1996 "Declaration of War

Against the Americans," in which he called on Muslims to deploy secret "fast moving light forces" to attack "the main enemy,"[32] and start nailing down the basic structure of what the 9/11 Commission would later describe as a "true global terrorist network."[33]

At the heart of this global jihad network, was a core organization structured along functional lines: at the top of the organization, similar to a corporate board of directors, was an advisory or *Shura council*; then there was a *Sharia committee* to ensure that policy decisions were in line with Islamic principles; a *military committee* to oversee operations; a *finance committee* to raise money and manage the flow of funds; a *procurement committee* to keep the organization's infrastructure running; and finally a *media relations committee* to get the group's message out. According to the 9/11 Commission, this inner core was largely composed of people who had sworn "fealty (or bayat) to Bin Ladin."[34]

Bin Laden's organizational genius lay not in the fact that he could build a classic hierarchical organization out of people who were willing to report to him. Rather, what was inspired about the way bin Laden structured al Qaeda was that in addition to the core organization, he was also able to brand a network of loosely affiliated organizations and individuals. Some have compared al Qaeda's structure to an international conglomerate, one former government official likened it the to Ford Foundation of Islamic terrorism.[35] Whatever the analogy, the fact was that by creating a network and not just a core organization, bin Laden was able to build a structure that could survive the loss of its headquarters, training camps, and most of its key personnel and yet still exist to carry on attacks.

Independent Affiliates

To understand how exactly bin Laden worked with his independent affiliates, take the case of Khalid Sheikh Mohammed (KSM), the mastermind of the 9/11 attacks. Much of what we know about KSM comes via interrogations as he has been in American custody in an undisclosed location since March 2003, as well as corroborating accounts of those who knew him, in most cases, themselves detainees. Keep in mind, however, as in the case of bin Laden, there is still a great deal to be learned about KSM's upbringing and family history, and even what exactly motivated him. The fact that so very few Americans can even identify KSM as the mastermind of the 9/11 attacks should suggest how very little investigative reporting has been done on him.

KSM, like his nephew Ramzi Yousef, the mastermind of the 1993 World Trade Center bombing, has so far maintained to authorities that he never pledged an oath of fealty to bin Laden until after the 9/11 attacks.[36] He claims that he insisted on maintaining his independence so that in the event bin Laden decided to back out of what he referred to as "the planes operations," he could still retain the option of being able to carry them out. He was willing to work with bin Laden and al Qaeda only because he perceived them as having the necessary resources to implement his plans and has indicated that he would have worked with anyone who could have helped him. This caused the 9/11 Commission panel to conclude that KSM, like his nephew Ramzi Yousef, was essentially a "terrorist entrepreneur" or "rootless but experienced" operative who never formally joined any organization but traveled the world "joining in projects that were supported by or linked to Bin Laden, the Blind Sheikh, or their associates."[37]

As was the case for most of their confederates in the core of al Qaeda, the road to jihad for both KSM and Yousef led through Afghanistan. KSM first heard about what was happening there from his older brother who was then the head of one of the largest charities involved in funding the effort, a Kuwaiti organization by the name of Lajnat al Dawa al Islamiyah (or the "Committee for Islamic Appeal").

Thus, in 1986, after graduating from North Carolina Agricultural and Technical State University in Greensboro, North Carolina, with a degree in mechanical engineering, KSM moved to Peshawar, Pakistan, where with his brother's connections, he was able to find work with Abdul Rasul Sayyaf, a prominent Pashtun military commander. Sayyaf had risen to his position because he was one of the very few Pashtuns, the dominant ethnic and linguistic group in Afghanistan, who spoke Arabic. Sayyaf had picked up the language while studying at the famous Al Azhar University in Cairo. Like most of the Arab jihadists, Sayyaf was also a member of the Muslim Brotherhood.

The Muslim Brotherhood (MB) occupies a special place in the global jihad movement. As we have already noted, many jihadists have been active in the MB at some point in their lives. KSM, for example, says that he became radicalized after he joined the Muslim Brotherhood at age 16 and attended youth camps in the desert.[38] His father, who was the imam at the local mosque in Kuwait, where he had migrated from his native Pakistan to improve his economic prospects, died while KSM was still a boy and he simply followed his older brothers into the Muslim Brotherhood. As we have already noted, its most famous ideologue, Sayyid Qutb, has had a profound influence on the global jihad movement through his writings. Dr. Mamoun Fandy, an Egyptian-American political scientist and expert on Islamic radicalism describes the MB as "the mother of all these [radical] movements, ideologically," and says that both "Salafist jihadism" and the concept of a coming conflict between Islam and the rest of the world "are the ideas that emerged from the writings and the teachings of the Muslim Brotherhood."[39]

The Muslim Brotherhood, which was founded in 1928 in Egypt, now has branches in some seventy countries throughout the world.[40] The MB is an amorphous organization, changing its shape and mission, depending on the political climate. Its overt mission is to prepare society for the restoration of Islam to political power and to accomplish this, the MB sponsors all sorts of activities including Koranic study circles, summer youth camps, professional unions, and other civic organizations. Covertly, the organization has been suspected of seditious activity, particularly by the Egyptian government.

When Egyptian president Gamal Abdel Nasser uncovered a MB plot to assassinate him in 1954, he banned the movement and imprisoned many of its members. This crackdown caused many members to flee to places like Saudi Arabia where they were warmly welcomed by the government as a counterforce to Nasser's rapidly spreading Arab nationalism. Moreover, the Saudi regime considered the Muslim Brothers, with their religious credentials, as ideal candidates to fill the many job openings in the kingdom's rapidly expanding educational system. Experts are now convinced that the prevalence of Muslim Brothers in the Saudi school system has significantly contributed to the radicalization of the Saudi public that began in the 1960s. Bin Laden, in fact, is a notable example of the first generation of Saudis whose education was left almost entirely in the hands of the Muslim Brothers.

Thus, using his Muslim Brotherhood connections, the Afghan commander Abu Sayyaf was able to secure funding to set up a network of training and refugee camps, publish a jihad newspaper, and even set up a jihad college outside Peshawar to train recruits how to use explosives, along with a regular curriculum of engineering, medicine, and science.[41]

It was there at Sayyaf's college, the University of Dawa al-Jihad, that KSM first found work as a fresh graduate on his way to Afghanistan. This was also where KSM become close to an Indonesian by the name of Hambali, who the world would later hear about when he emerged as the chief suspect in the 2002 Bali bombing.

In Afghanistan, KSM is also said to have participated in the famous Jaji battle, alongside Azzam and bin Laden, the battle in which the mujahidin forced the superior Soviet forces into retreat—or so the legend goes. For a time KSM even served as Azzam's personal assistant before he was pegged to run one of Sayyaf's NGOs.

Ramzi Yousef, his sister's son, who was a few years younger than KSM would not make it to Afghanistan until after the jihad against the Soviets had already wound down, though he claims to have received his explosives training in the Afghan camps.[42] It was after Yousef moved to Afghanistan, around 1991 or 1992, KSM told investigators, that he first heard about Yousef's plan to attack the United States.[43] Though KSM is not believed to have played a significant role in the 1993 WTC bombing, he did provide the only confirmed source of funding, a wire transfer of $660.[44]

After the 1993 WTC attacks, the next time investigators believe KSM linked up operationally with his nephew was in the Philippines in the mid-1990s. There the two men plotted to blow up a dozen commercial airliners as they flew over the Pacific (the "Bojinka plot") and assassinate both President Bill Clinton and Pope John Paul II on their upcoming visits to the Philippines. Their plans were aborted, however, when Yousef caused an explosion at his Manila apartment experimenting with bomb-making materials, and police investigators discovered what they were planning to do in a laptop computer he had abandoned when he fled the scene.

Though Yousef was ultimately convicted for the 1993 WTC bombing, much remains unknown about the crime. Yousef has never indicated who, if anyone was behind him, or where he got his funding aside from the small transfer from KSM. Nor do authorities really know how he managed to insert himself into the small group of the Blind Sheik's followers who were plotting to bomb New York only days after he initially arrived in the United States claiming that he was a refugee from Iraq.[45]As the judge who presided over his trial remarked at his sentencing, "We don't even know what your real name is."[46] After 9/11, when it emerged that it was Yousef's uncle who was the mastermind of the 9/11 attacks, authorities had to have realized the full impact of their dearth of knowledge about this early case and the conspiracy involved.

Both KSM and Yousef are believed to have grown up in the same town in Kuwait, though neither were Arabs, but rather Baluchis, a distinct people who traditionally inhabit the area which spans western Pakistan and eastern Iran. We also know that a childhood friend, Abdul Rahman Yasin, who confessed to mixing the chemicals for the bombing, told Leslie Stahl of "60 Minutes" that the reason Yousef targeted the World Trade Center was because he was told that a lot of Jews worked there.[47] In a similar vein, KSM has told interrogators that his animus toward the United States was based largely on its support of Israel.[48]

In any case, after leaving Afghanistan in the early 1990s, KSM fought jihad for awhile in Bosnia but eventually decided to accept an engineering position at the Qatari Ministry of Electricity and Water, a job that he found through one of the high-level connections he had formed in Afghanistan. Though he remained with the Qatari Ministry until 1996, the 9/11 Commission concluded that during his period of employ there, he appears to have spent most of his time traveling the world "in furtherance of terrorist activity."[49] In 1996 he would be forced to leave Qatar to evade the FBI who were now on his trail because of his suspected involvement in the Manila plots. U.S. investigators believe that he was alerted by someone in the Qatari government that an arrest was impending.

Now back in Afghanistan, KSM arranged to meet bin Laden. Though they are said to have fought together in the legendary battle of Jaji, KSM has told interrogators that he assumes that the only reason bin Laden agreed to meet him at this point was because of his notorious nephew.[50] At the meeting, according to the recollection of Abu Zubaydah, an al Qaeda military commander in U.S. custody, KSM proposed a "scaled-down version of the 9/11 plan," to which Zubaydah recalls bin Laden responding, "Why do you use an axe when you can use a bulldozer?"[51]

Rank and File

The 9/11 hijackers themselves are also prototypical members of the global jihad movement and we can learn more about the jihad movement by examining for a moment who they were and how they came to participate in the operation. Essentially there were two tracts: that of the pilots and that of the "muscle" or the men whose job it would be to overwhelm the cabin and crew in order to prepare the aircraft for takeover.

Three out of four of the pilots were members of the "Hamburg cell," so named because it was in the city of Hamburg in Germany that the young students from Egypt, the United Arab Emirates, and Lebanon first met.

Mohamed Atta, the Egyptian, who would become the lead hijacker, was the only son of a Cairo attorney. After completing his undergraduate studies in Egypt, he went to Germany to get a doctorate in urban planning. There, his German thesis advisor remembers him as a serious student. Though he was always religious, he did not appear to become particularly fanatic until the mid-1990s. After his death, law enforcement officials found a suitcase he left behind at Logan Airport in Boston before boarding the American Airlines jetliner he would later crash into the World Trade Center. In the suitcase was a will in which he made clear that his final act should be interpreted as an effort to serve God, and that at his funeral, "everybody should mention God's name and that I died as a Muslim," suggesting[52] that he may have been planning to martyr himself as early as April 1996, the date of the will.

Sometime during this period, Atta met a Yemeni student by the name of Ramzi Binalshibh, with whom he shared intense religious sentiments, in particular a growing belief in the importance of jihad. Though Binalshibh was also slated to become one of the 9/11 hijackers, he was never able to get the necessary visa and had to content himself making a solely logistical contribution to the operation.

At some point, Atta and Binalshibh met Marwan al Shehhi, another one of the pilots, who was a student from the United Arab Emirates. Eventually, the three men became roommates. They were drawn together in part by their shared belief in what Binalshibh liked to refer to as the "Jewish world conspiracy"[53] and their sympathy for the Palestinians. Shehhi was asked once why he and Atta never laughed, and he is said to have responded, "How can you laugh when people are dying in Palestine?"[54]

Over time the three men became friends with a Lebanese student by the name of Ziad Jarrah, who had come to Germany in 1996. Of all the members of the Hamburg cell, Jarrah seems to have been the least likely candidate for jihad. He attended private Christian schools in Lebanon and was in love with a Turkish-German girl who was studying to become a dentist. By 1996, he was noticeably becoming enamored of jihad, even going so far as to express a desire to become a martyr. In 1997, he transferred to Hamburg. While he told family and friends this was because he wanted to study aircraft engineering, now authorities suspect that his real motive may have been to move closer to his radical friends. As he became more and more religious, he tried to break off with his girlfriend because she did not share his piety, though he never really succeeded. It would only be on the eve of the 9/11 mission that he would write her a final farewell letter, a letter that she would receive by mail after his death, in which he tried to assure her, "I did not escape from you, but I did what I was supposed to. You should be very proud of me. It's an honor, and you will see the results, and everybody will be happy. God willing, I am your prince and I will pick you up. See you again!!"[55]

In late 1999 the four Hamburg students were now so committed to fighting jihad that they left Hamburg for Afghanistan, intending to make their way to the jihad then going on in Chechnya.[56] Instead, they were hand-picked by bin Laden himself to participate in the 9/11 operation. He reportedly singled them out from the other would-be jihadists because of their technical backgrounds and familiarity with the languages and customs of the West.

It is interesting to note that none of the jihadists we have profiled so far were in any way underprivileged. Rather, they all had access to education, family connections, and good if not superior career prospects. What is interesting to note, however, is that at the time most of these individuals decided to join al Qaeda, almost all were living far from home. Sageman, in fact, found 70 percent of global jihadists were living in a country in which they had not grown up at the moment they decided to join jihad—the newly enlisted mujahidin were foreign students, workers, refugees, or had come from other countries to fight the Soviets in Afghanistan. Eight percent were second generation immigrants living in the West. As Sageman notes, this means that "a remarkable 78 percent were cut off from their cultural and social origins, far from their families and friends."[57] Like the members of the Hamburg cell, Sageman also found that though most jihadists were raised as Muslims, almost all of those he studied became markedly more religious just prior to enlisting in jihad, and that their newfound faith was overwhelmingly a Salafi interpretation of Islam. Sageman speculates that these dislocated Muslims may have been drawn to the local mosque because it was "the most available source for companionship with people of similar background."[58]

The mother of the first descent European suicide bomber, a Belgian convert to Islam who blew herself up in Iraq in November 2005, noticed a similar deepening of faith in her daughter: "Muriel became more Muslim than a Muslim," her mother told Le Parisien newspaper. "When she first converted she wore a simple veil. But with her last husband she wore a (head to toe) chador."[59] It was with her last husband that she decided to carry out her martyrdom mission. As for her husband, he was shot and killed by American forces before he could detonate his explosives belt.

The fifteen "muscle hijackers," or those whose task it was to "storm the cockpit and control the passengers,"[60] came to jihad through a slightly different route than the members of the Hamburg cell. Fourteen of the fifteen muscle men were from Saudi Arabia.[61] Among the Saudis were two sets of brothers (Waleed and Wail al Shehri and Nawaf and Salem al Hazmi) and four members of the same tribe—the Ghamdis, along with Ahmad al-Haznawi. All were directly or indirectly recruited by one Tawfiq bin Attash, otherwise known as Khallad, who met up with them on their way to fight jihad in Chechnya, which is where Khallad claims to have first met them.

Khallad himself was introduced to jihad by a family connection, namely his father. Family and kinship connections, as we have seen, appear to have played an important part in the global jihad movement: KSM and Yousef, for example, were uncle and nephew—and another member of the family, Ammar al-Baluchi, emerged as a leading member of the 9/11 conspiracy during the Moussaoui trial.[62] Bin Laden's son Saad is supposedly a high-level al Qaeda manager. And now we have seen that many of the muscle hijackers were related as well.

Khallad's father was a Yemeni radical who ended up in Saudi Arabia where he connected with all the major players of the emerging global jihad movement—including bin Laden, Azzam, and the Blind Sheikh. Inspired by his father's example, Khallad left home at the age of fifteen to go fight jihad against the Northern Alliance in Afghanistan in 1994, where he lost his leg in battle and pledged fealty to bin Laden. When it became time to select the 9/11 hijackers, bin Laden immediately thought of Khallad. But because Khallad carried a

Yemeni passport, like Binalshibh, he could never get an American visa so he had to content himself with playing a logistical role in the 9/11 plot (and a lead role in the U.S.S. Cole bombing in Yemen in the fall of 2000).[63]

Saudi government officials have suggested that bin Laden intentionally used Saudis to carry out the 9/11 attacks because he wanted to drive a wedge between the two allied nations, the U.S. and Saudi Arabia.[64] According to KSM, however, the choice of Saudis was simply borne of practical considerations: they had the easiest time obtaining U.S. visas and also constituted, according to his estimates, about 70 percent of the recruitment pool at the training camps in Afghanistan.[65]

Like most of the jihadists we have seen so far, almost all of the Saudi hijackers came from middle class families. While they may not have had doctorates, almost all had at least some university education as did the majority in Sageman's study (60 percent). As he points out, this made them, "as a group more educated than the average person worldwide, and especially more educated than the vast majority of the people in the third world."[66]

It should be noted, however, that because journalists are still not given freedom of access inside Saudi Arabia, there is still much that remains unknown about the Saudi hijackers. As far as how they came to jihad, we do know that at least several of them had spent time in the Qassim province, which moderate clerics call the "terrorist factory" because it is a hotbed of radicalism.[67] There they are believed to have been directed to Afghanistan by al Qaeda recruiters, including Sulayman al Alwan, Abu Zubaydah's spiritual advisor.

Radical imams and clerics, in fact, have played a notorious role in channeling recruits to jihad. Sageman found that it was often an imam who served as the necessary human link that directed would-be jihadists to those who would help them find their way to training camps in Afghanistan. Magnus Ranstorp of the Centre for the Study of Terrorism and Political Violence at Scotland's St. Andrews University says that "these talent spotters and handlers are the really worrisome parts of *al-Qaeda*. They can tap into new recruits and dispatch them as well."[68]

The FBI described how the human chain that took hold in various mosques worked: Once a mosque was identified as hospitable, the memo said, an al Qaeda operative would then try to forge a friendship with anyone who seemed to express a deeper interest in Islam in order to identify the potential recruit's strength, vulnerabilities, and emotional state. Once he passed this initial evaluation, he would then be put through a period of indoctrination in which he would be inculcated with Islamic history, with a special focus on the battles of the Prophet and conflicts in which Muslims have been aggrieved by non-Muslims. Finally, the recruit would be asked whether he was willing to defend his religion and fight for jihad.[69]

A relief worker in the Palestinian territories, Nasra Hassan, who studied would-be suicide bombers during the late 1990s, saw evidence of a similar inculcation among the Palestinians she studied:

> Most were bearded. All were deeply religious. They used Islamic terminology to express their views, but they were well informed about politics in Israel and

throughout the Arab world . . . Many of these young men had memorized large sections of the Koran and were well versed in the finer points of Islamic law and practice. But their knowledge of Christianity was rooted in the medieval Crusades, and they regarded Judaism and Zionism as synonymous. When they spoke, they all tended to use the same phrases: "The West is afraid of Islam." "Allah has promised us ultimate success." "It is in the Koran." "Islamic Palestine will be liberated." And they all exhibited an unequivocal rage toward Israel. Over and over, I heard them say, "The Israelis humiliate us. They occupy our land, and deny our history."[70]

Experts have identified radical mosques all over the world. Among the most notorious is the Finsbury Park Mosque in London. In 1996, Abu Hamza al-Masri, a hook-fisted, one-eyed, former nightclub bouncer and engineering student from Cairo, began preaching at the mosque, using the pulpit to incite Muslims to kill Jews and non-Muslims, according to charges filed against him in October 2004 by British authorities. He is famous for his recruitment efforts. Among his followers were Djamel Beghal, who confessed to plotting to blow up the U.S. embassy in Paris; Nizar Trabelsi, the Tunisian former pro soccer player who is now serving a ten-year sentence for planning to drive a car bomb into a NATO air base in Belgium; Richard Reid, the "shoe-bomber"; Zacarias Moussaoui, the "twentieth hijacker" who later confessed to being a member of al Qaeda and to having trained for a plane operation, just not 9/11; Ahmed Ressam and a co-conspirator who were convicted of plotting to bomb the Los Angeles airport during millennium celebrations; Anas al-Liby, an al Qaeda leader wanted by the FBI in connection with the African embassies bombings; Earnest James Ujaama who was indicted for trying to set up a terrorist training camp in Oregon (he eventually agreed to plead guilty to lesser charges and help the government in terrorism investigations in exchange for a reduced sentence); and Rabah Kadre, accused of plotting to attack the traditional Christmas markets in Strasbourg, France.

Abu Hamza's reach extends even as far as the United States, where he has been accused of attempting to set up a terrorist training camp in Oregon and recruiting for al Qaeda and the Taliban; and even in Yemen, where he is suspected of having been involved in a kidnapping in which four foreign tourists were killed.

Other radicalized mosques that have been identified include: London's Baker Street and Brixton Mosques; Milan's Islamic Cultural Center; Madrid's Abu Baker Mosque; the St. Denis and Rue Myrrah mosques in Paris; al-Dawah Mosque in Roubaix, France; Montreal's Assuna Annabawiyh Mosque; and Brooklyn's al-Faruq Mosque, just to name a few.

There are also worrisome indications that jihad is being promoted in some moderate mosques. In 2005, Freedom House, an independent civil liberties monitor, released a study of promotional materials being distributed at fifteen American mosques by the Saudi government in which they found that Muslims were being urged to adopt:

[A] dualistic worldview in which there exist two antagonistic realms or abodes that can never be reconciled—*Dar al-Islam* and *Dar al-Har*, or Abode of War (also called *Dar al-Kufr*, Abode of the Infidel)—and that when Muslims are in the latter, they must behave as if on a mission behind enemy lines. Either they are there to acquire new knowledge and make money to be later employed in the *jihad* against the infidels, or they are there to proselytize the infidels until at least some convert to Islam. Any other reason for lingering among the unbelievers in their lands is illegitimate, and unless a Muslim leaves as quickly as possible, he or she is not a true Muslim and so too must be condemned.[71]

Moreover, the Saudi materials were promoting the idea that Muslims, no matter where they live, are obliged to reject democracy and actively work to install an Islamic state wherever they reside. In a book found at a Texas mosque, *To Be a Muslim*, for example, the Freedom House researchers found that Muslims were being taught that:

> [A]ll available political and economic systems and manmade laws are fundamentally anti-Islamic and "operate functionally to deny the wisdom of Allah on earth." The book states that the responsibility to change these systems is "binding in principle, in law, in self-defense, in community and as a sacred obligation of *jihad*." It is compulsory for every Muslim to establish an Islamic society "in every country on earth and to restore the Islamic way of life taught by all the prophets." This obligation must occur according to Islamic *shari'a* law because "Muslim countries have been ruled by manmade systems with elements borrowed from the Romans, Chinese, French, and many other cultures . . . This overlay of secular cultures makes it all the more necessary to abolish all traces of such primitive life (*jahiliyya*) and to reinforce the understanding and application of the eternal and universal Islamic *deen* [religion] until it becomes the ruling power throughout the world."[72]

To get a sense of how pervasive the distribution of such materials may be in American mosques, consider that the main vehicle the Saudis use to distribute their materials is an organization called the Islamic Society of North America (ISNA). J. Michael Waller, an expert in the political warfare of terrorist groups, has estimated that the "ISNA provides ideological material to about 1,100 of an estimated 1,500 to 2,500 mosques in North America," and that the North American Islamic Trust, a related entity, "finances, owns, and otherwise subsidizes the construction of mosques and is reported to own between 50 and 79 percent of the mosques on the North American continent."[73] In other words, the Saudis now have financial control of about 80 percent of American mosques.

Now to help work out the logistics of the 9/11 operations, KSM frequently called upon his old friend Hambali, now the head of Jemaah Islamiah in Indonesia. By this time, JI had already accepted bin Laden's operational and financial support in its jihad against Christians and Jews in Southeast Asia.[74] KSM would tell interrogators that it was he who ultimately convinced Hambali to also wage attacks on Americans, though no such plans were ever carried out.[75]

Hambali, the son of a peasant farmer, became radicalized in Malaysia during the 1980s during a work stint in Malaysia. There he fell under the influence of a radical cleric, Abdullah Sungkar, who wanted to establish an Islamist regime in Southeast Asia. It was Sungkar who sent him to Afghanistan in 1986, where he became friends with KSM.

Eventually Hambali returned to Southeast Asia and was appointed to run JI's operations in Malaysia and Singapore, the new terrorist organization that had been formed by his old mentor Sungkar, along with Abu Bakar Bashir, who describes himself as a teacher at an Islamic school in Java.[76] (Incidentally, though Hambali is still believed to have been responsible for the Bali attacks and is in U.S. custody, the United States has consented to extradite him to Indonesia to be tried because of the fear that he would receive a similar sentence to Bashir, the group's spiritual leader, who was found guilty of conspiring of in the attacks but who received a minor sentence—that was even commuted—so that ultimately, Bashir would serve a total of only four days for each person killed in the attacks. The United States, in fact, refuses even to disclose his whereabouts.)

It is interesting to note that while Hambali attended an Islamic boarding school, madrassahs and Islamic religious schools have not contributed as many members to the global jihad movement as one would suspect. While the madrassahs may have supplied fighters to the Taliban's war against the Northern Alliance, or to other Afghan warlords during the 1990s, and madrassah alumni may have comprised part of the rank and file during the jihad in Afghanistan, Sageman found that only 17 percent of the jihadists in his sample attended Islamic schools and of those, half were Southeast Asians or members of Hambali's group, Jemaah Islamiyah. Most jihadists in Sageman's study, including the Indonesians, were sent to these religious schools out of necessity, not because they or their parents wanted a strong religious education, necessarily, but because in many cases, the madrassahs were the only affordable educational option available.

Note, however, that in these numbers, Sageman did not include those who attended Saudi public schools in spite of the fact that the religious indoctrination in Saudi public schools is very intense—at the elementary level, for example, a third of the curriculum is reportedly devoted to religious studies. According to MEMRI, a think tank which monitors Arabic media, a sample Saudi textbook promotes the notion that "following the battle of Badr (the first victory of Muslims over the disbelievers) a new chapter in the Koran had descended on the Prophet which raised, in the eyes of Allah, the status of the mujahideen (Jihad warrior) and their preference over those who sit still" and then encourages "the mujahid to Jihad, and discourages those who sit still."[77]

Incidentally, Freedom House found that elements of the Saudi curriculum were even being taught in Islamic centers in the United States:

One example is a book for third-year high school students published by the Saudi Ministry of Education that was collected from the Islamic Center of Oakland in California. The text, written with the approval of the Saudi Ministry of Education, teaches students to prepare for *jihad* in the sense of war against Islam's enemies, and to strive to attain military self-sufficiency: "To be true Muslims, we must prepare and be ready for *jihad* in Allah's way. It is the duty of the citizen and the government. The military education is glued to faith and its meaning, and the duty to follow it."

The case of a U.S. citizen, and valedictorian of the Islamic Saudi Academy in Alexandria, Virginia, Ahmed Omar Abu Ali—who was convicted of plotting to assassinate President Bush, launch an attack similar to 9/11, and for performing reconnaissance on nuclear power plants in the U.S. for a possible terrorist strike suggests that there may well be reasons to be concerned about what is being taught in Saudi sponsored schools in the United States.[78] While the Saudi government claims that it has, in the words of Prince Turki, the Saudi ambassador to the United States, "eliminated what might be perceived as intolerance from old text-books that were in our system" and "implemented a comprehensive internal revision and modernization plan," according to a 2006 study of current textbooks produced by Freedom House, such claims are simply not true in that Saudi textbooks that teach Muslim supremacy and promote jihad are still circulating.[79]

Claude Berrebi, a Rand economist, studied the connection between education and poverty and Palestinian terrorism while he was a doctoral candidate at Princeton University. After analyzing data on 335 Palestinian terrorists (members and leaders of Hamas and PIJ) who were active during the period 1987–2002, he found that terrorists were more likely to be better-off financially, more educated, and to have had higher rates of employment than the comparable Palestinian population.

Specifically, Berrebi found that terrorists were generally a lot less poor than their comparable peer group: only 16 percent of the terrorists could be classified as poor versus 31 percent of comparable Palestinians.[80] They were also much better educated: 96 percent of the terrorists had had at least a high school education, compared to only 51 percent of the comparable population; and 65 percent of the terrorists were educated beyond the high school level, compared to only 15 percent of the comparable Palestinian population group. Finally, the terrorists also had higher rates of employment: 94 percent of the terrorists had jobs compared to only 69 percent of their Palestinian peers.[81]

When Berrebi singled out suicide terrorists in his study, the same comparisons held true: they were less poor than their peers (13 percent versus 32 percent); better educated (62 percent were educated beyond high school versus 16 percent of the comparable population) and had higher rates of employment (96 percent versus 61 percent).[82]

Hassan drew similar conclusions when she studied Palestinian would-be suicide bombers during the late 1990s:

> None of the suicide bombers—they ranged in age from eighteen to thirty-eight—conformed to the typical profile of the suicidal personality. None of them were uneducated, desperately poor, simple-minded, or depressed. Many were middle class and, unless they were fugitives, held paying jobs. More than half of them were refugees from what is now Israel. Two were the sons of millionaires. They all seemed to be entirely normal members of their families. They were polite and serious, and in their communities they were considered to be model youths.

As Sageman points out, the data appear to suggest that "far from being a product of falling expectations," jihad is the "result of the rising expectations among its members."[83] Even as early as 1958, Daniel Lerner, author of *The Passing of Traditional Society*,[84] observed that data collected on Middle East extremists suggested that these were not the "have-nots" of society but the "want-mores."[85]

Sageman also found that, for the most part, the jihadists he studied "were [described using] positive or neutral labels; shy, introverted, serious, quiet, bright, excellent student, loner, pleasant, easy-going, happy, gentle were recurrent descriptors," and concluded that this would make sense as, "On a logical basis, although antisocial people might become *individual* terrorists, they would not do well in a terrorist *organization*. Because of their personalities, they would not get along with others or fit in well in an organization, whether in the business world, the army, or a terrorist cell."[86]

Finally, both KSM and Khallad emphasized to interrogators that the main thing they looked for in selecting hijackers was a recruit's willingness to martyr himself. (Although Khallad was also careful to note that the second most important quality was patience as the attacks could take years to plan.[87] Indeed, by 1999 almost all of the hijackers had been selected but it would be two years before they would be able to carry out their mission.)

Martyrdom is so intrinsic to the jihad movement that Palestinian jihadists have managed to create an entire culture around celebrating it. In the Palestinian areas, observer after observer has noted that martyrdom is now so deified that it has become a route to fame and even relative fortune for the martyr's family. The martyr's image is posted all over the community, his funeral is celebrated as though it were a wedding, songs are sung in his honor, sometimes even streets are named after the him – or even in some cases her. Many families also receive some sort of reward, often donated by charities expressly set up to compensate the families of "martyrs" who sacrifice themselves in jihad.

Jessica Stern, a Harvard terrorism expert, reported that one mother whose son died fighting jihad in Kashmir told her that she would be happy to give up her other six sons as well because she believed that if her sons died in jihad they could help her "in the next life, which is the real life."[88]

So far we have seen that almost every member of the global jihad spent at least some time in Afghanistan either fighting jihad against the Soviets during the eighties or training in al Qaeda camps during the nineties before going on to fight jihad in other places. As Hegghammer notes, "the training camps generated an ultra-masculine culture of violence which brutalized the volunteers and broke down their barriers to the use of violence. Recruits increased their paramilitary skills while the harsh camp life built strong personal relationships between them. Last but not least, they fell under the ideological influence of Usama bin Ladin and Ayman al-Zawahiri, who generated a feeling among the recruits of being part of a global vanguard of holy warriors, whose mission was to defend the Islamic world against attacks by the Jewish-Crusader alliance.[89] Some 10,000 to 20,000 people are believed to have passed through these camps during the period 1996–2001.[90] While the destruction of this haven in 2001 weakened the global jihad movement, as Hegghammer goes on to point out, "an extremely diverse and loosely knit ideological movement emerged . . . bound together by little more than an extreme anti-Americanism and a willingness to carry out mass-casualty attacks on Western targets."[91]

Iraqi Jihadists

Analysts who have followed the global jihad movement have noted that every time a new jihad front has opened up—in Bosnia, in Chechnya, in Afghanistan, in Iraq—it has spurred a new wave of recruits. The new front that has opened up since the U.S.-led invasion of Iraq seems especially worrisome. The invasion of a Muslim country convinced many Muslims that Islam really was under attack. As al Qaeda expert Rohan Gunaratna wrote in 2004, "The very imams in Egypt that condemned the September 11 attacks as un-Islamic are now encouraging Muslim youth to go to Iraq and fight the invaders."[92] Such reactions raise the concern that the war in Iraq may be creating jihadists at a greater rate than it is eliminating them.

Some experts fear that those who will survive the jihad in Iraq will eventually represent an even greater menace than the mujahidin who got their experience fighting the Soviets, the Serbs, the Russians, or the Northern Alliance in Afghanistan because in Iraq this new generation will have learned the deadly skills of urban combat and gained a better understanding of improvised explosives.

As to who exactly is fighting the insurgency in Iraq, according to a study released by Anthony Cordesman of the Center for Strategic and International Studies, the bulk of the insurgency seems to be comprised of Sunni Muslims, including Iraqi Arab Sunnis who rightly sense that they will have a diminished role in the emerging Iraqi nation. Since its existence as a modern state, Arab Sunnis have been able to dominate Iraq in spite of the fact they comprise a minority of the population. Included in this group are the former regime elements unwilling to relinquish power. The balance of the insurgency is comprised of foreign jihadists, fighting to establish an Islamist state in the heart of the Arab world. Cordesman's analysis suggests that foreign jihadists number between 1,500 to 6,000 and represent less than 10 percent of the insurgency though they are believed to be responsible for most of the attacks on Iraqi civilians.[93] The Brookings Institution's "Iraq's Index" estimates the number of foreign insurgents to be in the range of 800 to 1,000, or less than 10 percent of the total number of insurgents.[94]

As to who are the foreigners fighting jihad in Iraq, Cordesman and Nawaf Obaid of the Saudi National Security Assessment Project concluded that as of Spring of 2005, Algerians seemed to comprise the largest component (20 percent), followed by Syrians (18 percent), Yemenis (about 17 percent), Sudanese (15 percent), Egyptian (13 percent), Saudis (12 percent), and the remaining 5 percent came from an assortment of other countries.[95] In October 2005, the U.S. military released statistics about foreign nationals that had been taken captive in Iraq; of the 312 detainees, Egyptians represented 25 percent, followed by Syrians (21 percent), Sudanese (13 percent), and Saudis (10 percent); the rest were from some 23 different mostly Muslim countries, though were also a few from Europe and even one American.[96]

It is difficult to get precise statistics on the number of jihadists in Iraq. "No one fully understands how many movements and cells are involved," as Cordesman observes, and "the high degree of compartmentalization, isolation, and independence" of the global jihad movement "enables them to operate as informal, distributed networks" and "makes their strength extremely hard to estimate."[97] Both the Obaid and Cordesman analysis and the U.S. military statistics contradict an earlier study by terrorism expert, Reuvan Paz, who analyzed death notices on Islamist websites during the period 2003–2005 and found that the majority of "martyrs" in Iraq were Saudi. Obaid and Cordesman claim that Paz's study was later discounted after it was determined that 22 percent of the Saudi martyrs listed were in fact alive and well in Saudi Arabia.[98]

Obaid and Cordesman suggest that the perception that Saudis are overrepresented in the foreign jihad movement in Iraq may be attributed to the fact that because they are Saudi they are simply able to bring more attention to their martyrdom. In their words:

> Saudis are the most sought after militants; not only because of their cash contributions [Saudis arrive in Iraq with an average of $10,000–15,000], but also because of the media attention their deaths as "martyrs" bring to the cause. This is a powerful recruiting tool. Because of the wealth of Saudi Arabia, and its well developed press, there also tends to be much more coverage of Saudi deaths in Iraq than of those from poorer countries.[99]

Assuming that Cordesman and Obaid are correct regarding the make-up of foreign jihadists in Iraq, it is worth observing that this would mean that there is no significant presence of fighters from any country that has experienced its own jihad in recent years—that is, there were no Afghans, Palestinians, Bosnians, Chechnyans, or Kashmiris to speak of in the CSIS analysis. The one notable exception to this pattern seems to be the Algerians, who again if the CSIS study is right, comprise the largest percent (20 percent) of the foreign fighters in Iraq.

Sageman's analysis of global jihadists, incidentally, also failed to unearth substantial numbers of jihadists from Afghanistan, Bosnia, Chechnya, Kashmir, or Palestine. He also found that Algerians were the exception. There may be several reasons for the Algerian exception. First, the Algerians may well be suffering from what Harvard terrorism expert Jessica Stern has characterized as an addiction to jihad. In the late 1990s, when Stern interviewed jihadists in Pakistan, she found that many seemed to be, as one mujahid fighting in Kashmir told her, "addicted to jihad" likening the feeling to a heroin addiction but observing that jihad was even harder to kick, "a person addicted to heroin can get off it if he really tries, but a mujahid cannot leave the jihad, I am spiritually addicted to Jihad."[100]

Second, in addition to not being able to wean themselves from the primal excitement of the battlefield or the sense of camaraderie they find there, Algerian jihadists may be simply unwelcome at home. Unlike other jihadists who for the most part fought non-Muslims or foreign occupying powers, Algerian jihadists waged jihad against their fellow Algerian Muslims. And a particularly brutal jihad it was, characterized by massive slaughters and throat-slittings. It would hardly be surprising to find that once the hostilities died down, those who had actively persecuted the jihad against their own countrymen and women—not to mention children—the vast majority of them fellow Muslims, would have been pressured to pack up and leave.

As to how Saudis find their way to jihad, Cordesman and Obaid provide a revealing case study in their analysis. They tell of a 24-year old Saudi student from one of the large tribes who, prior to the invasion, had no known history of radicalism. After he started paying attention to news reports of innocent Iraqis dying, however, the anti-U.S. rhetoric at the local mosque began to resonate with him and this reaction was noticed. Eventually he was invited to attend private sessions with a local cleric who began to inculcate him as well as other young men who had displayed a similar vulnerability with the notion that it was their religious duty to perform jihad in defense of Islam. Soon the recruits were being encouraged to contribute money or help in the actual fight. Eventually the cleric introduced his young followers to a Yemeni who began indoctrinating them about suicide operations. After a few weeks, the young men were then asked to purchase tickets to Damascus, Syria, where they were told they would be met by someone who would take them to Iraq.

From Damascus, the Saudis were taken to the Iraqi border where they were met by Iraqi handlers who brought them to Tikrit where there were other Saudis. There the young men were given their assignments—all suicide missions. Three of the four accepted their martyrdom missions but the fourth declined, realizing that he did not want to drive a truck full of explosives into a designated target. Eventually he realized that the only way that he would be able to escape his handlers alive however would be to pretend to accept another suicide mission and then use it as a cover to escape. Thus he was able to get back to Saudi Arabia, where he came to the attention of the authorities when he applied for a new passport, which triggered an automatic investigation. Both he and the cleric who originally recruited him face terrorism charges and could spend years in prison if convicted. The Yemeni, who it would turn out was a known member of al Qaeda, was killed by Saudi security forces following an attack on the Interior Ministry in December 2004.[101]

While foreign insurgents may comprise only a small fraction of the total insurgency in Iraq, by the fall of 2005, senior U.S. military commanders in Iraq were convinced that the insurgency had "been hijacked by a terrorist campaign," as Army Maj. Gen. Richard Zahner, the top U.S. military intelligence officer in Iraq put it. As Zahner noted, "by Zarqawi becoming the face of this thing, he has certainly gotten the funding, the media and, frankly, has allowed other folks to work along in his draft."[102]

Zarqawi was first introduced to the American public by Secretary of State Colin Powell during his February 2003 speech to the United Nations when he was described as an "associate and collaborator of bin Laden" and part of the "sinister nexus between Iraq and the al Qaeda terrorist network."[103] But it would not be until October 2004, according to Zarqawi's own statements, that he became the official leader of al Qaeda in Iraq.

A high school drop-out and one of ten children of a Bedouin herbal healer, *Newsweek* magazine reported that Zarqawi was first exposed to the ideology of jihad while serving time in prison in his native Jordan for sexual assault.[104] After his release, he eventually headed over to Afghanistan but by that time, the war was already over and instead of fighting jihad, he got a job at a jihadist newspaper. Eventually he returned to Jordan where he again landed in jail, this time for plotting to overthrow the monarchy. In 1999, after he was freed in an amnesty, he returned to Afghanistan where he ran his own training camp after reportedly being rejected for membership in al Qaeda.[105]

At some point, Zarqawi headed over to Iraq where, just as Colin Powell indicated in his United Nations address, he became the nexus of al Qaeda in Iraq. In addition to being believed to have been behind most of the insurgency violence directed against civilians in Iraq up until he was killed in June 2006, he was also linked to the assassination of an American diplomat, Lawrencey Foley in Jordan in October 2002, and was convicted of plotting to use chemical weapons to target Jordanian and U.S. government buildings in Jordan. Authorities speculate that the attacks could have resulted in some 80,000 deaths had the plot not been foiled.[106] Zarqawi is also believed to have personally beheaded a number of hostages including Nicholas Berg, an American civilian contractor;[107] South Korean, Kim Sun Il;[108] and British-Iraqi CARE worker, Margaret Hassan.[109] How Zarqawi got connected to al Qaeda reveals how interconnected this global movement really is.

According to an Internet statement written by Seif Al-Adl, variously described as al Qaeda's military commander or its head of security, it was he who introduced Zarqawi to the al Qaeda leadership.[110] Al-Adl says that he first heard about him from Abu Qatada, a Jordanian-Palestinian cleric then living in London who had followed Zarqawi's sedition proceedings during the 1990s. Eventually Zarqawi and Qatada had to have gotten together because both were eventually convicted in absentia in Jordan for plotting to blow up various U.S. and Jordanian targets during the millennium celebrations.[111]

Abu Qatada is a well-known figure in al Qaeda circles. Tapes of his sermons were found at the apartment of the 9/11 hijackers "Hamburg cell." Qatada was also a spiritual mentor of Zacarias Moussaoui, the "twentieth" hijacker, as well as Richard Reid, the "shoe-bomber."[112] He had links to the French cell that plotted to blow up the U.S. embassy in Paris.[113] And it was Abu Qatada that the Madrid commuter train bombers tried to contact to get permission to blow themselves in lieu of surrendering to the police lined up outside their safehouse. The Spanish judge who requested that he be extradited to Spain to stand trial for his role in the Madrid train bombings as well as the 9/11 attacks, described him as bin Laden's "spiritual ambassador to Europe."[114]

Jihadists in the West

If the Madrid commuter train bombings exposed new links between members of the global jihad movement, they, along with subsequent terrorist attacks in Europe, in Amsterdam and then in London, revealed that Europe faced the threat of jihadist sleeper cells located inside its own immigrant communities.

Law enforcement authorities in Spain tied the Madrid bombings to a group of mostly Moroccan immigrants; the man who killed Theo Van Gogh, the Dutch filmmaker who had made a film critical of Islam, was a second-generation dual-nationality Moroccan-Dutch citizen who Dutch authorities learned was connected to the European branch of the Moroccan Islamic Combatant Group; and three out of four of the London bombers were British citizens of Pakistani descent, while the fourth was a Jamaican-born convert to Islam.

Robert S. Leiken, an immigration specialist at The Nixon Center and the Brookings Institution studied the backgrounds of 212 terrorists who had been arrested or convicted of terrorist acts or plots targeting Western Europe and North America during the ten-year period 1993–2003 and discovered that an astonishing 86 percent were the work of Muslim visitors or first- or second-generation Muslim immigrants, many of them illegal, while the remainder were the work of converts to Islam (8 percent) or African-American Muslims (6 percent).[115] The results of his study led Leiken to conclude that "though most immigrants are not terrorists, most terrorists are immigrants."[116]

While the record does seem to suggest that Europe may indeed have sleeper jihadist cells resident in its midst, most jihadist plots that have been uncovered in the United States appear to be the work of foreign hit squads—many of them coming in from Europe. Al Qaeda expert Peter Bergen has documented this phenomenon; among the cases he cites include the 1993 World Trade Center bombing, in which the master bomber, Ramzi Yousef, came from Pakistan apparently with the express purpose of launching an attack; the 9/11 attacks as we have seen were carried out by a foreign hit squad; the millennium bomb plot against Los Angeles airport was the plan of an Algerian Ahmed Ressam radicalized in Italy who came to the United States from Canada to launch his attack; Richard Reid, the shoe-bomber, was a British citizen who tried to blow up an American Airlines flight en route to the United States from Paris with explosives hidden in his shoes; and Zacarias Moussaoui, the "twentieth" hijacker, who came to the United States from France specifically to advance a terrorist plot. The evidence, in fact, was so overwhelming that Bergen concluded that "the greatest threat to the United States from al Qaeda, its affiliated groups, or those animated by al Qaeda's ideology, emanates today from Europe."[117]

Some experts have tried to link Europe's radicalized Muslims to certain demographics. In Europe, Muslims comprise a much higher percentage of the general population relative to the United States. Muslims are now believed to represent 7–10 percent of France's total population; 4.4 percent of the Netherlands; 3.7 percent of Germany and Belgium; 2.7 percent of Britain; but less than 2 percent of the population in the United States.[118] (Since most of the above countries do not keep track of Muslims per se, most of these statistics have to be regarded as at best guesses.) Muslims in Europe have higher rates of unemployment than Muslims in the United States. In Britain, for example, the national unemployment rate is 5 percent but among Muslims it is 15 percent. British Muslim men between the ages of 16–24, the age group most likely to become radicalized, experience unemployment rates nearly six times the national average.[119] A study quoted by the *Economist* during the riots that spread across France's Muslim neighborhoods in November of 2005, estimated that in France the unemployment rate of "visible minorities" is three times the national average of 10 percent, or about 30 percent; another study quoted by the same magazine estimated that the unemployment rate for youth in "sensitive urban zones" (read areas with high concentrations of "visible minorities"—that is, generally people with roots in both Africa and Islam) runs as high as 40 percent.[120] Some 50 percent of the French prison population is Muslim.[121] In the Netherlands, immigrants have unemployment rates triple the national average.[122] By contrast, Muslim immigrants in America have higher average incomes and educational achievement than the average American.[123]

Curiously, while the above statistics would seem to suggest that there are reasons to be concerned that Europe's disenfranchised Muslims represent a pool of potential radicals, what is curious is that those who have actually carried out terrorist strikes in Europe were not particularly disenfranchised at all, except perhaps by their own volition.

The suspected leader of the Madrid cell, for example, was Sarhane Ben Abdelmajid Fakhet, a thirty-five-year-old real estate agent who originally came to Madrid from his native Morocco on a scholarship to study economics. Though he never appears to have completed his course of study, he found gainful employment selling real estate. Spanish newspapers reported that his boss regarded him as a "wonderful salesman," even at times a top salesman, though in the months before the attacks he had stopped coming to work.[124] If he held himself aloof from his coworkers, he did not appear to be particularly lonely given the fact that in the year prior to the attacks, as the *New Yorker* reported, he had married a sixteen-year-old Moroccan girl who appeared to share his beliefs as she cloaked herself entirely in black, even wearing the face veil and gloves, typical of a certain Salafi style.

Likewise, the twenty-six-year-old Dutch-Moroccan, Mohammed Bouyeri, who shot and then tried to saw off the head of Dutch filmmaker, Theo Van Gogh, in November 2004 for making a film critical of Islam, did not appear to be particularly disenfranchised except by choice.

Bouyeri was the son of Moroccan immigrants and had studied computer science at a Dutch university. He was by all accounts a good student. His high school teachers described him as having shown promise. He spent five years studying social work in college though he never obtained his degree. His radicalization, friends reportedly recalled, started with the 9/11 attacks and then accelerated after his mother's death from cancer in 2002, when he fell under the influence of a radical Syrian cleric.[125]

Months before the killing, Bouyeri had come to the attention of the Portuguese police when they discovered that suspects in a plot to murder the designated head of the European Union Commission were traveling in a VW van belonging to Bouyeri and one of the chief suspects had shared an apartment with him in Amsterdam. The authorities, however, discounted Bouyeri considering him to be an acquaintance of the so-called Hofstad group and did not put him under suspicion as someone who was capable of carrying out his own attack. Later, the Dutch police would conclude that the Hofstad group had in fact helped Bouyeri plan Van Gogh's murder. Investigators also linked the cell to the 2003 suicide attacks in Casablanca. In 2005, yet another member of this group would be arrested in Tours, France—a Russian who German authorities described as having "excellent contacts to Islamic extremists in Chechnya."[126]

At his trial, Bouyeri explained to the three-judge panel why he had shot the Dutch filmmaker multiple times and then tried to saw off his head with a knife, "I acted purely in the name of my religion," he was quoted as saying, and then added, "I can assure you that one day, should I be set free, I would do the same, exactly the same."[127] Then, turning to address the victim's mother directly, he stunned the courtroom by saying, "I don't feel your pain. I have to admit that I don't have any sympathy for you. I can't feel for you because you're a non-believer."[128]

Spanish and German counterterrorism authorities have concluded that Bouyeri's rapid descent into Islamic radicalism is not at all atypical and have seen cases where the radicalization took place in even less time—in weeks as opposed to months or years. German Interior Minister Otto Schily observes that this "metastasizing" makes it even more difficult to track Islamist extremists as law-enforcement agents are not dealing with a "hierarchical organization acting in a closed manner," but rather have to contend with groups that may or may not "act within a logistically linked network."[129] Counterterrorism officials and analysts reportedly see these small, autonomous cells such as those which carried out the Casablanca, the Madrid, and the London attacks as part of the "jihad of individualized terrorism," a tactical approach advocated by Mustafa Setmarian Nasar, the author of a 1,600-page document entitled "The Call for global Islamic Resistance," which has been widely circulated on jihadist websites. In the document, Nasar, who has been described by his fellow jihadists as "the greatest jihadi theoretician in our time," suggests that the because jihadist organizations can no longer count on state sanctuaries such as Afghanistan or Sudan now that there has been a full-scale war declared against them, they must increasingly adopt the approach of "*nizam, la tanzim*" or "system, not organization." Or, as Brynjar Lia, a Norwegian researcher who is writing a biography of Nasar, describes Nasar's theory,

> there should be "an operative system" or template, available anywhere for anybody, wishing to participate in the global jihad either on his own or with a small group of trusted associates, and there should not exist any, "organisation for operations." Hence, the global jihadist movement should discourage any direct or organisational bonds between the leadership and the operative units. Leadership should only be exercised through "general guidance" and the operative leaders should exist only at the level of small cells. The glue in this highly decentralised movement is nothing else than "a common aim, a common doctrinal program and a comprehensive (self-) educational program."[130]

The leader of the London subway and bus bombers, Mohammed Siddique Khan, 30, also seemed to be a fellow with plenty of opportunity. He was a well-regarded elementary school teacher and the married father of a small child. He was also active in his community, with an avid following at the local teenage-drop-in center, the place he is believed to have first met and recruited two of the other bombers, the two other British citizens, ages 18 and 22, also of Pakistani descent. It is so far unknown how the bombers came into contact with the fourth bomber, a married, twenty-year-old Jamaican convert to Islam and father of a one-year-old with another child on the way.

Authorities suspect that Khan and one of the others attended training camps in Pakistan and Afghanistan and may have met with members of al Qaeda.[131] The production style of the martyrdom videotape Khan left behind was consistent with other al Qaeda videos. In the video, which was broadcast on Al-Jazeera, he explained the reason for his intended action:

> I and thousands like me are forsaking everything for what we believe.
>
> Our driving motivation doesn't come from tangible commodities that this world has to offer.
>
> Our religion is Islam—obedience to the one true God, Allah, and following the footsteps of the final prophet and messenger Muhammad . . . This is how our ethical stances are dictated.
>
> Your democratically elected governments continuously perpetuate atrocities against my people all over the world.
>
> And your support of them makes you directly responsible, just as I am directly responsible for protecting and avenging my Muslim Brothers and sisters.
>
> Until we feel security, you will be our targets. And until you stop the bombing, gassing, imprisonment and torture of my people we will not stop this fight.
>
> We are at war and I am a soldier. Now you too will taste the reality of this situation.[132]

Shehzad Tanweer, the 22-year-old bomber, was described by those who knew him well as another unlikely candidate for a suicide operation. They said his real passion in life was cricket, though they did note that he idolized bin Laden as his "personal hero." According to a Pakistani cousin, he was obsessed by the idea that "America had made Muslims suffer all over the world."[133]

London authorities suspect that the London cell may have had links to a missionary group, the Tablighi Jamaat (TJ) ("Preaching Party" in Arabic), that is widely suspected of funneling potential recruits to militant jihad. Tanweer's family has already indicated that Shehzad was involved with the group and Khan lived near a Tablighi mosque.

TJ was founded in India in the 1920s to counter Hindu proselytizing and has since grown to become Islam's largest missionary group. It maintains a network of part-time preachers who travel around mosques and college campuses throughout the world preaching an interpretation of Islam not incompatible with Salafi jihadists. Like the Salafis, TJ rejects Shiism as a form of heresy and preaches that Islam must be the hegemonic religion in the world. Tablighis are also taught to reject most of the canon of Islamic jurisprudence and are told to instead rely only on their reading of the Koran—along with a few Tablighi texts, of course, to help them interpret it. TJ also teaches its adherents that it is necessary to disengage from society in order to strengthen themselves as Muslims.

The movement has grown so powerful that its annual gathering in India draws hundreds of thousands of adherents each year and is second only to the hajj in the number of adherents it attracts.[134] TJ's efforts have helped make Islam Europe's fastest-growing religion and the group is planning to erect a 40,000-person capacity mosque in London in time for the 2012 Olympic Games, which will make it the biggest mosque in Western Europe. Its architect, Ali Mangera, was quoted as saying that the mosque is intended to be "more than a mosque. The whole idea behind it is to break down barriers."[135]

The organization, which is led by a hereditary dynasty and has no formal organization, refrains from publishing any statements. Though it claims to have no political agenda and disavows armed struggle, many experts believe that radicals have used it in order to identify potential recruits. Khaled Abou El Fadl, a professor of Islamic law at UCLA who was himself a former member of the organization, says the TJ teaches its adherents "that the modern world is an aberration, an offense, some form of blasphemy." He cautions that "by preparing people in this fashion, you are preparing them to be in a state of war against this world." El Fadl suggests that there is a distinct possibility that militants may very well be "fishing in the Tablighi pond" as what he sees as the "alienated and withdrawn social attitude" the Tablighis foster presents them with an opportunity to be exploited.[136] As one senior U.S. law enforcement official observed, TJ functions as "a natural entree, a way of gathering people together with a common interest in Islam," providing an opportunity for extremists to use the organization as a kind of "assessment tool to evaluate individuals with particular zealousness and interest in going beyond what's offered."[137]

Not surprisingly, a number of TJ adherents have indeed found their way to the global jihad. Famous jihadists who have passed through the gates of TJ include John Walker Lindh, the "American Taliban"; Herve Loiseau, a French convert to Islam who froze to death fighting Americans in Afghanistan in late 2001; Zacarias Moussaoui, the "twentieth" hijacker; Richard Reid, the "shoe bomber"; Jose Padilla, the "dirty bomber"; the "Lackawanna Six," a group of Yemeni-Americans who went to al Qaeda training camps in Afghanistan in the spring of 2001; Jeffrey Leon Battle, an American citizen and member of the "Portland Seven," a group of Muslims from Oregon who were convicted of having tried to help the Taliban and al Qaeda after the 9/11 attacks; Iyman Faris, an Ohio truck driver, who pled guilty to having trained with bin Laden and plotted to blow up the Brooklyn Bridge—he was arrested after being named by KSM; Djamel Beghal, who confessed to plotting to blow up the U.S. embassy in Paris; and the Moroccans who carried out the May 16, 2003 synagogue bombing in Casablanca, Morocco; and the Moroccans were also linked to the Hofstad group in Holland which was behind the Van Gogh beheading. Terrorism expert B. Raman of the South Asia Analysis Group claims that TJ played a significant role in the founding of two terrorist groups, Harakat ul-Mujahideen and the Harakat ul-Jihad-i Islami.[138] Alex Alexiev, of the Center for Security Policy, contends that the TJ was also one of the founders of the Islamic Salvation Front in Algeria. TJ was also used as a cover for mujahidin traveling to Pakistan and Algeria during the 1980–1990s, where they would ultimately be funneled to active jihad fronts.

In the United States, the TJ actively recruits members in prisons and the African-American community. Michael J. Heimbach, the deputy chief of the FBI's international terrorism section told the *New York Times* that "We have a significant presence of Tablighi Jamaat in the United States," and said that there is evidence to suggest that al Qaeda has used the group and continues to use them to recruit members.[139]

Theodore Dalrymple, a psychiatrist who worked over a decade in a British prison explains the appeal of Islam to criminals who need a pretext to abandon their life of crime. Because Islam is "feared by society at large," he writes, by converting, "prisoners are killing two birds with one stone: they are giving themselves boundaries so that they can commit no more crimes—at least of the ordinary kind—and yet do not feel that they have capitulated to the demands of society."[140]

Reid and Padilla, it is noteworthy, converted to Islam while they were incarcerated. In August 2005, authorities in Los Angeles uncovered a terrorist plot that was conceived in a prison in California. Kevin James, who converted to Islam while serving time in the New Folsom State Prison in California planned to attack various targets including military facilities, the Israeli Consulate, El Al airlines offices, and Los Angeles area synagogues to commemorate the 9/11 attacks. In prison, prosecutors allege he organized a group called the Jam'iyyat Ul-Islam Is-Saheeh or the Assembly of Authentic Islam to recruit other inmates to wage jihad against the U.S. government and supporters of Israel.[141]

Most experts believe that prison recruits are highly prized by radical Islamists because of their already deeply ingrained hostility to the status quo. One expert, J. Michael Waller, cites the number of Muslim prison recruits in American prisons as somewhere between 15–20 percent of the total prison population. In his testimony before a U.S. Senate subcommittee he stated, "They are overwhelmingly black with a small, but growing Hispanic minority. It appears that in many prison systems, including Federal prisons, Islamist imams have demanded, and been granted, the exclusive franchise for Muslim proselytization to the forceful exclusion of moderates." In his testimony, Waller quotes a federal corrections official's comments regarding Islamist efforts to recruit violent felons in American prisons: "It's literally a captive audience, and many inmates are anxious to hear how they can attack the institutions of America."[142]

Daniel Pipes, an expert on radical Islamism, has documented many cases in which converts to Islam have been involved in terrorism related activities in countries as far a field as Australia, France, Germany, Italy, Netherlands, United Kingdom, the United States, and even non-Western countries such as the Philippines.[143]

On November 9, 2005, a female convert to Islam made a name for herself when she became the first European Muslim woman to carry out a suicide bombing. Muriel Degauque, a Belgian, aged 38 blew herself up in an attack on an American military patrol near Baquba, Iraq.

Degauque, who was thirty-eight at the time of her death, was raised in a Roman Catholic family and converted to Islam after a rebellious phase in which she dabbled in drugs and had a series of failed relationships, some of them with

Muslim men who exposed her to Islam. Her faith is believed to have taken a radical turn only after she met her husband, Issam Goris, who American forces shot and killed shortly after Degauque launched her suicide attack, before he could detonate the explosives he was wearing. The Belgian police were aware of the couple's radicalism and had warned authorities in Iraq that they had intercepted phone calls suggesting that a Belgian couple had entered Iraq and were planning to blow themselves up.[144]

Degauque's mother told a French newspaper that after her daughter married Goris, the son of a Belgian man and Moroccan woman, she became "more Muslim than the Muslims" and from then on seemed only to live for Islam, even learning Arabic.[145]

Throughout Europe, authorities are convinced that jihadists are increasingly trying to recruit European converts to Islam because of their ability to travel freely and blend into Western communities without arousing suspicion. There appear to be plenty of converts to draw from, if a report recently released by France's domestic intelligence agency and cited by *Le Figaro* is correct; some 30,000 to 50,000 French people convert to Islam every year.[146] Antoine Sfeir, a French scholar who closely follows this trend, says that there is cause for concern as many young Europeans see Islamic terrorism as "a kind of combat against the rich, powerful, by the poor men of the planet."[147]

Even some middle-aged and privileged European radicals seem to be unable to resist the allure of Islamic radicalism. Take the case of Isabelle Coutant-Peyre, an admittedly anti-American, anti-imperialist attorney in Paris, who married her client, the notorious Carlos the Jackal, the Venezuelan Marxist-Leninist who admitted to killing as many as 1,500 people on behalf of the Palestinian liberation movement.[148] Their wedding took place while they were both still married to other people and Carlos was serving out a life-sentence for a triple murder he had orchestrated in 1975. He converted to Islam in prison and wrote a book, *Revolutionary Islam*, in which he argues that only radical Islam has the "transnational force capable of standing up to the enslavement of nations."[149]

CHAPTER 5

Who Is Really Fighting Jihad?

And spend for God's cause.
The Koranic citation scrawled atop the "Golden Chain," a handwritten list of names found in Bosnia that U.S. prosecutors believe al Qaeda has called upon for the bulk of its financial support.

B in Laden became a person of intense national interest after he was implicated in the two embassies bombings in east Africa in 1998. To get a better grip on their understanding of the exiled Saudi and the extent of his resources, the Clinton administration created a joint task force composed of members of the National Security Council (NSC) as well as the CIA's Illicit Transactions Group (ITG) to look into the matter. Though the U.S. government assumed at this point that the multimillionaire bin Laden was the primary financier of the Islamic radicals that had carried out the attacks, Washington also had to rule out the possibility that there were other individuals or governments involved.

Thus, for the first time, the U.S. government launched an in-depth review of what was really known about bin Laden and his organization. The exercise would by no means be in vain. By the end of its investigation of all of the available intelligence, the task force would reach a startling conclusion: bin Laden was no where near as rich as everyone had assumed, nor was he the primary source of support for his terrorist organization.[1] Rather, as the task force's director, William Wechsler, put it, in reality al Qaeda was "a constant fund raising machine" and the bulk of its support came from a network of charities in Saudi Arabia.[2] The task force would also be astonished to learn that not only were these Saudi charities financing bin Laden's organization, but they were also funding jihadist groups in some twenty countries from Algeria, to Bosnia, to Chechnya, to Egypt, to Kashmir, to Pakistan, to the Philippines. Every where that jihad had been waged, the investigators were finding Saudi funds behind the effort. Naturally this raised some troubling questions: What exactly was Saudi Arabia doing underwriting all these various jihads and why hadn't America been apprised of its ally's activities?

Eventually the audit trail would lead back to the 1979 Islamic revolution in Iran and the radical takeover of the Grand Mosque in Mecca. These events took the Saudi regime totally by surprise and brought an end to the halcyon days when Saudi Arabia, the birthplace of Islam, really did seem to be well, not a harsh desert after all but uniquely blessed. Those were the days, in the aftermath of the oil embargo of 1973, when the world's demand for oil seemed to support almost any oil price and the kingdom's treasury was overflowing with petrodollars and Saudi princes were building palaces and yachts and blowing money like crazy in all the world's pleasure spots. While they may have been famous for their excesses in the West, back home, the royal family knew that they had to share at least some of their new wealth with the people of Saudi Arabia, many of whom could remember what it was like to have to survive on goats' milk and dates, and so they were also spending billions of their petrodollars building an infrastructure that would take the kingdom from a medieval-like tribal society straight into the modernity of the twentieth century, bypassing an industrial revolution and an enlightenment. While the Saudi people would not be able to participate in their own governance, or hold their rulers accountable through elections or a free press, the Koran would continue, at least in theory, to serve as the constitution, and they were happy to consent to the absolute rule of their monarch, in exchange for generous cradle-to-grave welfare benefits and the happy illusion that any difficult work to be done in the kingdom could be outsourced to guest workers who were now flooding the kingdom from the world's rich and poor countries alike.

But in 1979, the fantasy started to unravel. First the revolutionary leader in Iran, the Ayatollah Khomeini, displaced Iran's monarch and immediately started inciting the region's people to rise up against their unIslamic rulers, singling out the Saudi royals as particularly contemptible and corrupt given that they had the special responsibility of overseeing the holy places of Islam. Then, months later, radical Islamists, right under the nose of the monarchy, seized control of the Grand Mosque in Mecca and during the annual hajj no less. Suddenly the Saudi monarchy realized that it was in danger of losing its grip on power.

To fight this new revolutionary strain of Islam, it was clear to the Saudis that they would have to face off the radical Shiite element in Tehran with their own version of revolutionary Islam. Thus, to maintain their custodianship of the holy lands of Islam, not to mention the vast oil reserves that lay beneath their surface, the Saudi royals did just as their forebear had done before them: they used Islam as a weapon. Their unique interpretation of Islam, after all, had always been the royal family's source of power.

Recall that the Saud family originally seized control of the Arabian peninsula sometime in the late 1700s only after an ancestor, Muhammad bin Saud, had the genius to align himself with a radical Islamic cleric, Muhammad Abd Al-Wahhab. In the cleric's creed Saud saw exactly the type of ideology he needed to convince his fellow Muslims that they should rise up and follow his lead against the various rival warlords. This was because Wahhab preached a creed that said that anyone who did not practice his particular version of Islam was a heretic, an apostate, and should, according to Islamic law, be put to death. To Saud,

Wahhab provided all the justification he required to get his fellow Muslims to help him dispose of his enemies. And so, armed with this creed, Saud was able to seize control of much of the peninsula. Centuries later, in 1932 when one of his descendants, Abdul Aziz, declared the birth of the nation-state of Saudi Arabia, it was Wahhab's creed that would become the de facto state religion.

And so, in 1979, when the Saudi monarchy again needed to dispose of some enemies and bolster its legitimacy, the royal family did exactly as their ancestor before them had done: they set out to convince the Islamic world that theirs was the only true interpretation of Islam. Thus the Saudis began a massive campaign to spread Wahhabism throughout the world. Over the next twenty years they would spend some $70 billion to promote their message, publishing educational materials, funding missionaries, building mosques, and Islamic centers and funding schools and madrassahs and Muslim student associations.[3] To get a sense of just how much money the Saudis spent in this effort, compare the fact that at its peak, the Soviet Union never spent more than a billion dollars a year on propaganda, according to Alex Alexiev, an expert on religious and ethnic conflict at the Center for Security Policy.[4]

The U.S. government would eventually recognize that the Saudi effort was not just limited to missionary activities and educational programs. The Soviet invasion of Afghanistan on Christmas Eve of 1979 had provided another type of opportunity for the Saudis to enhance their standing in the Muslim world by coming to the defense of a Muslim nation. The idea of funding a modern Islamic army invigorated the Saudis. Royals and subjects alike were eager to make their own personal contribution to the cause, the jihad going on in Afghanistan. Over time, the Saudis found themselves financing jihads everywhere from Central Asia to the Philippines to the former Yugoslavia to the Russian republic of Chechnya. Saudi-financed jihadists would even target the United States and eventually even the kingdom itself. In short, Saudi Arabia became the primary source of financing of the global jihad movement.

Al Qaeda's Funding Sources

To track how exactly this situation came about, let us review the evolution of al Qaeda. At this point we know enough about its history to differentiate its development into four distinct phases:

1. *The founding phase* (1979–1989) during and just after the Soviet War in Afghanistan when the global Islamic army first assembled and later resolved not to dissolve even after the Soviets departed but to continue waging jihad throughout the globe until the Islamic caliphate was once again restored.
2. *The organizational phase* (1990–1996), or the period in Sudan, when al Qaeda was regrouping in Sudan, participating in its "Islamic experiment" and creating alliances with other organizations throughout the world.
3. *The militant phase* (1996–2001), or the period in Afghanistan, under the Taliban when al Qaeda officially declared war against Americans and Jews and began mounting its own terrorist operations.

4. *The defensive phase (2001–present)*, the period since the United States started retaliating for the attacks of 9/11, sending the core on the run and forcing the network to assume all of the operational aspects.

We can safely assume that each of the above phases had its own cost structure. During the *founding phase*, for example, when al Qaeda was still in its embryonic stage in Afghanistan, and was known only as the "Arab Afghans" or the mujahidin, the funding requirement was nevertheless substantial. The mujahidin, after all, were fighting an openly declared war against the Soviet Union. Muslim fighters were being recruited from all over the world, requiring help with travel expenses, and once assembled at the war's staging bases, in need of training, housing, food, and of course enough arms to confront the world's second greatest military power.

But because this was an open campaign and there was plenty of support for their struggle, this was a relatively easy time to secure funding. Both the United States and Saudi Arabia saw the Arab Afghans as freedom fighters, as a counterforce to communism and Arab nationalism (which had tilted toward the Soviet Union) and both countries were more than willing to commit substantial funds to jihad in Afghanistan. Over the course of the war, each country contributed about $3 billion though the Saudis may have even contributed a bit more.[5]

The United States distributed its funding through the Pakistani national security agency, the Inter-Services Intelligence (or ISI) as it wanted to maintain plausible deniability so as not to incite a direct confrontation with the Soviets. Saudi Arabia, on the other hand, sent much of its aid through state-controlled charities such as the Muslim World League, the International Relief Organization and the Islamic Relief Agency. As Jason Burke, author of *Al Qaeda: Casting a Shadow of Terror*,[6] put it, the kingdom "needed reliable and honest men on the ground to manage the flow of funds to their recipients," and "bin Laden was one [of them]."[7]

Rich Saudi donors, excited by the prospect of funding a modern jihad, were another important source of funding for the mujahidin. Many analysts believe that such private donations may have even exceeded the Saudi regime's official contribution. Like the Saudi government, these private individuals also generally donated through charities, though in some cases they may have made their contributions directly to leaders such as Azzam and bin Laden. As the 9/11 Commission found:

> Bin Ladin understood better than most of the volunteers the extent to which the continuation and eventual success of the jihad in Afghanistan depended on an increasingly complex, almost worldwide organization. This organization included a financial support network that came to be known as the "Golden Chain," put together mainly by financiers in Saudi Arabia and the Persian Gulf states. Donations flowed through charities or other nongovernmental organizations (NGOs). Bin Ladin and the "Afghan Arabs" drew largely on funds raised by this network, whose agents roamed world markets to buy arms and supplies for the mujahideen, or "holy warriors." Mosques, schools, and boardinghouses served as recruiting stations in many parts of the world, including the United States. Some

were set up by Islamic extremists or their financial backers. Bin Ladin had an important part in this activity. He and the cleric Azzam had joined in creating a "Bureau of Services" (Mektab al Khidmat, or MAK), which channeled recruits into Afghanistan.[8]

After the Soviets pulled out of Afghanistan in February 1989, the United States effectively abandoned the country as well, and Afghanistan quickly fell into a state of feuding warlords. Though Azzam had wanted to make sure an Islamic state was installed in Kabul before leaving, he was never able to accomplish this as he was killed in a car bombing on his way to a mosque that November. Bin Laden, for his part, was not really not interested in staying amid the chaos of the endlessly squabbling Afghans and though he had an outstanding invitation to move his organization to Sudan, where the Sorbonne-trained Hassan al-Turabi was in the midst of his own "Islamic experiment," he returned home to Saudi Arabia to work on a plan to install Islamic governance there.

Bin Laden's plans would have to change, however. Shortly after he returned to Saudi Arabia, in August 1990, Saddam Hussein invaded and the annexed a neighboring state, the petroleum monarchy of Kuwait. After bin Laden failed to convince the Saudi monarchy that the mujahidin veterans of the Soviets in Afghanistan should be the ones to guard the kingdom's oil wealth—as opposed to American infidel forces—bin Laden quickly made himself unwelcome in his homeland by publicly criticizing the royal family. The regime quickly cracked down. His passport was taken away and his family was pressured to rein him in. Knowing that he was now a marked man in the kingdom, in April 1991, bin Laden solicited the help of a sympathizer in the royal family and managed to get back his passport under the pretense that he was going to attend an Islamic conference in Pakistan.[9] Instead he headed straight for Sudan.

In exchange for safe harbor in Sudan, bin Laden agreed to help the newly established Islamic regime with its war against the Christian and animist south and with some of its infrastructure needs, such as the construction of a highway from the capital to the Red Sea. During this *organizational phase* in Sudan, bin Laden would also spend a considerable amount of his personal money to "set up a large and complex set of intertwined business and terrorist enterprises," according to the 9/11 Commission.[10] He then used these various businesses as a cover to accumulate weapons and ammunitions from all over the world—from western Europe, China, Malaysia, the Philippines, Ukraine, and Belarus.

During the years in Sudan (1991–1996), bin Laden set up a network of enterprises in the Balkans to support the mujahidin that were fighting jihad in Bosnia and when another front opened up in Chechnya, he established an NGO in Azerbaijan to support that conflict as well.[11] He also established ties with jihadist organizations in Saudi Arabia, Egypt, Jordan, Lebanon, Iraq, Oman, Algeria, Libya, Tunisia, Morocco, Somalia, and Eritrea; and less formal relationships with jihadist groups in Africa including Chad, Mali, Niger, Nigeria, and Uganda; and in Southeast Asia in, Burma, Thailand, Malaysia, and Indonesia. He referred to his network of alliances at this point in time as the "Islamic Army Shura," according to the 9/11 Commission.[12]

Under the tutelage of the Sudanese leader, Turabi, bin Laden was also willing at this stage to form alliances with Shiite as well as Sunni groups. He was in fact, very keen to establish a relationship with the Iranian-backed Hezbollah in order to learn how exactly they had carried out their suicide strikes on the U.S. and French peacekeeping forces in Lebanon in 1983.[13]

During the time in Sudan, bin Laden's organization did not mount any of its own terrorist operations, though bin Laden did issue a fatwa in 1992 that called for Muslims to wage jihad against the U.S. forces stationed in the Arabian peninsula and he would also later take credit for having trained the Somalian militias who killed eighteen U.S. famine-relief forces in Mogadishu in 1993.

How bin Laden funded his various enterprises during this period in Sudan remains something of a mystery. Recall that up until the NSC-CIA joint-task force investigation in the wake of the 1998 embassies bombings, U.S. government officials assumed that bin Laden was financing his terrorist network himself through his personal inheritance, widely estimated to be around $300 million. The task force, however, would reach a different understanding.

Through extensive interviews with bin Laden family members and Saudi government officials, the task force would conclude, to their surprise, that during this period, bin Laden was only receiving about a million dollars a year from his share of the family business and then only up until 1994 or so, at which point the Saudi government, angered by bin Laden's sedition, forced the bin Ladens to sell Usama's share of the family fortune only to freeze the proceeds of the sale, effectively cutting him off from his inheritance.[14]

Not surprisingly, this would cause a downward spiral in most of bin Laden's enterprises, most of which had not been set up to be viable businesses in the first place. Forced to drastically cut back his expenditures, this created a fair degree of dissent in his organization and there were complaints that bin Laden was miserly.[15]

In May 1996, after the UN imposed sanctions on Sudan for harboring bin Laden after it was discovered that he was implicated in a plot to kill Hosni Mubarak, the Egyptian president on a state visit to Ethiopia the year before, the Sudanese decided that they had enough of bin Laden and insisted that he leave. Since the Saudis had revoked his citizenship in 1994, bin Laden was now a man without a country and an international pariah at that.

His only option was to return to Afghanistan. What a low point this was for bin Laden. The negative turn in his financial condition had caused some of his followers to abandon him. Those who remained were now forced to follow him to Afghanistan where the future must have looked very uncertain. Bin Laden still had a few contacts among the warlords who were still fighting amongst themselves, now years after the Soviets had left, but by the time he moved back to Afghanistan, the country was rapidly falling under the rule of an extremist group of former madrassah students going by the name of the Taliban, with whom bin Laden had no prior relationship. Adding to the uncertainty was the grim fact that for the first time in his entire life he was truly broke.

Now back in Afghanistan in 1996, as the 9/11 Commission would later conclude, the only hope bin Laden had of resolving his desperate financial situation was to revive the network of wealthy financial donors that he had called upon to fund the mujahidin during their jihad against the Soviets.[16] In only a matter of months, thanks to the largesse of these wealthy donors, who he referred to as the "Golden Chain," he would be firmly back on his feet.[17]

Though the United States government would begin to piece together bin Laden's financial picture soon after the 1998 embassies attacks, it would not be until well after the 9/11 attacks, that the U.S. government would obtain any kind of understanding of al Qaeda's finances. To give the reader some idea just how little the intelligence community knew prior to 9/11, this is how the CIA characterized their knowledge of the situation in April of 2001 in an internal memo cited by the staff of the 9/11 Commission:

> Usama Bin Ladin's financial assets are difficult to track because he uses a wide variety of mechanisms to move and raise money[;] . . . he capitalizes on a large, difficult-to-identify network with few long-lasting nodes for penetration. It is difficult to determine with any degree of accuracy what percentage of each node contributes to his overall financial position. Gaps in our understanding contribute to the difficulty we have in pursuing the Bin Ladin financial target. We presently do not have the reporting to determine how much of Bin Ladin's personal wealth he has used or continues to use in financing his organization; we are unable to estimate with confidence the value of his assets and net worth; and we do not know the level of financial support he draws from his family and other donors sympathetic to his cause.[18]

Eventually, however, the 9/11 Commission would piece together enough information to lead them to conclude that during the militant phase, while al Qaeda was headquartered in Afghanistan under the Taliban, its annual budget was approximately $30 million a year. Two-thirds of the annual expenditures, or $20 million went to the Taliban alone, as a form of protection payment. The rest of the money was spent on al Qaeda's infrastructure—its training camps, living expenses, and salaries for its core staff and full-time operatives—and of course the investments the organization made to form various alliances and fund operations carried out by other groups, with whom it wanted to sustain an association to extend the organization's reach.

As the 9/11 Commission Staff noted, what was surprising about al Qaeda's budget was how minimal was the amount of money that was devoted to actual terrorist operations. The 9/11 attacks, for example, are estimated to have cost between $400,000 and $500,000;[19] while the 1998 U.S. embassies bombings are believed to have cost no more than $10,000; and the U.S.S. Cole bombing, only $5,000–$10,000.[20]

During this militant phase, bin Laden also funded other terrorist organizations in the Middle East and even as far away as Indonesia and the Philippines. Sometimes the funding would be used to found new jihadist groups, at other times, the al Qaeda monies went to fund actual operations. As the 9/11 Commission staff concluded:

> Al Qaeda's cash contributions helped establish connections with these groups and encouraged them to share members, contacts, and facilities. It appears that

al Qaeda was not funding an overall jihad program but was selectively providing start-up funds to new groups or money for specific operations. Generally, however, al Qaeda was more likely to provide logistical support and cover and to assist with terrorist operations than to provide money.[21]

Al Qaeda's primary interest when it came to funding independent groups was to fund operations targeting U.S. and Western interests, in which case it would rely on the affiliate to command and carry out the attack with their own personnel.

In the case of the millennium plots to bomb the Los Angeles airport (coordinated by Abu Zubaydah, a top military commander) and destroy tourist sites in Amman, Jordan (Zubaydah and Zarqawi were convicted and sentenced to death in absentia in connection with this second plan), for example, al Qaeda is believed to have lent the cells some financial support and to have allowed the conspirators to train at al Qaeda's facilities, although in neither case do authorities believe that bin Laden either commanded or controlled either operation directly.

It was bin Laden's very willingness to work with independent organizations that experts believe ultimately made al Qaeda strong and flexible enough to survive the post 9/11 destruction of most of its infrastructure as well as the capture and killing of so many of its core membership.

Islamic Charities

As to who was funding al Qaeda, eventually the 9/11 Commission would conclude that most of the organization's money came from a network of sympathetic or corrupted Islamic charities and "well-placed financial facilitators" who collected money from donors primarily in the Gulf region who in some cases knew where their funds were headed, but in many cases, the donors were unwitting and thought they were funding genuine relief missions.[22]

The network of charities that were funding al Qaeda first emerged during the jihad in Afghanistan. In addition to the funds that the Saudi government was providing, were private funds that people like Azzam and bin Laden solicited throughout the Islamic world, calling on fellow Muslims to funnel their *zakat*, or fundamental religious obligation to give charity, to their fellow Muslims in Afghanistan as they were now under attack by the Soviets. To handle the flow of donations, the Saudis used a variety of charities, some existing, some set up for this new purpose. The charities would funnel money provided by Saudi princes, businessmen and bankers, as well as the cash contributions made by ordinary citizens that were being placed in boxes that had been set up all over the kingdom for the purpose of collecting cash donations to go to the mujahidin. Every good Muslim was encouraged to help: the message was if they could not fulfill their individual duty to take up arms themselves in this defensive jihad on behalf of their fellow Muslims in Afghanistan, at least they could contribute some cash.

In fact, it was exactly one of these Saudi charities, the Muslim World League, that first set up Azzam in the jihad business. He was asked to head up their office in Peshawar, Pakistan, and from there coordinate the relief activities.[23] Other Saudi charities that also came to the aid of the mujahidin, included the International Islamic Relief Organization and the Saudi Red Crescent, a Muslim version of the Red Cross. Over time, however, much of the money destined for Afghanistan flowed through Azzam's MAK or "Bureau of Services," the organization that later metamorphosed into al Qaeda.[24]

While it is understandable that U.S. officials may not have paid much attention to the role Saudi charities were playing in Afghanistan given that the Americans were on the same side what they should have noticed was that even when the Soviets pulled out and the mujahidin dispersed to other battle fronts, the network of Saudi charities stayed in place and continued to fund new jihads.

It is important to understand that there was nothing nefarious about the Saudi relief efforts per se. Giving to charity is an ingrained part of Islam as well as Saudi culture. This is because zakat or alms-giving, is one of the "five pillars" of Islam, the set of fundamental obligations Muslims are expected to fulfill as the minimal demonstration of their faith (the other pillars include the oath of faith, daily prayers, fasting, and a once-in-a-lifetime pilgrimage to Mecca).

In Saudi Arabia, where the Koran is considered to be the country's basic system of law or constitution, zakat donations are regarded as a form of income tax or welfare or even foreign aid payment. In fact, there is no income tax in Saudi Arabia. Instead, individuals and businesses are expected to pay at least 2.5 percent of their net assets (think of it as a wealth as opposed to income tax) to support the Islamic community. (Foreign companies, on the other hand, are obliged to pay income taxes but not zakat.)

The Koran gives specific instructions as to whom Muslims are expected to give charity—namely, the poor, the captive, those in debt, those who fight jihad, and to travelers who do not have access to personal funds:

> As-Sadaqât (here it means Zakât) are only for the Fuqarâ' (poor), and Al-Masâkin (the poor) and those employed to collect (the funds); and for to attract the hearts of those who have been inclined (towards Islâm); and to free the captives; and for those in debt; and for Allâh's Cause (i.e. for Mujâhidûn—those fighting in the holy wars), and for the wayfarer (a traveller who is cut off from everything); a duty imposed by Allâh. And Allâh is All-Knower, All-Wise. (Sura 9:60)

Moreover, the Koran does not just encourage Muslims to perform their obligation of alms-giving, rather it warns them that serious consequences will follow if they do not spend their money in the "Way of Allah." Specifically, they are told that they should expect "a painful torment" on Judgment Day and that any gold and silver they may have hoarded will be used as a branding iron to negatively mark their foreheads, flanks, and backs on Judgment Day.

> O you who believe! Verily, there are many of the (Jewish) rabbis and the (Christian) monks who devour the wealth of mankind in falsehood, and hinder (them) from the Way of Allâh (i.e. Allâh's Religion of Islâmic Monotheism). And those who hoard up gold and silver [Al-Kanz:the money, the Zakât of which has

not been paid], and spend it not in the Way of Allâh, -announce unto them a painful torment. On the Day when that (*Al-Kanz*: money, gold and silver, etc., the *Zakât* of which has not been paid) will be heated in the Fire of Hell and with it will be branded their foreheads, their flanks, and their backs, (and it will be said unto them): "This is the treasure which you hoarded for yourselves. Now taste of what you used to hoard." (Sura 9:34–35)

Because Saudi Arabia has always counted on oil revenues to fund the bulk of its national budget, the kingdom has never really needed to put into place a system that would keep track of the zakat donations. People could pay their zakat in cash, anonymously, in boxes that were provided at mosques or even shopping malls. No accounting system was really necessary, not when the regime had petrodollars. It was God's work to punish those who failed to pay their zakat.

It is important to recognize that Saudi zakat donations were by no means all going to fund militant activities, not even in the various places that jihads were being fought, such as Bosnia and in the Palestinian areas. As the 9/11 Commission acknowledged, the kingdom's zakat donations have "long provided much-needed humanitarian relief in the Islamic world."

Al Qaeda facilitators were able to take advantage of the zakat obligation by approaching sympathetic worshippers or imams to ask them for help in funding the various jihads which they were always careful to characterize as defensive jihads. Thus they could capitalize on the Islamic principle that says that in the case of a defensive jihad, the contribution becomes incumbent on all Muslims, individually, and not just the Muslim community as a whole, as is the case with offensive jihad, or jihad to expand the realm of Islam.

Terry McDermott, author of *Perfect Soldiers*, a book about the 9/11 hijackers, interviewed an American official who worked in the Gulf during the 1990s and who had knowledge of how the al Qaeda facilitators:

> Throughout the region, there was this classic sort of money collector—the guy who was hanging out at the mosque, checking out the scene, basically casing the mark, who would invariably be some old guy with lots of money. A religious guy, probably. The collector would come up alongside him, make his pitch very persistently, and the mark would write him a check.[25]

The U.S. official also recalled that one of the collectors who worked his territory was none other than KSM, the mastermind of the 9/11 attacks. At the time, KSM was ostensibly employed by the Qatari Ministry of Electricity and Water, and living in Doha. However, now U.S. investigators believe that this was only the official story. In reality he appears to have spent most of his time when he was supposedly employed by the Qatari government, traveling around the Gulf, raising money for jihad. As the U.S. official would recall:

> Khalid Sheikh Mohammed was a collector, a guy who would collect the money from the street collectors. He was in and out, operating in Qatar, UAE, Bahrain. The money network was very informal. A guy in the Philippines would call a guy in Dubai who would call Khalid Sheikh Mohammed. It would be a chain of

telephone calls, and Khalid would send the money. . . . There were a very large volume of very small transactions involving several hundred people and he was in the middle of it. He's a mover of money. It was never clear if he was connected to anyone above, if there was a line going up . . . .Khalid Sheikh Mohammed would pop up in Dubai, Pakistan, occasionally Kuwait. He became an issue for me only because he was on my turf. So far as we could tell this was a bunch of individual actors.[26]

In addition to collectors like KSM, and from the above account it would seem that there were many such characters. Saudi charities would also actively solicit donations from wealthy donors themselves. The charities would then funnel the donations to branch offices they maintained in the various jihad hotspots. They would use these branch offices to send food, clothing and medicine. In many cases, mujahidin going to and from the front were provided cover by the charities to facilitate travel and other jihad activities like procurement. In places like Bosnia, it was not at all uncommon to find International Islamic Relief Organization (IIRO) identity cards on fallen mujahidin.[27]

Saudi zakat donations would usually peak during Ramadan, when Muslims are expected to fulfill another fundamental obligation and observe a month-long fast (during daylight hours) and faith becomes foremost on the Muslim mind. In fact, when the 9/11 Commission would later come to some understanding of al Qaeda's funding-raising cycle, they would notice that there did seem to be a Ramadan effect.[28]

According to a report published by U.S. News & World Report, as early as 1994, Riyadh began receiving complaints from French government officials that Saudi money was funding Algerian terrorists, and around the same time, complaints from the Clinton administration that Saudi funds were also fueling Hamas' suicide bombing campaign in Israel.[29] That same year, according to the magazine, Saudi embassy statements boasted that Saudi charities had sent some $150 million in aid to Bosnia, which was now a full blown jihad front.

As to how the Saudi charities came to be used to fund these various jihads, let us examine what investigators have managed to uncover so far about some of their activities. By now investigators have concluded that some charities appear to have been set up with the sole purpose of funneling money to al Qaeda, while others were simply infiltrated by al Qaeda operatives who set out to take advantage of the general lack of oversight in many foreign branches of the largest Saudi charities.[30] Most of the money that the charities collected came from wealthy Saudi donors, some of whom were aware of the ultimate destination of their contributions, others most certainly were not.

Some of the major charities that have been linked to funding al Qaeda include the umbrella organization, the Muslim World League (and its affiliate the Rabita Trust), the International Islamic Relief Organization, the al-Haramain Islamic Foundation, and the Benevolence International Foundation.

The offices of the IIRO, for example, were routinely used to coordinate the flow of fighters and weapons into Bosnia, Chechnya, and Kashmir and according to a former employee, some fifty percent of its annual budget went to fund training camps in Afghanistan and Kashmir.[31]

Bin Laden's brother-in-law, Mohammed Jamal Khalifa, ran a branch office in the Philippines, through which he funded local jihadist groups such as the Abu Sayyaf group and the Moro Islamic Liberation Front. Khalifa is also believed to have provided funds to Yousef and KSM while they were living in Manila, plotting to blow up a dozen trans-Pacific airliners (the Bojinka plot) and to assassinate President Clinton and Pope John Paul II on their upcoming visits to the Philippines.

The Manila office of IIRO also had "the majority of Hamas members in the Philippines" on its payroll according to a CIA report.[32] In 1994, Khalifa was arrested by the Jordanian government under suspicion that he had been involved in a plot to bomb public places, including movie theaters in Amman, the Jordanian capital. Though he would ultimately be acquitted, he would admit to knowing and having supplied money to the alleged bombers.[33]

After the 1998 embassies bombings in east Africa, Kenyan authorities shut down the local branch of the IIRO after they implicated it in the attacks. In 1999, police in India would arrest an IIRO employee, Sayed Abu Nasir, for plotting to bomb U.S. consulates in the subcontinent. Nasir told Indian investigators that the charity was funding dozens of jihad training camps in Pakistan and Afghanistan. Western intelligence officials would also eventually find IIRO payments funding Hamas operations in Gaza and the West Bank. Canadian intelligence would also uncover evidence suggesting that the IIRO was also funding Zawahiri's group, Islamic Jihad.[34]

There is even an IIRO link to 9/11: One of the Saudi "muscle" hijackers, Fayez Banihammad, told his father that he was going to work for the IIRO before he left home for the last time to participate in the 9/11 attacks.

The IIRO was established by its parent organization, the Muslim World League, in 1978 to provide financial assistance to Muslim victims of natural disasters. Headquartered in Jeddah, Saudi Arabia, the charity has branches all over the world. It reportedly receives some seventy percent of its estimated annual budget of $46 million directly from the Saudi government and relies on private contributions for the balance of its budget.[35]

The IIRO's parent organization, the Mecca-based Muslim World League (MWL), was founded by the Saudi government in 1962 to "promote Islamic unity." According to congressional testimony provided by Steven Emerson, the MWL promotes jihad, defends terrorism, criticizes Judaism and Christianity as "false" religions, and as late as 2005, its Canadian branch had a tract on its website which saying Jews "do not deserve to be human and naturally do not qualify to enter Heaven."[36] In March 1997, the head of the MWL stated that at that point in time the Saudi government had already provided the organization with more than $1.33 billion.[37]

According to Lorenzo Vidino, a terrorism analyst at Washington-based Investigative Project, the MWL was created by the Muslim Brotherhood, specifically Said Ramadan, son-in-law of Hassan al-Banna, the founder of the Muslim Brotherhood.[38] This is significant because, as we saw in the last chapter, the

Muslim Brotherhood has had a profound influence on the global jihad movement. Mamoun Fandy, an expert on radical Islam, described the role the Muslim Brotherhood played thus:

> The germs of many of these organizations we are dealing with, you can see the ideological strands coming from the teachings of the Muslim Brotherhood, the beginning that the world is one of jahiliyya, a world of ignorance that has to be changed and has to be changed by force, not changed by basically a da'wa, or a call; it had to be changed by the power of the gun.[39]

Recall also that it was the MWL that first sent Azzam to the jihad in Afghanistan, to run its branch office in Peshawar, Pakistan where he was expected to facilitate the flow of mujahidin to the Afghan front. Thanks to the largesse of the MWL, Azzam was able create the organization that would metamorphose into al Qaeda, the Maktab Al-Khidamat.

It was not until the mid-1990s that the MWL itself began to be linked to terrorism. In 1995, the MWL was found to have purchased the travel tickets and provided spending money to the would-be assassins of the Egyptian president Hosni Mubarak, who al Qaeda plotted to kill on an upcoming state visit to Ethiopia, according to one of the plotters.[40]

In 1998, one of the MWL's former employees, Wadih el-Hage, was implicated in the 1998 United States embassies bombings in Africa.[41] Another former MWL employee, Ihab Ali, was found to have trained to be bin Laden's personal pilot and would turn out to have taken flying lessons at the same flight school Zacarias Moussaoui, the "twentieth hijacker" did in Norman, Oklahoma.[42]

In 2001, an MWL affiliate, the Pakistani-based Rabita Trust was even designated as a sponsor of al Qaeda by the U.S. Treasury Department[43] and the United Nations.[44] In March 2002, a host of organizations associated with the Virginia-based branch of the MWL were raided in a terrorist-financing probe, Operation Green Quest.[45] In January 2004, the Senate Finance Committee asked the Internal Revenue Service for its records on the MWL, along with more than two dozen other Muslim charities "as part of an investigation into possible links between nongovernmental organizations and terrorist financing networks."[46] (Among the other Muslim charities the Senate Finance Committee named were the Rabita Trust and the IIRO.)

Another Saudi charity (also named by the Senate Finance Committee) alleged to have been heavily infiltrated by jihadists was the U.S. branch of Al-Haramain Islamic Foundation, a charity headquartered in Riyadh, and at least partially funded by the Saudi government. At its peak , Al-Haramain had over fifty branch offices worldwide and an annual budget between $30 and $80 million.[47] While the organization's ostensible mission was to spread the message of Saudi Islam, covertly it appears to have been involved in sponsoring terrorism.

As early as 1996, the CIA established that Al-Haramain was funding Egyptian radicals as well as the jihad in Bosnia. In 1999, Moscow was claiming that Al-Haramain was funneling money and arms to Chechen rebels under the cover of humanitarian relief. In 2002, Manila airport authorities in the

Philippines even found explosives in the baggage of one of the organization's employees. By 2003, counterterrorism officials could implicate over twenty of its branches in sponsoring terrorism either through cash contributions or weapons shipments.[48]

In addition to the Saudi-government sponsored charities, there were also charities set up by wealthy individuals that somehow got involved in sponsoring the global jihad movement. In 1987, Adel Batterjee, a wealthy Saudi businessman, founded a charitable organization, Lajnat al-Birr al-Islamiah, based in Jeddah with offices in Pakistan to provide humanitarian aid to refugees of the Soviet War in Afghanistan. The organization was a close affiliate of Maktab Al-Khidamat, the precursor organization of al Qaeda, the organization started by Azzam to provide financial and logistical support to the streams of Muslim fighters that were coming from all over the world to fight jihad in Afghanistan.

After Saudi authorities shut down Lajnat during one of the kingdom's crackdowns on suspected Islamist militants in the early 1990s,[49] Battarjee relocated the organization to Illinois under the name of Benevolence International Foundation (BIF). Eventually the BIF would have operations in some ten countries all ostensibly providing humanitarian relief.

In 1997 Batterjee resigned and named a close associate of bin Laden, Enaam Arnaout, to the head of the organization.[50] After Arnaout was indicted on terrorism-related charges, it would emerge that in March of 2002, in a raid of BIF's offices in Sarajevo, Bosnia, Bosnian authorities found what U.S. prosecutors later described as a "treasure trove" of information.[51] According to a court filing, "BIF had in its Sarajevo office a computer file labeled 'Tareekh Osama,' or 'Osama's History,' " which contained scanned images of documents that chronicled the "formation of al Qaeda," and included the minutes of its founding meetings, which contained the text of al Qaeda's original bayat:

> The pledge of God and His covenant is upon me, to listen and obey the superiors, who are doing this work, in energy, early-rising, difficulty, and easiness, and for His superiority upon us, so that the word of God will be the highest, and His religion victorious.[52]

Also in these digital files were newspaper clippings featuring stories about mujahiden, personnel memos, an organizational chart, and a handwritten list of the names of wealthy Gulf businessmen who, the U.S. government alleges, had funded the mujahidin and who were referred to inside al Qaeda as the "Golden Chain." As prosecutors noted, "At the top of the list is a Koranic verse which states: 'And spend for God's cause.' "[53] Twenty names were then listed and after each name there was another name in parenthesis, which according to prosecutors likely indicated the intended recipient of the "donors," funds. "Usam" appeared after seven of the listings, while "Baterji" (an alternative spelling for Batterjee, most likely referring to BIF's founder) appeared after six of the listings.[54] Aside from the Koranic inscription at the top of the list, the other indication that this may have been a list of donors al Qaeda called on was the fact that among the twenty names were six bankers, twelve businessmen, and including some of the wealthiest individuals in Saudi Arabia. Their combined net worth was estimated to be $85 billion, or 42 percent of the kingdom's gross domestic product in 2002. They were known to have given to charities, some of them having even founded their own foundations.[55]

The U.S. government would ultimately shut down the Benevolence International Foundation, designating it as a sponsor of terrorism in 2002. The government also accused Arnaout, in connection with BIF, with having funded al Qaeda and other jihadist activities in Afghanistan, Sudan, Bosnia, Chechnya and elsewhere during the 1980s–1990s.

After raising a vigorous defense in which his lawyers argued that "the United States intends to try Enaam Arnaout not for acts he committed in violation of United States laws, but rather for associations he had over a decade ago, before he relocated to this country, with people who were at the time America's allies but who are now its enemies," Arnaout ultimately pled guilty to non-terrorism-related charges of racketeering and conspiracy charges for his role in having diverted BIF funds to the mujahidin in Bosnia and Chechnya.[56]

As far as Batterjee was concerned, authorities would not catch up with him until December 2004, when the U.S. Treasury, pursuant to Executive Order 13224, finally succeeded in designating him as a sponsor of al Qaeda and bin Laden.[57] The Treasury's press release announcing the designation described BIF's founder like this: "Adel Batterjee has ranked as one of the world's foremost terrorist financiers, who employed his private wealth and a network of charitable fronts to bankroll the murderous agenda of al Qaida."[58] Soon after, the United Nations 1267 Committee would also add Batterjee's name to its list of terrorists linked to al Qaeda. However, in spite of these actions, which are supposed to result in all United Nations member states freezing the assets of and blocking any financial transactions with such sponsors of terrorism, Batterjee is believed to be living-at-large in Saudi Arabia.

The reader should note that when the "Golden Chain" was presented as evidence in a lawsuit initiated by the "9/11 Families United to Bankrupt Terrorism,"[59] the presiding judge in the case, U.S. District Judge Richard Casey, ruled that the document was inadmissible, finding, in his words, that it had "serious foundational flaws" in that there was "no indication of who wrote the list, when it was written, or for what purpose," and therefore he was forced to conclude that "the Court cannot make the logical leap that the document is a list of early al Qaeda supporters."[60] The judge's decision correctly underscored the fact that the 'Golden Chain' is at this point still no more than a list of some of the wealthiest individuals in Saudi Arabia—the individuals who al Qaeda would have undoubtedly tried to tap for financial support. To date, it should be understood, no evidence has been made public that any of the listed individuals knowingly sponsored or directly funded al Qaeda.

The difficultly in proving terrorism-financing cases has led to a certain degree of misunderstanding between the Islamic community and the American system of justice. When the judge in the Arnaout case announced his plea bargain, the court duly noted that "Arnaout does not stand convicted of a terrorism offense. Nor does the record reflect that he attempted, participated in, or conspired to commit any act of terrorism."[61] As the staff of the 9/11 Commission wrote, the judge's remarks generated a considerable amount of misperception, as "many people in the Islamic and Arab communities concluded that Arnaout had been vindicated of any charge of supporting terrorism. They interpreted the judge's refusal to apply the terrorism sentencing enhancement as a major defeat for the government."[62] However, as the Commission staff further noted, while senior FBI agents in the Chicago office agreed that accepting Arnaout's plea was the right decisions, they reportedly maintained their belief that "a trial would have allowed the government to lay out all its evidence against Arnaout in open court" and then the Muslim community would have seen for themselves as the staff reported, "what the agents saw—that Arnaout and BIF were supporting terrorism."[63]

The Saudis, it should be noted, were not the only financiers of the global jihad. The Global Relief Foundation (GRF), for example, was founded by one Rabih Haddad, a Christian Lebanese who converted to Islam, who like BIF's founder Batterjee, had worked at The Makhtab al-Khidamat, the precursor organization to al Qaeda in Pakistan in the early 1990s. The GRF was originally set up to raise money for Muslims in areas that had been devastated by war. Before it was shut down by the U.S. Treasury in October 2002 when it was linked to terrorist financing, the foundation had operations in 25 countries including the United States, Afghanistan, Kosovo, Lebanon, Bosnia, and Kashmir.[64]

As early as 1998, FBI agents in Chicago had come across evidence suggesting that GRF was not only offering humanitarian relief to fellow Muslims in war-torn regions; but it was also "actively involved in supplying and raising funds for international terrorism and Islamic militant movements overseas."[65]

By 2000, the FBI had linked GRF with such jihadist groups as the Algerian Armed Islamic Group, the Egyptian Islamic Jihad, Gama'at Al Islamyia, and the Kashmiri Harakat Al-Jihad El-Islam, as well as Al Qaeda and had evidence indicating that the GRF was providing the mujahidin "large quantities of sophisticated communications equipment."[66]

FBI investigators concluded that the GRF had essentially two types of donors: those who sincerely believed that they were providing charity to help the wounded, the widowed, and the orphaned of war and those who knew exactly where their money was really going—the latter group of donors could sometimes even be distinguished from the former by the pro-jihad messages they would scrawl on the memo lines of their contribution checks.[67]

GRF was also in the business of promoting the jihadist ideology. According to the U.S. Treasury:

GRF has stocked and promoted audio tapes and books authored by Sheikh Abdullah Azzam, who was co-founder, with UBL, of MK as well as spiritual founder of Hamas; these tapes and books glorified armed jihad. Despite Azzam's terrorist background, GRF enthusiastically promoted Azzam's materials to the public. GRF published several Arabic newsletters and pamphlets that advocated armed action through jihad against groups perceived to be un-Islamic.[68]

State Sponsorship

As we have previously noted, the full-scale investigation into bin Laden really did not begin until al Qaeda launched its first full-scale operation against American interests: the near simultaneous truck bombings of the American embassies in the East African cities of Nairobi, Kenya and Dar es Salaam, Tanzania, would occur in August 1998, and result in some 224 deaths and 5,000 injured, mostly Africans. Investigators would later conclude the attack cost no more than $10,000.[69]

Investigators would find indication that the planning for the attacks began years earlier, as early as 1993, when bin Laden was still in Sudan. This is supposedly when the targets were first selected. It would only be when investigators learned that everyone who had participated in the embassies operations had spent at least some time at al Qaeda's training camps in Afghanistan, that the U.S. government would begin to fully appreciate the true cost of the terrorist "Disneyland" bin Laden had built in Afghanistan.[70]

Now the U.S. government was much more interested in what the Saudi exile was doing in this remote and backward nation. Within weeks the National Security Council and the CIA would put together a task force to learn whatever could be found out about bin Laden—who was sponsoring him, where he was getting his money, and how big his terrorist enterprise really was.[71]

It would be years, however, before the U.S. intelligence community would gather a complete picture of the man and his operations—and not before the 9/11 attacks. The fact that terrorist operations were relatively cheap to launch would come as no surprise, but the cost of building and training a global jihad army were substantial and the amount of money bin Laden was able to raise was truly staggering to behold.

The CIA eventually estimated that prior to 9/11, al Qaeda's annual expenses were approximately $30 million, with about $10 million going toward maintaining the infrastructure—staffing and maintaining the training camps, feeding and housing the fighters, supplying the military apparatus, and funding the propaganda and public relations function outside of Afghanistan. The ideology had to be popularized; members had to be recruited, trained, and maintained; alliances had to be nourished. Even friendly regimes, like those in Khartoum and Kabul, had to be compensated for providing safe harbor. The balance of the organization's estimated annual budget—a whopping $20 million—went to pay off the Taliban for essentially as Rohan Gunaratna, author of *Inside Al Qaeda*, put it, allowing Afghanistan to be turned into a kind of "terrorist Disneyland."[72] While it may not have exactly pleased bin Laden to have to pay such exorbitant fees to Mullah Omar, the Taliban leader who liked to refer to himself as the "Commander of the Faithful," an Islamic title that no one had dared adopt for a thousand years,[73] and whose professed goal was to set up a pure Islamic state given the fact that bin Laden was supposed to be the head of the Islamic vanguard and his brother-in-arms, he really had no choice but to pony up or get out.

In spite of the costs, the benefits of having unfettered use of Afghanistan were incalculable. Whereas in Sudan, bin Laden was always forced to maintain a relatively low profile so as not to alienate the regime in Khartoum or jeopardize its standing in the international community, in Afghanistan, there was no central government either strong enough or interested enough in what the world thought to bother to keep bin Laden in check.

The Taliban did not seize control of Kabul until September 1996, a month after bin Laden issued his first public fatwa declaring war on the U.S. forces still remaining in the Arabian peninsula. And then, even when the Taliban did take over the remainder of the country, the former madrassah students would turn out to be far better hosts to the emerging global jihad movement than the Islamic regime in Khartoum.

First of all, the Taliban, like bin Laden, were serious about imposing an Islamic state. Though their vision of what this should be like would turn out to be a bit harsher than bin Laden would have preferred have (the Taliban shut girls out of all educational opportunities, which bin Laden reportedly opposed), and there was occasionally some friction, there was enough of a shared vision between the two parties that, according to the findings of the 9/11 Commission, bin Laden was willing to swear an oath of fealty to the Taliban leader, Mullah Omar, thus cementing his ties with the Afghan regime.[74]

The Taliban for the most part did not stand in bin Laden's way. They did not try to stop him from opening up training camps or inviting jihadists from all over the world to train in the al Qaeda facilities. The Taliban even capitalized on the situation, picking out reinforcements from the ranks of the mujahidin coming to train with al Qaeda to replenish its own ranks.[75] Because of this ever-ready supply of new enlistees, the Taliban would be able to maintain its advantage over rival factions who never ceased competing for control of Afghanistan, even after the Taliban had installed itself as the new government of Afghanistan. (John Walker Lindh, the "American Taliban," for example, claims that he joined the Taliban to take up arms against the Northern Alliance, one of the rival factions, and never the U.S. forces, as has widely been alleged.) The 9/11 Commission estimates that from the time bin Laden returned to Afghanistan in May 1996 until the American-led forces invaded in October 2001, at least 20,000 men passed through al Qaeda's training camps in Afghanistan.[76] Other analysts have put the figures much higher. According to a CRS Report for Congress, estimates ranged anywhere from 20,000 to 60,000.[77]

While there is some indication that the Taliban may have been somewhat alarmed after bin Laden issued his 1996 fatwa, and may even have exerted some effort to rein him in at this point, over time, thanks to the source of revenue he was able to provide the regime, the Taliban became his staunchest ally.[78]

Bin Laden's ability to develop was also enhanced by the fact that during the period 1996–1998, bin Laden was still not considered to be a major threat by the U.S. intelligence community, although the CIA had by then set up a "virtual station" to track his activities after he issued his 1996 fatwa urging Muslims to attack U.S. forces in Saudi Arabia. In April 1998, when U.S. Ambassador to the United Nations Bill Richardson led the first high-level U.S. delegation to Kabul to ask the Taliban to expel bin Laden in light of his recently issued fatwa, the Taliban declined, saying that bin Laden was not a threat to the United States[79] and nothing much appears to have been done beyond this minor diplomatic effort. As one Defense Intelligence Agency analyst who covered the Middle East during the period recalled, the general thinking in the intelligence community was that "the jihadists were like men from Mars"[80] and required little serious thought. That this was indeed the prevailing attitude in the intelligence community is evidenced by the fact that in not one of the National Intelligence Estimates issued by the community during the 1990s, as U.S. News & World Report would later report, did the U.S. intelligence community ever issue a single NIE on the global jihad movement or al Qaeda, as the threat they posed was apparently not considered to be of the magnitude posed by such threats as ballistic missiles, migration, infectious diseases—examples of other topics that merited their own special reports.[81]

Likewise, though the intelligence community may have possessed information indicating that wealthy Saudis were funding al Qaeda's training camps in Afghanistan, as well as other terror-related activities, particularly with respect to the Arab-Israeli conflict, according to some inside reports there was apparently minimal interest in confronting one of America's most important allies with such negative information.

When a Chicago-based terrorism-financing probe uncovered information that a $1.2 million payment to Hamas had been made from a Saudi charity in 1998, a prosecutor working on the case later recalled that he got the distinct impression he should drop the lead. "Did someone say to me we can't do this because it would offend the Saudis? No," Mark Flessner was quoted as saying, "But was that always an undertone? Yes."[82] Flessner's recollection seems to have been corroborated by the findings of the 9/11 Commission staff which concluded that during the 1990s, "terrorist financing was not a priority for either domestic or foreign intelligence collection."[83]

There has been speculation that many American government officials have been reluctant to confront the Saudis about sinister activities not because of concerns that any negative feelings that would result would upset delicate national security concerns, but because these American officials have been looking out for their own personal interest. The Saudis famously employ legions of former U.S. government officials in various capacities after they leave government. The *Washington Post*, for example, quoted one anonymous source who claimed that he had overheard the then Saudi ambassador to the United States, Prince Bandar, once brag: "If the reputation then builds that the Saudis take care of friends when they leave office, you'd be surprised how much better friends you have who are just coming into office."[84] Robert Baer, a former CIA operative and author of the book, *Sleeping with the Devil: How Washington Sold our Soul for Saudi Crude*, has written that so many politicians have availed themselves of such Saudi largesse that what the Saudis have done could be caricatured as "Washington's 401(k) Plan."

There may have even been a degree of political correctness at work that impeded investigations into terrorist financing. According to the 9/11 Commission staff, law enforcement agents recalled that the climate before 9/11 was such that "Indicting or even investigating an Islamic charity or group of high-profile Middle Easterners required special sensitivity. Fears of selective prosecution or inappropriate ethnic profiling were always a consideration in going after a high-profile and sensitive target. Certainly, the evidence had to be strong before a prosecution would be considered. As one highly experienced prosecutor told the Commission staff, if the FBI had aggressively targeted religious charities before 9/11, it would have ultimately had to explain its actions before a Senate committee."[85]

And so, for whatever reason, there was no shortage of money in the global jihad "movement" prior to 9/11. There was so much money in fact, that as *U.S. News & World* Report reported, a mid-level Pakistani jihadist could count on making seven times his nation's average wage fighting jihad, or, as the magazine wryly concluded, "jihad had become a global industry, bankrolled by the Saudis."[86]

This was the environment then in which bin Laden was able to turn Afghanistan under the Taliban into a virtual magnet, drawing young Muslims who wanted to fight jihad from all over the world. After they arrived there, thanks to the safe harbor provided by the Taliban, he then had the luxury of selecting out the best and the most zealous of these would-be Muslim warriors to groom them for special missions against Western targets or deploy them to other jihad fronts—such as the Taliban's jihad against their fellow Muslims in the Northern Alliance or the Kashmiri jihad against the Indian state—where many of the young men, now sufficiently indoctrinated, hoped to die as martyrs for the Islamic cause.[87] As we have already seen, it was in the camps of Afghanistan that he was able to find the 9/11 hijackers, as well as most of the others who have carried out other terrorist attacks from Bali to Tunisia to Morocco to Turkey to Saudi Arabia to Spain.

It is curious that the 9/11 Commission was never able to find evidence that the Saudi government or any of its senior officials knowingly provided funding to al Qaeda. As the Commission staff duly observed, "While there have been numerous allegations about Saudi government complicity in al Qaeda, the Commission staff has found no persuasive evidence that the Saudi government as an institution or as individual senior officials knowingly support or supported al Qaeda."[88] The only blame that the 9/11 Commission would assign Saudi Arabia for its role in funding al Qaeda was its failure to properly oversee its charities even after recognizing that they had become corrupted.[89]

Congressional Research Service analyst Alfred B. Prados, however, remains less convinced that any definitive conclusion can ever be reached, given the difficulties in tracking terrorist financing:

> First, the relatively small amounts of money required for terrorist acts can easily pass unnoticed. Second, the structure of the Saudi financial system makes financial transfers difficult to trace. Personal income records are not kept for tax purposes in Saudi Arabia and many citizens prefer cash transactions. Third, Muslim charitable contributions (*zakat*) are a religious obligation, constituting one of the five "pillars of Islam." Contributions are often given anonymously, and donated funds may be diverted from otherwise legitimate charities. Moreover, Saudi

funding of international Islamic charities is reportedly derived from both public and private sources which in some cases appear to overlap, further complicating efforts to estimate the amounts involved and to identify the sources and end recipients of these donations.[90]

According to Gerald Posner, author of the book *Why America Slept: The Failure to Prevent 9/11*,[91] there are some puzzling omissions in the 9/11 Commission's report. Relying on two "government sources," Posner claims that during the interrogation of Abu Zubaydah, a high-ranking al Qaeda commander captured in Pakistan in 2002, U.S. authorities, in an effort to get Zubaydah to open up, pretended that he had been rendered to his native Saudi Arabia where, his interrogators hoped, because he would assume that he could face torture should he decide not to talk he would be more forthcoming. To the Americans great surprise, instead of becoming alarmed upon seeing the "Saudi" interrogators, he exhibited great relief and immediately gave them the phone numbers of a Saudi prince who he said would tell them what to do. The numbers turned out to be those of Prince Ahmed, a nephew of King Fahd, and the owner of the 2002 Kentucky Derby winner, War Emblem. When his interrogators challenged him on what he was saying, he tried to convince them that his connection was real by offering up the names of two additional princes and the chief of Pakistan's air force, who Zubaydah said had all known prior September 11, 2001 that an attack on America was planned for that day.

U.S. investigators were never able to fully pursue this lead, Posner claims, as within four months, the three Saudi princes would all die, and all in extraordinary circumstances. First, Prince Ahmed died of a heart attack—at the age of 43. Then, the next day, the second prince, Prince Sultan bin Faisal bin Turki al-Saud, 41, died in a car crash, on the way to Ahmed's funeral no less. Then, a week later, the third, Prince Fahd bin Turki bin Saud al-Kabir, 25, reportedly "died of thirst" alone in the Saudi desert. Finally, some seven months later, the Pakistani air force commander died in a plane crash on a clear day, according to Posner, along with his wife and fifteen top aides. As Posner would later write in a *New York Times* editorial following the publication of the 9/11 Commission Final Report, the government's supposedly exhaustive study of the 2001 attacks never addressed these allegations:

> Not only does the 9/11 report fail to resolve the matter of whether Mr. Zubaydah—who featured prominently in the now infamous Presidential Daily Briefing of Aug. 6, 2001—was telling the truth when he named Prince Ahmed and several other princes as his contacts, but they do not even mention the prince in the entire report. The report does have seven references to Mr. Zubaydah's interrogations, yet not a single one is from March, the month of his capture, and the time he made his startling and still unproven accusations about high- ranking Saudi royals.[92]

Posner's assertion is not entirely correct however. Prince Ahmed was one of the Saudi nationals who was flown out of the United States shortly after September 11, 2001. This is what the Commission had to say about allegations that some of these Saudis were linked to terrorism:

> The FBI interviewed all persons of interest on these flights prior to their departures. They concluded that none of the passengers was connected to the 9/11 attacks and have since found no evidence to change that conclusion. Our own independent review of the Saudi nationals involved confirms that no one with known links to terrorism departed on these flights.[93]

Moreover, there has been no further corroboration or substantiation of Posner's account to date, some three years after it first surfaced. Many close Saudi watchers have expressed extreme skepticism regarding Zubaydah's supposed allegations and at least one analyst has suggested that Posner's sources may be engaging in a disinformation campaign aimed at destroying U.S.-Saudi relations.[94]

Whatever the veracity of Posner's account, in the face of mounting pressure and once the kingdom began experiencing terrorist attacks at home, the Saudi government eventually did start cracking down on its out-of-control charities and terrorism sponsors. It began shutting down branches of Al-Haramain in 2002, starting with the branches in Somalia and Bosnia. The process would continue until finally, in 2004, the Saudi government found that so many branches of Al-Haramain—not to mention its other charities—had been corrupted that it announced that it was now not only dissolving the entire charity but that it was now putting in place an oversight entity that would "assume responsibility for the distribution of [all] private charitable donations from Saudi Arabia."[95] As of January 2006, however, the *Los Angeles Times* was reporting that senior U.S. counterterrorism officials were still complaining that Riyadh had yet to establish this oversight entity as promised.[96]

The 9/11 Commission would rule out official Saudi sponsorship of al Qaeda, and assert that "other than support provided by the Taliban in Afghanistan, there is no persuasive evidence of systematic government financial sponsorship of al Qaeda by any country either before or after 9/11."[97]

However, states have certainly sponsored other aspects of what we call the global jihad movement. As the U.S. State Department noted in its *Patterns of Global Terrorism—2003* in the case of Iran:

> Iran's record against al-Qaida remains mixed. After the fall of the Taliban regime in Afghanistan, some al-Qaida members fled to Iran where they have found virtual safe haven. Iranian officials have acknowledged that Tehran detained al-Qaida operatives during 2003, including senior members. Iran's publicized presentation of a list to the United Nations of deportees, however, was accompanied by a refusal to publicly identify senior members in Iranian custody on the grounds of "security." Iran has resisted calls to transfer custody of its al-Qaida detainees to their countries of origin or third countries for further interrogation and trial.[98]

Moreover, Iran's sponsorship of Palestinian jihadist groups has even been financial as the same State Department report noted:

> During 2003, Iran maintained a high-profile role in encouraging anti-Israeli activity, both rhetorically and operationally. Supreme Leader Khamenei praised Palestinian

resistance operations, and President Khatami reiterated Iran's support for the "wronged people of Palestine" and their struggles. Matching this rhetoric with action, Iran provided Lebanese Hizballah and Palestinian rejectionist groups—notably HAMAS, the Palestine Islamic Jihad, and the Popular Front for the Liberation of Palestine–General Command—with funding, safehaven, training, and weapons. Iran hosted a conference in August 2003 on the Palestinian *intifadah*, at which an Iranian official suggested that the continued success of the Palestinian resistance depended on suicide operations.[99]

Palestinian jihadist groups also obtain considerable support from Syria, another designated state sponsor of terrorism. Syria permits the various Palestinian groups to maintain "political and informational" offices in Damascus including the jihadist groups Hamas and Palestinian Islamic Jihad, even though the regime announced in May 2003 that the groups had "voluntarily" closed their offices in response to mounting international pressure.[100]

The Palestinian Authority using funds provided by Israel, the United States, and the European Union even contributes a portion of its revenues to the jihad against Israel. In December 2005, the Palestinian Authority approved a new law that provides monthly stipends to families of "shahids" or those who have given their lives to the Palestinian struggle. As an Israeli newspaper correctly reported, essentially the Palestinian Authority was approving monthly grants to the families of suicide bombers.[101]

Yet, as the U.S. Department of Treasury stated when it designated five charities as terrorism sponsors for providing financial supports to Hamas, the bulk of the organization's sponsorship comes from "donations from Palestinian expatriates around the world and private benefactors located in moderate Arab states, Western Europe and North America" and that like al Qaeda, the Palestinian organization "uses a web of charities to facilitate funding and to funnel money."[102] Such charitable sources allow Hamas to "hide the money trail" and, as Treasury noted, "While some donors may be aware of the intended use of their donations, too many innocent donors who intend for their money to be used to provide humanitarian services here or abroad, are unwittingly funding acts of violence when these funds are diverted to terrorist causes."[103]

The Council on Foreign Relations, a nonpartisan think tank that analyzes foreign policy issues, contends that the fact that jihadist groups have arranged their own nongovernmental sources of financing makes them more and not less robust than their state-sponsored peers. As the Council stated in a 2002 study:

Al-Qaeda differs from traditional, state-sponsored terrorist groups in one critical way: it is financially robust. Having developed multiple sources of support, it is free from the control of any government and able on its own to maintain its organizational infrastructure, communications systems, training programs, and operations. As such, it historically has been able to operate from failed or dysfunctional states. Indeed, when it was headquartered in Sudan and then Afghanistan, the al-Qaeda terrorist organization provided important financial support to its host state—instead of the other way around.[104]

Whether or not Saddam Hussein had any relationship with al Qaeda prior to the 9/11 attacks is not fully understood at this point, contrary to press reports. The 9/11 Commission, for example, has acknowledged that while there were various intelligence reports describing points of contact between the Iraqi regime and al Qaeda in the decade prior to 9/11, the panel was unable to conclude that any of these "contacts [had] ever developed into a collaborative operational relationship" and the panel reported that it had seen no "evidence indicating that Iraq cooperated with al Qaeda in developing or carrying out any attacks against the United States."[105]

In 2004, *Newsweek* reporter Christopher Dickey came across his files from when he was a reporter in Baghdad in 1993. In one memo he described attending a "jihad conference in Baghdad" also attended by, in his words, "Islamic radicals who hailed 'from Jakarta to Dakar,' as they liked to say. We're talking Chechens and Moroccans, Filipinos and Algerians—all sorts. There were so many of them, I couldn't even get a room at the Rashid Hotel where they were staying." Dickey also found newspaper clippings indicating that this was the second such conference and that the prior year's event had been attended by jihadists from all over the world including Sudan, which was then hosting bin Laden and Algeria, where there was a brutal jihad going on against the regime. One clipping even mentioned that the conference director, Izzat Ibrahim, a high-ranking Iraqi official in Saddam's regime, was urging Muslims worldwide "to conduct holy jihad against the U.S. and its allies." After the U.S.-led invasion, Ibrahim became No. 6 on the coalition's list of most-wanted Iraqis and was believed to be a leading figure in the insurgency until his death in 2005. As Dickey goes on to observe, "It's also worth remembering that at this point, in early 1993, Saddam had managed to keep his extensive biological weapons production capacity entirely hidden from the United Nations inspections team. They didn't even begin to get the goods on the germs until late 1994, and they couldn't prove he had a bioweapons program until 1995." As Dickey concludes, "So, let's not say there was no reason to worry about Saddam Hussein and terrorism. There was. And anyone who questions the war would be foolish to assume no weapons of mass destruction will be found, or to insist that no links with Al Qaeda could possibly exist. That's why you will note many politicians and pundits saying, very carefully, there seem to be no 'stockpiles' of weapons. There appear to be no 'collaborative' or 'operational' links to Al Qaeda."[106]

Any comprehensive analysis of former Iraqi regime documents and files has yet to be conducted, and there is still no consensus on the matter among those who have had access to confidential intelligence reports. For example, in January 2006, *Newsweek* magazine posted a 2002 briefing by the Pentagon on its website that described the problems the Pentagon was having at that point with the way the intelligence community (the IC) was assessing what was known about high-level contacts between the Iraqi regime and al Qaeda. In this report, written during the lead-up to the war, the Pentagon concluded that the intelligence community was now applying a new standard of rigor—in the Pentagon's words—a "standard that would not normally obtain—IC does not normally require judicial evidence to support a finding," and, according to the Pentagon, the IC was now consistently underestimating the "importance that would be attached by al Qaeda and Iraq to hiding a relationship." The Pentagon further charged that the IC was basing its assessments on the assumption that "secularists and Islamists will not cooperate even when they have common interests."[107] While the mainstream media has consistently reported that no link existed between Saddam Hussein and al-Qaeda, it is, in fact, too early to tell what the real story is. Most of the files recovered from the Baathist regime have yet to be translated much less analyzed and there is still not enough information available yet to reach any kind of definitive conclusion at this point in time.

Illegal Enterprise and Other Sources

While there have been several reports suggesting that al Qaeda has relied on a variety of illegal enterprises to fund its activities—opium production in Afghanistan, for example, or trading in illegal gemstones—the 9/11 Commission was unable to find, in its words, "persuasive evidence" that "al Qaeda relied on the drug trade as an important source of revenue, had any substantial involvement with conflict diamonds, or was financially supported by any foreign government." Or, as the Staff reported:

> In addition to the lack of affirmative evidence, there are substantial reasons to believe that al Qaeda has no role in drug trafficking: al Qaeda members are geographically hemmed in and are unable to travel as the narcotics business demands. Trafficking would unnecessarily expose al Qaeda operatives to risks of detection or arrest. Moreover, established traffickers have no reason to involve al Qaeda in their lucrative businesses; associating with the world's most hunted men would attract unwanted attention to their activities and exponentially increase the resources devoted to catching them. Furthermore, Al Qaeda neither controls territory nor brings needed skills and therefore has no leverage to break into the sector.
>
> Allegations that al Qaeda has used the trade in conflict diamonds to fund itself similarly have not been substantiated. Commission staff has evaluated the sources of information for these various public reports raising the diamond allegations. These include reports of journalists, the United Nations, and certain nongovernmental organizations investigating this issue. The FBI conducted an intensive international investigation of the conflict diamond issue, including interviews of key witnesses with direct knowledge of the relevant facts, and found no evidence of any substantial al Qaeda involvement; the CIA has come to the same judgment. Additionally, detained operatives have since reported that al Qaeda was not involved in legal or illegal trading in diamonds or precious stones during its Afghan years. We have evaluated the U.S. government investigations in light of the public reports to the contrary, the relative veracity of the sources of information, and the best available intelligence on the subject, and see no basis to dispute these conclusions. There is some evidence that specific al Qaeda operatives may have either dabbled in trading precious stones at some point, or expressed an interest in doing so, but that evidence cannot be extrapolated to conclude that al Qaeda has funded itself in that manner.[108]

The 9/11 Commission also discredited the theory that the Muslim community in the United States has been a substantial source of al Qaeda's funding, finding, in the panel's words, that "the United States is not, and has not been, a substantial source of al Qaeda funding, although some funds raised in the United States may have made their way to al Qaeda and its affiliated groups."[109] The panel also rejected the notion that al Qaeda had shared financing networks with the Palestinian jihadists, who investigators do believe, have raised substantial funds in the United States.

Moving Money

As to how al Qaeda actually moved its money during the militant phase in Afghanistan, the 9/11 Commission found that it most likely used a combination of bank transfers, the *hawala* system (an ancient form of money transfer used in the Middle East and South Asia) and cash couriers.

Understanding how the hawala system works sheds some light on how terrorists are able to move money to and from remote areas, areas out of reach of the international banking system (Afghanistan, for example) and ultimately evade detection. Hawala is an informal, unregulated network that relies completely on personal trust. Someone interested in sending money to a remote location—a friend or relative in a foreign country, for example—brings his remittance to a hawaladar, someone known to perform this kind of transaction. For a small fee, the hawaladar will give the sender a code which the intended recipient will need in order to claim the funds at the other end of the transaction. The hawaladar will then arrange with a counterpart at the destination to distribute the correct amount of funds upon the receipt of this code. The hawaladars at each end of the transaction will have a long-term personal or family relationship and will work out the accounting for the transaction between themselves. Once the transaction has been completed—that is, the recipient has picked up the funds using the code—there is no record kept to indicate that the transaction ever took place.

In many countries in the Middle East, North Africa, and South Asia, the hawala system is faster, cheaper, and more convenient than the international banking system and a substantial portion of funds transfers in developing countries go through the hawala system. Even in the United States, there are now some 20,000 hawaladars operating informal remittance businesses out of shops and restaurants, usually in immigrant neighborhoods to facilitate funds transfers to loved ones and friends back home.[110]

While hawalas have been suspected of playing a role in terrorist financing, it is extremely difficult to prove that this is indeed the case, given the lack of standard recordkeeping or audit trail. Take the case of the U.S.-based Somalian hawala, Al-Barakaat.

Even before 9/11, U.S. intelligence sources believed that bin Laden had set up and was using Al-Barakaat to fund his operations.[111] By 2000, the FBI was in the middle of a criminal investigation of its U.S. offices. The 9/11 attacks caused the government to essentially shut down the operation by freezing Al-Barakaat's assets and blocking any transactions. However, after an extensive investigative operation, the FBI was ultimately unable to establish a link between Al-Barakaat and al Qaeda or any other terrorist organization that would hold up in court. Thus the government was forced to unfreeze Al-Barakaat's assets even though the U.S. Treasury Department was still claiming that it had "met the evidentiary standard for designations."[112]

The 9/11 Commission brought up this case in its *Monograph on Terrorist Financing* to illustrate the difficulties prosecutors face when it comes to proving that entities or individuals are involved in terrorist financing and to show how it is very easy for a terrorist organization to hide its sources of financing by simply failing to keep ordinary, auditable business records. This, unfortunately, remains as true today as it was before 9/11, though there is a general recognition that more oversight and regulation is necessary both at the United Nations level and among member countries. (For example, see the work of the United Nations Counter Terrorism Committee, available online at http://www.un.org/Docs/sc/committees/1373/).

Since 9/11

Since the 9/11 attacks, the intelligence community is of the belief that al Qaeda's expenses have been significantly reduced. For one, al Qaeda no longer needs to pay protection money to the Taliban. Second, affiliate organizations (al-Qaeda in Iraq) now seem to be financing their own operations. While al Qaeda still obviously needs to feed and shelter whoever remains at large among its core organization, including most notably bin Laden and Zawahiri, according to the 9/11 Staff, al Qaeda's annual expenses are probably now no more than a few million dollars per year.[113]

While al Qaeda may indeed no longer need to pay protection monies to the Taliban, it does not strike these authors as entirely reasonable to assume that this then means they do not have to make any protection payments at all. Think about the problem. Both bin Laden and Zawahiri are now each in the position of having to secure safe harbor in an environment where the FBI has a well-publicized (presumably) outstanding cash offer of $25 million for any information leading to their capture. If their like-minded co-religionists, the Taliban, were not willing to provide sanctuary gratis, why would Afghan tribals or warlords? And at considerably more personal risk given the presence of coalition and Pakistani forces on the hunt for the al Qaeda leadership.

In any case, al Qaeda's ability to secure funds has most likely been significantly reduced if only because of the increased regulation and scrutiny that have since been imposed on the organization's funding sources—that is, the Saudi charities and rich Gulf donors. The pressure on such Saudi resources has most assuredly increased since Saudi Arabia experienced its own terrorist attacks on May 12, 2003. Since then, authorities almost universally acknowledge that the Saudi regime has become far more serious about crushing radicalism and stemming the flow of terrorist financing. Many corrupt charities have been shut down; cash donations at mosques and shopping malls in Saudi Arabia have been banned; several known financial facilitators have been captured or killed. While once al Qaeda could openly solicit donations in Saudi Arabia, such efforts must now, for the most part, be clandestine. Even more important, now that al Qaeda has hit home, some Saudi donors may themselves be less willing to fund an organization that is destabilizing the kingdom in a way that can only ultimately hurt their personal interests.

Jihad in Iraq

While the so-called core of al Qaeda may not need much money these days, al-Qaeda in Iraq, its affiliate, a leading player in the insurgency in Iraq is certainly in need of substantial funds.

Again, this is a jihad that is being conducted using mostly terror attacks, operations that are cheap to launch. The going-rate for planting roadside bombs, for example, is said to cost somewhere between $100 and $300.[114] Nevertheless, fighters have to be recruited, many require that their transportation costs be paid, and once in Iraq they have to be trained, clothed, fed, deployed, and in the event they survive whatever mission they are assigned (and many of the foreign fighters are used in the suicide missions), some may even require medical care. Then there are the costs associated with purchasing ordnance, weapons, and ammunition. Who is funding these costs?

Most experts are of the opinion that the insurgency in Iraq is being funded by a combination of Iraqis—including former regime loyalists, Sunnis fearful of being dispossessed of power by a democratic government over which they would very likely not be able to exert their customary control, and foreign jihadists who see the insurgency in Iraq as the latest front in the global jihad.

There have been reports suggesting that the bulk of the insurgency's Iraqi funding and logistical support comes from relatives of the deposed Iraqi leader and former regime loyalists. Specifically, some of Saddam's cousins are believed to be leading the effort to smuggle guns, people, and money into Iraq from Syria and Jordan, according to newspaper reports quoting unnamed American officials. One of Saddam's cousins, Fatiq Suleiman al-Majid, a former officer in his Special Security Organization who fled to Syria just after the U.S.-led invasion in March 2003, is alleged to be a key leader in this effort. He is also assisted by another cousin of Saddam's, Majid, who is a nephew of Ali Hassan al-Majid, the former Iraqi general otherwise known as Chemical Ali for having commanded chemical gas attacks against the Kurds in the 1980s.[115] U.S. military and government officials reportedly believe that Saddam's relatives and various former regime loyalists have "unlimited money" supplies. The Iraqi regime is known to have sent funds to Syria prior to the invasion. Corrupt oil-for-food transactions may also be a significant source.[116]

Because the Iraqi economy is currently conducted almost entirely in cash, U.S. government officials are concerned that some of the money the U.S. military is paying its contractors may also be being diverted to fund the insurgency, according to U.S. Treasury official Daniel Glaser.[117] Other sources of money may include criminal enterprise such as extortion, counterfeiting, car smuggling and hostage-taking-for-profit. Some analysts believe that sympathetic mosques, businessmen, local tribes, and other locals in Iraq may also be contributors.

Many experts believe that rich Saudis are sponsoring the foreign jihadists, maybe even some of the same corrupt Islamic charities and financiers who have funded al Qaeda in the past, who Anthony Cordesman and Nawaf Obaid derisively term "arm chair militants."[118] Some Saudis fighters may even be using their own personal funds to come to Iraq to wage jihad. Cordesman and Nawaf report that many are said to arrive, usually carrying personal funds in the range of $10,000–15,000.[119]

Funds are not just coming from the Middle East, either. According to U.S. Representative Jim Saxton (R-NJ), "there are credible reports of open fundraising for the insurgency being conducted in western Europe and more clandestine fundraising in the Middle East and even here at home [in the U.S.]."[120] For example, one far-left group in Europe waged a campaign called "Ten Euros for the Resistance" to aid those fighting what the group was calling "occupanti imperialisti" (or the "occupying imperialists") according to one Italian website. The groups funding the jihad in Iraq are described by terrorism expert Lorenzo Vidino as "being part of the old anticapitalist, anti-U.S., anti-Israel crowd," and Vidino contends that "the glue that binds them together is anti-Americanism."[121] Though the money raised is supposed to be used to buy medicine, one of the movement's leaders reportedly boasted to Vidino that "the campaign will send 'everything it takes' for the resistance to win, including weaponry."[122] Col. Ron Makuta, the chief intelligence officer for the First Marine Expeditionary Force contends that support for the insurgency comes from "a loose confederation of interests" many involving "marriages of convenience."[123]

One overriding fact seems clear: al Qaeda is still apparently able to raise funds and with relative ease, even in its defensive posture. In addition to its usual network of wealthy donors and sympathetic Muslims, al Qaeda can now also apparently call upon former regime elements in Iraq, Arab nationalists, and a hard-core left that seems to be willing to fund any force it believes is willing to stand up to what it sees as the twin evils: capitalism and imperialism. As the Council on Foreign Relations concluded in its 2002 report on terrorist financing:

> Building al-Qaeda's financial support network was Osama bin Laden's foremost accomplishment, and the primary source of his personal influence. Unlike other terrorist leaders, he was not a military hero, nor a religious authority, nor an obvious representative of the downtrodden and disillusioned. He was a rich financier, both a scion of one of Saudi Arabia's most influential families and a challenger to Saudi Arabia's existing system of governance, distinguished by his ability to organize an effective network.[124]

Thus as the Council duly observed, "As long as al-Qaeda retains access to a viable financial network, it remains a lethal threat to the United States."[125]

CHAPTER 6

How Is Global Jihad Being Countered?

This is an enemy without conscience—and they cannot be appeased. If we were not fighting and destroying this enemy in Iraq, they would not be idle. They would be plotting and killing Americans across the world and within our own borders. By fighting these terrorists in Iraq, Americans in uniform are defeating a direct threat to the American people. Against this adversary, there is only one effective response: We will never back down. We will never give in. And we will never accept anything less than complete victory.

> President George W. Bush, United States Naval Academy,
> November 30, 2005

The Nonmilitary Response

Interestingly enough, the administration's "first strike in the war on terror"[1] (its characterization) was not the military campaign that began in October 2001 in Afghanistan, but rather, a financial strike intended to cripple terrorists by cutting off their sources of financing. On September 23, 2001, President Bush signed into effect Executive Order 13224, in which he authorized the government to designate and block the assets of any foreign individuals or entities engaging in or otherwise supporting terrorism. Essentially this order would give law enforcement agents the ability to treat sponsors of terrorism the exact same way they dealt with terrorists themselves. U.S. persons were now strictly barred from having anything to do with terrorism and the U.S. government would be able to freeze the assets of and block any transactions with any entity or person determined to be linked in any way to terrorists. Under this order, the U.S. government was able to lock the assets of and block hundreds of individuals, groups, charities, and other front organizations designated to have sponsored terrorism out of the U.S. financial system.

E.O. 13224 was not a perfect tool, however, in that it only applied to assets and transactions that came into contact with the United States economy. Terrorist sponsors would still be able to continue their activities abroad. To remedy this situation, the Bush administration pushed for and quickly obtained a similar resolution at the United Nations. On September 28, 2001, the United Nations Security Council passed Resolution 1373 which compelled all 191 member states to ban terrorists from their financial systems, prevent any arms sales with them, and prohibit them from transiting through their borders. Designated terrorists could not be driven from their homes without a judicial trial, but they could be stopped in their tracks with this new process. Within weeks of the attacks, some one hundred nations had passed these additional measures to curb terrorist activities within their jurisdictions.[2]

There were of course critics of the new rules who charged that now both the United States and the United Nations were enabling states and the international community to shut down enterprises or cause financial harm to individuals based simply on suspicions of terrorism, in that the designation process did not require the burden of having to prove such associations in any recognized court of law. What happened to Al-Barakat and the Benevolence International Foundation, as we saw in the last chapter, were famously cited examples of what critics claimed was a process that did not have sufficient checks and balances. However, proponents of the measures argued that few if any truly innocent parties would find themselves listed as terrorist sponsors given the high-level agreement among competing authorities that was required to designate an entity. The Bush administration further made the case that if the goal was to disrupt terrorist financing before another major attack could occur, the world no longer had the luxury to wait while such cases made their way through the world's court systems. While none of these arguments completely satisfied the critics, the measures remained in effect and, to date, have not been successfully challenged.

While coalition forces routed out terrorist havens in Afghanistan, Congress and the Bush administration beefed up law enforcement's ability to track down terrorists on the domestic front. In October 2001, both houses of the U.S. Congress voted overwhelming to pass the "Patriot Act."[3] The 342-page act gave the government expanded surveillance powers and provided the FBI and the CIA legal cover to share information and cooperate in terrorism-related investigations.

The USA Patriot Act also gave U.S. law enforcement updated investigative tools to investigate and disrupt terrorist plots.[4] For example the act would now allow law enforcement agents the ability to intercept, via a single court order, all of the communications devices used by a terrorism suspect (e.g., his cell phone as well as his home phone), as opposed to having to obtain separate warrants for each of his phones as government agents had to do before the legislation. Such tools had for years been available to investigators in organized crime and racketeering cases, or those involving a foreign threat to national security posed by a foreign power.

The act also gave law enforcement the ability to examine business and other records of suspects in terrorism cases without having to immediately alert the target that such an investigation was taking place. This gave investigators the chance to examine a suspect's records in cases where it was determined that such knowledge would impede the investigation.[5] Before the Patriot Act, such "sneak and peek" search warrants were available but only in cases where investigators

could show a special Foreign Intelligence Surveillance Act (FISA) cou
terrorist was receiving support from a foreign country. FISA powers w
preted to be useless when it came to investigating al Qaeda, for example,
because investigators could not link the organization to a foreign governmental
sponsor. Though this narrow interpretation of the law would later be challenged, this was the sort of perceived shortcoming in existing legislation that
Congress sought to correct with the USA Patriot Act.

At the time the Patriot Act was passed, civil libertarians including Muslim
civil rights advocates expressed concerns that the Patriot Act would infringe on
fundamental civil liberties and would create an environment which could very
well lead to governmental abuse of power. Especially alarming to civil libertarians was that, persons suspected of terrorism could now be held for up to seven
days for questioning without being charged and law enforcement would have
the ability to probe into a suspect's library records or bookstore purchases based
on only suspicions of links to terrorism. Though the Patriot Act would come
under intense national scrutiny and criticism, Congress renewed the act before
its scheduled expiration March 16, 2006.

Civil libertarians would only have more cause to be outraged when on
November 13, 2001 President Bush, acting in his capacity as commander-in-
chief of the U.S. armed forces, signed an order reserving the right to use special
military tribunals as opposed to war crimes tribunals or criminal courts to try
noncitizens suspected of terrorism so that the government would not be put in
the position of having to divulge intelligence sources or methods in the discovery process that is the standard part of a criminal trial and have greater latitude
in what could be considered criminal. Under the order, the president designated
himself as the sole authority able to determine when such tribunals would be
used. Critics claimed that such tribunals would violate the fundamental human
right to due process and gave the executive undue privilege without the necessary checks and "balances." Proponents, not surprisingly, argued that this was
necessary to safeguard the nation's security in a time of war.

The very same day President Bush made his decision reserving the right to use
military tribunals, in what critics would charge was yet another assault on cher-
ished American values, the Justice Department asked some 5,000 mostly Middle
Eastern men between the ages of eighteen to thirty-three who had entered the
country on nonimmigrant visas since 2000 to come in to their local FBI and
law-enforcement offices for voluntary questioning related to terrorism issues.
While the Justice Department gave assurances that none of the individuals it was
asking to come in to submit to the voluntary questioning would automatically
be arrested, the American Civil Liberties Union (ACLU), a leading civil rights
advocate, quickly condemned the request because of its overtones of "racial and
ethnic profiling."[6] The Arab and Muslims being targeted, most of whom came
from countries with poor human rights records, understandably jumped to the
conclusion that their civil rights were now going to be violated in America as
well and the shock wave reverberated throughout the Muslim world. Now the
United States, long the beacon of freedom in the world, was in the grip of an
irrational hysteria and Muslims would surely suffer disproportionately.

Though the government would ultimately arrest and detain some 1,100 persons, according to a *New York Times* report,[7] most would be held only briefly, just long enough for federal agents to establish that they had no known connections to terrorism and no apparent information to offer. Because there was no central recordkeeping effort, accurate statistics on the detentions were not readily available, the government was unable to respond on a timely basis to the wildly exaggerated claims that the United States was now officially engaging in mass detentions of Muslims and Arabs. Thus the damage was done though both Human Rights Watch, an independent monitor, and the ACLU, would ascertain that only some seventy persons had been detained for longer than just a few days. In only one case was a detainee held for more than a year, and then only because authorities had determined that he was a "material witness" and could under an existing federal law provision, be legally detained without charge or access to counsel as the government gathered information about the underlying crime to which he was a witness.[8]

In the fall of 2002, there were additional discriminatory measures put in place. Adult males from twenty-five Arab and Muslim countries were asked to register with the Immigration and Naturalization Service or face misdemeanor criminal charges and deportation. According to a *New York Times* report, under the program, the Justice Department collected information on some 83,000 people and deported some 13,000 illegal immigrants.[9] While civil libertarians were again appalled that such ethnic profiling was going on proponents of the measures argued that such measures were only reasonable given that it was Arabs and Muslims who had planned and carried out the 9/11 attacks. Even though ethnic profiling would indeed be unacceptable in peace time, proponents of the program acknowledged that, such drastic measures were entirely reasonable given that the country was at war with a declared enemy that was claiming to be acting under the banner of Islam. Moreover, as the 9/11 Commission reported, a senior al Qaeda detainee told his interrogators that the increased scrutiny of Muslim immigration files after 9/11 had curtailed to some extent al Qaeda's ability to operate.[10] Nevertheless, the program was discontinued in late 2003 because any information the registration process was yielding was ultimately deemed not worthy enough to compensate for the strain the program was putting on the United States' relations with key allies and its Muslim and Arab immigrant communities at home.

In December 2005, the *New York Times* published a report revealing that in the months after the 9/11 attacks, President Bush authorized the National Security Agency (NSA) to monitor the international phone calls and email messages of people inside the United States believed to be linked to al Qaeda and other terrorist groups without first obtaining warrants.[11]

According to the *New York Times*, the president authorized such wiretaps to monitor telephone numbers and addresses that CIA agents obtained from the seized cell phones and computers of captured al Qaeda leaders, such as Abu Zubaydah.[12] The administration believed that they had only so much time to exploit such information before word would get out that the al Qaeda operative had been captured and other terrorists would stop using the operative's telephone numbers and addresses. Officials claimed that the eavesdropping program had foiled at least two terror plots, including one by Iyman Faris, an Ohio truck driver who later pled guilty to having planned to bring down the Brooklyn Bridge using blowtorches; and another plot in which terrorists planned to bomb British pubs and train stations.[13]

Justice Department lawyers asserted that the president had the power to authorize such warrantless searches under the September 2001 Congressional resolution that granted him broad powers to wage war on al Qaeda and other terrorist groups.[14] Generally, the government is required to obtain a court order from a special court, the Foreign Intelligence Surveillance Court, before tapping communications in the United States. Critics of the warrantless wiretaps pointed out they were unnecessary because the FISA court could grant warrants within hours in emergency situations and that such courts required a lower standard of proof than an ordinary criminal court does. In short, critics wondered why the Bush administration resorted to such drastic measures and implied that it was only to expand the executive's powers. However, in practice, even as late as April of 2004, the FISA process was reported as being "long and slow," according to Christine Healy, a staff member of the 9/11 Commission who told reporters in a press briefing that "Requests for such approvals are overwhelming the ability of the system to process them and to conduct the surveillance."[15]

A memorandum written for Congress by the Congressional Research Service that summarized the issues surrounding the executive's authority to authorize such wiretaps stated: "Critics challenge the notion that federal statutes regarding government eavesdropping may be bypassed by executive order, or that such laws were implicitly superceded by Congress's authorization to use military force. Others, however, have expressed the view that established wiretap procedures are too cumbersome and slow to be effective in the war against terrorism, and that the threat of terrorism justifies extraordinary measures the President deems appropriate, and some agree that Congress authorized the measures when it authorized the use of military force."[16]

John Schmidt, an associate attorney general in the Clinton administration, weighed in on the debate to say that the legal issues had already been settled. In an editorial for the Chicago Tribune, he wrote: "Four federal courts of appeal subsequently faced the issue squarely and held that the president has inherent authority to authorize wiretapping for foreign intelligence purposes without judicial warrant" quoting as support for his position the opinion of the FISA court which in 2002 ruled that "We take for granted that the president does have that authority."[17]

However, as the Congressional Research Service stated, the president's authority to authorize these secret wiretaps without judicial oversight was far from far from obvious to all legal experts. In the words of the memorandum: "While courts have generally accepted that the President has the power to conduct domestic electronic surveillance within the United States inside the constraints of the Fourth Amendment, no court has held squarely that the Constitution disables the Congress from endeavoring to set limits on that power. To the contrary, the Supreme Court has stated that Congress does indeed have power to regulate domestic surveillance, and has not ruled on the extent to which Congress can act with respect to electronic surveillance to collect foreign intelligence information."[18]

In June 2006, the New York Times, the Los Angeles Times, and the Wall Street Journal published more classified information regarding the government's counterterrorism efforts. The newspapers revealed a secret program in which the government was collecting data on terrorist financing using records maintained by Swift, an electronic system based in Belgium that manages and records the flow of international funds transfers. Administration officials say the information obtained from this program led to the capture of Hambali, the terrorist behind the 2002 Bali bombings, yielded significant leads regarding the London bombers, and led to the arrest and conviction of a Brooklyn man who was trying to help an al Qaeda operative enter the United States to commit a terrorist act.[19]

Many Americans were outraged that the papers had divulged this classified program in a time of war. Some even went so far as to suggest that those responsible should be tried for treason and cited numerous other times the media had compromised counterterrorism efforts. In 2001, for example, two reporters had alerted two charities that an FBI raid was pending. In response to the Swift leak, the House passed a resolution condemning the disclosure of classified information and called on the media to help as opposed to harm the nation's counterterrorism efforts.

The New York Times defended its decision to publish the Swift story in an editorial. The editors warned of the dangers of "mission creep" in granting unchecked powers even in wartime. While they acknowledged that they had no reason to believe that such searches were going beyond terrorism suspects at this point, there was always inherent danger when there is no oversight of an investigation. Given that "the United States is trying to learn how to live in a perpetual war on terror," the editors argued, counterterrorism "efforts need to be done under a clear and coherent set of rules, with the oversight of Congress and the courts."[20]

The Military Response

On the evening of the 9/11 attacks, President Bush addressed the American people in a televised address and declared that the United States was now at "war against terrorism," and that the nation would no longer make any "distinction between the terrorists who committed these acts and those who harbor them."[21]

This was an abrupt departure from what had previously been America's approach to terrorism. In the 1990s, when Islamic terrorists attacked various U.S. persons and interests, the attacks were always prosecuted through the criminal justice system. Even when the evidence suggested a wider conspiracy, there seemed to be a systemic resistance to pursuing the leads, the goal apparently being to keep the case simple in order to put the terrorists behind bars as soon as possible.

One notable case where this was the approach taken involved the fatal shooting of a Jewish rabbi, Meir Kahane, in New York. In spite of the fact that the NYPD investigators found that the gunman, an Egyptian, El Sayyid Nosair, had boxes of literature in his apartment suggesting that he may have acted as a member of a jihadist cell led by the Blind Sheik, Omar Abdel Rahman, investigators decided not to pursue this angle in the interest of keeping the case as simple as possible and to avoid having to explain to a jury the complicated history of the Islamist movement in the Middle East.[22]

Authorities would realize in early 1993 that this had been a grave mistake when they discovered that Nosair, from inside his jail cell no less, had various ties to the 1993 World Trade Center bombers—also followers of the Blind Sheik—and that he had tried to recruit at least one of them to help him wage a war of urban jihad against New York City.[23] Unfortunately, investigators would fail to pursue another lead in this investigation as well. It would turn out that the uncle of the master bomber in this case, and the only known source of financing in the bombing, would go on to mastermind the 9/11 attacks. After uncovering his links to the World Trade Center bombers, the FBI determined that Nosair was involved in yet a third terrorist conspiracy, also centered around the Blind Sheik. This time it was a plot to blow up various New York landmarks, including the United Nations headquarters. Only at this point would the government finally have to acknowledge that there really was a "Jihad organization" that planned to terrorize New York City.[24]

Ironically, the governments' original strategy, to simplify the Kahane case and only charge Kahane as a lone gunman, did not even yield the expected result in that case. Instead of being convicted of murder, Nosair was acquitted, a verdict that the judge even felt compelled to deride as "against the overwhelming weight of evidence" and "devoid of common sense and logic."[25] The only thing he could do to rectify the situation, however, was to issue the maximum sentence possible for the lesser weapons-possession and assault charges for which Nosair was convicted. After Nosair's role in the Sheik's "Jihadist organization" was uncovered and other evidence surfaced, he would be convicted of Kahane's murder as well.

When in 1998, after bin Laden declared jihad against the United States and then launched his first major assault on American interests, bombing the embassies in east Africa, the Clinton administration ordered a couple of missiles strikes to be fired at a training camp in Afghanistan where bin Laden was supposed to have been at that moment (it would turn out he was already gone) and at a suspected chemical-weapons factory in Sudan (that turned out to be a pharmaceutical factory). Again, the intelligence was wrong. Though CIA director George Tenet wrote his high-level staff officials a memo in December of 1998 saying, "We are at war" and "no resources or people" should be "spared in this effort," as the 9/11 Commission pointed out, the memo "had little overall effect on mobilizing the CIA or intelligence community."[26]

Ultimately many of those responsible for the U.S. embassies bombings would be rounded up and put on trial. In other words, the attacks were once again prosecuted as a criminal justice crime and not an act of war.

The 9/11 attacks would, however, force the United States to change its approach. The number of casualties incurred—some 3,000 people were killed—meant that al Qaeda could no longer be regarded as tantamount to a criminal gang. Nor would the Bush administration be able to limit its response to terrorism to a retaliatory strike or two. Now the nation was at war. As President Bush said in a speech to the American people on September 20, 2001:

> Americans should not expect one battle, but a lengthy campaign, unlike any other we have ever seen. It may include dramatic strikes, visible on TV, and covert operations, secret even in success. We will starve terrorists of funding, turn them one against another, drive them from place to place, until there is no refuge or no rest. And we will pursue nations that provide aid or safe haven to terrorism. Every nation, in every region, now has a decision to make. Either you are with us, or you are with the terrorists.[27]

The War in Afghanistan

For a few weeks after the attacks at least, America's friends and allies also seemed to realize that the United States was at war and had to strike back in order to defend itself. On September 12, 2001, the day after the attacks, NATO, for the first time its history, invoked article 5 of the North Atlantic Treaty and declared that because the United States had been attacked, all nineteen member states should react as though they had been attacked as well.[28] On the same day, the UN Security Council, expressing solidarity with America, unanimously passed resolution 1368 which characterized the attacks as a "threat to international peace and security," and recognizing "the inherent right of individual or collective self-defense in accordance with the Charter," provided the United States with the international legal cover to respond to the attacks with force.[29]

Within three days, on September 14, 2001, Congress would also authorize the use of force, by a vote of 98:2 in the Senate and 420:1 in the House, and give the president the authority to "use all necessary and appropriate force against" any nation, organization, or person that he determines planned, authorized, committed, or aided the terrorist attacks . . . or harbored such organizations or persons."[30]

On September 18, 2001, the U.N. Security Council President Jean-David Levitte of France for his part sent a strong message warning the Taliban that it should "immediately and unconditionally . . . turn over Usama bin Laden" so that he could be brought to justice.[31]

Thus less than two weeks after the attacks, President Bush, in a televised address to the American people, declared that the United States was now engaged in a "war on terror"[32] against "a radical network of terrorists, and every government that supports them." He avoided casting the conflict as a war against either Islam or Muslims. He would go on to specify, however, that the evidence suggested that the enemy was al Qaeda which he described as "a collection of loosely affiliated terrorist organizations" and that these terrorists had hijacked the teachings of a "good and peaceful" religion to "practice a fringe form of Islamic extremism" that "commands them to kill Christians and Jews, to kill all Americans, and make no distinction among military and civilians, including women and children."

Some experts—notably Daniel Pipes, author of the book *Militant Islam Reaches America*,[33] who had long been warning of the threat coming from militant Islam, took issue with the administration's decision to cast the enemy as terrorism. As Pipes later wrote, "the notion of making war on a military tactic" is "euphemistic, inaccurate, and obstructive and that it was critical for Americans to understand that this was a war against 'radical Islam' an ideology whose goal it was to 'replace the U.S. Constitution with Shariah.' "[34]

While President Bush's characterization of the enemy may have been intentionally vague, his actions were certainly clearer. In his September 20th address, he issued an ultimatum to the Taliban: "Deliver to United States authorities all the leaders of al Qaeda who hide in your land . . . Close immediately and permanently every terrorist training camp in Afghanistan, and hand over every person in their support structure, to appropriate authorities. Give the United States full access to terrorist training camps, so we can make sure they are no longer operating. These demands are not open to negotiation or discussion. The Taliban must act, and act immediately. They will hand over the terrorists, or they will share in their fate."[35]

The Taliban's only response to President Bush's ultimatum was to demand to see proof of bin Laden's culpability, and then insist that in any case he should be tried in an Islamic court. As the Taliban envoy, Mullah Zaeef, stated, "The Americans are flying in the sky, and we are on the earth . . . President Bush should respect Islam and Islamic principles if he wants to deal with the Muslims."[36]

When, less than two weeks later, the Taliban realized that a U.S.-led attack was now imminent they tried to have bin Laden extradited to a neutral country but by then their offer was deemed to be too little and too late.[37] And so just three weeks after having issued his ultimatum to the Taliban, on October 7, President Bush ordered the commencement of "Operation Infinite Justice," a campaign of air strikes against Afghanistan. When it was pointed out that this name might just be interpreted in the Muslim world as a declaration of a holy war, the campaign was quickly renamed, "Operation Enduring Freedom."

In spite of the many negative predictions that the invasion would result in a quagmire, in the end, as invasions go, this one went extremely well. Operating from nearby bases in Uzbekistan and Pakistan, the U.S.-led coalition deployed CIA and Special Operations forces, and aligned with an Afghan faction, the Northern Alliance, a rival Afghan gang that had been fighting the Taliban for years. In fact, just before the 9/11 attacks, some analysts have speculated that al Qaeda assassinated the Northern Alliance's military commander, Ahmed Shah Massoud, in preparation for the retaliation that they assumed would follow in the wake of the 9/11 attacks. Nevertheless, the Taliban and al Qaeda forces proved a less formidable enemy than expected. In less than two months, the coalition forces had seized control of almost all major Afghan cities.

By the end of December, on December 22, 2001, a new interim government was installed under the leadership of Hamed Karzai, a Pashtun from Kandahar.

However, most of the Taliban and al Qaeda leadership, including Mullah Omar, head of the Taliban and bin Laden and his key associates managed to escape capture or death and are still presumed to be living at large, probably somewhere in the tribal areas of Pakistan or Afghanistan.

In terms of civilian casualties, the cost of the war was also relatively low. Marc W. Herold, an economist from the University of New Hampshire, estimates that some 3600 Afghan civilians were killed during the U.S.-led bombings;[38] though the *Los Angeles Times* places the figure somewhere between 1,067 and 1,201.[39] None of the estimates are any where near, for example, the million Afghans that are believed to have been killed as a result of the jihad against the Soviets in the 1980s.[40]

Perhaps the most controversial aspect of the administration's prosecution of the war in Afghanistan was its decision regarding what to do with those it captured, the combatants caught fighting for the Taliban and al Qaeda in Afghanistan.

The Bush administration decided that it would not extend these "enemy combatants" protection under the Geneva Conventions, though the administration did take pains to assert they would be treated humanely. John Yoo, a U.S. deputy assistant attorney general from 2001 to 2003, and the principal author of Justice Department memos that outlined the Bush administration's position on this issue recalled the issues that the United States faced:

> If you're a prisoner of war under the Geneva Conventions, you can only be asked questions and you cannot be treated any differently based on whether you answer them or not. And in a way, it's a much tougher standard than we even apply here at home. So, for example, the Geneva standard would prohibit the government from offering plea bargains to people. So you couldn't say, "If you cooperate, we're not going to try you, and if you cooperate, we'll move you to a better prison with better facilities." Things that are commonly offered in American police houses to get cooperation from suspects are prohibited under the Geneva Conventions.[41]

To make sure that the worst of these enemy combatants could never make their way back to the battlefield, the administration made another controversial decision—it decided to house the most dangerous of the captured al Qaeda and Taliban prisoners in a location as far as possible from the battlefield. To this end, a military installation located in Guantanamo Bay, Cuba, was selected as the site of the detention facility. Critics contended that this particular location was chosen only to enable intelligence agents to interrogate the detainees outside the purview of the U.S. legal system, so that they could bypass American laws which prohibit the use of torture.

The Bush administration took the position that the detainees had to be interrogated because, as Yoo put it, the only "way to stop future terrorist attacks" was to obtain information from the captured members of al Qaeda.[42] Moreover, the administration contended that the al Qaeda terrorists were not guaranteed protections under the laws of war, because, as *Washington Post* columnist Charles Krauthammer would later argue in a widely quoted essay they did not *observe* the laws of war:

> A terrorist is by profession, indeed by definition, an unlawful combatant: He lives outside the laws of war because he does not wear a uniform, he hides among

civilians, and he deliberately targets innocents. He is entitled to no protections whatsoever. People seem to think that the postwar Geneva Conventions were written only to protect detainees. In fact, their deeper purpose was to provide a deterrent to the kind of barbaric treatment of civilians that had become so horribly apparent during the first half of the 20th century, and in particular, during the Second World War. The idea was to deter the abuse of civilians by promising combatants who treated noncombatants well that they themselves would be treated according to a code of dignity if captured—and, crucially, that they would be denied the protections of that code if they broke the laws of war and abused civilians themselves.[43]

The case of the Taliban was more complicated in that the Taliban had been the de facto rulers of Afghanistan, a country that was itself a party to the Geneva Conventions. Here, Bush administration lawyers argued that the Taliban fighters were not covered by the conventions because the Taliban was not widely recognized as the official government of Afghanistan (only Pakistan, Saudi Arabia, and the United Arab Emirates had recognized their rule). Moreover, the Taliban fighters, just like the al Qaeda fighters, also routinely violated the rules of war and therefore, the Justice Department argued, had long ago forfeited any right to their protection.

In June 2006, the Supreme Court overturned the Bush administration's decision not to extend protection under the Geneva Conventions to al Qaeda and Taliban detainees and outlawed the use of special military tribunals for terrorism suspects.[44] This meant that the United States would have to follow the advice of the United Nations Committee Against Torture, which had asked the U.S. to stop using interrogation techniques such as sexual humiliation, water boarding (to induce near drowning), short shackling (to keep the detainee in uncomfortable positions), or dogs (to induce fear). Moreover the UN asked the U.S. to stop using all degrading, cruel or inhuman interrogation techniques and to stop rendering terrorism suspects to countries where they could be tortured, which the CIA was alleged to be doing in order to force captured terrorists to divulge details of on-going plots.[45] The Committee then further stated that the United States "should cease to detain any person at Guantanamo Bay and close this detention facility, permit access by the detainees to judicial process or release them as soon as possible."[46]

The Bush administration still maintains the position that "The law of war allows the United States—and any other country engaged in combat—to hold enemy combatants without charges or access to counsel for the duration of hostilities. Detention is not an act of punishment, but of security and military necessity. It serves the purpose of preventing combatants from continuing to take up arms against the United States."[47] As State Department spokesman Sean McCormack put it, "we at some point in the future would very much like to see Guantanamo Bay closed down, but at the moment it's housing some dangerous people."[48]

Preventative War

In September 2002, President Bush would introduce the first major change in U.S. foreign policy in fifty years in a document, *The National Security of the*

United States. In this document, also referred to as the Bush Doctrine, the administration announced that because of the 9/11 attacks, the United States was no longer going to rely on its Cold War foreign policy of deterrence, which was premised on the notion that no nation would dare attack the world's greatest military power. While "enemies in the past needed great armies and great industrial capabilities to endanger America," the Bush administration argued, "Now shadowy networks of individuals can bring great chaos and suffering to our shores for less than it costs to purchase a single tank."[49] This new threat, according to the Bush administration, required a new strategy: now the United States would exercise its fundamental right to protect itself by engaging, unilaterally, if necessary, in preemptive or even preventative war.

The Bush Doctrine stated that the official position of the United States was now to "target any state or non-state entity that attempted to obtain or use weapons of mass destruction" because, in the administration's estimation, the United States was now "threatened less by conquering states than . . . by failing ones . . . [and] less by fleets and armies than by catastrophic technologies in the hands of the embittered few."[50]

During the Cold War, the United States' main foes, the Soviet Union and communist China, had been kept at bay using the threat of mutually assured destruction. Both of these powers knew that any direct attack on U.S. interests would trigger an all-out war and vice versa—the United States realized that any direct attack on the interests of the Soviet Union or China would similarly invite disaster. The Bush Doctrine was now asserting that this logic would no longer work to contain a stateless enemy "whose so-called soldiers seek martyrdom in death."[51] Now, it was believed, the United States needed to "prevent rogue states and terrorists from acquiring the materials, technologies, and expertise necessary for weapons of mass destruction."[52] This meant that now the United States would reserve the right to act—unilaterally, if necessary—to prevent a rogue regime or a terrorist entity from obtaining weapons of mass destruction.

Iraq

Even before the U.S.-led coalition decided to invade Afghanistan, the Bush administration wondered what to do about the regime in Iraq. As soon as he had heard that a third plane had hit the Pentagon, President Bush told the 9/11 Commission, one of the first suspects that came to his mind was Iraq.[53] When members of his cabinet and other senior administration officials met at Camp David in the days following the attacks, they were presented with a Defense Department report that focused on the three greatest threats America was believed to face. In addition to al Qaeda and the Taliban, the report named Iraq, and of the three, Iraq was presented as the greatest strategic threat because of its long history of supporting terrorism and its track record of having both used and tried to acquire weapons of mass destruction.[54]

Iraq's support for terrorism was a well-established fact. For years, Iraq had been listed by the U.S. State Department as one of seven state sponsors of terrorism. Iraq was believed to be harboring at least three famous terrorists, Abu Abbas, Abu Nidal and Abdul Rahman Yasin.

Abu Abbas, a former secretary of the Palestine Liberation Front, gained international notoriety when he masterminded the October 1985 hijacking of the Achille Lauro, an Italian cruise ship in the Mediterranean, in which a wheelchair bound American retiree, Leon Klinghoffer, was thrown overboard for the simple reason that he was Jewish. Though Abbas was taken into Italian custody during the course of the Achille Lauro hijacking, because he was holding an Iraqi diplomatic passport, by international law, the Italian government had no choice but to set him free because of his diplomatic immunity. The Italian courts would later convict Abbas in absentia and sentenced him to five consecutive life terms in prison, a sentence he would never serve, however, as up to the time he was captured by U.S. Special Forces in Iraq on April 14, 2003, weeks after the U.S. launched its invasion, he had been living freely in Iraq, where Saddam had given him refuge.[55]

Saddam had also provided safe haven to the Palestinian terrorist Abu Nidal from the late 1990s, until his death in 2002. Nidal was an international fugitive wanted for his role in the death of hundreds of persons in some twenty countries. He was perhaps most widely known for having bombed a TWA jet en route from Israel to Greece in 1974, in which all eighty-eight people on board were killed. According to the official Iraqi report, Nidal committed suicide after learning that he was about to be arrested for spying on Iraq on behalf of an unnamed Arab nation.

Saddam was also harboring Abdul Rahman Yasin, one of the bomb makers in the 1993 World Trade Center bombing.[56] After carrying out the attack, he reportedly fled to Iraq where he was said to live freely, even receiving a monthly government stipend according to documents unearthed by the coalition forces.[57] His current whereabouts are unknown.

Saddam was also known for his generous contributions to the families of Palestinian suicide bombers. Toward the end of his regime especially, Saddam would make a public display of handing out $25,000 checks to the families of suicide bombers who carried out attacks against Israelis, according to press reports.[58]

Iraq's sheltering of terrorists was just one of many reasons that on October 2, 2002, both houses of Congress voted overwhelmingly in favor of authorizing the use of force against Iraq. Additional reasons listed in the 23-clause resolution included Iraq's refusal to give up its WMD programs, its various human and civil rights violations, and its almost daily attacks on U.S. and British air forces protecting the no-fly zones, which had been instituted to protect Iraqi Kurds and Shiites from Saddam's assaults.[59]

When it came time to present the case for invasion before the United Nations, however, the United States would largely focus its presentation on Iraq's WMD programs as the major reason for the invasion. This was because for over a dozen years, Iraq had been violating U.N. resolutions requiring it to abandon its WMD programs. Now in November 2002, the United Nations Security Council, pressured by the United States and Britain, finally agreed to pass a binding resolution that threatened Iraq with "serious consequences" if it did not finally put a stop to its illegal proliferation activities.

Even after Iraq submitted a 12,000-page declaration to the UN Security Council asserting that it no longer had WMD stores that December, to keep the pressure mounting and because he skeptical that Saddam was really cooperating, Bush deployed some 200,000-war-ready forces to the Persian Gulf.

At the end of January, after having examined Iraq's declaration, the head United Nations weapons inspector, Hans Blix, declared that he could not confidently state that Iraq had taken its disarmament obligations seriously.[60] His counterpart responsible for monitoring Iraq's nuclear programs, Dr. Mohamed ElBaradei, reached a similar conclusion, stating that as far as he could tell, Iraq had not provided "any new information relevant to certain questions that have been outstanding since 1998," the last time United Nations inspectors had been permitted access to Iraq.[61] In other words, neither monitoring agency was willing to give Iraq a clean bill of health.

The United States was growing impatient, and as far as the Bush administration was concerned, the United States already had all the authority it needed to act with resolution 1441 in hand. However, a key ally, the British prime minister, Tony Blair, was meeting a great deal of resistance back home. In January, hundreds of thousands of antiwar protestors had taken to the streets in Britain to mark their opposition to an impending invasion. Blair convinced Bush that he needed him to go back to the United Nations again and get them to specifically authorize an invasion so that he could get the support of the British people behind the plan.

Thus on February 10, 2003, Secretary of State Colin Powell, at Blair's request, made another case for war in front of the United Nations Security Council. After presenting the administration's evidence of Iraq's WMD activities, Powell stated that "the information and intelligence we have gathered point to an active and systematic effort on the part of the Iraqi regime to keep key materials and people from the inspectors in direct violation of Resolution 1441."

A few days later, on February 4, the weapons inspectors came back to the UN to report their status. While they acknowledged that many of Iraq's proscribed weapons and items had yet to be accounted for, so far they had been unable to find any "evidence of ongoing prohibited nuclear or nuclear-related activities in Iraq." The weapons inspectors did caution that Iraqi scientists were still declining to be interviewed unless an Iraqi official was present or they could tape record their conversations and that not a single scientist was willing to be taken out of Iraq for inspectors to conduct secure interviews.[62]

On March 7, the UN weapons inspectors again delivered a status report on their activities. Now both inspectors were allowing that, under the threat of force, Iraq was increasing its level of cooperation but months were still required for them to complete their assessment and ElBaradei noted that only a few Iraqi scientists had come forward to be interviewed, in his words, "without escort and without a taped record."[63]

Aside from describing Saddam's WMD activities, in his February speech to the United Nations, Powell also outlined what the United States knew about Saddam's relationship with al Qaeda. What was concerning U.S. officials most, he said, was that Saddam was providing safe harbor to one Abu Musab

Al-Zarqawi, who at that point was still a little known figure outside of intelligence circles.

In his address, Powell described Zarqawi as a poisons expert and "collaborator of Osama bin Laden and his al Qaeda lieutenants," and said that Saddam was providing Zarqawi and his group safe haven in an area controlled by Ansar al-Islam, a radical organization that controlled a corner of the northern Kurdish region of Iraq.

Powell said that much of the information on Zarqawi's network had come from a captured assassin of the U.S. diplomat who was gunned down in Jordan in October 2002. The assassin claimed that he had received money and weapons from Zarqawi to carry out the plot. Powell also said that European authorities believed that Zarqawi and his network had been behind terrorist plots involving bombs and poisons that had been uncovered in countries as far a field as France, Britain, Spain, Italy, Germany, and Russia.

According to Powell, an al Qaeda detainee in U.S. custody was claiming that al Qaeda associates were being trained by Iraqi government personnel in the use of poisons and gases as early as December 2000. The detainee, later identified as Ibn al-Shaykh al-Libi, would recant his claims in January 2004.[64]

Powell spent some time in his speech addressing those who doubted that an avowed secularist such as Saddam would ally with religious extremists such as al Qaeda. Powell stated that he believed that Saddam would indeed ally with radical Islamists, as, in his words, "Ambition and hatred are enough to bring Iraq and al Qaeda together." He cited as evidence Saddam's established record of having supported other Islamist terrorist organizations including Hamas, which was known to have had a presence in Baghdad since 1999, as well as the Palestine Islamic Jihad, an organization which for years had participated in Baghdad's annual terrorism conference.

After citing Saddam's various crimes against humanity, including his use of chemical weapons against the Iraqi Kurds, Powell concluded his presentation to the U.N. by stating that the United States could no longer risk "leaving Saddam Hussein in possession of weapons of mass destruction for a few more months or years" in the "post-September 11th world" and urged the United Nations to act.

Contrary to popular belief, neither Powell nor any other senior member of the Bush administration ever made the assertion that there was any firm evidence of a link between Iraq and 9/11. As President Bush himself later said, while "we did say there were numerous contacts between Saddam Hussein and al Qaeda,"—contacts that were also confirmed by the 9/11 Commission[65]— "this administration never said that the 9/11 attacks were orchestrated between Saddam and al Qaeda."[66]

Whatever the merits of the administration's case regarding Saddam's sponsorship of terrorism, the issue that would come to dominate worldwide opinion in judging the legitimacy of the invasion would be the missing WMDs. To date, no large stockpiles of chemical or biological weapons or signs of any kind of advanced nuclear weapons program have been unearthed in Iraq. While security conditions have no doubt impeded search efforts, at the time of writing this book, most experts—and the Bush administration—are now of the persuasion that the intelligence estimates regarding Iraq's WMD programs and stockpiles were simply wrong.

In September 2004, the 1,200-member team of investigators, the Iraq Survey Group, which was sent by the CIA to search for WMDs, issued a 1,000-page "Comprehensive Report" in which the group concluded that the reason most intelligence assessments were so wrong was because once Saddam kicked the UN inspectors out in 1998, all analysis had to be done remotely and because of this handicap, "incorrect conclusions" had been made.[67] Once back in Iraq, the inspectors noted, it was still difficult, if not impossible to gather conclusive evidence because of the way in which the former regime worked. As Charles Duelfer, head of the ISG concluded, "in the security-conscious world of Saddam, *it would be surprising to find explicit direction related to sensitive topics like WMD*"[68] [emphasis in the original]. Duelfer also stated that "many years of inspections [had] taught the Iraqi WMD counterparts how their country was being examined. It might well be expected that they would seek to elude such examination as a result."[69] As Duelfer duly noted, instead of finding no evidence, "it may be that a more accurate formulation might be we recognized no evidence. This is a fundamental conundrum in assessing alien circumstances."[70]

Critics of the war in Iraq continue to claim that the Bush administration misled the public in casting the threat as imminent. What the Bush administration actually argued, however, was that in the post-9/11 environment the United States had to act *before* the threat became imminent. As President Bush's stated in his 2003 State of the Union Address:

> Some have said we must not act until the threat is imminent. Since when have terrorists and tyrants announced their intentions, politely putting us on notice before they strike? If this threat is permitted to fully and suddenly emerge, all actions, all words, and all recriminations would come too late. Trusting in the sanity and restraint of Saddam Hussein is not a strategy, and it is not an option.[71]

As far as keeping Saddam contained through the oil-for-food sanctions program, by 2002, almost no one was willing to argue that continuing the sanctions was a sustainable approach. As *Fareed Zakaria* of Newsweek wrote:

> Those who now oppose the war must recognize that there was no stable status quo on Iraq. The box that Saddam Hussein had been in was collapsing. Saddam's neighbors, as well as France and Russia, were actively subverting the sanctions against Iraq. And yet, while the regime was building palaces, the restrictions on Iraqi trade had a terrible side effect. UNICEF estimated that the containment of Iraq was killing about 36,000 Iraqis a year, 24,000 of them children under the age of 5. In other words, a month of sanctions was killing far more Iraqis than a week of the war did. This humanitarian catastrophe was being broadcast nightly across the Arab world.[72]

Bin Laden repeatedly cited the devastating impact of the Iraq sanctions as one of his casus belli against the United States. First, in a 1998 interview with ABC's John Miller,[73] and then again, four years later, in a November 2002 letter address to the American people, he chastised Americans for not showing concern when "more than 1.5 million Iraqi children . . . died as a result of your sanctions."[74] In short, continuing with the sanctions policy would have hardly been the way to appease the jihadists.

According Duelfer, Saddam maintained his hopes that the sanctions would be lifted right up until he heard Bush give his 2002 State of the Union address. This was the speech in which President Bush identified Iraq as part of an "axis of evil." Duelfer says that it was only at this point that Saddam finally understood that the rules of the game had changed. Only upon hearing Bush plainly state that "the United States of America will not permit the world's most dangerous regimes to threaten us with the world's most destructive weapons,"[75] did Saddam finally realize, that there had been a profound shift in the American psyche. As Duelfer wrote, he now saw a "seriousness [that] he had not earlier recognized." Still, old habits would die hard, and he would continue to try to negotiate with the United Nations Security Council and, as Duelfer wryly observed, this "dithering cost him."[76]

On March 20, 2003, an international coalition of forty-nine countries, led by the United States and Britain, invaded Iraq.[77] In less than three weeks, on April 9, U.S. forces seized Baghdad and, in front of the world's television cameras, toppled a statue of Saddam in the central square of the Iraqi capital. The Iraqi army seemed to have simply melted away. None of the most dire prewar predictions came to pass: coalition forces did not become entangled in a war of urban combat; casualties were kept to a minimum; the invasion generated very few refugees; there were no major ecological disasters; and finally, the good news about the intelligence failure regarding WMDs was that Saddam did not have any stockpiles to deploy against the coalition forces.

And so, some five weeks after the invasion, on May 1, 2003 aboard the USS Abraham Lincoln, under a banner declaring "Mission Accomplished" President Bush declared that major combat operations were over. In the aftermath, some Iraqis descended into looting and lawlessness, and devastated such national treasures as Iraq's museum of antiquities and its national library. When asked on April 11, 2001, why U.S. forces were not doing more to stop the chaos, Secretary of Defense Donald Rumsfeld seemed almost nonchalant in his assessment, "Freedom's untidy, and free people are free to make mistakes and commit crimes and do bad things. They're also free to live their lives and do wonderful things, and that's what's going to happen here."[78] In spite of the chaos, for a moment, at least, most Americans believed the war in Iraq had gone amazingly well.

When Saudi Arabia experienced its own terror attacks at the hands of jihadists in May 2003, even the reluctant kingdom seemed to become a more reliable ally, finally cracking down on the jihadists at home, having realized that it had no special immunity. Despite these initial hopeful signs in the war on terror, however, by end of Summer 2003, it was clear that the jihad in Iraq had just beginning. Now the main debate in jihadist circles would center around whether jihadists should remain at home and destabilize their local regimes or whether they should go and join the battle in Iraq.[79] With a year, the answer would be clear: most jihadists seemed to be opting in favor of the front in Iraq.

Thomas Hegghammer, a Norwegian expert on the global jihad movement has even gone so far as to make the case that the war in Iraq actually undermined other jihad fronts. As he writes "It is reasonable to assume that radical forces are being diverted away from other terrorist campaigns that are considered by many as being strategically unproductive or theologically controversial."[80] He does caution that "[t]his does not mean, however, that other fronts are being abandoned. Many global jihadists still believe that it is perfectly possible to fight on several fronts at simultaneously."[81]

The Human Rights of Terrorists

The war on terror would force Americans to confront various moral dilemmas as they tried to achieve a balance between civil liberties and security. On April 28th, CBS Sixty Minutes broadcast photographs obtained from an ongoing Pentagon investigation showing prisoners being abused at the Abu Ghraib prison in Baghdad, now operating under the U.S. military.[82] The Pentagon investigation would ultimately conclude that some individual American soldiers and officers had indeed committed various offenses ranging from slapping Iraqi prisons to using dogs to intimidate them to simulating electric torture to stripping them and then forcing them to perform sexually explicit or humiliating acts while videotaping and photographing them.[83] The Pentagon determined that the abuses represented violations of the military's own code of conduct and were committed by individual soldiers and officers and were not the product of the military's interrogation policies.

Though the Abu Ghraib abuses were found to have occurred because of a breakdown in the military discipline and not in the course of any interrogations—none of the prisoners involved were considered to be of any intelligence value—the photos opened up debate about the appropriateness of the use of torture. Americans now had to think about just how far they were willing to go to extract critical information from terrorists.

In response to a CIA request for guidance on conducting interrogations, in August 2002, the administration's lawyers wrote a memo outlining what they believed was permissible under U.S. law and international conventions. The memo interpreted torture to mean only "extreme acts" causing pain of such intensity that it is "akin to that which accompanies serious physical injury such as death or organ failure." If the torture is psychological, it must cause harm of long duration—post-traumatic stress syndrome, for example—and must arise from threats of imminent death, torture, or mind altering drugs. Merely "cruel, inhuman, or degrading treatment or punishment fail to rise to the level of torture." Even with this leeway, the memo argued that "under the current circumstances" the existing bans on torture could be construed as unconstitutional and that "necessity and self-defense could provide justifications that would eliminate any criminal liability" later.[84]

Though it is unclear that this guideline information was ever widely disseminated, as the memo was written exclusively for the CIA, and military personnel and lawyers with knowledge of the interrogation process have stated that they were unaware of any of its contents, Seymour Hersh who wrote an influential story on what had occurred at Abu Ghraib, labeled it the "most suggestive document," implying that the memo contained the real story on what was actually going on inside America's military prisons and detention centers.[85]

The Abu Ghraib scandal ultimately resulted in the U.S. Senate passing legislation in October 2005 that explicitly banned not just torture but also the use of "cruel, inhuman or degrading treatment or punishment" by the U.S. military any where in the world. The legislation also strictly limited the types of interrogation techniques the U.S. military could use to those authorized in the Army field manual – such as exploiting a source's passions, fears, pride, or sense of futility.

Senator John McCain, a Republican who was one of the senators who authored the bill because he himself had been tortured while held captive during the Vietnam War, summed up why he felt the measures were necessary: "Many of my comrades were subjected to very cruel, very inhumane and degrading treatment, a few of them even unto death. But every one of us—every single one of us—knew and took great strength from the belief that we were different from our enemies."[86]

The White House tried to carve out an exception for "clandestine counterterrorism operations conducted abroad, with respect to terrorists who are not citizens of the United States, that are carried out by an element of the United States government other than the Department of Defense and are consistent with the Constitution and laws of the United States and treaties to which the United States is a party, if the president determines that such operations are vital to the protection of the United States or its citizens from terrorist attack."[87] In other words, the White House wanted certain CIA operations to be excluded from regulation under the bill.

Charles Krauthammer, in a widely quoted essay in the *Weekly Standard*, suggested that those who would ban torture had to consider what they would legally sanction doing to extract information from a terrorist who, to quote Krauthammer, "has planted a nuclear bomb in New York City. It will go off in one hour. A million people will die. You capture the terrorist. He knows where it is. He's not talking. Question: If you have the slightest belief that hanging this man by his thumbs will get you the information to save a million people, are you permitted to do it?"[88]

Krauthammer concluded that not only was it permissible to use torture in this particular case but that it was the moral imperative. Taking the case of KSM, the mastermind of the 9/11 attacks, he argued that "It would be a gross dereliction of duty for any government not to keep" him "isolated, disoriented, alone, despairing, cold and sleepless, [and] in some godforsaken hidden location in order to find out what he knew about plans for future mass murder."[89] As he framed the issue: "Have we learned nothing from 9/11? Are we prepared to go back with complete amnesia to the domestic-crime model of dealing with terrorists, which allowed us to sleepwalk through the nineties while al Qaeda incubated and grew and metastasized unmolested until on 9/11 it finished what the first World Trade Center bombers had begun?"[90]

Instead of the McCain amendment, Krauthammer proposed banning, in his words, "all forms of torture, coercive interrogation, and inhuman treatment, except in two contingencies: (1) the ticking time bomb and (2) the slower-fuse high-level terrorist (such as KSM)" and suggested that

> In the case of the ticking time bomb, the rules would be relatively simple: Nothing rationally related to getting accurate information would be ruled out. The case of the high-value suspect with slow-fuse information is more complicated. The principle would be that the level of inhumanity of the measures used (moral honesty is essential here—we would be using measures that are by definition inhumane) would be proportional to the need and value of the information. Interrogators would be constrained to use the least inhumane treatment necessary relative to the magnitude and imminence of the evil being prevented and the importance of the knowledge being obtained.[91]

Krauthammer suggests that only "highly specialized agents who are experts and experienced in interrogation" be given the authority to resort to torture and then only under the supervision of cabinet level officials or under the purview of a body similar to the existing FISA court which now oversees the granting of what would otherwise be illegal searches and seizures in special circumstances. In cases where there is a ticking bomb however, Krauthammer argues that interrogators would have to be given enough leeway to act on their own. To ensure that this provision could never be abused, however, he suggests that the law require there to be a post-facto authorization process and in a reasonably short period after the interrogation took place.[92]

In a widely disseminated article in *The New Republic*, Andrew Sullivan made the counterargument—that torture should never be legalized, regardless of any moral imperative to use it, and compared torture to civil disobedience:

> In that case, laws are indeed broken, but that does not establish that the laws should be broken. In fact, civil disobedience implies precisely that laws should *not* be broken, and protesters who engage in it present themselves promptly for imprisonment and legal sanction on exactly those grounds. They do so for demonstrative reasons. They are not saying that laws don't matter. They are saying that laws do matter, that they should be enforced, but that their conscience in this instance demands that they disobey them.[93]

In extreme cases where torture is the right thing to do, Sullivan argues that a president should simply break the law:

> In the Krauthammer scenario, a president might well decide that, if the survival of the nation is at stake, he must make an exception. At the same time, he must subject himself—and so must those assigned to conduct the torture—to the consequences of an illegal act. Those guilty of torturing another human being must be punished—or pardoned ex-post-facto. If the torture is revealed to be useless, if the tortured man is shown to have been innocent or ignorant of the information he was tortured to reveal, then those responsible must face the full brunt of the law for, in Krauthammer's words, such a "terrible and monstrous thing." In Michael

Walzer's formulation, if we are to have dirty hands, it is essential that we show them to be dirty.[94]

It is interesting to note that this is essentially the approach Israel has taken. The use of torture has been illegal in Israel since 1999 when the Israeli supreme court explicitly banned its use in interrogations. However, as Glenn Frankel of the *Washington Post* observed,

> after the second Palestinian uprising broke out a year later, and especially after a devastating series of suicide bombings of passenger buses, cafes and other civilian targets, Israel's internal security service, known as the Shin Bet or the Shabak, returned to physical coercion as a standard practice, according to human rights lawyers and detainees. What's more, the techniques it has used command widespread support from the Israeli public, which has few qualms about the mistreatment of Palestinians in the fight against terrorism. A long parade of Israeli prime ministers and justice ministers with a variety of political views have defended the security service and either denied that torture is used or defended it as a last resort in preventing terrorist attacks.[95]

Sullivan contends that once the use of torture is permitted, "it has a habit of spreading."[96] Mark Bowden, author of *Black Hawk Down*, made the same case in an *Atlantic Monthly* article:

> It may be clear that coercion is sometimes the right choice, but how does one allow it yet still control it? Sadism is deeply rooted in the human psyche. Every army has its share of soldiers who delight in kicking and beating bound captives. Men in authority tend to abuse it—not all men, but many. As a mass, they should be assumed to lean toward abuse. How does a country best regulate behavior in its dark and distant corners, in prisons, on battlefields, and in interrogation rooms, particularly when its forces number in the millions and are spread all over the globe? In considering a change in national policy, one is obliged to anticipate the practical consequences. So if we formally lift the ban on torture, even if only partially and in rare, specific cases (the attorney and author Alan Dershowitz has proposed issuing "torture warrants"), the question will be, How can we ensure that the practice does not become commonplace—not just a tool for extracting vital, life-saving information in rare cases but a routine tool of oppression?[97]

Sullivan further argues that "Enemy combatants need not be accorded every privilege granted legitimate prisoners of war; but they must be treated as human beings. This means that, in addition to physical torture, wanton abuse of their religious faith is out of bounds. No human freedom is meaningful without religious freedom. The fact that Koran abuse has been documented at Guantánamo; that one prisoner at Abu Ghraib was forced to eat pork and drink liquor; that fake menstrual blood was used to disorient a strict Muslim prisoner at Guantánamo—these make winning the hearts and minds of moderate Muslims far harder."[98] He argues further that

> The war on terrorism is, after all, a religious war in many senses. It is a war to defend the separation of church and state as critical to the existence of freedom,

including religious freedom. It is a war to persuade the silent majority of Muslims that the West offers a better way—more decency, freedom, and humanity than the autocracies they live under and the totalitarian theocracies waiting in the wings. By endorsing torture—on anyone, anywhere, for any reason—we help obliterate the very values we are trying to promote. You can see this contradiction in Krauthammer's own words: We are "morally compelled" to commit "a terrible and monstrous thing." We are obliged to destroy the village in order to save it. We have to extinguish the most basic principle that defines America in order to save America.[99]

Norwegian researcher Thomas Hegghammer, a noted expert on the global jihad movement, also believes that the reports of abuse or war crimes at Guantanamo and Abu Ghraib have become icons of Muslim suffering and have helped turn Iraq into, in his words, "the most important battlefront for the global jihad movement."[100]

Europe's Response

If, as Hegghammer writes, few people "had expected that Iraq would be so attractive as a battle front that it would weaken, at least in the short-run, terrorist campaigns elsewhere," "nobody could know that Spain would be the country in Europe to be hit first and hardest by Iraq-inspired terrorism."[101] At the height of rush hour traffic on the morning of March 11, 2004, ten nearly simultaneous explosions occurred aboard four commuter trains in the Spanish capital of Madrid, killing 191 and injuring some 1,400. At first the Spanish government blamed the usual suspects—Basque separatists, who had been terrorizing Spain for decades. Two days after the bombings, however, a man called a Madrid television station to say that he had found a videotape in a wastebasket near a Madrid mosque showing a man identifying himself as the military spokesman for al Qaeda in Europe who was saying that the attacks were a response to Spain's "collaboration with the criminals Bush and his allies . . . to the crimes you have caused in the world, and specifically in Iraq and Afghanistan."[102]

In what would be widely characterized as an act of appeasement, three days later the Spanish electorate voted the party that had gotten it into Iraq out of office. The wisdom of Spain's reaction would be challenged later, when Spanish law enforcement agents found that those responsible for the bombings, a group of mostly Moroccan immigrants, had begun planning for the attacks in the year before the 9/11 attacks, before the war in Iraq had even been contemplated.[103]

Interestingly, though the United States has been widely criticized for its detentions in the wake of the 9/11 attacks, suspects in Spain's terrorism cases can be held up to three years (with the possibility of an extension), without access to lawyers or family, while Spanish authorities go about gathering evidence.

Recall that the members of the Madrid cell who blew themselves up during a police stand-off had called a cleric in London, Abu Qatada, to ask for permission to kill themselves in lieu of being taken captive. At the time of the call, Qatada was in a high-security prison in London where he had been held since 2002. According to his arrest records he was "suspected of being at the center of al Qaeda in the United Kingdom."[104] Under British antiterrorism laws passed in the wake of the 9/11 attacks, foreigners suspected of terrorism could be detained indefinitely without being charged or having to undergo trial.

However by December 2004, with the passage of time and the fact that no major act of terrorism had occurred, in spite of everything that was known about Qatada—and there was plenty of evidence connecting him to everyone from the 9/11 hijackers to Zacarias Moussaoui, the "twentieth hijacker," to Richard Reid, the "shoe-bomber," to Zarqawi—Britain's highest court of appeals ruled that the counterterrorism measures that Britain had passed in haste after the attacks on New York and Washington encroached on fundamental civil liberties and that the British government could no longer detain foreign terrorism suspects indefinitely without charging or trying them. And so in March 2005, though he was believed to be somehow linked to the Madrid attacks, Abu Qatada was released from high-security prison and placed under house arrest, where he could live at home with his family but all his coming and goings were to be monitored.

As Michael Clarke, director of the International Policy Institute at King's College in London, observed, the Madrid train bombings simply did not impact on Europeans the way the 9/11 attacks had had on Americans who now took a whole new approach to the world. According to Clarke, even after what happened in Madrid, the general consensus in Europe was still, "We've got to do more of the same, only a bit more vigorously."[105] Or as *Newsweek* wryly noted in the summer after the attacks, "If there's been a wake-up call in Europe, then many of its officials are taking it under a beach umbrella."[106]

It is noteworthy that France, arguably America's staunchest critic regarding its Iraq policies is, among European countries, the one that takes the hardest line when it comes to counterterrorism efforts. The French routinely use techniques that would be repugnant to most Americans, including measures such as ethnic profiling, preemptive arrests and the monitoring of mosques and cultural centers. French authorities can also detain terrorism suspects for up to six days of questioning without providing any access to lawyers and for up to three years without charging them. In 2004, the French went even further and passed a law allowing the government to expel any foreigner caught preaching "discrimination, hatred or violence" against any group.[107]

French counterterrorism officials defend their policies by arguing that they have enabled them to preempt terrorism plots not just at home but also abroad. Terrorism is "a new form of war and we should be flexible in how we fight it," Jean-Louis Bruguiere, a senior French anti-terrorism judge was quoted as saying by the *Washington Post*. As he observed: "When you have your enemy in your own territory, whether in Europe or in North America, you can't use military forces because it would be inappropriate and contrary to the law. So you have to use new forces, new weapons."[108]

France first began ramping up its antiterrorism laws in the mid-1990s when it was being targeted by Algerian terrorists. According to Bruguiere, the French saw the attacks on the World Trade Center and the Pentagon as a part of an already long-running campaign by radical Islamists against Western civilization.[109]

French counterterrorism authorities are reportedly considered by U.S. intelligence agencies to be the most helpful of any European law-enforcement agents when it comes to pursuing terrorists. According to U.S. government officials, after the 9/11 attacks, the French president, Jacques Chirac, gave instructions to his intelligence agents to treat their U.S. counterparts "as if they were your own service."[110]

In 2002, the CIA and French intelligence services even set up a joint top-secret center in Paris, which they code-named the Alliance Base, to facilitate the sharing of information and to coordinate counterterrorism efforts, according to the *Washington Post*, which broke the news of the joint effort.[111] France is also the only one of six European nations who continues to hold its citizens in detention once they have been repatriated from Guantanamo, according to the same report. It is noteworthy that jihadists have not been able to successfully carry out any mass-casualty attacks in France, though individual Jews have suffered at the hands of radicalized Muslims—and in some particularly gruesome attacks.

Britain had to reexamine many of its domestic policies in the wake of the July 7, 2005 subway and bus attacks that took place in London. When news emerged that the bombers were British nationals, it became clear that the threat from Islamic extremism was no longer remote but now frighteningly local. As Sheik Omar Bakri Mohammed, a radical cleric in London explained it "[Osama bin Laden] is showing that he can use British Muslims, who are living on your own doorstep, to harm you. He doesn't have to bring people all the way from Medina and Saudi Arabia to fly over here. . . . If this attack was Al Qaeda, then I think it can be considered a great success for them."[112]

Bakri was already a well-known figure to British counterterrorism officials. Some of his followers had even been indicted for plotting to bomb various targets in the United Kingdom using a half-ton of ammonium nitrate they had stored for the occassion. A relative of one of the would-be bombers told a reporter that his nephew was "a normal kid" until he came into contact with Bakri's group.[113]

The London attacks finally compelled British authorities to reconsider their long-standing policy of offering safe haven to Islamic radicals like Omar Bakri. He had been granted asylum by British authorities in 1985 after having been deported from Saudi Arabia for radical activities. For years Britain had been welcoming Islamist radicals from all over the Middle East—even some that had been convicted of capital offenses back home. There were so many Islamic radicals operating out of London in the 1990s, that counterterrorism officials had taken to calling it "Londonistan." In "Londonistan" these Islamic radicals had for years been free to operate websites, publish newspapers, hold conferences, speak freely at mosques and Islamic centers and otherwise rally young Muslims to jihad, incite them to hate Israel and America, and organize seditious Islamist movements back home. Many did not even have to work, courtesy of the British government which provided these "refugees" with generous welfare benefits. Some observers have suggested that by providing safe harbor to the radicals, British authorities may have even believed they were purchasing immunity from Islamic terrorist attacks inside Britain.

But when the London subway and bus bombings occurred, the British home secretary, Charles Clarke, reflected a broad swath of public sentiment, when he announced that the government would no longer tolerate the messages of hate that were being propagated by refugee guests such as Bakri. Clarke announced that under the authority provided by existing laws, the country would now exercise its right to deport any foreigner who preached or in any way advocated terrorism.[114] Omar Bakri, who was visiting relatives in Lebanon at the time of the announcement was denied reentry to Britain, and other radicals, including Abu Qatada, the spiritual advisor to the 9/11 Hamburg cell and the Madrid train bombers were rounded up for deportation processing.

When a United Nations torture specialist, Manfred Nowak, expressed concerns that Britain was now going to be sending people back to countries with poor human rights records, Clarke responded icily, "The human rights of those people who were blown up on the tube in London on July 7 are, to be quite frank, more important than the human rights of the people who committed those acts."[115] Nevertheless, the British government, in order to comply with the European Court of Human Rights, would still have to prove that anyone it deported would not face death or torture upon deportation and as of May 2006, was still trying to sort out the legal issues to be able to deport Qatada. Some 230 individuals linked to terrorism by Scotland Yard and MI5 have reportedly already been allowed to remain in Britain as asylum seekers because the government could not meet the human rights standard in these cases.[116]

While deporting radical clerics and eradicating the safe harbor that was once "Londonistan" would presumably help counter Islamic radicalism, just as eliminating the terrorist refuge in Afghanistan has diminished al Qaeda's ability to operate, Europe must still contend with the fact that many of its young Muslims are enamored with the global jihad movement. Thousands are suspected of having been radicalized. Scott Atran, the director of research in anthropology at France's Centre National de la Recherche Scientifique, who is an expert on suicide bombing, warns that

[i]n Muslim countries and across western Europe, bright and idealistic Muslim youth, even more than the marginalized and dispossessed, internalize the jihadi story, illustrated on satellite television and the Internet with the ubiquitous images of social injustice and political repression with which much of the Muslim world's intimately identifies. From the suburbs of Paris to the jungles of Indonesia, I have interviewed culturally uprooted and politically restless youth who echo a stunningly simplified and decontextualized message of martrydom for the sake of global jihad as life's noblest cause. They are increasingly as willing and even eager to die as they are to kill.[117]

Because of Europe's open borders and the failure of European intelligence agencies to adopt uniform counterterrorism strategies, the movements of these radicals are extremely difficult to track.

While the most radical mosques are known to and may be being monitored by counterterrorism investigators, Britain has, at the time of writing this book abandoned earlier plans to shut down radical mosques after it received too many complaints from the police and the Muslim community that this was only serving to alienate ordinary Muslims and drive the extremists further underground, according to the London *Times*.[118]

It bears noting that even mainstream mosques both in Europe and the United States may bear some responsibility in fomenting radicalism. In early 2005, a New York-based think tank, Freedom House, published a study of Saudi material being disseminated at fifteen mosques around the United States.[119] In the books and pamphlets that Freedom House found, which are also being distributed at Islamic bookstores and cultural centers, Muslims are told that Christians worship an infidel God; infidels should be hated for their religion; women should be veiled; Muslims should not become citizens of any country "governed by infidels because this is a means of acquiescing to their infidelity and accepting all their erroneous ways"; and, finally, that jihad is the duty of all Muslims and Muslim governments. The authors of the study were forced to conclude that such materials "pose a grave threat to non-Muslims and to the Muslim community itself."

James Woosley, former head of the CIA during the Clinton administration, compared the hateful ideology being promoted in the Saudi educational materials to "the extremely angry form taken by much of German nationalism in the period after WWI." As he noted, "not all angry and extreme German nationalists (or their sympathizers in the U.S.) in that period were or became Nazis. But just as angry and extreme German nationalism of that period was the soil in which Nazism grew, Wahhabi and Islamist extremism today is the soil in which al Qaeda and its sister terrorist organizations are growing. We need to recognize the problem posed by the international spread of this hate ideology."[120]

While the notion of having to monitor religious institutions including mosques is normally repugnant, the presence of the Saudi materials at American institutions does, however, seem to suggest that the West may indeed have to face at least the prospect that some percentage of its Musilim population is now being encouraged to represent a fifth column. Perhaps a lesson can be extracted from Atran's work. As he writes: "What has struck me in my interviews with mujahideen who have rejected suicide bombing is that they remain very committed to Salifi principles, with firm and deep religious beliefs. Those who seem to succeed best at convincing their brethren to forsake wanton killing of civilians do so by promoting alternative interpretations of Islamic principles that need not directly oppose Salafi teachings."[121]

The Forward Strategy of Democratization

After the invasion of Iraq, the American-led provisional government set about implementing the next phase of the Bush administration's war on terror: replacing the Iraqi dictatorship with a democracy, a move that the Bush administration hoped would unleash a domino effect whose end result would be the eventual democratization of the entire Middle East.

In a speech in London in November 2003, President Bush explained why he believed that democracy would eliminate one of the major root causes of Islamic terrorism:

> In democratic and successful societies, men and women do not swear allegiance to malcontents and murderers; they turn their hearts and labor to building better lives. And democratic governments do not shelter terrorist camps or attack their peaceful neighbors; they honor the aspirations and dignity of their own people.[122]

In his speech, President Bush also acknowledged that for fifty years the United States had mistakenly tolerated dictatorships and tyrannies in the Middle East in the interest of stability, but the 9/11 attacks had taught the nation a lesson and now the United States was going to pursue "a different course, a forward strategy of freedom in the Middle East."[123] Moreover, according to Bush, if democracy failed to take hold in Iraq, he feared that Iraq would become a terrorist stronghold.[124]

Strangely, al Qaeda's representative in Iraq, Abu Musab al-Zarqawi, shared President Bush's assessment of the situation.

In a letter intercepted by American forces in January 2004, Zarqawi explained why Iraq was such a central front in the global jihad movement: "We know from God's religion that the true, decisive battle between infidelity and Islam is in this land, i.e., in [Greater] Syria and its surroundings. Therefore, we must spare no effort and strive urgently to establish a foothold in this land."[125] In a message he posted on the Internet just before Iraq's historic January 2005 elections, he explained in detail what he sees to be the seven fundamental flaws of democracy. His analysis reveals a great deal about the ideology of the global jihad movement.

First: Democracy is based on the principle that the people are the source of all authority, including the legislative [authority]. This is carried out by choosing representatives who act as proxies for the people in the task of legislating and making laws. In other words, the legislator who must be obeyed in a democracy is man, and not Allah. That means that the one who is worshiped and obeyed and deified, from the point of view of legislating and prohibiting, is man, the created, and not Allah. That is the very essence of heresy and polytheism and error, as it contradicts the bases of the faith [of Islam] and monotheism, and because it makes the weak, ignorant man Allah's partner in His most central divine prerogative—namely, ruling and legislating. Allah said: "Sovereignty is Allah's alone. He has commanded you to worship none but Him" [Koran 12:40]. "He allows none to share His sovereignty" [Koran 18:26] . . .

Second: Democracy is based on the principle of freedom of religion and belief. Under democracy, a man can believe anything he wants and choose any religion he wants and convert to any religion whenever he wants, even if this apostasy means abandoning the religion of Allah . . . This is a matter which is patently perverse and false and contradicts many specific [Muslim] legal texts, since according to Islam, if a Muslim apostatizes from Islam to heresy, he should be killed, as stated in the *Hadith* reported by Al-Bukhari and others: "Whoever changes his religion, kill him." It does not say "leave him alone."

One may not make a [peace] treaty with an apostate, nor grant him safe passage or protection. According to Allah's religion, he has only one choice: "Repent or be killed."

Third: Democracy is based on considering the people to be the sole sovereign, to whom all juridical matters and conflicts should be referred, and if there is any controversy or conflict between governor and governed, each of them threatens the other to refer to the will of the people and its choice, so that the people should decide on the matter on which is disagreed. This conflicts with and is contradictory to the principles of monotheism, which determines that the arbiter, deciding by His judgment in matters of discord, is Allah and none else. Allah said [Koran 42:10]: "And in whatever thing you disagree, the judgment thereof belongs to

Allah." Democracy, on the other hand, says: "And in whatever things you disagree, the judgment thereof belongs to the people and to none beside the people . . ."

Fourth: Democracy is based on the principal of "freedom of expression," no matter what the expression might be, even if it means hurting and reviling the Divine Being [i.e. Allah] and the laws of Islam, because in democracy nothing is so sacred that one cannot be insolent or use vile language about it.

Fifth: Democracy is based on the principle of separation between religion and state, politics, and life; what is Allah's is rendered unto Allah, which is just worship in the places designed for it. All other aspects of life—political, economic, social, etc.—are the people's prerogative . . .

Sixth: Democracy is based on the principle of freedom of association and of forming political parties and the like, no matter what the creed, ideas, and ethics of these parties may be. This principle is null and void according to [Islamic] law for a number of reasons . . . One of them is that voluntary recognition of the legality of heretical parties implies acquiescence in heresy . . . Acquiescence in heresy is heresy . . .

Seventh: Democracy is based on the principle of considering the position of the majority and adopting what is agreed upon by the majority, even if they agree upon falsehood, error, and blatant heresy . . . This principle is totally wrong and void because truth according to Islam is that which is in accordance with the Koran and the *Sunna* [i.e., the tradition of the Prophet], whether its supporters are few or many; and that which contradicts the Koran and the *Sunna* is false even if all the people of the world agree on it . . .[126]

To disrupt the democratic process in Iraq, Zarqawi proposed in early 2004 that the mujahidin should incite a sectarian war between Iraq's Sunni and Shiite Muslims. Anticipating criticism that this would, in his words, lead "the [Islamic] nation into a battle for which it is not ready, [a battle] that will be revolting and in which blood will be spilled," he argued that "right and wrong no longer have any place in our current situation . . . God's religion is more precious that lives and souls."[127]

In spite of Zarqawi's considerable efforts to disrupt the electoral process through threats and attacks against Iraqi civilians on January 30, 2005, a majority of the Iraqi population braved what would turn out to be the bloodiest day of the insurgency to that date in order to participate in their nation's first free elections in half a century. The images of Iraqis holding up their ink-stained fingers for all the world to celebrate unleashed a flurry of messages on Islamist websites encouraging foreign jihadists not to despair and give up their fight. As Ritz Katz of the SITE Institute, an organization that monitors such websites observed, the elections seemed to make the jihadists "very nervous about the future."[128] Zarqawi would be so desperate he would even be moved to produce a full-blown Internet magazine, *Zurwat al Sanam* ("the top of the camel's hump"), to shore up support, an effort *The New York Times* would characterize as a "full-scale propaganda war."[129]

Other signs of democracy also seemed to be sprouting elsewhere in the region. In February 2005, for the first time in their history, Saudi men went to the polls to cast their ballot in nationwide municipal elections. Though women could not vote participate and these were only local as opposed to national elections, they still represented the first nationwide democratic exercise in the kingdom's history.

A few days after the Saudi elections, on February 14, the Lebanese prime minister, Rafiq Hariri, was assassinated in a car bombing in Beirut. The good news was that the assassination provoked so much outrage among the Lebanese public who suspected that Syrian forces were behind the killing that they took to the streets in massive protests against the sinister influence and finally forced Syria to withdraw the troops and intelligence agents it had stationed in Lebanon since 1989. (A U.N. investigation later confirmed the Lebanese public's suspicions when it implicated high-level Syrian officials in the assassination, including a brother-in-law of the Syrian president.[130])

In February, Egyptian president Hosni Mubarak announced that for the first time in history, Egypt would allow its first contested presidential elections. (Mubarak still won however and the elections could handly be characterized as fair.)

Then in April 2005, Kuwait also made history when, for the first time, it allowed women to participate in the country's municipal elections. Again, though this was an imperfect victory, it was at least a start. As President Bush observed in a speech at the National Defense University in March, for decades the "chances for democratic progress in the broader Middle East" had seemed frozen . . . Yet, at last, clearly and suddenly, the thaw has begun."[131]

Walid Jumblatt, the leader of the Lebanese Druze community, would confirm to *Newsweek*, that the Middle East was finally changing. "The Arab people want to join the rest of the civilized world. They want freedom. I have denounced the American invasion of Iraq, but I also admit that the Iraqi people are now free."[132] Earlier he commented, that when he saw "the Iraqi people voting, 8 million of them," what occurred to him was that "this signaled the start of a new Arab world," adding, "the Berlin Wall has fallen."[133]

In its annual report for 2006, Freedom House, an independent monitor of civil rights and political liberties in the world observed that:

> The global picture thus suggests that 2005 was one of the most successful years for freedom since Freedom House began measuring world freedom in 1972. . . .
>
> The Freedom in the World 2006 ratings for the Middle East represent the region's best performance in the history of the survey. . . . Since the events of 9/11, the United States has made the promotion of democracy—in the Middle East primarily but in other regions as well—a greater priority among the broad mix of foreign policy goals. . . . the administration of George W. Bush, building on policies initiated by his predecessors, has pushed forward an agenda in which the advancement of freedom plays a tangible role. . . . While the precise impact of democracy promotion policies is often difficult to measure, it is by now clear that the efforts by the established democracies to expand freedom's reach are paying dividends. Democracy promotion has always had its critics, and the critics' objections, as might be expected, have been amplified during a controversial war. But if the gains for freedom revealed in this survey tell us anything, it is that the policies of the United States, Europe, and other free societies are achieving some crucial goals.[134]

Even some of Bush's most severe critics were suddenly asking, as Claus Malzahn phrased the question in the German newsweekly *Der Spiegel*, "Could

George W. Bush Be Right?"[135] or as Guy Sorman, writing for the Paris daily *Le Figaro*, asked: "And if Bush Was Right?"[136]

Rami G. Khouri, editor of the *Beirut Daily Star*, suggested that Bush—and Arab democrats—did indeed deserve credit for the "Arab spring." He said that "the presence of the U.S. and other foreign forces in Iraq also certainly has played a role in focusing the minds of various Arab leaders on their need to change and modernize quickly." He added that for the first time, Arabs and the U.S. government share the same goal of replacing dictatorships with democracy and the rule of law, "This has never happened in recent memory, which is why it is important now to focus on what needs to be done by all concerned parties, rather than argue about who started the ball rolling. We both did."[137]

In August and September, in an effort to secure peace with the Palestinians after enduring four years of the intifada. Israel withdrew its forces and settlements from Gaza, the narrow strip of land it had conquered in the 1967 war. Israel's unilateral move was supposed to give the 1.3 million Palestinians living in Gaza their first opportunity to build their own state since they rejected the United Nation's 1947 Partition Plan. Critics of the disengagement, most notably Daniel Pipes, warned that, "[t]o Palestinian rejectionists, an Israeli retreat under fire sends an unambiguous signal: Terrorism works. Just as the Israeli departure from Lebanon five years earlier provoked new violence, so too will fleeing Gaza. Palestinians ignore all the verbiage about 'disengagement'and see it for what it really is, an Israeli retreat under fire. Indeed, Palestinian leaders have already broadcast their intent to deploy Gaza-like aggression to pry the West Bank and Jerusalem from Israeli control. Should that campaign succeed, Haifa and Tel Aviv are next, after which Israel itself disappears."[138]

"Of course terror has a role in the disengagement," the *New York Times* quoted Michael Oren, a senior fellow at the Shalem Institute, a Jerusalem research group, as saying, "It convinced us that Gaza was not worth holding onto and awakened us to the demographic danger. It took two intifadas for a majority of Israelis to decide that Gaza is not worth it."[139]

A senior Israeli official, who according to the *New York Times* had close associations with Likud leaders, reportedly reached a similar conclusion: "The fact that hundreds of them are willing to blow themselves up is significant," he was reported as saying. "We didn't give them any credit before. In spite of our being the strongest military power in the Middle East, we lost 1,200 people over the last four years. It finally sank in to Sharon and the rest of the leadership that these people were not giving up."[140]

Meanwhile, in spite of the democratic process going on in Iraq, the insurgency continued. By the fall of 2005, opinion polls were indicating that American support for the war in Iraq was flagging in the face of mounting casualties. In the last week of October, the number of American military forces who had died in Iraq reached the widely reported "grim milestone" of 2,000.

Recognizing that Americans were losing heart, in a speech to the National Endowment for Democracy in October, President Bush urged his fellow citizens not to be persuaded by those who "claim that America would be better off by cutting our losses and leaving Iraq now." This type of thinking, he suggested was a "dangerous illusion" that could be "refuted with a simple question: Would the United States and other free nations be more safe, or less safe, with Zarqawi and bin Laden in control of Iraq, its people, and its resources?" Acknowledging that war always has its difficult stretches, "There's always a temptation, in the middle of a long struggle, to seek the quiet life, to escape the duties and problems of the world, and to hope the enemy grows weary of fanaticism and tired of murder." "This would be a pleasant world, but it's not the world we live in," he said, cautioning. "The enemy is never tired, never sated, never content with yesterday's brutality. This enemy considers every retreat of the civilized world as an invitation to greater violence. In Iraq, there is no peace without victory."[141]

In October 2005, Iraqis again braved threats of violence and came out to vote on a constitutional referendum. Though al Qaeda in Iraq threatened to kill anyone who participated in the process, 70 percent of Iraq's eligible voters cast their ballots. Iraq's Sunnis, among whom Zarqawi was drawing most if not all of his local support, even made a surprise showing, turning out in significantly higher numbers than they had for the January elections. Abu Theeb, a Sunni who was described by a London newspaper as a man who had previously "devoted himself and his resources to fighting the Americans" in Iraq, told *The Guardian* that he had finally decided to enter the electoral process because "Politics for us is like filthy dead meat. We are not allowed to eat it, but if you are passing through the desert and your life depends on it, God says its OK."[142]

In the national parliamentary elections held on December 15, 2005, the Sunnis turned out in even greater numbers and this time the insurgent violence was less than anticipated. As one Sunni Iraqi told *The New York Times*, "Last time, if you voted, you died." Abdul Jabbar Mahdi, was quoted as saying, "God willing, this election will lead to peace."[143]

While the Bush administration was basing its forward strategy on the idea that democracy would ultimately stifle Islamic extremism by engaging people in the political process as opposed to frustrating them to the point that wanted to destroy it, there was still plenty of evidence suggesting that unleashing the rule of the people in the region would only bring about governments that were even more Islamist, more hostile to U.S. interests and no less susceptible to Islamic terrorism.

In a *Foreign Affairs* article published in the fall of 2005, political scientist F. Gregory Gause III examined this fundamental premise of the Bush Doctrine by asking: "Is it true that the more democratic a country becomes, the less likely it is to produce terrorists and terrorist groups?"[144]

Gause argued that recent elections results throughout the Middle East had shown that, in his words, "Islamists of various hues score well in free elections." This suggested to Gause that "further democratization in the Middle East would, for the foreseeable future," be more and not less likely to "generate Islamist governments" and these new Islamist government could most likely be counted on to be even "less inclined to cooperate with the United States on important U.S. policy goals, including military basing rights in the region, peace with Israel, and the war on terrorism."[145] Indeed, in the Lebanese parliamentary elections in May 2005, the Iranian-backed Hezbollah won 23 out of 128 seats—its largest election win ever and enough seats to secure at least two ministerial positions in the Lebanese government. Then in Egypt, the Muslim

Brotherhood won a substantial number of seats in the parliamentary elections in late 2005 threatening the National Democratic Party's decades-long hold on power. Qatar, by now fearing its own Islamist victory, postponed its inaugural parliamentary elections, pushing them back to 2007. Jordan also decided to table a planned reform agenda after being hit by multiple terrorist attacks in November 2005, orchestrated by Zarqawi. In January 2006, the jihadist terror organization, Hamas, came to power in the Palestinian Authority, winning 74 out of 132 seats in the January 2006 Palestinian Authority legislative elections forcing Israel to suspend payment of $50 million in tax receipt after the Palestinian Authority named a Hamas leader Ismail Haniya to be the new prime minister of the PA. Israel had made clear that it would refuse to fund a government controlled by a party that called for its destruction. The United States, the European Union, and the United Nations had also warned the Palestinians that they would not supply aid if Hamas did not renounce violence, recognize Israel's right to exist, and agree to continue to advance the peace process. The only member of the Quartet that appeared to be willing to work with the new Hamas-led Palestinian Authority was Russia. Though Hamas leaders indicated that they might be willing to observe a temporary ceasefire, they refused to repudiate terrorism or back away from their calls for the destruction of Israel. To make up the aid deficit in aid, the Hamas leaders called on Arab and Muslim countries. Gause's predictions did seem to be coming true.

However, a leading Arab democrat, Saad Eddin Ibrahim who himself spent years in Egyptian prison for promoting democracy, offered an opposing viewpoint:

Based on my 30 years of empirical investigation into these [Islamist] parties—including my observations of fellow inmates during the 14 months I spent in an Egyptian prison—I can testify to a significant evolution on the part of political Islam. In fact, I believe we may be witnessing the emergence of Muslim parties that are truly democratic, akin to the Christian Democrats in Western Europe after World War II.[146]

According to Ibrahim, Islamists should be encouraged to participate in the political process, because in his view, "As long as these groups don't have to deal with the complicated business of forging actual political policies, their popularity remains untested. The challenge, therefore, is to find a formula that includes them in the system, but that prevents a 'one man, one vote, one time' situation."[147]

In his speech to the National Endowment for Democracy, President Bush compared the threat posed by the global jihad movement to the West's earlier struggle against the spread of communism:

The murderous ideology of the Islamic radicals is the great challenge of our new century. Yet, in many ways, this fight resembles the struggle against communism in the last century. Like the ideology of communism, Islamic radicalism is elitist, led by a self-appointed vanguard that presumes to speak for the Muslim masses. Bin Laden says his own role is to tell Muslims, quote, "what is good for them and what is not." And what this man who grew up in wealth and privilege considers good for poor Muslims is that they become killers and suicide bombers. He assures them that his—that this is the road to paradise—though he never offers to go along for the ride.

Like the ideology of communism, our new enemy teaches that innocent individuals can be sacrificed to serve a political vision. And this explains their cold-blooded contempt for human life. We've seen it in the murders of Daniel Pearl, Nicholas Berg, and Margaret Hassan, and many others. In a courtroom in the Netherlands, the killer of Theo Van Gogh turned to the victim's grieving mother and said, "I do not feel your pain—because I believe you are an infidel." And in spite of this veneer of religious rhetoric, most of the victims claimed by the militants are fellow Muslims.

When 25 Iraqi children are killed in a bombing, or Iraqi teachers are executed at their school, or hospital workers are killed caring for the wounded, this is mur-der, pure and simple—the total rejection of justice and honor and morality and religion. These militants are not just the enemies of America, or the enemies of Iraq, they are the enemies of Islam and the enemies of humanity. We have seen this kind of shameless cruelty before, in the heartless zealotry that led to the gulags, and the Cultural Revolution, and the killing fields.

Like the ideology of communism, our new enemy pursues totalitarian aims. Its leaders pretend to be an aggrieved party, representing the powerless against impe-rial enemies. In truth they have endless ambitions of imperial domination, and they wish to make everyone powerless except themselves. Under their rule, they have banned books, and desecrated historical monuments, and brutalized women. They seek to end dissent in every form, and to control every aspect of life, and to rule the soul, itself. While promising a future of justice and holiness, the terrorists are preparing for a future of oppression and misery.

Like the ideology of communism, our new enemy is dismissive of free peoples, claiming that men and women who live in liberty are weak and decadent. Zarqawi has said that Americans are, quote, "the most cowardly of God's creatures." But let's be clear: It is cowardice that seeks to kill children and the elderly with car bombs, and cuts the throat of a bound captive, and targets worshippers leaving a mosque. It is courage that liberated more than 50 million people. It is courage that keeps an untiring vigil against the enemies of a rising democracy. And it is courage in the cause of freedom that once again will destroy the enemies of freedom.

And Islamic radicalism, like the ideology of communism, contains inherent contradictions that doom it to failure. By fearing freedom—by distrusting human creativity, and punishing change, and limiting the contributions of half the population—this ideology undermines the very qualities that make human progress possible, and human societies successful. The only thing modern about the militants' vision is the weapons they want to use against us. The rest of their grim vision is defined by a warped image of the past—a declaration of war on the idea of progress, itself. And whatever lies ahead in the war against this ideology, the outcome is not in doubt: Those who despise freedom and progress have con-demned themselves to isolation, decline, and collapse. Because free peoples believe in the future, free peoples will own the future.[148]

While the newly-elected Iraqi parliament took its time forming a new government, sectarian violence continued, leading some observers to claim that the country had now descended into a civil war. Zarqawi's group, interestingly enough, announced in January 2006 that it was now part of the Mujahhedeen Shura or Council of Holy Warriors under the leadership of an Iraqi, Abdullah Rashid al-Baghdadi, and for a change, the Jordanian seemed to stop taking credit for large-scale mass-casualty attacks against civilians (although experts believe he was behind the bombing of the Shiite shrine in Samarra that set off a new round of sectarian violence in March).[149] Many analysts believe that Zarqawi may have been forced to modify his behavior on the advice of Zawahiri and because of the negative public reaction to hotel bombings he orchestrated in November that left some sixty people dead and more than a hundred injured, including thirty-eight guests attending a Muslim wedding in Jordan.

In early June, U.S. forces killed Zarqawi in an air strike. At the time of writing this book, it is still to early to assess the impact that Zarqawi's death will have on the insurgency. A few days after his death, a jihadist website posted a statement naming his successor. American officials say that al Qaeda in Iraq's new leader is Abu Ayyub al-Masri, an Egyptian believed to be in his late 30's who met Zarqawi at a training camp in Afghanistan in 1999. He is believed to have been a member of Zawahiri's organization, Egyptian Islamic Jihad, though officials do not know whether he is close to Zawahiri, now serving as bin Laden's second-in-command. Officials say Masri claims to have come to Iraq in 2003 expressly to set up a branch of al Qaeda in anticipation of a U.S. invasion. Around the same time, the Iraqi government released a document purportedly written by al Qaeda in Iraq that calls for the need to incite war between America and Iran. "Time is now beginning to be of service to the American forces and harmful to the resistance," the document said. "We mean specifically attempting to escalate the tension between America and Iran, and America and the Shiites in Iraq."[150]

The Shiite-led government in Iraq has so far failed to pacify the situation and has also contributed to concerns about the ascendance of a "Shiite Crescent" in the region, especially since the Iranians elected a hard-liner, Tehran's mayor Mahmoud Ahmedinejad, as their president in June 2005, and thus ended eight years of "reform" under Mohammad Khatami.

Nuclear Iran?

As soon as Ahmedinejad assumed office, he declared that "a new Islamic revolution has arisen."[151] This was the same Ahmedinejad that had been identified by several of the hostages taken in the 1979 American embassy seizure as one of their student captors.[152] Once in office, Ahmedinejad continued to reawaken nightmares of the Islamic revolution by proceeding to make several alarming statements regarding Iran's nuclear-power activities, increasing U.S. suspicions that Iran was secretly building a nuclear bomb in violation of the Nuclear Non-Proliferation Treaty. When on April 11, 2006, President Ahmedinejad announced that Iran had at last succeeded in enriching uranium, even the IAEA, the UN body which monitors nuclear activities, moved closer to the U.S. position and recommended that Iran be referred to the UN Security Council to determine the next course of action, as the enrichment of uranium is considered to be a crucial first step in building a bomb.

Iran, for its part, has denied such allegations and claims that it needs to enrich uranium in order to develop nuclear energy so that it can meet its growing domestic demand for electricity and save its plentiful oil and gas resources for much needed foreign exchange. The official position of the U.S. government is that Iran has enough natural gas and petroleum resources for all its needs and that its activities are in fact a cover for its illicit weapons program. Moreover, as Robert Joseph, a spokesman for the State Department has summed up the U.S. position, "a nuclear-armed Iran [would be] intolerable."[153]

After President Ahmadinejad gave a speech to the United Nations in September 2005 asserting Iran's right to develop nuclear energy, a film was distributed by an Iranian news organization that showed Ahmedinejad telling senior Iranian clerics that when he was in front of the United Nations, someone told him he had been surrounded by a halo of light. Ahmadinejad can be seen in the video saying, "I felt it myself, too. I felt that all of a sudden the atmosphere changed there, and for 27–28 minutes all the leaders did not blink."[154] Ahmedinejad's remarks raised concerns that the Iranian leader may believe that he has been called by God to fulfill a special destiny to prepare the world for the return of the Twelfth Imam, the Shiite leader who is believed to have gone into hiding in the ninth century and is supposed to return after a period of cosmic war in order to lead the world into its final state of Islamic peace and justice.

Adding to such concerns, were the various statements that President Ahmedinejad was making regarding Israel. In an address he made to a "World Without Zionism" conference hosted in Tehran in 2005, he declared that "the Qods-occupying regime [Israel] should be wiped off the map of the world."[155] In December 2005, he stated that the Holocaust had been exaggerated, and as recently as April 14, 2006, he declared that "the Zionist regime is on the road to being eliminated."[156]

President Ahmedinejad is by no means the first Iranian leader to have made bellicose statements regarding Israel. The Islamic revolutionary leader, the Ayatollah Khomeini, famously stated that Israel "should be wiped off the map." In 2001, another Iranian leader, the Chairman of Iran's powerful Expediency Council, Ali Akbar Rafsanjani, declared that "If one day, the Islamic world is also equipped with [nuclear] weapons like those that Israel possesses now, then the imperialists' strategy will reach a standstill because the use of even one nuclear bomb inside Israel will destroy everything," but a nuclear strike would "only harm [as opposed to destroy] the Islamic world" and thus "it is not irrational to contemplate such an eventuality."[157] In military parades, Iranian missiles are often covered with banners reading, "We will crush America" and "Wipe Israel off the map."

As opposed to alienating the largely Sunni population of the Middle East, such inflammatory rhethoric seemed to be winning the Iranian president a great deal of support in the region, particularly on the "Arab street." As the *New York Times* reported in February 2006, "with President Mahmoud Ahmadinejad bashing the United States and Europe, calling for Israel to be wiped off the map and claiming that the Holocaust is a myth, many people from taxi drivers in Morocco to street sweepers in Cairo are saying that they like the man and his vision."[158] Sheik Adel al-Mawada, a member of Bahrain's parliament, and a leader of the Sunni fundamentalist Salafi bloc went on record to say, "If Iran acted like an Islamic power, just Islam without Shiism, then Arabs would accept it as a regional Islamic power."[159]

At least some Sunni Islamists, however, registered alarm about the prospect of a nuclear-armed Iran. "If Iran developed a nuclear power, then it is a big disaster because it already supports Hezbollah in Lebanon, Hamas in Palestine, Syria and Iraq," Essam el-Erian, a spokesman for the Muslim Brotherhood of Egypt, told the New York Times, adding "we would [then] have the Shiite crescent that the Jordanian king [has] warned [about]."[160] In January 2006, Saudi Arabia's foreign minister Prince Saud al-Faisal was reported as saying that Tehran's nuclear ambitions "threaten disaster in the region."[161]

Not surprisingly, Israel was particularly alarmed about the threatening remarks coming from the Iranian president. The same day that Tehran threatened to pull out of the NPT were it forced to abandon its uranium enrichment activities, Israel's defense minister, Shaul Mofaz, declared that the Iranian regime was now one of the greatest threats the Jews had faced since Adolf Hitler and described Iran as "an existential threat on three levels: Extreme leadership, missile capability, and intent to acquire nuclear weapons." Referring to Iran's sponsorship of terrorist groups, the Iranian-born Israeli posed the rhetorical question: "[How] can we relay the message to the people of Iran that their regime could devastate them?"[162] If the Shiite regime in Iran had played a key role in the birth of the global jihad movement back in 1979, by 2006, it seemed like once again it was going to become a significant player.

In June 2006, Hamas militants, now in control of Gaza, tunneled into Israel and captured an Israeli soldier in an effort to free Palestinians sitting in Israeli prisons. Israel refused to negotiate and Hamas proceeded to kidnap an Israeli settler. Israel then bombarded Gaza and rounded up dozens of Hamas leaders. After the settler was found dead, Israel hit the Palestinian Interior Ministry. Hamas retaliated by sending a rocket into Israel and over the next week, Israeli forces killed some fifty Palestinians. The conflict widened when Lebanese Hezbollah captured two Israeli soldiers inside Israel, a move which Israel interpreted as an "act of war." Israel retaliated by bombarding Lebanon while Hezbollah launched hundreds of missile strikes at Israel. While the "Arab street" was outraged by what they saw as Israel's "disproportionate" response to the hostage taking, most Arab leaders placed the blame on Hezbollah, and suspected that it was really Iran who was pulling the strings in a bid for regional hegemony. The Hezbollah's leader for his part characterized his actions as seizing the opportunity on behalf of the Islamic world to achieve "a historic victory against the Zionist enemy." As this book went to press it was impossible to know the real story or see where this was heading. Was this a conventional war or a new front in the global jihad? As to whether the Bush administration was right or wrong to invade Iraq, or whether its strategy of democratizing the Middle East will in the end free up the region—and the world—from the threat of Islamic terrorism remains to be seen. As the Dalai Lama said in September 2003 when he was asked if the United States was right to invade Iraq, "I feel only history will tell," he said. "Terrorism is the worst kind of violence, so we have to check it, we have to take countermeasures."[163]

Notes

Chapter 1   Where Is Jihad Being Fought?

1. Dan Balz and Bob Woodward, "America's Chaotic Road to War," *The Washington Post*, January 27, 2002.
2. *The 9/11 Commission Report* (New York: W.W. Norton Co, 2004), 45.
3. The fatwa was originally published in *Al-Quds Al-Arabi* (London), February 23, 1998, a translation of the fatwa can be found http://www.military.com/Resources/ResourceFileView?file=fatwa1998.htm.
4. *The 9/11 Commission Report*, 45.
5. "Address to a Joint Session of Congress and the American People," Speech by President George W. Bush, September 20, 2001, available online at http://www.whitehouse.gov/news/releases/2001/09/20010920-8.html.
6. A translation of bin Laden's fatwa is available online at http://www.pbs.org/newshour/terrorism/international/fatwa_1998.html.
7. John J. G. Jansen, *The Neglected Duty: The Creed of Sadat's Assassins and Islamic Resurgence in the Middle East* (New York: Macmillan, 1986), 8.
8. Bin Laden's interview with Al-Jazeera television correspondent Tayseer Alouni in October 2001, available online at http://archives.cnn.com/2002/WORLD/asiapcf/south/02/05/binladen.transcript/index.html.
9. See Francis Fukuyama, *The End of History and the Last Man* (New York: The Free Press, 1992).
10. *The 9/11 Commission Report*, 101.
11. Sura 9:5 of the Koran.
12. "Interview with bin Laden," *Time Magazine*, January 11, 1999, http://www.time.com/time/asia/news/printout/0,9788,174550,00.html.
13. "*The 9/11 Commission Report*: About" http://www.gpoaccess.gov/911/about.html.
14. *The 9/11 Commission Report*, 357.
15. Ibid., 198.
16. Ibid., 343.
17. Ronald Sullivan, "Code of Silence Threatens Trade Center Investigation," *The New York Times*, March 17, 1993.
18. Ned Zemen, "The Path to 9/11; Lost Warnings and Fatal Errors," *Vanity Fair*, November 2004.
19. United Stated District Court, Southern District of New York, United States of America v. Usama bin Laden, Indictment, 98 CR, available online at http://www.fas.org/irp/news/1998/11/indict1.pdf, accessed September 6, 2005.

20. *The 9/11 Commission Report*, 60.

21. *BBC Summary of World Broadcasts*, (Source: "National Voice of Iran," in Persian) January 21, 1979), January 23, 1979.

22. As quoted by Angus Deming, "The Khomeini Enigma," *Newsweek*, December 31, 1979.

23. As quoted by Zawahiri in "Al-Sharq Al-Awsat Publishes Extracts from Al-Jihad Leader Al-Zawahiri's New Book," *FBIS-NES-2002-0108*, December 2, 2001, 24.

24. Lawrence Wright, "The Man Behind Bin Laden," *The New Yorker*, September 16, 2002.

25. As quoted by Khaled M. Abou Fadi, *The Great Theft: Wrestling Islam from the Extremists* (NY: HarperCollins, 2005), 54.

26. Mark Fineman, "Next Step; Have Guns, Will Travel; Thousands of Muslims Learned Guerrilla War in Afghanistan. Where Will They Go Next?" *Los Angeles Times*, April 7, 1992.

27. "Al-Sharq Al-Awsat Publishes Extracts from Al-Jihad Leader Al-Zawahiri's New Book," *FBIS-NES-2002-0108*, December 2, 2001, 13.

28. As quoted in Peter L. Bergen, *Holy War Inc.: Inside the Secret World of Osama bin Laden* (New York: Free Press, 2002), 53.

29. Jason Burke, *Al-Qaeda: Casting a Shadow of Terror* (London: I.B. Tauris, 2003), 6. contends that prior to 9/11, there is little evidence to support the notion that bin Laden himself regularly used the term *al Qaeda* to refer to his organization prior to September 11, 2001.

30. Milton Bearden, "Afghanistan, Graveyard of Empires," *Foreign Affairs*, November/December 2001.

31. *The 9/11 Commission Report*, 467.

32. Beardebm "Afghanistan, Graveyard of Empires."

33. Available online at http://news.findlaw.com/cnn/docs/binladen/binladenintvw-cnn.pdf.

34. *The 9/11 Commission Report*, 56.

35. Wright, "The Man Behind Bin Laden."

36. Harry Anderson, "The End of the Khomeini Era," *Newsweek*, June 12, 1989.

37. Loren Jenkins, "Iraqi Leader Claims to Be Fighting Holy War," *The Washington Post*, November 10, 1980.

38. Ibid.

39. Terence Smith, "Iran: Five Years of Fanaticism," *The New York Times*, February 12, 1984.

40. "Comprehensive Report of the Special Advisor to the DCI on Iraq's WMD," September 30, 2004, available online at http://www.cia.gov/cia/reports/ iraq_wmd_2004/Comp_Report_Key_Findings.pdf.

41. Dilip Hiro, *The longest war: the Iran-Iraq military conflict* (NY: Routledge, 1991) 250.

42. Peter Steinfels, "Calls for Holy War Reveals Fissures in Islamic World," *The New York Times*, October 7, 1990.

43. Judith Miller, "Muslims; Saudis Decree Holy War on Hussein," *The New York Times*, January 20, 1991.

44. Milton Viorst, "Sudan's Islamic Experiment," *Foreign Affairs*, May, 1995; June, 1995.

45. "Sudanese Fundamentalists Demonstrate for Islamic Law," The Xinhua General Overseas News Service, April 15, 1989.

46. " 'The Tears of Orphans': No Future without Human Rights," *Amnesty International*, January 1995.

47. Jemera Rone, Human Rights Watch, testimony, July 29, 1998, http://hrw.org/campaign/sudan98/testim/house-05.htm.

48. Julie Flint, "Hidden Holy War in the Hills," *The Guardian* (London), July 22, 1995.

49. Wright, "The Man Behind Bin Laden."

50. USA v. Omar Ahmad Ali Abdel Rahman et al., S5 93 Cr.181, United States District Court, Southern District of New York, pages 18649 and 18920.

51. Wright, "The Man Behind Bin Laden."

52. Ibid.

53. Clyde R. Mark, "Egypt-United States Relations," Congressional Research Service issue brief, Oct. 10, 2003.

54. *The 9/11 Commission Report*, 72.

55. "Lessons of First WTC Bombing," *BBC News*, February 26, 2003, http://news.bbc.co.uk/2/hi/americas/2800297.stm.

56. Terry McDermott, "The Plot; How Terrorists Hatched a Simple Plan to Use Planes as Bombs," *Los Angeles Times*, September 1, 2002.

57. Richard Bernstein, "U.S. Portrays Sheik as Head of a Wide Terrorist Network," *The New York Times*, May 6, 1994.

58. Ibid.

59. U.S. v. Sattar et al., S1 02 Cr. 395 (JGK), 7126, also referenced as Government Exhibit, 2638, 11122; Videotape, CNN, August 20, 2002, http://archives.cnn.com/2002/US/08/19/terror.tape.main/ and *The New York Post*, October 8, 2004.

60. *The 9/11 Commission Report*, 63.

61. Ibid., 64.

62. Kim Murphy, "Algeria Cracks Down, Targets Islamic Front," *Los Angeles Times*, February 10, 1992.

63. "Algerian Fundamentalist Promises More Massacres," *Agence France-Presse*, January 21, 1997.

64. Christopher Burns, "Militants' New Target: Students," *Associated Press Worldstream*, August 6, 1994.

65. *BBC Summary of World Broadcasts*, (Source: *Al-Hayat*, "London," in Arabic, November 4, 1996), November 5, 1996.

66. As quoted by Quintan Wiktorowicz and John Kaltner, "Killing in the Name of Islam: Al-Qaeda's Justification for September 11," *Middle East Policy*, vol. X (Summer 2003). Language taken from a GIA communiqué dated April 18, 1996, according to the authors.

67. Statistics from Onwar.com, http://www.onwar.com/aced/chrono/c1900s/yr90/falgeria1992.htm.

68. Pierre Verger, William Dab, Donna L. Lamping, Jean-Yves Loze, Céline Deschaseaux-Voinet, Lucien Abenhaim, and Frédéric Rouillon, "The Psychological Impact of Terrorism: An Epidemiologic Study of Posttraumatic Stress Disorder and Associated Factors in Victims of the 1995–1996 Bombings in France," *American Journal of Psychiatry*, vol. 161, no.8 (August 2004): 1384–1389.

69. Kim Murphy, "Tunisia Raises Stakes against Islamic Fundamentalists," *Los Angeles Times*, August 30, 1992.

70. Ibid.

71. Quintan Wiktorowicz, "The New Global Threat: Transnational Salafis and Jihad," *Middle East Policy*, vol. 8, no. 4 (December 1, 2001): 18.

72. First published August 31, 1996, *Al Quds Al Arabi* (London), available online: http://www.pbs.org/newshour/terrorism/international/fatwa_1996.html.

73. Emil A. Payin and Arkady A. Popov, "Chechnya," U.S. and Russian Policymaking with Respect to the Use of Force (Santa Monica, CA: Rand, 1996), http://www.rand.org/pubs/conf_proceedings/CF129/CF-129.chapter2.html.

74. "*Agence France-Presse*, August 11, 1994.

75. Wiktorowicz, "The New Global Threat," 18.

76. Ibid.

77. "Al-Sharq Al-Awsat Publishes Extracts from Al-Jihad Leader Al-Zawahiri's New Book," *FBIS-NES-2002-0108*, December 2, 2001, 44.

78. Michael Mainville, "Trained by Arabs, 'Black Widows' a Terrifying New Weapon," *The New York Sun*, December 10, 2003.

79. *BBC News*, September 2, 2005, available online at http://news.bbc.co.uk/1/hi/world/europe/4207112.stm.

80. *CNN Live Today*, September 7, 2004.

81. Kim Murphy, "Chechnya Conflict Seeps Over Border," *Los Angeles Times*, February 26, 2005.

82. Matthew Brzezinski, "Surrealpolitik; How a Chechen Terror Suspect Wound Up Living on Taxpayers' Dollars near the National Zoo," *The Washington Post*, March 20, 2005.

83. Terry McDermott, Josh Meyer, and Patrick J. McDonnell, "The Plots and Designs of Al Qaeda's Engineer," *Los Angeles Times*, December 22, 2002.

84. Terry McDermott, "How Terrorists Hatched a Simple Plan to Use Planes as Bombs," *Los Angeles Times*, September 1, 2002.

85. "Profile: Abu Sayyaf," Online News Hour, January 2002, http://www.pbs.org/newshour/terrorism/international/abu_sayyaf.html, accessed September 7, 2005.

86. "Asia's Terrorist Haven," *The Wall Street Journal*, April 14, 2005.

87. "US Warns Philippines South Could Become New Afghanistan," *Agence France-Presse*, April 11, 2005.

88. Robert Fisk, "Why We Reject the West—By the Saudis' fiercest Arab Critic; At Home in his Afghanistan Fastness, Osama Bin Laden Tells Robert Fisk Why He Wants to Drive the Americans and British Out of the Gulf," *The Independent* (London), July 10, 1996.

89. Fisk, "Muslim Leader Warns of New Assault on US Forces," *The Independent* (London), March 22, 1997.

90. Fisk, "Saudi Calls for Jihad against US 'Crusader'; Iraq is not the Only Source of Concern for America in the Gulf," *The Independent* (London), September 2, 1996.

91. Peter Bergen, *Holy War, Inc.: Inside the Secret World of Osama Bin Laden* (New York: Free Press, 2001).

92. *The 9/11 Commission Report* (New York: W.W. Norton Co, 2004), pages 65–66.

93. *BBC Summary of World Broadcasts*, Source: 'Al-Hayat', (London) (August 6, 1998), August 8, 1998.

94. Wright, "The Man Behind Bin Laden."

95. Ibid.

96. Council on Foreign Relations, http:www//cfr.org/publication/9135/kashmir_militant_extremists.html, accessed July 6, 2006.

97. Jessica Stern, "Pakistan's Jihad Culture," *Foreign Affairs*, November 2000–December 2000.

98. United States Department of Justice, Press Release, April 9, 2004, available online at http://www.usdoj.gov/criminal/press_room/press_releases/2004_3655_

RANDALL_TODD_ROYER_AND_IBRAHIM_AHMED_ALHAMDI_SEN-TENCED_FOR_PARTICIPATION_IN_VIRGINIA_JIHAD_NETWORK.htm.

99. Vernon Loeb, "Attack Carefully Planned, Experts Say," *The Washington Post*, October 13, 2000.

100. U.S. v. Sattar et. al., S1 02 Cr. 395 (JGK), 2148 and 10967–10968.

101. According to B. Raman, "Attack on USS Cole: Background," Institute for Topical Studies, Chennai, October 16, 2000, http://www.saag.org/papers2/paper152.html.

102. Ibid.

103. The next most lethal attack on the United States was the Japanese bombing of Pearl Harbor on December 7, 1941, which resulted in approximately 2,400 deaths.

104. Judith Achieng, "Muslims Protest U.S. Air Strikes in Afghanistan," IPS-*Inter Press Service*, October 12, 2001.

105. "Malaysia's Islamic Party Declares Jihad Over Afghanistan," Agence France-Presse, October 10, 2001.

106. Stewart Bell, "Some Canadians Tried to Join Taliban: CSIS: Agency Uncertain whether Militants Reached the Front," *National Post* (Canada), March 27, 2002.

107. "Coalition Targets Ex-Afghan Premier Hekmatyar after Jihad Threat," *Agence France-Presse*, May 30, 2002.

108. *BBC Worldwide Monitoring*, (Source: *Al-Hayat* (London), in Arabic, November 2, 2002), November 3, 2002.

109. John Gershman, "Is Southeast Asia the Second Front?" *Foreign Affairs*, July 2002–August 2002. Gershman is senior analyst at the Interhemispheric Resource Center and the Asia/Pacific Editor for *Foreign Policy in Focus* (www.fpif.org).

110. Simon Elegant/Pattani, "Southern Front; Muslims have been Fighting for Decades for a Separate State in Thailand's South," *Time International*, October 18, 2004.

111. "Bin Laden Tape: Text," *BBC*, February 12, 2003, http://news.bbc.co.uk/2/hi/middle_east/2751019.stm.

112. Craig Whitlock, "Al Qaeda Leaders Seen in Control," *The Washington Post*, July 24, 2005.

113. Philip Mattar, *The Mufti of Jerusalem: Al-Hajj Amin al-Husayni and the Palestinian National Movement* (New York: Columbia University Press, 1988), 103.

114. Abraham J. Edelheit and Hershel Edelheit, *History of the Holocaust A Handbook and Dictionary* (Boulder, CO: Westview Press, 1994), 120.

115. Shlomo Aronson, *Hitler, the Allies, and the Jews* (Cambridge: Cambridge University Press, 2004), 60.

116. Francine Friedman, *The Bosnian Muslims: Denial of a Nation* (Boulder, CO: Westview Press, 1996), 124.

117. Aronson, *Hitler, the Allies, and the Jews*, 53.

118. As quoted by Rudolph Peters, *Jihad in Classical and Modern Islam; A Reader* (Princeton: Markus Wiener Publishers, 1996), 105.

119. Don Oberdorfer, "U.S. Offers Plan to End Impasse in Mideast Talks," *The Washington Post*, November 13, 1978.

120. U.S. State Department, *Patterns of Global Terrorism 2003*, http://www.globalsecurity.org/security/library/report/2004/pgt_2003/index.html.

121. MIPT Terrorism Knowledge Base, http://www.tkb.org/Group.jsp?groupID=82, accessed July 6, 2006.

122. John L. Esposito, *Unholy War: Terror in the Name of Islam* (New York: Oxford University Press, 2002), 7 and Steve Coll, *Ghost Wars: The Secret History of the CIA, Afghanistan and bin Laden from the Soviet Invasion of Afghanistan to September 11, 2001* (New York: Penguin Press, 2004), 204.

123. See a translation of the Hamas Charter at http://www.fas.org/irp/world/para/docs/880818.htm.

124. From the Hamas website: http://www.hamasonline.com/ indexx. php?page=Hamas/hamas_covenant.

125. MIPT Terrorism Knowledge Base, http://www.tkb.org/Group.jsp?groupID=49, accessed April 14, 2005.

126. Talima Essam, "Resisting Invaders Individual Duty: Qaradhawi." Islam Online, March 8, 2003, http:// www.islamonline.net/ english/News/2003-03/08/ article09. shtml. From MEMRI, Inquiry and Analysis Series, No. 145, http://www.memri.org/bin/ articles.cgi?Page=s ubjects&Area=jihad&ID= IA14503.

127. Mohammed Almezel, "Lawmakers Slam Attack on Iraq," *Gulf News*, March 22, 2003.

128. Ibid.

129. "Al-Azhar Calls for Jihad over Iraq War." *Ummah News Online*, March 26, 2003, from MEMRI, Inquiry and Analysis Series, No. 145, http://www.memri.org/bin/articles.cgi?Page=subjects&Area=jihad&ID=IA14503.

130. April 6, 2003, http://www.albawaba.com/countries/index.ie.php3?country= egypt & lang =as reported by MEMRI, Inquiry and Analysis Series, No. 130, April 8, 2003.

131. Neil MacFarquhar, "For Arabs, New Jihad Is in Iraq," *The New York Times*, April 2, 2003.

132. *BBC Monitoring International Reports*, March 28, 2003.

133. Michael Wines, "2 Leaders of Russia's Muslims Split Over Jihad Against U.S.," *The New York Times*, April 4, 2003.

134. Sabrina Tavernise, "25 Are Killed As Insurgents Press Attacks on Shiites," *The New York Times*, September 17, 2005.

135. Coalition Provisional Authority English translation of terrorist Musab al Zarqawi letter obtained by United States Government in Iraq, February 2004, http://www.state.gov/p/nea/rls/31694.htm.

136. Nasra Hassan, "Al-Qaeda's Understudy," *The Atlantic Monthly*, June 1, 2004.

137. Jessica Stern, "Pakistan's Jihad Culture," *Foreign Affairs*, November 2000–December 2000.

138. "FFI Explains Al Qaeda Document," March 19, 2004, http://www.mil.no/felles/ffi/ start/article.jhtml?articleID=71589.

139. Lawrence Wright, "The Terror Web," *The New Yorker*, August 2, 2004.

140. Ibid.

141. Petter Nesser, "Jihad in Europe—A Survey of the Motivations for Sunni Islamist Terrorism in Post-Millennium Europe," FFI Rapport, Norwegian Defence Research Establishment, 2004, 9–10.

142. Ibid., 12.

143. "Open Letter Warns of Blood and Revenge," *Expatica*, May 3, 2005.

144. "London Bomber: Text in Full," BBC News, September 1, 2005 available at http://news.bbc.co.uk/1/hi/uk/4206800.stm.

145. *Associated Press*, November 11, 2005.

146. "Interview with bin Laden," *Time Magazine*, January 11, 1999, http://www.time.com/time/asia/news/printout/0,9788,174550,00.html.

Chapter 2   What Is The Ideology of Jihad?

1. "Fact Sheet: President Bush Remarks on the War on Terror," The White House, http://www.whitehouse.gov/news/releases/2005/10/print/20051006-2.html, accessed July 6, 2006.

2. President George W. Bush, "Address to a Joint Session of Congress and the American People," September 20, 2001, available online at http://www.whitehouse.gov/news/releases/2001/09/20010920-8.html.

3. Ibid.

4. David Cook, *Understanding Jihad* (Berkeley and Los Angeles: University of California Press, 2005), 6.

5. Ibid., 2–3.

6. Michael Isikoff and John Barry, "Gitmo: SouthCom Showdown," *Newsweek*, May 9, 2004.

7. Peter Edidin, "Taking Care of the Koran," *The New York Times*, May 22, 2005.

8. Michael B. Schub, "That Which Gets Lost in Translation," *The Middle East Quarterly*, Fall 2003, vol. x, no. 4.

9. For a discussion of the various English translations of the Koran, see Khaleel Mohammad, "Assessing English Translations of the Qur'an," *The Middle East Quarterly*, vol. XII, no. 2 (Spring 2005), http://www.meforum.org/article/717.

10. "Jihad and its Solution Today," Kavkaz.center, November 26, 2003, posted at http://kavkazcenter.com/eng/content/2003/11/26/2028.shtml, accessed May 10, 2005.

11. Cook, *Understanding Jihad*, 35.

12. Douglas E. Streusand, "What Does Jihad Mean," *The Middle East Quarterly*, vol. IV, no. 3 (September 1997).

13. Sayyid Qutb, *Milestones* (Karachi: International Islamic Federation of Student Organizations, 1978), 114–115.

14. Sura 2:194.

15. Excerpted in Jansen, *The Neglected Duty*, 195–196.

16. Sura 9:29–31.

17. Sura 49:15.

18. Suras 18:31, 47:15, 44:53–54, 52:20.

19. R. Hrair Dekmejian, *Islam in Revolution* (Syracuse: Syracuse University Press, 1985) 40, 92–95 for a discussion on takfir in general.

20. Wiktorowicz, Quintan, "The Salafi Movement: Violence and the Fragmentation of Community," in Miriam Cooke and Bruce B. Lawrence, eds., *Muslim networks from Hajj to hip hop* (Chapel Hill and London: University of North Carolina Press, 2005), 221–222.

21. Bruce Lawrence, ed., *Messages to the World: The Statements of Osama Bin Laden* (London: Verso, 2005), 5.

22. As quoted by Quintan Wiktorowicz, "The New Global Threat: Transnational Salafis and Jihad," *Middle East Policy*, vol. 8, no. 4 (December 1, 2001): 18.

23. Shaikh Abdul Aziz ibn Abdullah Ibn Baz, "Imaam Muhammad Ibn Abdul Wahhab—His Life and Mission," AHYA.ORG, http://www.ahya.org/amm/modules.php?name = Sections&op=viewarticle&artid=180, accessed September 13, 2005.

24. Excerpted in Peters, *Jihad in Classical and Modern Islam*, 47–49.

25. Bin Laden's 1996 fatwa, available online at http://www.pbs.org/newshour/terrorism/international/fatwa_1996.html.

26. "Bin Laden message mystery," *BBC News*, April 11, 2001, http://news.bbc.co.uk/2/hi/world/south_asia/1269655.stm.

27. For a scholarly analysis and translation of the pamphlet, see John J. G. Jansen, *The Neglected Duty: The Creed of Sadat's Assassins and Islamic Resurgence in the Middle East* (New York: Macmillan, 1986).

28. Ibid., 8 and 172–173.
29. Ibid., 2.
30. Ibid., 5.
31. Ibid., 15.
32. Coalition Provisional Authority English translation of terrorist Musab al Zarqawi letter obtained by United States Government in Iraq, February 2004, http://www.state.gov/p/nea/rls/31694.htm.
33. Sura 9:36, Yusuf Ali translation.
34. Sura 8:39, Yusuf Ali translation.
35. Fatwa available online at http://www.fas.org/irp/world/para/docs/980223-fatwa.htm.
36. Sura 8:24, Yusuf Ali translation of the Quran, available online at http://www. harunyahya.com/Quran_translation/Quran_translation8.php.
37. Sura 9:38–39, Yusuf Ali translation of the Quran, available online at http://www.harunyahya.com/Quran_translation/Quran_translation9.php.
38. Sura 3:139, Yusuf Ali translation of the Quran, available online at http://www.harunyahya.com/Quran_translation/Quran_translation3.php.
39. Jansen, *The Neglected Duty*, 199.
40. Ibid., 193.
41. John Kelsay, "Bin Laden's Reasons: Interpreting Islamic Tradition," *The Christian Century*, February 27–March 6, 2002.
42. Jansen, *The Neglected Duty*, 203.
43. Sheikh Abdullah Azzam, *Defense of Muslim Lands*, chapter 4, available online at http://www.islamistwatch.org/texts/azzam/defense/defense.html.
44. Ibid., chapter 2.
45. Ibid.
46. Office of the Director of National Intelligence, ODNI News Release No. 2-05, October 11, 2005, available at http://www.fas.org/irp/news/2005/10/letter_in_english.pdf.
47. Ibid.
48. Thomas Hegghammer, "Global Jihadism After the Iraq War," *Middle East Journal*, vol. 60, no. 1 (Winter 2006).
49. Thomas Hegghammer, Al-Qaida Statements 2003–2004, Kjeller: FFI/Rapport 01428, 2005, p. 64, available at http://rapporter. ffi.no/rapporter/2005/01428.pdf.
50. Hegghammer, "Global Jihadism After the Iraq War."
51. Hegghammer, Al-Qaida Statements 2003–2004.
52. Bin Laden interview with Al-Jazeera, Tayseer Alouni, October 2001.
53. Palestinian Friday Sermon by Sheik Ibrahim Mudeiris: *Muslims Will Rule America and Britain, Jews Are a Virus Resembling AIDS*, MEMRI TV Monitor Project, May 13, 2005, Clip No. 669, http://memritv.org/Transcript.asp?P1=669.
54. Sayyid Qutb, *Milestones* (Karachi: International Islamic Federation of Student Organizations, 1978), 207.
55. David Zeidan, "The Islamic Fundamentalist View of Life as a Perennial Battle," *Middle East Review of International Affairs Journal*, vol. 5, no. 4 (December 2001).
56. As quoted by Cook, *Understanding Jihad*, 101.
57. From Abu l-A la—Mawdudi, Al-jihad fi sabil Allah, 12–13, as quoted by Peters, *Jihad in Classical and Modern Islam*, 128.
58. Qutb, *Milestones*, 135.
59. Ibid., 136.
60. Ibid., 246.
61. Ibid., 260–261.

62. Ibid., 7–9.
63. Ibid., 109.
64. Ibid., 111.
65. Ibid., 16–17.
66. Ibid., 17–18.
67. Abdullah Azzam, "Al-Qaeda al-Sulbah (The Solid Base)", al-Jihad (Afghanistan), No. 41 (April 1988), 46–49, as quoted by Reuven Paz, see http://meria.idc.ac.il/journal/2003/issue 4/jv7n4a5.html.
68. Interview with John Miller, *ABC News*.
69. Interview with *Time Magazine*, December 23, 1998.
70. Interview with John Miller, *ABC News*.
71. Ayman al-Zawahiri, *Knights Under the Prophet's Banner*, published by Al-Sharq Al-Awsat, December 2, 2001, translated and reprinted, FBIS-NES-2002–0108, December 2, 2001, 75.
72. Ibid.
73. Ibid., 70.
74. Ibid., 77.
75. Ibid., 39.
76. Interview with John Miller, *ABC News*.
77. Jansen, *The Neglected Duty*, 6.

Chapter 3   How Is Jihad Being Fought?

1. Aparisim Ghosh, "Inside the Mind of an Iraqi Suicide Bomber," *Time Magazine*, July 4, 2005.
2. For a general discussion see Helen Duffy, *The 'War on Terror' and the framework of international law* (Cambridge: Cambridge University Press, 2005).
3. For a succinct discussion of this topic, see Boaz Ganor, "Defining Terrorism: Is One Man's Terrorist Another Man's Freedom Fighter?" *ICT*, September 24, 1998.
4. This is the definition that has been employed by the U.S. government for statistical and analytical purposes since 1983. http://www.state.gov/s/ct/rls/pgtrpt/2000/2419.htm.
5. Bin Laden interview with John Miller, *ABC News*, May 1998.
6. USA v. Omar Ahmad Abdel Rahman et al., S5 93 Cr. 181, United States District Court Southern District of New York, page 20088 of the trial transcripts.
7. Ghosh, "Inside the Mind of an Iraqi Suicide Bomber."
8. thereligionofpeace.com records all reported incidents of terror attacks committed in the name of Islam. On September 18, 2005, the recorded tally of such incidents was 2,947. The author of the website informed one of these authors that not all incidents particularly those occurring in the Islamic world are necessarily tallied. These numbers should be viewed as approximate.
9. http://www.thereligionofpeace.com/Pages/TheList.htm, accessed November 25, 2005.
10. Statement of September 13, 2001. http://www.islamonline.net/English/News/2001-09/13/article25.shtml. Arabic original at http://www.qaradawi.net/site/topics/article.asp?cu_no=2&item_no=1665&version=1&template_id=130&parent_id=17.
11. Statement of September 15, 2001, http://saudiembassy.net/Publications/Magsummer02/CONDEMS.htm.
12. "Saudi cleric condemns 'attacks on innocent people,'" Agence France-Presse, December 4, 2001.

13. "Islamic Statements Against Terrorism," compiled by Charles Kurzman, available at: http://www.unc.edu/~kurzman/terror.htm.

14. Martyn Leek Angry, "The Sick Poster that Celebrates Sept 11 Outrage," *Sunday Mercury*, August 24, 2003.

15. Joyce M. Davis, "Muslims Condemn Attacks, Insist Islam not Violent Against Innocents," Knight Ridder/Tribune News Service, September 13, 2001.

16. *The Dawn*, Karachi, Pakistan, October 8, 2001, http://www.dawn.com/2001/10/08/op.htm#2.

17. See "Islamic Statements Against Terrorism," http://www.unc.edu/~kurzman/terror. htm; Kurzman also refers to several other such compilations including, Omid Safi, Colgate University, "Scholars of Islam & the Tragedy of Sept. 11th," http://groups. colgate.edu/aarislam/response.htm; Tim Lubin, Washington and Lee University, "Islamic Responses to the Sept. 11 Attack," http://home.wlu.edu/~lubint/ islamonWTC.htm; The Becket Fund, "Osama Bin Laden Hijacked Four Airplanes and a Religion," October 17, 2001, http://www.becketfund.org/other/ MuslimAd.html; Islam for Today, "Muslims Against Terrorism," http://www.islam-fortoday.com/terrorism.htm; ReligiousTolerance.org, "Aftermath of the 9-11 Terrorist Attack: Voices of Moderate Muslims," http://www.religioustolerance.org/ reac_ter16.htm; Islamic Stand on Terrorism: An International Conference, Al-Imam Muhammad Ibn Saud Islamic University, Riyadh, Saudi Arabia, 20–22 April 2004, http://www.islamstand.org/english/abaakail.htm.

18. http://www.thereligionofpeace.com/, accessed November 28, 2005.

19. From *Sahih Muslim*, translated by Abdul Hamid Siddiqui, available at http://www.usc.edu/dept/MSA/fundamentals/hadithsunnah/muslim/019.smt.html.

20. Translation of April 24, 2002 al-Qaeda document, *Middle East Policy Council Journal*, http://www.mepc.org/public_asp/journal_vol10/0306_alqaeda.asp.

21. "Qaradawi Criticizes Al-Azhar for Condemning Jerusalem Attacks," December 5, 2001, http://www.islam-online.net/English/News/2001-12/05/article6.shtml.

22. Ibid.

23. Nasra Hassan, "An Arsenal of Believers," *The New Yorker*, November 19, 2001.

24. James Bennet, "U.N. Report Rejects Claims Of a Massacre Of Refugees," *The New York Times*, August 2, 2002.

25. Bin Laden, Interview with John Miller, *ABC News*, May 1998.

26. Quintan Wiktorowicz and John Kaltner, "Killing in the Name of Islam: Al Qaeda's Justification for September 11," *Middle East Policy Council Journal*, vol. X, no. 2 (Summer 2003) http://www.mepc.org/public_asp/journal_vol10/0306_ wiktorowiczkaltner.asp.

27. Bin Laden's interview with Tayseer Alouni, *Al-Jazeera*, October 2001.

28. Bukhari vol. 5, no. 362, Book 59, http://www.usc.edu/dept/MSA/fundamentals/ hadithsunnah/bukhari/059.sbt.html.

29. Dan Eggen and Scott Wilson, "Suicide Bombs Potent Tool of Terrorists," The Washington Post, July 17, 2005.

30. See "Refuting Suicide Bombing as Martyrdom Operations in Contemporary Jihad Strategy," "The Hijacked Caravan," available at: http://www.ihsanic-intelligence. com/dox/The_Hijacked_Caravan.pdf, accessed July 6, 2006.

31. Ibid.

32. Ibid.

33. See http://www.pbs.org/newshour/terrorism/international/fatwa_1998.html, accessed December 12, 2005.

34. Ibid.

35. Ibid.

36. MEMRI Special Dispatch Series—No. 457, January 9, 2003, http://memri.org/bin/articles.cgi?Page=subjects&Area=jihad&ID=SP45703.

37. David B. Cook, "Suicide Attacks or 'Martyrdom Operations' in Contemporary Jihadist Literature," *Nova Religio*, October 2002, vol. 6, no. 1: 7–44. A copy of the fatwa is available online at http://www.cdfe.org/martyrdom_operations.htm.

38. Hoffman, "The Logic of Suicide Terrorism."

39. Hassan, "An Arsenal of Believers."

40. Eggen and Wilson, "Suicide Bombs Potent Tools of Terrorists."

41. Audrey Kurth Cronin, *CRS Report for Congress: Terrorists and Suicide Attacks*, August 28, 2003, http://www.uspolicy.be/issues/terrorism/CRS_24049.pdf.

42. Eggen and Wilson, "Suicide Bombs Potent Tools of Terrorists."

43. Because these were attacks against armed forces (though most were asleep in their bunks and stationed in Beirut as part of a U.S.-French peacekeeping force) there is debate about whether it was a terrorist or a guerilla attack.

44. As cited in Hoffman, "The Logic of Suicide Terrorism."

45. Ibid.

46. Eggen and Wilson, "Suicide Bombs Potent Tools of Terrorists."

47. Cited in Bruce Hoffman, "The Logic of Suicide Terrorism."

48. Robert Pape, *Dying to Win: The strategic Loss of Suicide Terrorism* (New York: Random House, 2005).

49. Yuba Bessaoud, "Biggest Suicide Wave in a Bloody 2,000-Year History," *The Sunday Times* (London), July 31, 2005.

50. Assaf Moghadam, "Palestinian Suicide Terrorism in the Second Intifada: Motivations and Organizational Aspects," *Studies in Conflict & Terrorism*, vol. 26, no. 2 (March–April 2003), 65.

51. MEMRI, '72 Black Eyed Virgins': A Muslim Debate on the Rewards of Martyrs, Inquiry and Analysis Series-No. 74, October 30, 2001, available at http://memri.org/bin/articles.cgi?Page=subjects&Area=jihad&ID=IA7401.

52. Ibid.

53. Ibid.

54. Hassan, "An Arsenal of Believers."

55. David Brooks, "The Culture of Martyrdom; How Suicide Bombing Became Not Just a Means but an End," *The Atlantic Monthly*, June 2002.

56. Ibid.

57. Coalition Provisional Authority English translation of terrorist Musab al Zarqawi letter obtained by United States Government in Iraq, February 2004, http://www.state.gov/p/nea/rls/31694.htm.

58. *The 9/11 Commission Report* (New York: W.W. Norton Co, 2004), 54.

59. "Sunni Muslim authority condemns Iraq beheadings," *Agence France-Presse*, September 22, 2004.

60. "Bomb Rips through Algiers, Hours after Warning of Bloodbath," *Agence France-Presse*, January 21, 1997

61. GIA communiqué, issued April 18, 1996 cited in Quintan Wiktorowicz and John Kaltner, "Killing in the Name of Islam: Al Qaeda's Justification for September 11," *Middle East Policy Council Journal*, vol. X, no. 2 (Summer 2003), http:// www.mepc.org/ public_ asp/ journal_ vol10/ 0306_ wiktorowiczkaltner.asp.

62. Steven Mufson, "A Brutal Act's Long History," *The Washington Post*, July 4, 2004.

63. Carey Scott and Mark Franchetti, "Horror in Chechnya," *The Sunday Times* (London), December 13, 1998.

64. Yochi J. Dreazen, "Beheadings Become Tactic of Choice," *The Wall Street Journal*, September 3, 2004.

65. John Daniszewski, "Beheading for the Sake of Fear, Not Islam," *Los Angeles Times*, June 22, 2004.

66. Gregory Crouch, "Man on Trial Accepts Blame in Dutch Killing," *The New York Times*, July 13, 2005.

67. Abdullah Yusuf `Ali, trans., *The Meaning of the Holy Qur'an* (Beltsville, MD: Amana publications, 2001), 1315.

68. See Timothy Furnish, "Beheading in the Name of Islam," *The Middle East Quarterly*, vol. XII, no. 2 (Spring 2005).

69. `Ali, *The Meaning of the Holy Qur'an*, 417.

70. Jami' al-Bayan fi Tafsir al-Qur'an (Beirut: Dar al-Ma`rifah, 1972), 26 as cited by Timothy Furnish, "Beheading in the Name of Islam," *The Middle East Quarterly*, vol. XII, no. 2 (Spring 2005), http://www.meforum.org/article/713.

71. 'Abd al-Malik Ibn Hisham, *The Life of Muhammad: A Translation of Ishaq's Sirat Rasul*, introduction and notes by A. Guillaume (Karachi: Oxford University Press, 2004 [reprint of the 1955 ed.]), 461–469; 'Abd al-Malik Ibn Hisham, As-Sirah an-Nabawiyah, vol. 3, ed. Mustafa as-Saqqa and Ibrahim al-Hafiz Shalabi (Misr: Mustafa al-Babi al-Halabi, 1936), 251–254, as cited by Furnish, "Beheading in the Name of Islam," http://www.meforum.org/article/713.

72. Paul Fregosi, *Jihad in the West: Muslim Conquests from the Seventh to the Twenty-first Centuries* (Amherst, NY: Prometheus Books, 1998), 160.

73. Ibid., 228, 246, 261, 374.

74. Furnish, "Beheading in the Name of Islam."

75. Ibid.

76. Dreazen, "Beheadings Become Tactic of Choice."

77. See "Dirty Bombs," Council of Foreign Relations, at http://cfrterrorism.org/weapons/dirtybomb.html.

78. Ibid.

79. Philip Shenon, "Qaeda Leader Said to Report A-Bomb Plans," *The New York Times*, April 23, 2002.

80. November 17, 2005 "Superceding Indictment" available at http://wid.ap.org/documents/051122padilla_indictment.pdf, accessed July 6, 2006.

81. Adam Liptak, "In Terror Cases, Administration Sets Own Rules," *The New York Times*, November 27, 2005.

82. United States of America v. Usama bin Laden et. al., 1998, http://cns.miis.edu/pubs/reports/pdfs/binladen/indict.pdf.

83. "Exclusive Interview: Conversation with Terror," *Time Magazine*, January 11, 1999, http://www.time.com/time/asia/news/interview/0,9754,174550-1,00.html.

84. "Egypt Rethinks its Nuclear Program," MEMRI—Inquiry and Analysis, January 22, 2003.

85. "I Have Nuclear Weapons, Bin Laden," *The Times* (London), November 10, 2001.

86. United States of American v. Usama bin Laden et. al, trial transcripts, February 7, 2001 and February 13, 2001 available at http://cns.miis.edu/pubs/reports/pdfs/binladen/070201.pdf and http://cns.miis.edu/pubs/reports/pdfs/ binladen/ 130201.pdf, respectively.

87. Anthony Loyd, "Bin Laden's nuclear secrets found in al-Qaeda's Kabul safe house," *The Times* (London), November 15, 2001.

88. "National Security Strategy of the United States of America," September 2002, http://www.whitehouse.gov/nsc/nss5.html.

89. "Joint Resolution to Authorize the Use of United States Armed Forces Against Iraq," October 2, 2002, available online at http://www.whitehouse.gov/news/releases/2002/10/20021002–2.html.

90. "Egypt Rethinks its Nuclear Program," MEMRI—Inquiry and Analysis Series No. 120, January 22, 2003.

91. Nasir bin Hamid al-Fahd, "A Treatise on the Legal Status of Using Weapons of Mass Destruction Against Infidels," May 2003 available on-line at http:// www. carnegieendowment.org/static/npp/fatwa.pdf, accessed May 30, 2006.

92. CNN.com, April 26, 2004, http://www.cnn.com/2004/WORLD/meast/04/26/jordan.terror.

93. Ibid.

94. Michael Slackman, "Iraqi Qaeda Leader Is Said to Vow More Attacks on Jordan," The New York Times, November 19, 2005.

95. CNN.com, November 18, 2005, http://www.cnn.com/2005/WORLD/meast/11/18/zarqawi.jordan/.

96. "Al-Zarqawi disowned by his tribe in Jordan," BBC Monitoring Middle East, November 20, 2005

97. Text of the letter available at http://www.fas.org/irp/news/2005/10/letter_in_english.pdf, accessed July 6, 2006.

Chapter 4   Who Is Fighting Jihad?

1. David Rennie, "Face of Europe's First Woman Suicide Bomber," The Daily Telegraph (London), December 2, 2005.

2. Ahmed Rashid, Taliban (London: Pan Books, 2001), 129.

3. Many of the details of bin Laden's life that have been supplied here were found in Jason Burke, "The Making of the World's Most Wanted Man," The Observer (London), October 28, 2001. The reader should note, however, that accounts of bin Laden's biographical details vary quite a bit.

4. Peter Bergen, The Osama bin Laden I know: An Oral History of al Qaeda's Leader (New York: Free Press, 2006), 1.

5. Burks, "The Making of the World's Most Wanted Man."

6. Ibid.

7. As excerpted in "From the Shadows: An Oral History of Osama bin Laden, Vanity Fair, January 2006.

8. Steve Coll, "Young Osama," The New Yorker, December 12, 2005.

9. Ibid.

10. See for example, Geneive Abdo, "Islam in Egypt," Inside Islam: The Faith, the People and the Conflicts of the World's Fastest Growing Religion (New York: Marlowe & Company, 2002), 122.

11. Burke, "The Making of the World's Most Wanted Man."

12. Lawrence Wright, "The Man Behind bin Laden," The New Yorker, September 16, 2002.

13. Lawrence Wright, "The Man behind Bin Laden," The New Yorker, September 16, 2002.

14. Susan B. Glasser, " 'Martyrs' in Iraq Mostly Saudis; Web Sites Track Suicide Bombings," The Washington Post, May 15, 2005.

15. CNN, June 8, 2005, http://www.cnn.com/2005/LAW/06/08/florida.doctor.terrorism/.

16. Michael Whine, "The Mode of Operation of Hizb ut Tahrir in an Open Society," ICT, February 20, 2004, http://www.ict.org.il/articles/articledet.cfm?articleid= 515.

17. "Top Zarqawi Aide 'Killed' in US Attack," *Khaleej Times Online*, June 26, 2005, http://www.khaleejtimes.com/DisplayArticle.asp?xfile=data/middleeast/2005/June/middleeast_June743.xml&section=middleeast&col.

18. Marc Sageman, *Understanding Terror Networks* (Philadelphia: University of Pennsylvania Press, 2004), 75–76.

19. Ibid., 92.

20. Josie Glausiusz, "Discover Dialogue: Anthropologist Scott Atran; The Surprises of Suicide Terrorism. It's Not a New Phenomenon, and Natural Selection May Play a Role in Producing It," *Discover*, vol. 24, no. 10 (October 2003). http://www.discover.com/issues/oct-03/departments/featdialogue/.

21. Wright, "The Man Behind Bin Laden."

22. Lawrence Wright, "Update: Zawahiri's Whereabouts," *The New Yorker*, September 16, 2002.

23. Wright, "The Man Behind Bin Laden."

24. Sageman, *Understanding Terror Networks*, 71–72.

25. Ibid., 71–72.

26. Wright, "The Man Behind Bin Laden."

27. Ibid.

28. Ibid.

29. Ibid.

30. Ibid.

31. *The 9/11 Commission Report* (New York: W.W. Norton Co, 2004), 123.

32. Available online at http://www.pbs.org/newshour/terrorism/international/fatwa_1996.html.

33. *The 9/11 Commission Report*, 58.

34. Ibid., 67.

35. Karen DeYoung and Michael Dobbs, "Bin Laden: Architect of New Global Terrorism," *The Washington Post*, September 16, 2001.

36. "Substitution for the Testimony of Khalid Sheikh Mohammed," in USA v. Zacarias Moussaoui, U.S. District Court for the Eastern District of Virginia Alexandria Division, 1:01cr455 (LMB), available at http://www.rcfp.org/moussaoui/pdf/DX-0941.pdf.

37. *The 9/11 Commission Report*, 59.

38. Ibid., 145.

39. Bruce Livesy, "The Salafist Movement," http://www.pbs.org/wgbh/pages/frontline/shows/front/special/sala.html.

40. "The Muslim Brotherhood Movement Homepage" at http://www.ummah.net/ikhwan/, accessed July 9, 2006.

41. Terry McDermott, *Perfect Soldiers* (New York: HarperCollins Publishers Inc., 2005), 103.

42. Ibid., 128.

43. *The 9/11 Commission Report*, 147.

44. Ibid.

45. See Laurie Mylroie, "The Baluch Connection," *The Wall Street Journal*, March 18, 2003.

46. John J. Goldman, "Bomb Plot Architect Gets Life Term," *Los Angeles Times*, January 9, 1998.

47. "60 Minutes," *CBS News*, June 2, 2002.

48. *The 9/11 Commission Report*, 147.

49. Ibid., 146.

50. Ibid., 148.

51. Ibid., 491.

52. Philip Shenon and David Johnston, "Suspect's Will Suggests a Longtime Plan to Die," *The New York Times*, October 4, 2001.

53. *The 9/11 Commission Report*, 161.

54. Ibid., 162.

55. McDermott, *Perfect Soldiers*, 230–231.

56. *The 9/11 Commission Report*, 165–167.

57. Sageman, *Understanding Terror Networks*, 92–93.

58. Ibid., 93.

59. Nicholas Watt, "From Belgian Cul-De-Sac to Suicide Bomber in Iraq: Troubled Life of Woman Who Converted to Islam Mother Grieves for 'Brainwashed' Daughter," *The Guardian* (London), December 2, 2005.

60. *The 9/11 Commission Report*, 227.

61. The only exception was Fayez Banihammad, who was from the UAE and who was recruited by one of the plot's facilitators, Mustafa al Hawsawi, who along with KSM's nephew, Ali Abdul Aziz Ali (and first cousin of Yousef), provided the hijackers with things like plane tickets, hotel reservations, funding, and other logistical requirements.

62. Richard A. Serrano, "Al Qaeda Agent's 9/11 Role Comes Into Focus," *Los Angeles Times*, May 21, 2006.

63. *The 9/11 Commission Report*, 151–159, 190.

64. *The 9/11 Commission Report*, 232.

65. Ibid.

66. Sageman, *Understanding Terror Networks*, 75.

67. *The 9/11 Commission Report*, 233.

68. Helen Gibson, "Looking for Trouble," *Time Magazine* (Europe), January 21, 2002.

69. Matthew Purdy and Lowell Bergman, "WHERE THE TRAIL LED: Between Evidence and Suspicion; Unclear Danger: Inside the Lackawanna Terror Case," *The New York Times*, October 12, 2003.

70. Nasra Hassan, "An Arsenal of Believers," *The New Yorker*, November 19, 2001.

71. "Saudi Publications on Hate Ideology Fill American Mosques," Center for Religious Freedom, Freedom House, 2005, http://www.freedomhouse.org/religion/publications/Saudi%20Report/FINAL%20FINAL.pdf, 13.

72. Ibid., 43–44.

73. Testimony of J. Michael Waller before the Senate Judiciary Subcommittee on Terrorism, Technology, and Homeland Security, October 14, 2003.

74. *The 9/11 Commission Report*, 151.

75. Ibid.

76. *BBC News*, March 3, 2005.

77. MEMRI, Special Report No. 12, December 20, 2002, available at http://memri.org/bin/articles.cgi?Page=archives&Area=sr&ID=SR01202.

78. David Stout, "Student from Virginia is Convicted of Plotting with Al Qaeda to Assassinate Bush," *The New York Times*, November 23, 2005.

79. Nina Shea, "This is a Saudi Textbook (After the Intolerance Was Removed)," *The Washington Post*, May 21, 2006

80. Claude Berrebi, *Evidence about the Link Between Education, Poverty and Terrorism among Palestinians* (Department of Economics, Princeton University), 42.

81. Ibid., 43.

82. Ibid, Tables 1–2.

83. Sageman, *Understanding Terror Networks*, 94–95.
84. Daniel Lerner, *The Passing of Traditional Society* (The Free Press, 1958).
85. As quoted by Berrebi, *Evidence about the Link between Education, Poverty and Terrorism among the Palestinians*, 5.
86. Sageman, *Understanding Terror Networks*, 81, 85.
87. *The 9/11 Commission Report*, 234.
88. Jessica Stern, "Pakistan's Jihad Culture," *Foreign Affairs*, vol. 79, no. 6 (November–December 2000).
89. Thomas Hegghammer, Global Jihadism After the Iraq War," *Middle East Journal*, vol. 60, no. 1 (Winter 2006).
90. *The 9/11 Commission Report*, 67.
91. Hegghammer, "Global Jihadism After the Iraq War."
92. Rohan Gunaratna, "The Post-Madrid Face of Al Qaeda," The Center for Strategic and International Studies and the Massachusetts Institute of Technology, *The Washington Quarterly*, vol. 27, no. 3 (Summer, 2004), 91.
93. Anthony H. Cordesman, "Iraq's Evolving Insurgency and the Risk of Civil War," Center for the Strategic and International Studies, Working Draft, Revised June 22, 2006, http://www.csis.org/media/csis/pubs/060622_insurgency.pdf, 191. [CSIS is a think tank].
94. The Brookings Institution, "The Iraq Index," June 1, 2006, www.brookings.edu/iraqindex, 18.
95. Nawaf Obaid and Anthony Cordesman, "Saudi Militants in Iraq: Assessment and Kingdom's Response," Center for Strategic and International Studies, September 19, 2005, http://www.csis.org/media/csis/pubs/050910_saudimilitantsiraq.pdf, 6.
96. Brookings, "The Iraq Index," 19.
97. Cordesman, "Iraq's Evolving Insurgency and the Risk of Civil War," 191.
98. Obaid and Cordesman, "Saudi Militants in Iraq."
99. Ibid., 10.
100. Stern, "Pakistan's Jihad Culture."
101. Cordesman and Obaid, "Saudi Militants in Iraq," 18–19.
102. Bradley Graham, "Zarqawi 'Hijacked' Insurgency," *The Washington Post*, September 28, 2005.
103. Official White House Transcript of Colin Powell's speech to the United Nations, February 5, 2003, http://www.whitehouse.gov/news/releases/2003/02/print/20030205-1.html, accessed June 15, 2005.
104. Rod Nordland and Christopher Dickey, "Hunting Zarqawi," *Newsweek*, November 1, 2004.
105. Ibid.
106. Michael Isikoff and Mark Hosenball, "The World's Most Dangerous Terrorist," *Newsweek*, June 23, 2004, http://www.msnbc.msn.com/ id/ 5280219/ site/ newsweek/.
107. Jeffrey Gettleman, "Zarqawi's Journey: From Dropout to Prisoner to an Insurgent Leader in Iraq," *The New York Times*, July 13, 2004.
108. Isikoff and Hosenball, "The World's Most Dangerous Terrorist."
109. Nordland and Dickey, "Hunting Zarqawi."
110. Mohammed Al Shafey, "Seif Al-Adl: Al-Qaeda's Ghost," *Asharq al-Awsat*, June 1, 2005.
111. "Jordan Will Ask Britain to Extradite Militant Cleric," *Jordan Times*, August 14, 2005; and Vanora McWalters and Sebastian Rotella, "10 Extremists Arrested in British Crackdown," *Los Angeles Times*, August 12, 2005.

112. Michael Isikoff and Mark Hosenball, "Terror Threat?" *Newsweek*, March 9, 2005.

113. Terrorism Research Center, http://www.homelandsecurity.com/modules.php? op= modload&name=Intel&file=index&view=649, accessed September 23, 2005.

114. David Sharrock in Madrid and Daniel McGrory, "Caged by Glass: The Men Facing Europe's Biggest al-Qaeda Trial," *The Times* (London), April 23, 2005.

115. Robert S. Leiken, "Bearers of Global Jihad? Immigration and National Security after 9/11," Nixon Center, 2004, http://www.nixoncenter.org/publications/ monographs/Leiken_Bearers_of_Global_Jihad.pdf, 6.

116. Ibid., 14.

117. "Islamic Extremism in Europe," Testimony by Peter Bergen before House International Relations Committee, Subcommittee on Europe, Federal Document Clearing House Congressional Testimony, April 27, 2005.

118. Leiken, "Bearers of Global Jihad? Immigration and National Security after 9/11," Nixon Center, 2004, http://www.nixoncenter.org/ publications/ monographs/ Leiken_Bearers_of_Global_Jihad.pdf, 72–73.

119. "Islamic Extremism in Europe," Testimony by Peter Bergen.

120. "An Underclass Rebellion—France's Riots," *The Economist*, November 12, 2005.

121. Ibid.

122. Country Reports on Human Rights Practices—2005: The Netherlands, Bureau of Democracy, Human Rights, and Labor, U.S. State Department, March 8, 2006, available at http://www.state.gov/g/drl/rls/hrrpt/2005/61666.htm.

123. "A Cable Home for Muslims," *Buffalo News* (New York), December 13, 2004.

124. Lawrence Wright, "The Terror Web," *The New Yorker*, August 2, 2004.

125. Ian Buruma, "Final Cut; After a Filmmaker's Murder, the Dutch Creed of Tolerance Has Come Under Siege," *The New Yorker*, January 3, 2005.

126. "German Report Analyzes Al-Qa'idah Activities in Europe," *BBC Monitoring International Reports*, July 12, 2005.

127. David Rennie, "I'd Do It All Again, Says Filmmaker's Killer," *The Daily Telegraph* (London), July 13, 2005.

128. Ibid.

129. "German Report Analyzes Al-Qa'idah Activities in Europe."

130. Brynjar Lia, "The al-Qaida Strategist Abu Mus`ab al-Suri: A Profile," The Transnational Radical Islamism Project, Norwegian Defence Research Establishment (FFI), Presentation, OMS-Seminar March 15, 2006, Oslo, Norway.

131. Alan Travis and Rosie Cowan, "July 7 Reports: Bombs in the Bath: How Gang Plotted Attacks," *The Guardian* (London), May 12, 2006.

132. BBC News, September 1, 2005; tape transcript available online at http://news.bbc.co.uk/1/hi/uk/4206800.stm.

133. Peter Foster and Nasir Malick, "Bomber Idolised bin Laden, Says Pakistan Family," *The Daily Telegraph* (London), July 21, 2005.

134. Craig S. Smith, "Muslim Group in France is Fertile Soil for Militancy," *The New York Times*, April 28, 2005.

135. Abul Taher, "Giant Mosque for 40,000 May be Built at London Olympics," *Sunday Times* (London), November 27, 2005.

136. Susan Sachs, "A Muslim Missionary Group Draws New Scrutiny in U.S.," *The New York Times*, July 14, 2003.

137. Ibid.

138. B. Raman, "Dagestan: Focus on Pakistan's Tablighi Jamaat," *South Asia Analysis Group*, September 15, 1999.

139. Sachs, "A Muslim Missionary Group Draws New Scrutiny in U.S."

140. Theodore Dalrymple, "Our prisons are fertile ground for cultivating suicide bombers," *The Times* (London), July 30, 2005.
141. Eric Lichtblau, "4 Men in California Accused Of Plotting Terrorist Attacks," *The New York Times*, September 1, 2005 and Solomon Moore, "Radical Islam an Issue in Prisons," *Los Angeles Times*, August 20, 2005.
142. Testimony of J. Michael Waller, Annenberg Professor of International Communication at the Institute of World Politics, before the Senate Judiciary Committee Subcommittee on Terrorism, Technology, and Homeland Security, Federal Document Clearing House Congressional Testimony, October 14, 2003.
143. See Daniel Pipes, "Converts to Terrorism," and "More Converts to Terrorism," FrontPageMagazine.com, December 6 and 7, 2005.
144. Craig S. Smith, "Raised Catholic in Belgium, She Died a Muslim Bomber," *The New York Times*, December 6, 2005.
145. Rennie, "Face of Europe's First Woman Suicide Bomber."
146. Craig S. Smith, "Europe Fears Islamic Converts May Give Cover for Extremism," *The New York Times*, July 19, 2004.
147. Ibid.
148. Kim Willsher, "My Love for Carlos the Jackal," *Sunday Telegraph* (London), March 21, 2004.
149. As cited in Mustafa Akyol, "Bolshevism in a Headdress: Islamic Fundamentalism has more to do with Hatred of the West than with Religion," The American Enterprise Online, April 1, 2005, http://www.taemag.com/issues/articleID.18464/article_detail.asp.

Chapter 5   Who Is Really Fighting Jihad?

1. *The 9/11 Commission Report (New York: W.W. Norton Co, 2004)*, 122.
2. David E. Kaplan, Monica Ekman, and Aamir Latif, "The Saudi Connection," U.S. News & World Report, December 15, 2003.
3. "Wahhabism: State-Sponsored Extremism Worldwide," Testimony of Alex Alexiev before the United States Senate Judiciary Committee, June 26, 2003.
4. Ibid.
5. Claitor's Publishing Division, *Afghanistan: A Country Study* (Baton Rouge, LA: Claitor's Publishing Division, 2001), xxxii and Neamatollah Nojumi, *The Rise of the Taliban in Afghanistan: Mass Mobilization, Civil War and the Future of the Region* (New York: Palgrave, 2002), 188.
6. Jason Burke, *Al Qaeda: Casting a Shadow of Terror* (New York: Palgrave Macmillan, 2003).
7. Burke, *Al-Qaeda: The True Story of Radical Islam* (London: I.B. Tauris, 2004), 60.
8. *The 9/11 Commission Report* (New York: W.W. Norton Co, 2004), 55.
9. Ibid., 57.
10. Ibid., 57.
11. Ibid., 58.
12. Ibid.
13. *The 9/11 Commission Report*, 61, 470.
14. John Roth, Douglas Greenburg, and Serena Wille, Monograph on Terrorist Financing, National Commission on Terrorist Attacks Against the United States, Special Report to the Commission, 2004, 20.
15. *The 9/11 Commission Report*, 62.
16. Ibid., 170.

17. Ibid, 66.
18. Roth, Greenburg, Wille, Monograph on Terrorist Financing, 18.
19. Ibid., 4.
20. Ibid., 27–28 and Jean Charles Brisard, "Terrorism Funding," NY: JCB Consulting. A copy of his article can be found here http://www.nationalreview.com/document/document-un122002.pdf.
21. Roth, Greenburg, and Wille, Monograph on Terrorist Financing, 28.
22. Ibid., 4.
23. "Prepared Testimony of Steven Emerson and Jonathan Levin," United States Senate Committee on Governmental Affairs, July 31, 2003.
24. Ibid.
25. Terry McDermott, *Perfect Soldiers* (New York: Harper Collins Publishers Inc., 2005), 163–164.
26. Ibid.
27. Matthew Epstein, "Trails Lead to Saudis," *National Review*, May 21, 2003.
28. Roth, Greenburg, and Wille, Monograph on Terrorist Financing, 20–21.
29. Kaplan, Ekman, and Latif, "The Saudi Connection."
30. Roth, Greenburg, Wille, Monograph on Terrorist Financing, 21.
31. Testimony of Matthew Epstein with Evan Kohlmann on "Arabian Gulf Financial Sponsorship of Al-Qaida via U.S.-Based Banks, Corporations and Charities," before the House Committee on Financial Services Subcommittee on Oversight and Investigations, March 11, 2003, http://financialservices.house.gov/media/pdf/031103me.pdf, 6.
32. David Kane, "Declaration in Support of Pre-Trial Detention," USA v. Soliman S. Bihieri, Case No. 03-365-A, U.S. District Court for the Eastern District of Virginia, Alexandria Division, available online at http://fl1.findlaw.com/ news.findlaw.com/hdocs/docs/terrorism/usbiheiri81403knaff.pdf.
33. Burke, *Al-Qaeda*, 110–111.
34. BURNETT et. als. v AL BARAKA INVESTMENT et. als., Civil Action, Case Number 1:02CV01616(JR), Third Amended Complaint, November 22, 2002, http://www.motleyrice.com/911_victims/FinalThirdAmendedComplaint.pdf, 285.
35. Epstein and Kohlmann, on "Arabian Gulf Financial Sponsorship of Al-Qaida via U.S.-Based Banks, Corporations and Charities," 2–3.
36. Steven Emerson, "Saudi Arabia and the War on Terror," testimony before the U.S. Senate Judiciary Committee, November 8, 2005, http://judiciary.senate.gov/testimony.cfm?id=1669&wit_id=4791.
37. Steven Emerson and Jonathan Levin, "Terrorism Financing: Origination, Organization, and Prevention: Saudi Arabia, Terrorist Financing, and the War on Terror," testimony before the U.S. Senate Committee on Governmental Affairs, July 31, 2003, http://hsgac.senate. gov/_files/073103emerson.pdf.
38. Lorenzo Vidino, "The Muslim Brotherhood Conquest of Europe," *The Middle East Quarterly*, volume XII, no. 1 (Winter 2005).
39. PBS: Frontline, "Al Qaeda's New Front; Interview: Mamoun Fandy," October 18, 2004, http://www.pbs.org/wgbh/pages/frontline/shows/front/interviews/fandy.html.
40. BURNETT et. als. v AL BARAKA INVESTMENT et. als., Civil Action, Case Number 1:02CV01616(JR), Third Amended Complaint, November 22, 2002, http://www.motleyrice.com/terrorism/downloads/FinalThirdAmendedComplaint.pdf, 288.
41. Ibid., 287.
42. Ibid., 288.

43. Treasury Department Statement on the Designation of Wa'el Hamza Julidan, http://www.treas.gov/press/releases/po3397.htm.

44. See "List of Individuals Belonging to or Associated with al Qaida," available at http://www.un.org/Docs/sc/committees/1267/pdflist.pdf, accessed December 13, 2005.

45. BURNETT et al. v AL BARAKA INVESTMENT et al., 287.

46. "Senators Request Tax Information on Muslim Charities for Probe," U.S. State Department news release, Jan. 14, 2004, available online at http://usinfo.state.gov/ei/Archive/2004/Jan/15-147062.html.

47. Kaplan, Ekman, and Latif, "The Saudi Connection."

48. Ibid., 12.

49. BURNETT et. als. v AL BARAKA INVESTMENT et. als., 267–268.

50. "U.S. Treasury Designates Two Individuals with Ties to al Qaeda, UBL; Former BIF Leader and al-Qaida Associate Names Under E.O. 13224," The United States Treasury Department, THE OFFICE OF PUBLIC AFFAIRS, December 21, 2004, JS-2164, http://www.treas.gov/press/releases/js2164.htm.

51. United States of America v. Enaam M. Arnaout, United States District Court Northern District of Illinois, Eastern Division, No. 02 CR 892, "Government's Proffer Supporting the Admissibility of Co-Conspirator Statements," available online at http://news.findlaw.com/hdocs/docs/bif/usarnaout10603prof.pdf.

52. Ibid.

53. Ibid.

54. Ibid.

55. J. Millard Burr and Robert O. Collins, *Alms for Jihad: Charity and Terrorism in the Islamic World* (Cambridge: Cambridge University Press, 2006), 51.

56. Defendant's Motion in Limine to Exclude Evidence of Historical Events (January 13, 2003), as cited by Roth, Greenburg, Wille, Monograph on Terrorist Financing, 108.

57. "U.S. Treasury Designates Two Individuals with Ties to al Qaeda, UBL; Former BIF Leader and al-Qaida Associate Names Under E.O. 13224."

58. Ibid.

59. Information about this case is available online at http://www.motleyrice.com/911_victims/911_victims_saudi_case.html.

60. Case 03 MDL 1570 (RCC) IN RE: TERRORIST ATTACKS ON SEPTEMBER 11, 2001 ECF Case, Opinion and Order, http://www.nysd.uscourts.gov/rulings/03MDL1570_RCC_011905.PDF.

61. United States v. Arnaout, 282 F. Supp. 2d at 843 as cited by Roth, Greenburg, and Wille, Monograph on Terrorist Financing, 108–109.

62. Roth, Greenburg, and Wille, Monograph on Terrorist Financing, 109.

63. Ibid.

64. "U.S. Treasury Department Statement Regarding the Designation of the Global Relief Foundation," PO-3553, October 18, 2002, http://www.treasury.gov/press/releases/po3553.htm.

65. Roth, Greenburg, and Wille, Monograph on Terrorist Financing, 90.

66. Ibid., 91.

67. Ibid.

68. United States Treasury Department, "Additional Background Information on Charities Designated Under Executive Order 13224," http://www.treasury.gov/offices/enforcement/key-issues/protecting/charities_execorder_13224-e.shtml#g.

69. Roth, Greenburg, and Wille, Monograph on Terrorist Financing, 27–28.
70. "The Rise and Decline of Al Qaeda," third public hearing of the National Commission on Terrorist Attacks Upon the United States, Statement of Rohan Gunaratna to the National Commission on Terrorist Attacks Upon the United States, July 9, 2003.
71. Kaplan, Ekman, and Latif, "The Saudi Connection."
72. "The Rise and Decline of Al Qaeda," July 9, 2003.
73. Robert Marquand, "The Reclusive Ruler who Rules the Taliban," *The Christian Science Monitor*, October 10, 2001.
74. National Commission on the Terrorist Attacks Upon the United States, Overview of the Enemy, Staff Statement No. 17, page 7, available at http://www.9-11 commission.gov/staff_statements/staff_statement_15.pdf.
75. Ibid., 10.
76. Overview of the Enemy, Staff Statement No. 15, 9/11 Commission, 10.
77. Audrey Kurth Cronin, "Al Qaeda after the Iraq Conflict," *CRS Report for Congress*, May 23, 2003.
78. *The 9/11 Commission Report* (New York: W.W. Norton Co, 2004), 65.
79. Ibid., 111.
80. Kaplan, Ekman, and Latif, "The Saudi Connection."
81. Ibid.
82. Ibid.
83. Roth, Greenburg, and Wille, Monograph on Terrorist Financing, 4.
84. Robert G. Kaiser and David Ottaway, "Oil for Security Fueled Close Ties," *The Washington Post*, February 11, 2002.
85. Roth, Greenburg, and Wille, Monograph on Terrorist Financing, 31.
86. Kaplan, Ekman, and Latif, "The Saudi Connection."
87. Overview of the Enemy, 10.
88. Roth, Greenburg, and Wille, Monograph on Terrorist Financing, 24.
89. Ibid., 8.
90. Alfred B. Prados, "Saudi Arabia: Terrorist Financing Issues," *CRS Report for Congress*, March 1, 2005, http://fpc.state.gov/documents/organization/45189.pdf.
91. Gerald Posner, *Why America Slept: The Failure to Prevent 9/11* (New York: Randon House, 2003).
92. Gerald Posner, "Scrutinizing the Saudi Connection." *The New York Times*, July 27, 2004.
93. *The 9/11 Commission Report*, 330.
94. Mark Follman, "Did the Saudis know about 9/ 11?" October 18, 2003, salon. com.
95. Roth, Greenburg, and Wille, Monograph on Terrorist Financing, 12.
96. Josh Meyer, "U.S. Faults Saudi Efforts on Terrorism," *Los Angeles Times*, January 15, 2006.
97. Ibid., 24.
98. Patterns of Global Terrorism—2003, Released by the Office of the Coordinator for Counterterrorism, United States State Department, April 29, 2004, http://www.state.gov/s/ct/rls/pgtrpt/2003/31644.htm.
99. Ibid.
100. Ibid.
101. Scott Shiloh, "Abbas Approves Monthly Grants to Family of Suicide Bombers," *Arutz Sheva*, December 11, 2005.

102. "U.S. Designates Five Charities and Six Senior Hamas Leaders as Terrorists Entities," JS-672, From the Office of Public Affairs, United States Treasury Department, August 22, 2003, http://www.ots.treas.gov/docs/4/48937.html.

103. Ibid.

104. "Terrorist Financing: Report of an Independent Task Force," Council on Foreign Relations, 2002, 5.

105. *The 9/11 Commission Report*, 66.

106. Christopher Dickey, "Shadowland: The Saddam Files," *Newsweek*, June 22, 2004.

107. http://www.msnbc.msn.com/id/10652305/site/newsweek/.

108. Roth, Greenburg, and Wille, Monograph on Terrorist Financing, 22–23.

109. Ibid., 4.

110. Michael K. Freedman, "The Invisible Bankers," Forbes.com, October 17, 2005.

111. Roth, Greenburg, and Wille, Monograph on Terrorist Financing, 10.

112. Ibid.

113. Ibid., 28.

114. Eric Schmitt and Thom Shanker, "Estimates by U.S. See More Rebels with More Funds," *The New York Times*, October 22, 2004.

115. Douglas Jehl, "U.S. Aides Say Kin of Hussein Aid Insurgency," *The New York Times*, July 5, 2004.

116. Schmitt and Shanker, "Estimates by U.S. See More Rebels with More Funds."

117. Testimony of Daniel L. Glaser before the House Armed Services Committee Terrorism, Unconventional Threats and Capabilities Subcommittee, July 28, 2005.

118. Anthony Cordesman and Nawaf Obaid, "Saudi Militants in Iraq: Assessment and Kingdom's Response," The Center for Strategic and International Studies, September 19, 2005.

119. Ibid.

120. Testimony Jim Saxton, U.S. Representative, Committee on House Armed Services Subcommittee on Terrorism, Unconventional Threats and Capabilities, July 28, 2005.

121. David E. Kaplan, "National Security Watch: Eurolefties fund Iraq insurgency," *U.S. News & World Report*, June 23, 2005.

122. Ibid.

123. Schmitt and Shanker, "Estimates by U.S. See More Rebels with More Funds."

124. "Terrorist Financing: Report of an Independent Task Force," 5.

125. Ibid.

Chapter 6   How Is Global Jihad Being Countered?

1. "The Global War on Terrorism: The First 100 Days," The White House, December 2001, http://www.whitehouse.gov/news/releases/2001/12/100dayreport.html.

2. John Roth, Douglas Greenburg, and Serena Wille, Monograph on Terrorist Financing, National Commission on Terrorist Attacks Against the United States, Special Report to the Commission, 2004, 45.

3. The Senate passed the USA Patriot Act by a vote of 98-1; in the House it passed by a vote of 357–66.

4. See the government's case at the USA Patriot Act: Preserving Life and Liberty, http://www.lifeandliberty.gov/highlights.htm, accessed August 29, 2005.

5. Section 213 of the Patriot Act.

6. Elisabeth Bumiller and David Johnston, "Bust Sets Option of Military Trials in Terrorist Cases," *The New York Times*, November 14, 2001.

7. Christopher Drew and William K. Rashbaum, "Opponents' and Supporters' Portrayals of Detentions Prove Inaccurate," *The New York Times*, November 3, 2001.

8. "Witness to Abuse: Human Rights Abuses under the Material Witness Law since September 11," Human Rights Watch and the American Civil Liberties Union, June 27, 2005.

9. Rachel L. Swarns, "Program's Value in Dispute as a Tool to Fight Terrorism," *The New York Times*, December 21, 2004.

10. *The 9/11 Commission Report* (New York: W.W. Norton Co, 2004), 328.

11. James Risen and Eric Lichtblau, "Bush Lets U.S. Spy on Callers Without Courts," *The New York Times*, December 15, 2005.

12. Ibid.

13. Ibid.

14. Ibid.

15. "Thomas Kean holds a public hearing on reforming law enforcement, counterterrorism and intelligence collection in the United States," FDCH Political Transcripts, April 14, 2004.

16. Memorandum by Congressional Research Service, "Presidential Authority to Conduct Warrantless Electronic Surveillance to Gather Foreign Intelligence Information," January 5, 2005, available online at http://www.fas.org/sgp/crs/intel/m010506.pdf.

17. John Schmidt, "President has Legal Authority to OK Taps," *Chicago Tribune*, December 21, 2005.

18. "Presidential Authority to Conduct Warrantless Electronic Surveillance."

19. Eric Lichtblau and James Risen, "Bank Data Sifted in Secret by U.S. to Block Terror," *The New York Times*, Glenn R. Simpson, "Treasury Tracks Financial Data in Secret Program," *The Wall Street Journal*, and Josh Meyer and Greg Miller, "U.S. Secretly Tracks Global Data," *Los Angeles Times*, all on June 23, 2006.

20. Editorial, "Following the Money, and the Rules," *The New York Times*, June 24, 2006.

21. "Statement by the President in his Address to the Nation," September 11, 2001, http://www.whitehouse.gov/news/releases/2001/09/20010911-16.html.

22. John Miller and Michael Stone with Chris Mitchell, *The Cell: Inside the 9/11 Plot, and Why the FBI and CIA Failed to Stop It* (New York: Hyperion, 2002).

23. Ralph Blumenthal, "Bombing Defendant Had Been in Egypt, FBI Was Told," *The New York Times*, November 2, 1993.

24. Perez-Rena, "Government Revises Case on Terrorism," *The New York Times*, October 20, 1994.

25. Ronald Sullivan, "Judge Gives Maximum Term in Kahane Case," *The New York Times*, January 30, 1992.

26. *The 9/11 Commission Report*, 357.

27. http://www.whitehouse.gov/news/releases/2001/09/20010920-8.html.

28. The North Atlantic Treaty, April 4, 1949, http://www.nato.int/docu/basictxt/treaty.htm.

29. Security Council Resolutions 2001, http://www.un.org/Docs/scres/2001/sc2001.htm.

30. Congress Authorizes Use of Force Against Those Responsible for Terrorist Attacks, September 14, 2001, http://www.house.gov/ryan/press_releases/2001pressreleases/useofforce91401.html.

31. "UN Security Council to Taliban: Deliver bin Laden," September 18, 2001, http://www.usembassy.it/file2001_09/alia/a1091801.htm.

32. President George W. Bush, "Address to a Joint Session of Congress and the American People," September 20, 2001, http://www.whitehouse.gov/news/releases/2001/09/20010920-8.html.

33. Daniel Pipes, *Militant Islam Reaches America* (New York: W. W. Norton & Company, 2002).

34. Daniel Pipes, "Bush Declares War on Radical Islam," *New York Sun*, October 11, 2005.

35. Bush, "Address to a Joint Session of Congress and the American People."

36. John F. Burns, "Taliban Say They Hold Bin Laden, for His Safety, But Who Knows Where," *The New York Times*, October 1, 2001.

37. Douglas Frantz, "Taliban Say They Want to Negotiate With the U.S. Over bin Laden," *The New York Times*, October 3, 2001.

38. Marc W. Herold, "A Dossier on Civilian Victims of United States' Aerial Bombing of Afghanistan," http://pubpages.unh.edu/~mwherold/.

39. David Zucchino, " 'The Americans . . . They Just Drop Their Bombs and Leave,' " *Los Angeles Times*, July 2, 2002.

40. See "Soviet Invasion of Afghanistan," Wikipedia, http://en.wikipedia.org/wiki/Soviet_invasion_of_Afghanistan, accessed October 17, 2005.

41. Interview: John Yoo, PBS Frontline, available online at http://www.pbs.org/wgbh/pages/frontline/torture/interviews/yoo.html, July 19, 2005.

42. Ibid.

43. Charles Krauthammer, "The Truth about Torture," *The Weekly Standard*, December 5, 2005.

44. Richard A. Serrano, "Guantanamo Military Tribunals Are Upheld," *Los Angeles Times*, July 16, 2005.

45. Committee Against Torture, 36th Session, May 1–19, 2006, Advance Unedited Edition, "Consideration of Reports Submitted by States Parties Under Article 19 of he Convention, Conclusion and Recommendations of the Committee Against Torture: USA, May 18, 2006, report available at http://www.ohchr.org/english/bodies/cat/docs/AdvanceVersions/CAT.C.USA.CO.2.pdf.

46. Ibid.

47. Maggie Farley, "Report: U.S. is Abusing Captives," *Los Angeles Times*, February 13, 2006.

48. Colum Lynch, "Military Prison's Closure is Urged," *The Washington Post*, May 20, 2006.

49. National Security Strategy of the United States, September 17, 2002, http://www.whitehouse.gov/nsc/nssall.html.

50. Ibid.

51. Ibid.

52. Ibid.

53. *The 9/11 Commission Report*, 333.

54. Ibid., 335.

55. CNN, April 16, 2003.

56. CBC News, May 31, 2002.

57. John Diamond, "US: Iraq sheltered suspect in '93 WTC attack," *USA Today*, September 17, 2003.

58. Dana Priest and Toby Warrick, "Observers: Evidence for War Lacking," *The Washington Post*, September 15, 2002 and *Fox News*, March 26, 2002.

59. "Joint Resolution to Authorize the Use of United States Armed Forces Against Iraq," October 2, 2002.

60. "Remarks of Hans Blix," CNN, January 27, 2003, available online at http://www.cnn.com/2003/US/01/27/sprj.irq.transcript.blix/.

61. IAEA Director General Mohamed ElBaradei Delivers Remarks to the U.N.," FDCH Political Transcripts, January 27, 2003.

62. "Reports to the Security Council by the Chief U.N. Weapons Inspectors," *The New York Times*, February 15, 2003 and Mohamed ElBaradei, "Excerpts from the U.N. Reports," *Los Angeles Times*, February 15, 2003.

63. "In a Chief Inspector's Words: 'A Substantial Measure of Disarmament," *The New York Times*, March 8, 2003.

64. Douglas Jehl, "High Al Qaeda Aide Retracted Claim of Link with Iraq," *The New York Times*, July 31, 2004.

65. *The 9/11 Commission Report*, 66.

66. Dana Milbank, "Bush Defends Assertions of Iraq-Al Qaeda Relationship," *The Washington Post*, June 18, 2004.

67. Comprehensive Report of the Special Advisor to the DCI on Iraq's WMD, September 30, 2004, 6.

68. Ibid., 7.

69. Ibid.

70. Ibid.

71. Speech available online at http://www.whitehouse.gov/news/releases/ 2003/01/20030128-19.html.

72. Fareed Zakaria, "Why the War was Right," *Newsweek*, October 20, 2003.

73. John Miller, "Greetings America. My name is Osama bin Laden . . .," PBS Website, http://www.pbs.org/wgbh/pages/frontline/shows/binladen/who/miller.html, accessed August 26, 2005.

74. "Full Text: bin Laden's 'Letter to America,' " *Observer Worldview*(London), November 24, 2002, http://observer.guardian.co.uk/worldview/story/ 0,11581, 845725,00.html.

75. State of the Union Speech, January 29, 2002, http://www.whitehouse.gov/news/releases/2002/01/20020129-11.html.

76. Comprehensive Report of the Special Advisor to the DCI on Iraq's WMD, September 30, 2004, 12.

77. For a list of the coalition as of March 27, 2003, see http://www.whitehouse.gov/news/releases/2003/03/20030327-10.html.

78. "Rumsfeld's Words on Iraq: 'There is Untidiness,' " *The New York Times*, April 12, 2003.

79. Thomas Hegghammer, Global Jihadism After the Iraq War," *Middle East Journal*, vol. 60, no. 1 (Winter 2006).

80. Ibid.

81. Ibid.

82. Seymour Hersh, "Torture at Abu Ghraib," *The New Yorker*, May 4, 2004, available at http://www.newyorker.com/fact/content/?040510fa_fact.

83. Article 15-6 Investigation of 800th Military Police Brigade, http://news.findlaw.com/nytimes/docs/iraq/tagubarpt.html, 17.

84. Office of the Assistant Attorney General, Memorandum for Alberto R. Gonzalez: Counsel to the President, August 1, 2002 http://news.findlaw.com/wp/docs/doj/bybee80102mem.pdf.

85. Heather MacDonald, "How to Interrogate Terrorists," *City Journal* (Winter 2005).

86. Eric Schmitt, "Senate Moves to Protect Military Prisoners Despite Veto Threat," October 6, 2005.

87. Schmitt, "Exception Sought in Detainee Abuse Ban," *The New York Times*, October 25, 2005.

88. Charles Krauthammer, "The Truth about Torture," *The Weekly Standard*, December 5, 2005.

89. Ibid.

90. Ibid.

91. Ibid.

92. Ibid.

93. Andrew Sullivan, "The Abolition of Torture," *The New Republic*, December 7, 2005.

94. Ibid.

95. Glenn Frankel, "Prison Tactics A Longtime Dilemma For Israel," *The Washington Post*, June 16, 2004.

96. Sullivan, "The Abolition of Torture."

97. Mark Bowden, "The Dark Art of Interrogation," *The Atlantic Monthly*, October 2003.

98. Sullivan, "The Abolition of Torture."

99. Ibid.

100. Hegghammer, "Global Jihadism After the Iraq War."

101. Ibid.

102. "Full Text: Madrid Claim," BBC News, March 14, 2004, http://news.bbc.co.uk/2/hi/europe/3509556.stm.

103. Lawrence Wright, "The Terror Web," *The New Yorker*, August 2, 2004.

104. Peter Bergen and Paul Cruickshank, "Militant London Clerics," PeterBergen.com, July 29, 2005, http://www.peterbergen.com/bergen/articles/ details.aspx?id=225.

105. Glenn Frankel, "Europe, U.S. Diverge on How to Fight Terrorism," *The Washington Post*, March 28, 2004.

106. Eric Pape and Christopher Dickey, "Does Terror Take a Holiday?" *Newsweek*, August 9, 2004.

107. Craig Whitlock, "French Push Limits in Fight on terrorism," *The Washington Post*, November 2, 2004.

108. Ibid.

109. Dana Priest, "Help From France Key In Covert Operations," *Washington Post*, July 3, 2005.

110. Ibid.

111. Ibid.

112. Peter Bergen and Paul Cruickshank, "Militant London Clerics."

113. Ibid.

114. Alan Cowell, "Britain and Jordan Agree on Expulsion of Terror Suspects," *The New York Times*, July 21, 2005.

115. Ibid.

116. David Leppard, "More than 230 Terror Suspects Free to Stay in Britain," *Sunday Times* (London), May 21, 2006.

117. Scott Atran, "The Moral Logica and Growth of Suicide Terrorism," *The Washington Quarterly*, vol. 29, no. 2 (Spring 2006).

118. "Home Office Dumps Plans to Close Mosques," *Times Online* (London), December 15, 2005.

119. "Saudi Publications on Hate Ideology Fill American Mosques," available at http://www.freedomhouse.org/religion/publications/Saudi%20Report/FINAL%20FINAL.pdf.

120. Ibid., 9.
121. Cite Scott Atran, "The Moral Logica and Growth of Suicide Terrorism," *The Washington Quarterly*, vol. 29, no. 2 (Spring 2006).
122. President Bush Discusses Iraq Policy at Whitehall Palace in London, Office of the Press Secretary, The White House, text available at http://www.whitehouse.gov/news/releases/2003/11/20031119-1.html, November 19, 2003.
123. Ibid.
124. Ibid.
125. See text of letter http://www.state.gov/p/nea/rls/31694.htm.
126. MEMRI Special Dispatch No. 856, February 1, 2005.
127. See text of letter http://www.state.gov/p/nea/rls/31694.htm.
128. Robert F. Worth, "Jihadists Take Stand on Web And Some Say It's Defensive," *The New York Times*, March 13, 2005.
129. Ibid.
130. Maggie Farley, "U.N. Links Syria to Lebanon Slayings," *Los Angeles Times*, October 21, 2005.
131. Jim VandeHei, "Bush Calls Democracy Terror's Antidote," *The Washington Post*, March 9, 2005.
132. Christopher Dickey, "An Arabian Spring," *Newsweek*, March 14, 2005.
133. Sarah Baxter, "Bush Basks in that Reagan Glow," *Sunday Times* (London), February 27, 2005.
134. Arch Puddington, "Freedom in the World 2006; Middle East Progress Amid Global Gains," http://www.freedomhouse.org/research/freeworld/2006/essay2006.pdf.
135. Claus Christian Malzahn, "Could George W. Bush Be Right?" *Der Spiegel*, February 23, 2005, http://service.spiegel.de/cache/international/0,1518, 343378, 00. html.
136. As quoted in Jefferson Morley, "Is Bush Right?" Washingtonpost.com, March 8, 2005.
137. As quoted in Jefferson Morley, "Is Bush Right?" Washingtonpost.com, March 8, 2005.
138. Daniel Pipes, "A Democracy Killing Itself," *USA Today*, August 15, 2005.
139. Ethan Bronner, "Why 'Greater Israel' Never Came to Be," *The New York Times*, August 14, 2005.
140. Ibid.
141. President Discusses War on Terror at National Endowment for Democracy, October 6, 2005, available online at http://www.whitehouse.gov/news/releases/2005/10/ 20051006-3.html.
142. Ghaith Abdul-Ahad, "We don't need al-Qaida," *The Guardian* (London), October 27, 2005.
143. Dexter Filkins, "Iraqis, including Sunnis, Vote in Large Numbers on Calm Day," *The New York Times*, December 16, 2005.
144. F. Gregory Gause III, "Can Democracy Stop Terrorism?" *Foreign Affairs*, September–October 2005.
145. Ibid.
146. Saad Eddin Ibrahim, "Islam Can Vote, If We Let it," *The New York Times*, May 21, 2005.
147. Ibid.
148. President Discusses War on Terror.
149. Dexter Filkins, "Tactics: Iraq Qaeda Chief Seems to Pursue a Lower Profile," *The New York Times*, March 25, 2006.

150. Dexter Filkins, "U.S. Portrayal Helps Flesh Out Zarqawi's Heir," *The New York Times*, June 16, 2006.

151. Ramita Navai, "Leader Invokes New Islamic Wave," *The Times* (London), June 30, 2005.

152. The hostages' allegations have not been confirmed by the U.S. government.

153. Robert G. Joseph, "Under Secretary for Arms Control and International Security Statement Before the House International Relations Committee," Washington, DC, March 8, 2006, available at http://www.state.gov/t/us/rm/63121.htm.

154. Golnaz Esfandiari, "Radio Free Europe Radio Liberty," November 29, 2005, http://www.rferl.org/featuresarticle/2005/11/184cb9fb-887c-4696-8f54-0799df747a4a.html.

155. "Iranian TV broadcasts what Ahmadinezhad actually said on Israel," BBC Worldwide Monitoring, October 29, 2005.

156. Nazila Fathi, "Iranian Leader Renews Attack on Israel at Palestinian Rally," *The New York Times*, April 15, 2006.

157. "Voice of the Islamic Republic of Iran, Tehran," in Persian 1130 gmt, BBC Worldwide Monitoring, December 15, 2001.

158. Michael Slackman, "Iran the Great Unifier? The Arab World is Wary," *The New York Times*, February 5, 2006.

159. Michael Slackman, "Iran the Great Unifier? The Arab World is Wary," *The New York Times*, February 5, 2006.

160. Michael Slackman, "Iran the Great Unifier? The Arab World is Wary," *The New York Times*, February 5, 2006.

161. Hassan M. Fattah, "Gulf States Join Call for Tougher Action Toward Tehran," *The New York Times*, February 1, 2006.

162. Roee Nahmias, "Defense minister rejects Gaza killings criticism, says protesters should visit bereaved families first," ynetnews.com, April 24, 2006, http://www.ynetnews.com/articles/0,7340,L-3243262,00.html.

163. Laurie Goodstein, "Dalai Lama Says Terror May Need a Violent Reply," *The New York Times*, September 18, 2003.

Bibliography

Algar, Hamid, *Wahhabism: A Critical Essay* (North Haledon, NJ: Islamic Publications International, 2002)

Al-Zayyat, Montasser, *The Road To Al-Qaeda: The Story of Bin Laden's Right-Hand Man* (London: Pluto Press, 2004)

Anonymous, *Through Our Enemies' Eyes; Osama bin Laden, Radical Islam, and the Future of America* (Washington, DC: Brassey's, Inc., 2002)

Ayoubi, Nazih, *Political Islam; Religion and Politics in the Arab World* (New York: Routledge, 1998, fourth edition)

Azzam, Abdullah, *Join the Caravan* (1987), via Islamistwatch http://www.islamistwatch. org/texts/azzam/caravan/intro.html

Baer, Robert, *See No Evil: The True Story of a Ground Soldier in the CIA's War on Terrorism* (New York: Crown Publishers, 2002)

Benjamin, Daniel and Steven Simon, *The Age of Sacred Terror* (New York: Random House, 2002)

Bergen, Peter, *Holy War Inc. Inside the Secret World of Osama bin Laden* (London: Phoenix, 2002)

Blanchard, Christopher, "Al Qaeda: Statements and Evolving Ideology," *CRS Reports for Congress*, June 20, 2005

Bonney, Richard, *Jihad: From Qur'an to bin Laden* (New York: Palgrave Macmillan, 2004)

Bostom, Andrew G., ed., *The Legacy of Jihad: Islamic Holy War and the Fate of Non-Muslims* (Amherst, NY: Prometheus Books, 2005)

Bradley, John R., *Saudi Arabia Exposed; Inside a Kingdom in Crisis* (New York: Palgrave Macmillan, 2005)

Brisard, Jean-Charles, Zarqawi: *The New Face of al-Qaeda* (Cambridge, England: Polity, 2005)

Bronson, Rachel, *Thicker Than Oil: America's Uneasy Partnership with Saudi Arabia* (New York: Oxford University Press, 2006)

Burgat, Francois, *Face to Face with Political Islam* (London and New York: I. B. Tauris, 2003)

Burke, Jason, *Al-Qaeda, Casting the Shadow of Terror* (London and New York: I.B. Tauris, 2003)

Coll, Steve, *Ghost Wars: The Secret History of the CIA, Afghanistan, and Bin Laden, from the Soviet Invasion to September 11, 2001* (New York: Penguin Books, 2004)

Cook, David, *Understanding Jihad* (Berkeley, LA, and London: University of California Press, 2005)

Cook, Michael, *The Koran: A Very Short Introduction* (Oxford: Oxford University Press, 2000)

Corbin, Jane, *Al-Qaeda: The Terror Network that Threatens the World* (New York: Thunder's Mouth Press, 2002)

Dahlby, Tracy, *Allah's Torch; A Report from Behind the Scenes in Asia's War on Terror* (New York: William Morrow, an Imprint of HarperCollins, 2005)

Ehrenfeld, Rachel, *Funding Evil: How Terrorism is Financed—And How to Stop It; The Book the Saudis Don't Want You to Read* (Chicago and Los Angeles: Bonus Books, 2005)

El-Fadl, Khaled Abu, *The Great Theft: Wrestling Islam From the Extremists* (San Francisco: HarperSanFrancisco, 2005)

Emerson, Steven, *American Jihad: The Terrorists Living Among Us* (New York: The Free Press, 2002)

Esposito, John L., *Unholy War; Terror in the Name of Islam* (New York: Oxford University Press, 2002)

Fielding, Nick and Yosri Fouda, *Masterminds of Terror: The Truth behind the Most Devastating Terrorist Attack the World Has Ever Seen* (Edinburgh and London: Mainstream Publishing, 2003)

Firestone, Reuven, *Jihad; The Origin of Holy War in Islam* (New York: Oxford University Press, 1999)

Fregosi, Paul, *Jihad in the West: Muslim Conquests from the 7th to the 21st Centuries* (Amherst, NY: Prometheus Books, 1998)

Gerges, Fawaz A., *The Far Enemy: Why Jihad Went Global* (New York: Cambridge University Press, 2005)

Gordon, Michael R. and Bernard E. Trainor, *Cobra II: The Inside Story of the Invasion and Occupation of Iraq* (NY: Pantheon, 2006)

Greenberg, Karen J., ed., *Al Qaeda Now: Understanding Today's Terrorists* (Cambridge University Press, 2005)

Gunaratna, Rohan, *Inside Al-Qaeda* (London: Hurst, 2002, first edition)

Habeck, Mary, *Knowing the Enemy: Jihadist Ideology and the War on Terror* (New Haven: Yale University Press, 2006)

Hayes, Stephen F., *The Connection: How al Qaeda's Collaboration with Saddam Hussein Has Endangered America* (New York: HarperCollins, 2004)

Hegghammer, Thomas, "Al-Qaida Statements 2003–2004—A Compilation of Translated Texts by Usama bin Ladin and Ayman al-Zawahiri," *FFI Rapport*, June 24, 2005

Hoffman, Bruce, *Inside Terrorism* (New York: Colombia University Press, 1998)

Huntington, Samuel P., *The Clash of Civilizations and the Remaking of the World Order* (New York: Touchstone, 1997, first edition)

Jansen, Johannes J.G., *The Dual Nature of Islamic Fundamentalism* (Ithaca, NY: Cornell University Press, 1997)

———, *The Neglected Duty* (New York: Macmillan Publishing Company, 1986)

Johnson, James Turner, *The Holy War Idea in Western and Islamic Traditions* (Pennsylvania: The Pennsylvania State University Press, 1997)

Karsh, Efraim, *Islamic Imperialism: A History* (New Haven: Yale University Press, 2006)

Katzman, Kenneth, "Al Qaeda: Profile and Threat Assessment," *Congressional Research Service*, August 17, 2005

Kelsay, John and James Turner Johnson, eds., *Just War and Jihad: Historical and Theoretical Perspectives on War and Peace in Western and Islamic Traditions* (Westport, CT: Greenwood Press, 1991)

Kohlmann, Evan F., *Al-Qaida's Jihad in Europe; The Afghan-Bosnian Network* (Oxford: Berg, 2004)

Kushner, Harvey with Bart Davis, *Holy War on the Home Front; The Secret Islamic Terror Network in the United States* (New York: Sentinel, 2004)

Lawrence, Bruce, ed., *Messages to the World: The Statements of Osama bin Laden* (London and New York: Verso, 2005)

Lia, Brynjar, *The Society of the Muslim Brothers in Egypt: The Rise of an Islamic Mass Movement, 1928–1942* (Reading, UK: Ithaca, 1998)

Mackey, Chris and Greg Miller, *The Interrogators; Task Force 500 and America's Secret War Against Al Qaeda* (New York: Back Bay Books, 2004)

McDermott, Terry, *Perfect Soldiers; The Hijackers: Who They Were, Why They Did It* (New York: HarperCollins Publishers, 2005)

Miniter, Richard, *Shadow War; The Untold Story of How Bush is Winning the War on Terror* (Washington, DC: Regnery Publishing, Inc., 2004)

Moussalli, Ahmad S., *Radical Islamic Fundamentalism: The Ideological and Political Discourse of Sayyid Qutb* (Syracuse, NY: Syracuse University Press, 2003)

Moussaoui, Abd Samad, Zacarias, *My Brother: The Making of a Terrorist* (New York: Seven Stories Press, 2003)

Musallam, Adnan A., *From Secularism to Jihad: Sayyid Qutb and the Foundations of Radical Islam* (Westport, CT: Praeger Publishers, 2005)

Mylroie, Laurie, *Bush vs. the Beltway: How the CIA and the State Department Tried to Stop the War on Terror* (New York: HarperCollins, 2003)

Napoleoni, Loretta, *Modern Jihad; Tracing the Dollars Behind the Terror Networks* (London: Pluto Press, 2003)

Nesser, Petter, "Jihad in Europe—A Survey of the Motivations for Sunni Islamist Terrorism in Post-Millennium Europe," *FFI Rapport*, Norwegian Defence Research Establishment, 2004

Pape, Robert, *Dying to Win: The Strategic Logic of Suicide Terrorism* (New York: Random House, 2005)

Peters, Rudolph, *Jihad in Classical and Modern Islam* (Princeton: Marcus Wiener Publishers, 1996)

Phares, Walid, *Future Jihad: Terrorist Strategies Against America* (New York: Palgrave, 2005)

Pipes, Daniel, *Militant Islam Reaches America* (New York: W.W. Norton & Company, 2002)

Posner, Gerald, *Secrets of the Kingdom; The Inside Story of the Saudi-U.S. Connection* (New York: Random House, 2005)

Qutb, Sayyid, *Milestones* (International Islamic Federation of Student Organizations, n.d.)

———, *In the Shade of the Qur'an*; vol. 30 (New Delhi: Islamic Book Service, 2001)

Rashid, Ahmed, *Jihad. The Rise of Militant Islam in Central Asia* (New Haven and London: Yale Nota Bene, 2002)

———, *Social Justice in Islam* (North Haledon, NJ: Islamic Publications International, revised edition 2000)

Roy, Olivier, *Globalized Islam; The Search for a New Ummah* (New York: Columbia University Press, 2004)

Rubin, Barry and Judith Colp Rubin, eds., *Anti-American Terrorism and the Middle East: A Documentary Reader* (New York: Oxford University Press, 2002)

Ruthven, Malise, *A Fury for God; The Islamist Attack on America* (London: Granta Books, 2004, second edition)

Sageman, *Understanding Terror Networks* (Philadelphia: University of Pennsylvania Press, 2004)

Schanzer, Jonathan, *Al-Qaeda's Armies; Middle East Affiliate Groups & The Next Generation of Terror* (Washington, DC: Washington Institute for Near East Policy, 2004)

Sharansky, Natan and Ron Dermer, *The Case for Democracy: The Power of Freedom to Overcome Tyranny and Terror* (Cambridge, MA: Public Affairs, 2004)

Sivan, Emmanuel, *Radical Islam; Medieval Theology and Modern Politics* (New Haven and London: Yale University Press, 1990)

Sperry, Paul, *Infiltration; How Muslim Spies and Subversives Have Penetrated* Washington (Nashville, TN: Nelson Current, 2005)

Stern, Jessica, *Terror in the Name of God: Why Religious Militants Kill* (New York: HarperCollins, 2003)

Streusand, Douglas E., "What Does Jihad Mean?" *Middle East Quarterly*, vol. IV, no. 3 (September 1997)

U.S. State Department, Patterns of Global Terrorism 2003, released April 2004

Weaver, Mary Anne, *A Portrait of Egypt; A Journey Through the World of Militant Islam* (New York: Farrar, Straus and Giroux, 2000, 1st revised paperback edition)

Weaver, Mary Anne, Pakistan: *In the Shadow of Jihad and Afghanistan* (New York: Farrar, Straus and Giroux, 2002)

Wiktorowicz, Quintan, *Global Jihad; Understanding September 11* (Falls Church, Virginia: Sound Room Publishers, Inc., 2002)

———, *Radical Islam Rising: Muslim Extremism in the West* (Rowman & Littlefield Publishers, 2005)

Woodward, Bob, *Bush at War* (New York: Simon and Schuster, 2002)

Wright, Robin, *Sacred Rage; The Wrath of Militant Islam* (New York: Touchstone, [1985] 2001 edition)

Index